THE CARPATHIANS

THE
CARPATHIANS

DISCOVERING THE
HIGHLANDS OF
POLAND AND
UKRAINE

PATRICE M. DABROWSKI

NORTHERN ILLINOIS UNIVERSITY PRESS
AN IMPRINT OF CORNELL UNIVERSITY PRESS
Ithaca and London

A volume in the NIU Series in Slavic, East European, and Eurasian Studies
Edited by Christine D. Worobec
For a list of books in the series, visit our website at cornellpress.cornell.edu.

COVER AND FRONTISPIECE: At Morskie Oko. Photo by Awit Szubert, 1871. From the collection of the Documentation Center of the Tatra National Park, image in the public domain.

First published 2021 by Cornell University Press

Printed in the United States of America

Library of Congress Cataloging-in-Publication Data
Names: Dabrowski, Patrice M., 1960– author.
Title: The Carpathians : discovering the highlands of
    Poland and Ukraine / Patrice M. Dabrowski.
Description: Ithaca, [New York] : Northern Illinois University
    Press, an imprint of Cornell University Press, 2021. |
    Series: NIU Series in Slavic, East European, and Eurasian
    studies | Includes bibliographical references and index.
Identifiers: LCCN 2020056458 (print) | LCCN 2020056459
    (ebook) | ISBN 9781501759673 (hardcover) |
    ISBN 9781501759680 (ebook) | ISBN 9781501759697 (pdf)
Subjects: LCSH: Carpathian Mountains—Discovery and
    exploration. | Tatra Mountains (Slovakia and Poland)—
    Discovery and exploration. | Beshchady Mountains
    (Poland and Ukraine)—Discovery and exploration. |
    Carpathian Mountains—History—19th century. |
    Carpathian Mountains—History—20th century. |
    Tatra Mountains (Slovakia and Poland)—History—
    19th century. | Tatra Mountains (Slovakia and Poland)—
    History—20th century. | Beshchady Mountains (Poland
    and Ukraine)—History—19th century. | Beshchady
    Mountains (Poland and Ukraine)—History—
    20th century.
Classification: LCC DJK71 .D33 2021 (print) |
    LCC DJK71 (ebook) | DDC 947.7/908—dc23
LC record available at https://lccn.loc.gov/2020056458
LC ebook record available at https://lccn.loc.gov/2020056459

JJ

My first, and favorite, mountain guide

❧ Contents

❧ ILLUSTRATIONS

Maps

Figures

✖ ACKNOWLEDGMENTS

While still the greenest of graduate students, I once chatted with Simon Schama, who at the time was working on his pathbreaking *Landscape and Memory*, about what landscape Poles identified with most. He postulated that the primeval forest of Białowieża took precedence, yet I thought that perhaps it was Poland's mountains that figured most prominently (no pun intended). The seed for this book, thus, was planted, although it would take many years to germinate, not to mention mature.

Given the elapsed time, I could easily write a full-length chapter acknowledging all the help and support I have received over the years. Research for this book was supported in part by a fellowship from IREX (International Research and Exchanges Board), with funds provided by the United States Department of State through the Title VIII Program. Neither of these organizations is responsible for the views expressed herein. In addition to the IREX fellowship, a generous Senior Grant as part of the Thesaurus Poloniae Fellowship Program, run by the International Cultural Centre in Kraków, likewise took me to Poland. I thank the helpful leadership and staff of numerous archives, museums, libraries, and centers, in particular Andrzej Czesław Żak of the Central Military Archive in Rembertów, Lieutenant Andrzej Wesołowski of the Central Military Library in Warsaw, and Jerzy Kapłon and Wiesław A. Wójcik of the Centralny Ośrodek Turystyki Górskiej PTTK in Kraków.

I also received fellowship support for two research trips to Ukraine: a summer traveling grant courtesy of the Harvard Ukrainian Research Institute as well as a Fulbright grant. I am grateful to the staffs of the various archives in L'viv and Ivano-Frankivs'k, the Stefanyk Library in L'viv, and the Hutsul Museum in Kolomyia.

An early home base for me was the Watson Institute for International Studies at Brown University, where I worked under Omer Bartov on a project entitled "Borderlands: Ethnicity, Identity, and Violence in the Shatterzone of Empires Since 1848." A Eugene and Daymel Shklar fellowship at the Harvard Ukrainian Research Institute (HURI) provided me with the time to get down to serious writing as well as present an aspect of my work as part of HURI's lecture series. My decades-long affiliation with HURI has been wonderful and stimulating. I also spent several years in Vienna, Austria, as part of the Doktoratskolleg "Das österreichische Galizien und sein multikulturelles Erbe," under the inspiring and able leadership of Alois Woldan and Christoph Augustynowicz.

Special lecture invitations led me to Hamburg for the Third International Perspectives on Slavistics conference, to Nancy Shields Kollmann's seminar at Stanford, to the University of Chicago, to the Polish Academy of Arts and Letters (PAU) in Kraków, to the University of Basel, and to the Vienna branch of the Polish Academy of Sciences, where the audiences posed stimulating questions. I profited from comments made at a number of specialized conferences and workshops: the Polish Studies Conference at the University of Michigan; the international interdisciplinary conference Multiculturalism: The Central European Experience and Its Impact on Identity-Formation in a Globalized World in Bellagio, Italy; the workshop Modern German Environmental History in European Perspective at the Center for European Studies at Harvard University; and the Mountain Landscapes Workshop at GWZO, Leipzig. Helpful feedback from both panelists and the audience was forthcoming at a number of panels held at the conventions of the Association for Slavic, East European, and Eurasian Studies, the Association for the Study of Nationalities, the Deutscher Historikertag, and the Polish Institute of Arts and Sciences of America. I am indebted to Professor Jacek Kolbuszewski and Ewa Grzęda of the Pracownia Badań Humanistycznych nad Problematyką Górską (The Workshop of Humanistic Research on Mountain Issues) in Wrocław for their years of support and opportunities to present at their annual conference and publish in their periodical *Góry—Literatura—Kultura*.

Sections of the text will be familiar to some readers, although much has been reworked and recontextualized. Pieces of Part I originally appeared in "Constructing a Polish Landscape: The Example of the Carpathian Frontier," *Austrian History Yearbook* 39 (2008): 45–65; and "Between Highlanders and Lowlanders: Perceptions of the Jewish Presence in the Tatras in the Nineteenth Century," in *Galizien in Bewegung: Wahrnehmungen—Begegnungen—Verflechtungen*, edited by Magdalena Baran-Szołtys, Olena Dvoretska, Nino Gude, and Elisabeth Janik-Freis (Wiener Galizien-Studien, 1) (Vienna: V & R unipress, 2018), 141–53. Reprinted with permission, chapter 5 is a modified version of "'Discovering' the Galician Borderlands: The Case of the Eastern Carpathians," *Slavic Review* 64, no. 2 (summer 2005): 380–402. Chapter 6 contains fragments of "The 'Polish Switzerland': The Rise of the High-Altitude Health Resort of Jaremcze before World War I," in *Polacy i świat, kultura i zmiana. Studia historyczne i antropologiczne ofiarowane Profesor Halinie Florkowskiej-Frančić*, edited by Jan Lencznarowicz, Janusz Pezda, and Andrzej A. Zięba (Kraków: Księgarnia Akademicka, 2016), 165–74; and "Jak Hucułowie ze Wschodnich Karpat stali się . . . Europejczykami," in *Imperia, narody i społeczeństwa Europy Wschodniej i Środkowej na progu pierwszej wojny światowej*, edited by Andrzej Nowak and Mikołaj Banaszkiewicz (Warsaw: Centrum Polsko-Rosyjskiego Dialogu i Porozumienia, 2016), 69–78. Bits of chapter 7 appeared in "Multiculturalism, Polish Style: Glimpses from the Interwar Period," in *Understanding Multiculturalism and the Habsburg Central European Experience*, edited by Gary B. Cohen and Johannes Feichtinger (New York: Berghahn Press, 2014), 85–100: and "Poles, Hutsuls, and Identity Politics in the Eastern Carpathians after World War I," in special issue "War and Identity," edited by Stephan Lehnstaedt and Marta Ansilewska-Lehnstaedt, *Zeitschrift für Genozidforschung* 16, no. 1 (2018): 19–34. Pieces of chapters 9 and 10 were originally published as "Encountering Poland's 'Wild West': Tourism in the Bieszczady Mountains under Socialism," in *Socialist Escapes: Breaks from the Everyday in Cold War Eastern Europe*, edited by Cathleen Giustino, Catherine Plum, and Alexander Vari (New York: Berghahn Press, 2013), 75–97.

Timely and much valued assistance from Petro Arsenych, Hennadii Boriak, Wit Busza, Krzysztof Buczek, Roman Gąsiorowski, Yaroslav Hrytsak, Maciej Krupa, Mateusz Mroz, Jacek Purchla, Andrzej Ruszczak, Janusz Rygielski, Roman Syrota, Dmytro Vatamaniuk, Andrzej Wielocha, and Andriy Zayarnyuk afforded me access to archives, libraries, museums, and private collections, as well as other important sources of information for my work (including fieldwork). Cartographer Daniel P. Huffman turned my rough sketches into a set of beautiful maps.

Unfortunately, neither Mykola Sankovych of Vorokhta nor Ihor Pelypeiko of Kosiv lived to see the fruits of our conversations.

I thank friends, colleagues, and mentors for their generous assistance, helpful comments, and encouragement along the way: Olga Andriewsky, Justyna Bajda, Omer Bartov, David Blackbourn, Brian Boeck, Miśka Bremer, Krzysztof Broński, Keith Brown, Deborah Coen, Gary Cohen, John Connelly, John Czaplicka, Christine Dabrowski, Halina Florkowska-Frančić, Alison Frank Johnson, Cate Giustino, Jan Gross, Lubomyr Hajda, Leonid Heretz, Bianca Hoenig, Dietlind Hüchtker, Krzysztof Jasiewicz, Hugo Lane, John LeDonne, Stephan Lehnstaedt, Thomas Lekan, Jacek Lubecki, Małgorzata Łoboz, Bob Magocsi, Sean Martin, Małgorzata Mroz, Iris Rachamimov, Martin Rohde, Leszek Rymarowicz, Frithjof Benjamin Schenk, Jan Skłodowski, Ewa Sławińska, Timothy Snyder, Maria Sonevytsky, Frank Sysyn, Roman

Szporluk, Olaf Terpitz, Heléna Toth, Corinna Treitel, Sandor Vari, Marylina Weintraub, Jagoda Wierzejska, Larry Wolff, and Tara Zahra. Anna Müller was the first to read and comment on a full draft of the manuscript; I owe her more than I can say. Amy Farranto, Eagle Glassheim, Brendan Karch, and indexer Basia Nowak's insightful comments helped me hone the final product. All errors and shortcomings are mine, and mine alone.

Only in the course of writing this book did I realize how much it reflected part of my own past. For I, too, have been touched by the mountains. They were an integral part of the Poland I came to know and love in the early 1980s. My first ever *rajd* (group hiking excursion) was in the Bieszczady Mountains—one of the regions featured in this book. On my second rajd, in the Sudety Mountains along the Polish-Czechoslovak border, I met my future husband. It is to him—the person with whom I also first traversed the Tatras—that I dedicate this book.

🍂 ABBREVIATIONS

AAN	Archive of New Acts, Warsaw (Archiwum Akt Nowych)
AGK ZHP	Archive of the Main Quarters of the Union of Polish Scouting, Warsaw (Archiwum Głównej Kwatery Związku Harcerstwa Polskiego)
APRz	State Archive in Rzeszów (Archiwum Państwowe w Rzeszowie)
APRz PTTK	State Archive in Rzeszów, Polish Society of Tourism and Local Studies, Regional Executive in Rzeszów 1950–76 (Archiwum Państwowe w Rzeszowie, Polskie Towarzystwo Turystyczno-Krajoznawcze, Zarząd Okręgowy w Rzeszowie 1950–76)
APRz-Sanok	State Archive in Rzeszów—Sanok Branch (Archiwum Państwowe w Rzeszowie, Oddział w Sanoku)
APRz-Skołyszyn	State Archive in Rzeszów—Skołyszyn Branch (Archiwum Państwowe w Rzeszowie, Oddział w Skołyszynie)
AT-OeSTA	Austrian State Archive (Österreichisches Staatsarchiv)
CAW	Central Military Archive, Rembertów (Centralne Archiwum Wojskowe)
DAIFO	The State Archive of the Ivano-Frankivs'k Oblast (Derzhavnyi Arkhiv Ivano-Frankivs'koi Oblasti)
DALO	The State Archive of the L'viv Oblast (Derzhavnyi Arkhiv L'vivs'koi Oblasti)
GOPR	Mountain Volunteer Search and Rescue Organization (Górskie Ochotnicze Pogotowie Ratunkowe)
IKC	*Illustrated Daily Courier* (Ilustrowany Kurier Codzienny)

Muzeum Tatrzańskie	Archive of the Tatra Museum, Zakopane (Archiwum Muzeum Tatrzańskiego)
Ossolineum	Manuscript Collection of the Ossolineum, Wrocław (Zakład Narodowy im. Ossolińskich)
OUN	Organization of Ukrainian Nationalists (Orhanizatsiia Ukraïns'kykh Nationalistiv)
Pam. Tow. Tatrz.	*Tatra Society Yearbook* (Pamiętnik Towarzystwa Tatrzańskiego)
PGR	State Agricultural Farm (Państwowe Gospodarstwo Rolne)
PRL	Polish People's Republic (Polska Rzeczpospolita Ludowa)
PTTK	Polish Society of Tourism and Local Studies (Polskie Towarzystwo Turystyczno-Krajoznawcze)
PZPR	Polish United Workers' Party (Polska Zjednoczona Partia Robotnicza)
SKPB	Student Club of Beskid Guides (Studenckie Koło Przewodników Beskidzkich)
TsDIAL	The Central State Historical Archive in L'viv (Tsentralnyi Derzhavnyi Istorychnyi Arkhiv u L'vovi)
UPA	Ukrainian Insurgent Army (Ukraïns'ka Povstans'ka Armiia)
USSR	Union of Soviet Socialist Republics
Wielka Encyklopedia Tatrzańska	Zofia Radwańska-Paryska and Witold Henryk Paryski, *Wielka Encyklopedia Tatrzańska* [Great Tatra Encyclopedia] (Poronin: Wydawnictwo Gorskie, 1995)

❧ THE CARPATHIANS

Introduction

What does it mean to discover mountains that are already to some extent known, even inhabited? Why have Polish claims of "discovering" various mountain ranges within the vast Carpathian Mountain system—their southern border, after all—been made well into the nineteenth and twentieth centuries? What impact did these particular encounters with the mountains have on the discoverers as well as the mountains and the indigenous mountain folk?

Readers of this book will find answers to these and other, sometimes paradoxical, questions. Perhaps this befits the Carpathian Mountains, which themselves abound in paradoxes. Although they are Central and Eastern Europe's most prominent physical feature, one that bisects the region and serves as the watershed to the Baltic and Black Seas, politically they are peripheral. Various ranges within the Carpathian Mountain system (and there more than a few of these) delineate the frontier of two countries (present-day Poland and Slovakia) while lying on the outskirts of others (Austria, Czechia, Ukraine, Romania, Serbia). Likewise, despite the fact that the Carpathians are essentially a continuation of the Alps of west-central Europe and are the second most extensive range in Europe after them, they are infinitely less well known.

Witness the response of the historical profession. "Mountains come first": so claimed Fernand Braudel, at the beginning of his great work on

MAP 1. The Carpathians in Poland and Europe. Map by Daniel P. Huffman.

the Mediterranean. However, he also admitted that the historian tends "to linger over the plains, which is the setting for the leading actors of the day, and does not seem eager to approach the high mountains nearby."[1] Although many books on mountains have been published since Braudel's time, with the Alps particularly well covered, even the acclaimed author of *The Third Dimension: A Comparative History of Mountains in the Modern Era* found no room for the Carpathians.[2] Perhaps he would agree with the anonymous author who, writing about the Carpathians in the *Saturday Review* in 1867, observed, "The mountains have no history, have never come forward on the theatre of the world, or become associated in our minds with great men and great events, like the Alps and Pyrenees and Apennines."[3] The Carpathians as a whole seem to have been overlooked and ignored, something that the present book hopes in part to remedy.

If historians have generally been mute on the Carpathians, travelers have not. Although the northern slopes of the Carpathians featured in this book have been called severe, cold, gloomy, and desolate, the warmer southern slopes were penetrated by a handful of curious climbers already in the seventeenth century. Even some fifty years earlier, a Polish countess, Beata Łaska née Kościelecka, made the first recorded excursion to the Snowy Mountains (High Tatras, where the highest Carpathian peaks are to be found), although she and her entourage likely only reached the foot of the mountains—and this from the south.[4] That is not to say that shepherds, hunters, brigands, fugitives, medicine men, miners, and treasure seekers did not frequent the mountains, even the northern slopes, still earlier. Who, then, can say when the mountains were really discovered, and by whom?

Yet claims of discovery were made, and in a much later period than one might imagine. The discoverers of concern to us here came long after the first recorded climbs of certain peaks, after the first scientists came and took measurements.[5] They came even after the fashion for the Alps saw those mountains overrun with tourists in the mid-nineteenth century, prompting some intrepid British travelers to seek adventure further east—with one going so far as to exhort his readers in 1872 to "try Cracow and the Carpathians."[6] How paradoxical that the trip of a certain Warsaw physician to the Tatras made the year *after* the publication of that travelogue would go down in Polish history as the "discovery" of the Tatras.

Again, that did not mean that no one had been there before, that the region was devoid of life, or even that all memory of earlier explorations had been lost. That was not true for the Poles, a number of whom had climbed the mountains since the early nineteenth century, still less for other populations with easier access to them. Indeed, in 1873, right across what was then the Hungarian border, the Hungarian Carpathian Society was established; it was part of the string of alpine clubs—British (1857), Austrian (1862), Italian (1863), Swiss (1863), German (1869)—that had been popping up all over Europe.[7] Perhaps the time simply was ripe to follow in their footsteps?

There was more to the discovering than just establishing an alpine club, although that too could be important. That much of the Carpathians remained terra incognita to all but those in the surrounding piedmont (and sometimes even to them) allowed my protagonists, lowlanders who came to visit the mountains and fell in love with them, to dream big dreams and work to realize them. In different periods various individuals or institutions strove to place discrete ranges of this vast mountain system on the mental maps of their compatriots—to construct a recognizable, native, even national landscape.[8] They sought to turn the mountains, different in so many ways from the rest of the Polish lands, into a special kind of vacation destination, to popularize them, even to transform them and their inhabitants in specific ways—all part of the "discovering" project. This is not to say that there was no disconnect between these lowland outsiders' perceptions of the highlands and the indigenous highlanders—those whose very essence was shaped by the harsh mountain environment—and the reality on the ground. Likewise, tensions rose between the desire to make the highland wilderness more accessible to lowlanders and the desire to preserve what remained of these remote and wild spaces. This book combines elements of environmental history, borderlands studies, tourism and leisure studies as well as political, cultural, and social history.

Readers will find out that Poles at particular moments in time had the chutzpah to claim that certain discrete mountain ranges within the vast Carpathian Mountain system—the Tatras, the Hutsul region of the Eastern Carpathians, and the Bieszczady Mountains—had "been discovered" or were "being discovered," even "repeatedly discovered." This conscious invoking of the term *discovering* validates the book's treatment of several different episodes, varied in time and space, in each of which Poles claimed to discover a new mountain range.

That Poles discovered these mountain ranges and turned them into extremely popular vacation destinations is in various ways paradoxical.[9] When one thinks of Poland—historically as well as today—one thinks of a land of fields and plains, whence the name Poland (from *pole*, or field). The same holds true for Ukrainians, more identified with the steppe. Yet the quintessentially lowland Poles—as readers will see, especially those from Warsaw—came to be particularly enamored of mountains. In the episodes of discovery under investigation they took an inordinate interest in their own distant and remote mountains, far from the national center. (Discoverers rarely hailed from the piedmont.) In the process, the highland periphery moved to the center of the discoverers' mental maps as well as those of a broader swath of society. Yet another paradox is that the highlands discovered and popularized in this way were the less hospitable northern slopes of the Carpathians, more often than not gloomy, rainy, cold—if strikingly beautiful. This is why the dramatis personae of the book are predominantly Poles and Ukrainians, not Slovaks, Hungarians, or Romanians, the latter three being peoples who lived in more mountainous terrain or whose Carpathians consisted of the sunnier, and more easily accessible, southern slopes.[10] It also suggests that a greater effort was required of the discoverers who figure here. The penetration of the mountains was far from easy; their initial popularizers had to be particularly motivated individuals.

What, then, motivated the discoverers to speak of their encounter with the mountains in these terms? The trope of discovery is no stranger to world history. To the American ear it has the ring of a Columbian expedition—the conscious pursuit of the exotic and unknown, in the hopes of reaping the profits thereof. Elsewhere around the globe it likewise carries connotations of colonialism or imperialism.[11] Indeed, empires have long been engaged in discovering lands and peoples: to cite but two well-researched examples on the Eastern Hemisphere, witness gigantic Russia's expansion into the northern reaches of Eurasia as described by Yuri Slezkine, or tiny Venice's discovery of Dalmatia so engagingly elucidated by Larry Wolff.[12]

How do the Polish discoveries compare? There are undoubted similarities. Each episode of discovering has an air of intentionality. Discoverers do not generally stumble across the territory in question but rather pursue it in programmatic fashion. Each discovery is also asymmetrical, if not entirely unidirectional. It may be helpful to think of it in terms of a center discovering a periphery. The center is the source of the discovering impetus, which goes out and seeks the unknown, in order to peripheralize it—that is, to relate it to the center. It moves something previously off the center's radar screen onto it: it puts the periphery in its place, one often subordinate to the center.

Yet there are also important differences. The Russian and Venetian discoveries were imperial in scope, with the people from the center relating in predictable ways to what and whom they found in the periphery. In these two cases, the little peoples of the Arctic north and the Morlacchi highlanders of the Dalmatian hinterland, while serving as a mirror for the Russians' and Venetians' own sense of being civilized, were nonetheless seen as being fully "Other"—as *inozemtsy* or *inorodtsy*—or, as in the case of Venice, simply barbarous. By contrast, the distinction between "barbarism" and "civilization" is much attenuated in the Carpathians, with the discoverers intent on claiming the "Other" as an exotic—certainly outlying—subset of themselves. The Polish episodes of discovery were more national than imperial in character, although shades of imperialism may be perceived in places where distinctly different highlanders were being appropriated for the nation (however defined).

In the Polish case, the discoveries would result in special projects for the mountain regions. These travelers to the Carpathians who were involved in the discovery of the mountains were men and women with a mission: to uncover the wonders of the mountains to the broader world, in particular to their own imagined community (however it was imagined). At the same time, their mission of popularization brought them into contact, and often conflict, with different constituencies, consisting of other newcomers as well as the natives. "The embrace of tourism," as Hal Rothman has noted, "triggers a contest for the soul of a place."[13] It should come as no surprise, then, that, in the process of constructing a more broadly recognizable, native/national landscape out of these remote mountains, the various parties affected by the discovery occasionally argued over the very nature of the Carpathians (no pun intended).

Yet the pun is apt, for nature also plays a role on these pages.[14] The book's juxtaposition of tourism (mountain climbing, spa going, and vacationing in nature) and the natural world of the mountains sheds light on the relationship between man and the environment.[15] Discovering naturally had an impact, positive and negative, on the mountain regions, even when the latter were touted—rightly or not—as primeval wilderness.[16] After all, the mountains were pockmarked in places by mining, quarrying, and logging. In the wake of discovering came development, be it in the form of roads, railways, or trails to facilitate the penetration of the mountains or even a tourist and resort infrastructure to satisfy the needs of more sedentary lowlanders. In the process, the environment—human as well as natural—changed, sometimes in ways that perturbed those who were behind the popularization in the first place. This is also a story of how "modernity—and its attendant benefits and problems"—came to the mountains.[17]

That the mountains became part of the mental map of the Central and East European intelligentsia (that is, its educated stratum)—the people most often associated with nation building in this region—is significant. I would argue that one of the hallmarks of a genuine discovery is what transpires in its wake. It is far from a passive encounter. Instead, the outsiders who begin to stream into a territory that had not drawn significant attention previously acquire purpose once they have laid their fresh eyes on the region. The encounter inspires them to act—and to act in ways that significantly alter the relationship of lowlands and highlands, lowlanders and highlanders. That the encounter takes place in a historically heterogeneous/multiethnic borderland—one in which quintessentially mountain people such as the Górale, Hutsuls, Lemkos, and Boikos dwelled—lends an element of contestation, which often throws into relief the positions of the various groups inhabiting and visiting the region; this interplay can inspire previously nonnational folk to become national or otherwise effect changes in the relations between groups. Not for nothing did Peter Sahlins call frontier regions "privileged sites for the articulation of national distinctions."[18] True discoveries are transformative—and not just in the sense of terra incognita becoming tourist destination but in making these remote highlands and highlanders part of a larger narrative: regional, national, or perhaps even international/global.

It should come as no surprise that the Carpathian region, a frontier and borderland par excellence, should figure in this way. That the mountains comprised the southern frontier of so many permutations of Poland is significant. Always on the edge of something, frontiers like the Carpathians have long been places of refuge for many a renegade or nonconformist. They are also places of encounter. Despite its location in a Europe of sharply delineated (if sometimes contested) borders, the heterogeneous Carpathian frontier shares qualities with the frontiers of Latin America, which have been called "places where cultures contend with one another and with their physical environment to produce a dynamic that is unique to time and place."[19] This function of a frontier is not unlike that of a borderland. Borderlands have been defined as ethnically or religiously heterogeneous "spaces-in-between," areas far enough away from the political centers, whether imperial or national, to be ripe for contestation and conquest. This peripheral nature and the concomitant fantasizing about the borderlands on the part of those from or in the center often leads to these lands being subjected to myriad projects, in the process becoming places not only of coexistence but also—at times—of conflict.[20] Here, the discovery of Carpathian highlanders often resulted in attempts at reconciling the all-too-obvious difference between the people of the lowland center and the people of the highland borderland by emphasizing an essential underlying commonality of interests.

The challenging and capricious Carpathians were the perfect place for the center to indulge in introspection. Whether gazing upward—mountainward—or looking down from the heights, the center gained a different perspective on itself, its dilemmas, and how to resolve them. A new sense of the highland landscape, of its relevance as well as valuable qualities, emerged. Perhaps that should not come as much of a surprise, if we, like environmental historian Richard White, understand that spatial arrangements not only matter a great deal in human history but also reveal the social arrangements that help produce them.[21] The periphery can indeed be central.

This book consists of three parts, each in turn comprised of four chapters, representing different discoveries. The first part focuses on the Tatra Mountains from the 1870s to the first years of the twentieth century. Historically the Tatras had marked the southern border of the large East-Central European country known as the Polish-Lithuanian Commonwealth, a country partitioned out of existence at the end of the eighteenth century. Subsequently, the Carpathians, including the Tatras, formed the border of the Habsburg province of Galicia—part of the "Austrian" half of Austria-Hungary—with Hungary, the other half, the border line running through the mountains.[22] Nationally conscious Poles—especially those from the Russian zone of partition—were concerned about the state of both nation (partitioned, and still in the process of transitioning from the historic "noble nation" to something socially more comprehensive) and state (nonexistent). They would create a miniature Poland of the mind in the Tatra Mountain region, a place where Poles could congregate and experience freedom. By the outbreak of World War I, the Tatras had become a permanent fixture on the mental maps of

Poles, and the sleepy village of Zakopane, with its indigenous Górale (high-landers), had been transformed into the most famous high-altitude resort village in the Polish lands. This "discovery" was the benchmark for the others.

The second part heads further east, to the end of the Galician Carpathians, a region known as the Eastern Carpathians (vel Beskids) or, more precisely, the land of the Hutsuls (Huculszczyzna/Hutsul'shchyna), Hutsuls being the indigenous highlanders who dwelled there. It witnessed two periods of popularization. The first took place prior to World War I, when this section of the Carpathian Mountains was part of the Habsburg province of Galicia. Although it came on the heels of the Tatra discovery, for various reasons it was never directly proclaimed to be such by those who discovered it. These included Poles as well as Ruthenes/Ukrainians of varying stripes, all claiming the Hutsuls for their larger national projects. The various high-altitude resorts and sanatoria that emerged exemplify the different Galician, Polish, and Ukrainian approaches to the mountain region. The second popularization—and first proclaimed discovery—of the Hutsul region took place after World War I under very different circumstances. A bone of contention between Poles and Ukrainians, the wilderness that was the Eastern Carpathians ended up a part of the Second Polish Republic. Polish concerns for the integrity and security of the borders of their new and unquestionably

MAP 2. The "Polish" Carpathians, in the Kingdom of Galicia and Lodomeria (pre-1914). Map by Daniel P. Huffman.

heterogeneous state inspired a full-fledged, if militarily inflected, discovery of the Hutsuls and their region. The modernization of the region proceeded apace, bringing more and more tourists to this southeastern corner of the Second Polish Republic. Yet development came to an abrupt end with the outbreak of World War II, which would forever change the region.

The final part of the book veers back westward, as did the borders of postwar Poland, to a segment of the Carpathians known as the Bieszczady (Beshchady) Mountains. Although interest in this region and its native inhabitants, Lemkos and Boikos, began in the 1930s, its true discovery and popularization came only after World War II, under very different conditions, within the Polish People's Republic, now part of the Soviet bloc and feeling the pressure to modernize/industrialize after the fashion of the USSR. With the Tatras transformed into a national park, there was precious little wilderness left to explore in the country. Only then did the newly wild Bieszczady, Poland's "Wild East" (or "Wild West"?), become a popular tourist destination for urban Poles, millions of whom visited annually. In the 1970s a new postwar generation of ecologically minded trekkers expressed its concerns for the ever shrinking patch of wilderness, without which modern man would have no respite from an increasingly industrialized country and world. They sought to rescue the region for themselves and for posterity. That this mountain region was discovered repeatedly during the decades of state socialism, even before the advent of the Solidarity movement, and saw more than its share of contestation, is but one of the interesting aspects of this little known story.

This book's set of microhistories are all temporally situated within what Charles Maier has called the epoch of "territoriality," ranging from about 1860 to 1980.[23] It was a period in which nations and states—the Poles and Poland (in its various permutations) included—concerned themselves with the "frontier at the edge."[24] Space and spatial relations took on a new significance for those who claimed to discover the mountains. Catapulting the respective regions into unheard-of popularity, the discoveries also had important repercussions for the discoverers as well as the indigenous highlanders. Each self-proclaimed discovery was purpose driven, with those inspired by the highland periphery seeking to provide a solution to a pressing issue of the day. Claiming the mountains for nation, state, or posterity, they busied themselves with constructing a modern nation in the absence of independent state existence; buttressing the frontiers of a new, fragile, and nationally heterogeneous state in a world that privileged nation-states; or presenting plans for sustainable modernization in an increasingly industrialized world.

All this is one reason why anthropologist James C. Scott's observation rings true: "It is not possible to write a coherent history of the hills that is not in constant dialogue with lowland centers; nor is it possible to write a coherent history of lowland centers that ignores its hilly periphery."[25] Scott's contention regarding Southeast Asia admonishes those historians of Poland who would rather linger over the plains—the greatest part of the country, to be sure—instead of considering as well the unique vantage point and rarefied air of the physically peripheral Carpathian borderland. Turned into iconic native/national landscapes, they in turn shed light on the people and polity of a given age. One might also conclude from this that we ignore the intersection of nature and nation, and of nature and culture, at our own peril.

Part I

The Tatra Mountains of Galicia

❧ CHAPTER 1

Where Freedom Awaits

The first mountainous territory to figure in the consciousness of those who lived to its north, the Tatra Mountains comprise the highest and visually most distinctive part of the vast Carpathian range. Located in the western part of the Carpathians, bordering modern Poland and Slovakia, they can be thought of as a miniature Alps. With more than 60 peaks at around 8,000 feet, and a combined area of 303 square miles—less than one-quarter of which falls on the northern, Polish side—the Tatras are the most conspicuous geographical formation of the Carpathian Mountain system.

Essentially an uninhabited borderlands in the medieval period, the Tatra region became more of a genuine "frontier" (in the American understanding of the word) only as of the thirteenth century.[1] Pioneers came from all directions: in ethnic terms, colonists would be identified as Polish, Slovak, Ruthenian (Ukrainian and other East Slavs), Hungarian, "Saxon" (German) peasants, artisans, and pastoralists, as well as Wallachian (Romanian) shepherds migrating with their herds from the east. Many originally resided at the foot of the mountains: in Podhale (translated as "beneath the alpine meadows") on the northern, colder, Polish side of the border; in Orawa (Orava, Arva, Árva), Liptów (Liptov, Liptau, Liptó) and Spisz (Spiš, Zips, Szepes) on the warmer southern side, today part of Slovakia, although it historically had been part of Hungary.[2] The result of centuries of mixing, the highlanders—the word for

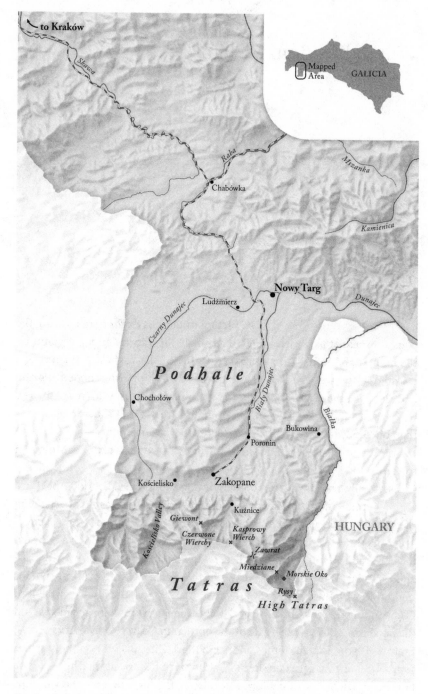

MAP 3. Podhale and the Tatra Mountains (pre-1914). Map by Daniel P. Huffman.

highlander in Polish was *góral*, from the term *góra* (mountain)—were shaped by various forces: their experience of the terrain, the migrations to the region, particularly from east to west, as well as by the mutual interaction of the different ethnic groups.[3] They were a borderland population par excellence.

While relatively small in scope and inhabited by a population of undeniably mixed provenance, the "Polish" Tatras are nonetheless the most significant mountainous terrain ever associated with any state that could be labeled Polish: these included the Polish-Lithuanian Commonwealth, the large, multiethnic, noble-dominated state that in the wake of three partitions disappeared from the map of Europe in 1795 (see map 1.) The seizure of the Polish Tatras in 1770 by Habsburg empress Maria Theresa had foreshadowed the "first" partition of 1772, in which not only Austria but Prussia and Russia helped themselves to large swaths of the country.[4] Following the first partition, the Carpathians formed the frontier between two provinces of the Habsburg (Austrian) lands: Hungary (to the south—a province which included today's Slovakia) and, to the north, the Polish territories annexed by Austria, which were christened the Kingdom of Galicia and Lodomeria.[5]

In the nineteenth century, the impact of this alpine borderland region, located far to the south of the vast plains of the Polish heartland (under Russian and Prussian/German rule), would transcend its geographical remoteness. Poles from across the partitioned lands would not only visit the Tatras; they would come to know, even identify strongly with the mountains and the highlanders who dwelled at their foot. The latter enjoyed a freedom of movement that was the envy of lowlanders, worn down by the cares of a civilization that came courtesy of the partitioning powers. That a rugged alpine territory should come to play an important role for the inhabitants of former Poland, the very name of which designates the territory as quintessential flatlands, is but one of the many paradoxes of this story.

Despite the fact that the Tatras were to some extent already known, a different encounter with the highlands and the indigenous highlanders was to take place in the last third of the nineteenth century.[6] This discovery, which had ramifications for how the Tatras were experienced, was of significance not only for the mountain environment. It would, as we shall see, have repercussions for the nation as well as for nature.

Early Encounters

The process of nationally conscious Polish elites encountering the Tatras started at the very beginning of the nineteenth century. The earliest to leave his mark on the region was the Enlightenment figure Stanisław Staszic (1755–1826), the first Polish scientist to investigate the Tatra Mountains. Now known as the "father of Polish geology," Staszic visited the Western, High, and Biel-skie Tatras as well as various valleys, climbed a number of mountain peaks, even spending the night on one so as to take scientific measurements.

Despite his scientific concerns, Staszic was also moved by his encounter with the mountains. An excerpt from his book, *On the Geology of the Carpathians, and Other Polish Mountains and Plains*, hints at the type of impression that the region was yet to make on his fellow countrymen. Staszic's trips—in 1802, 1804, and 1805—came at a difficult time for the Poles: they had just lost their independence as a result of the partitions of the late eighteenth century. Staszic projected onto the mountains he "conquered" an undeniably Polish message. As if addressing the very mountains themselves, he intoned: "You enormous cemetery of past centuries, you most lasting monuments for future centuries, in an inaccessible elevated height, your peaks filling the clouds, you will preserve the indestructible name of the Poles. Unreachable by any human violence, you will preserve this sign and convey it to the next centuries as testimony that the first one to stand on this your polished summit was a Pole."[7] The natural feature that was the Tatra Mountains thus became a metaphor for the Polish nation. By leaving his mark on Łomnica (Lomnický štít), thought at the time to be the Tatras' highest peak, Staszic was, in essence, demonstrating that the nation still existed: the memory of the stateless, territoryless Polish nation would somehow endure. That the mountain fell on the Hungarian side of the border, and that Staszic was not actually the first, but the second person—after the English naturalist Robert Townson—to reach the summit, made the observation all the more bittersweet.[8]

This example shows how, from the outset, even those inclined to see the Carpathians as a site of scientific inquiry were not immune to its potential national symbolism. Coming generations would continue Staszic's scientific investigations. This was especially true of the period of Romanticism. Here one might mention the multifaceted work of geologist and paleontologist Ludwik Zejszner (1805–71); Seweryn Goszczyński (1801–76), the "father of Podhale ethnography"; or the poet, geographer, and ethnographer Wincenty Pol (1807–72), who escorted students to the Tatras in 1852.[9]

Yet the Tatras were more than just a destination for scientists. These mountains, which later generations would come to see as unspoiled wilderness, were paradoxically the site of early industrial development. During the first half of the eighteenth century, an ironworks was established in the locality that would come to be known as Kuźnice (after the Polish word for ironworks). Henceforth mining and metallurgy would be developed in the region by a succession of landowners, with varying degrees of success. In the late eighteenth century, the Habsburg court sent Balthasar Hacquet into the Carpathian Mountains that formed the southern border of this new province of Galicia to investigate its newly acquired territory. Hacquet wrote a multivolume work detailing what he learned from his trips, beginning in 1788, through the "Dacian and Sarmatian or Northern Carpathians," this designation coming from his title.[10] This first major work of scholarship on the Carpathians did not convince the Habsburgs that they should involve themselves in the mining or metallurgy industries in the Tatras. Ultimately the Kuźnice and Kościelisko ironworks were purchased by the Homolacses, a Hungarian family who later bought the adjacent Zakopane demesne, with its extensive forests, in 1824.[11]

The two landholdings of the Homolacses, Kuźnice and Zakopane, the latter of which would figure importantly in the later discovery, would develop in different ways. The Homolacses settled in Kuźnice, in the vicinity of the forge, building a manor house with a garden and animal park, where the occasional traveler to the region would be housed and entertained.[12] Foreign workers were brought in to administer the iron works. Those highlanders from the village of Zakopane who found work with the Homolacses figured mainly within the cohort of miners, some 120 strong, although foreign miners from Bohemia and the German lands were also employed. Others served as drivers, carting the iron ore mined in the Kościelisko and other valleys to Kuźnice to be processed.

Mining and metallurgy shaped the look of the land. In the Tatras, it pockmarked the sections of the valleys where the ore was mined. Trees from the Zakopane forests, in the form of charcoal made on the spot, fueled the forge's fire, resulting in their gradual depletion and, in places, deforestation. The functioning of the forge doubtless had an impact on air quality, at least in the vicinity of Kuźnice. And primitive roads were created in this mountain wilderness where there had been none before. The wide gentle trail now known by hikers as Droga pod Reglami was created over time by the carters transporting the iron ore to Kuźnice. So much for a pristine wilderness!

Still, around midcentury the occasional intrepid traveler did come to the region.[13] These included members of the "gentler" sex: the noblewoman Łucja Rautenstrauchowa of the princely Giedroyć family, the inveterate hiker Maria Steczkowska of Kraków, and the Warsaw writer known as Deotyma all published books or articles about their experiences.[14]

Visitors also included Roman Catholic priests. In addition to the thrill of mountain climbing, these clergymen doubtless found attractive the possibility of being closer to heaven, atop what later would be referred to as "altars of freedom."[15] Of the priests to come midcentury there was one who, on summiting a great Tatra peak, would put on his surplice and stole and solemnly intone the Te Deum, his highland guides on their knees. This was Father Józef Stolarczyk (1816–93).[16]

Invited by the Homolacses to establish a parish in the Zakopane demesne in 1848, the thirty-two-year-old priest arrived to find a flock of unchurched highlanders, for whom the fat of the marmot held more miraculous power than did any Christian prayer.[17] Of peasant stock himself, the clergyman—an imposing figure who towered over the highlanders—got his parishioners to build him what he needed. Delivering his sermons in highland dialect, Stolarczyk tried to instill Christian morals in the folk, knowing full well that, after Mass, they often headed to the nearby tavern or went a'wooing. (Already Zejszner noted that the passionate as well as gregarious highlanders seemed to accept premarital sex, love affairs, and children out of wedlock as nothing out of the ordinary.)[18] Stolarczyk would rule Zakopane for a full forty-five years—ample time to tame his wild flock, turning poachers and brigands into regular law-abiding churchgoers.[19]

Stolarczyk immediately took to mountain climbing and proved to be more than a match for his highlanders.[20] Few of them could serve as competent guides for him. As odd as it may seem, Zakopane highlanders did not necessarily know "their" mountains. A shepherd might be familiar with the area where he pastured his sheep, and other highlanders knew a peak or two. The only men who had any deeper knowledge of the mountainous terrain were poachers and brigands. The first pursued with abandon chamois and marmots—rare and endangered animals—and would shoot any bear that should cross their path. And brigands clearly needed to know how to make themselves scarce after an attack on a cottage or tavern. Such men were the company of the priests who scaled the Tatra peaks.

At this time the highlanders, with their marginal, hardscrabble fields, were in need of supplementary employment, as highlander Wojciech Brzega explained in his memoirs.[21] Their problems increased after midcentury, when the mining of iron ore on the northern slopes of the Tatras ceased to be profitable. Once Kuźnice and Zakopane came into the possession of the German banker Baron Ludwig Eichborn in 1869, the local highlanders were increasingly forced to look for work elsewhere. Their jobs at the rolling mill and forges, making charcoal, or transporting iron to lowland destinations having dried up, the men were faced with few options. They could mow hay in season wherever necessary in the lowlands, or seek work in Hungarian mines or in construction. Young highland girls were sent to work as servants in Kraków. This they all did "for bread," to quote the title of an 1866 poem by

Michał Bałucki that became a song still sung today.[22] The highlanders, many of whom faced food insecurity even in good years, had fallen on hard times.

Yet a new source of income was on the horizon. It came courtesy of a twenty-year-old artist from Kraków, Walery Eljasz, who in 1861 began to make what would be annual trips to Zakopane and the Tatras. Eljasz and his family came to spend their summers in the village of Zakopane. Other Cracovians followed. This proved to be an inexpensive vacation, if not a particularly luxurious one, the accommodations being in highlander cottages.[23] Not only could one climb the mountains and inhale the fresh alpine air, which was already being "commodified" in the Alps, it was also the right place to go for those interested in the curative properties of the whey of ewe's milk, which could be obtained from highland shepherds.[24] With the intent of popularizing the Tatras among fellow Poles, in 1870 Eljasz published a guidebook of sorts entitled *Illustrated Guidebook to the Tatras, the Pieniny, and Szczawnica*.[25] This publication helped to acquaint his compatriots with the highland region and the possibilities of climbing mountains in Galicia, along whose southern border the mountains lay.

While this was not the first Polish-language guidebook to make note of the region, the timing was propitious for Eljasz and the invention of Zakopane as a tourist destination.[26] In 1870 the Galicians were in the process of securing for themselves a degree of autonomy within Austria-Hungary. By 1873, the province was the freest part of the former Polish lands, a place where one could not only feel but act like a Pole. That the most economically challenged of the former Polish lands—at one point nicknamed "Golicja i Głodomeria," essentially "the land of the naked and the starving"—was to become the most attractive Polish vacation destination is yet another paradox involving the borderland province.

The Discovery of the Tatras

In the summer of 1873 something so significant occurred as to be recorded in Father Stolarczyk's parish chronicle: some three hundred summer visitors were to be found in Zakopane.[27] This marked a quantitative leap forward, insofar as interest in and travel to the remote region was concerned. A middle-aged Polish physician from Warsaw, Dr. Tytus Chałubiński, made the trek to the Tatras that summer. This universally liked and respected doctor, who had just resigned his post at the university in Warsaw because he was being asked to teach in Russian, has gone down in Polish history as the discoverer of the Tatras.[28]

Chałubiński's portentous trip in the summer of 1873 represented his first family vacation in Zakopane, if not his first visit to the Tatras.[29] The Warsaw doctor came to Zakopane with a mission. During his stay, Chałubiński commissioned an iron cross to be erected on the nearby hill of Gubałówka, from which one has an excellent view of the Tatras.[30] The very choice of the Tatras as the proper place for such a cross—a place where Poles from any part of the world could leave their mark—prefigures the attraction this place would soon have for Chałubiński's compatriots. Many would soon be making what one might term a national pilgrimage, despite the fact that there were no historical monuments here.

The year 1873 was also marked by an outbreak of cholera in the mountains. Spreading from the Galician lowlands, the disease made its way to Zakopane at the beginning of September.[31] Chałubiński could have opted to escape the epidemic and depart for home with other lowland guests.[32] Instead, over the next five weeks the good doctor cared for the sick—many highlanders, and also Father Stolarczyk—practically around the clock.[33] Doctor Chałubiński won eternal gratitude from the highlanders.[34]

The cult of the man later to be labeled "King of the Tatras" was initiated by Father Stolarczyk, who suggested to the highlanders the following year that they erect a triumphal arch and greet the doctor upon his arrival. The gratitude of the highlanders was genuine and needed no prompting. Chałubiński would forevermore be treated like a celebrity in Zakopane, greeted with fanfare by masses of highlanders every time he visited. Indeed, a wild cavalry of mounted highland horsemen would ride out to meet Chałubiński's wagon and escort him to the village.[35] As one highlander recalled, in those lean years they awaited his arrival "as if he were to bring them good fortune from Warsaw."[36] For it was Chałubiński who recommended the Tatras and Zakopane to his patients (and others) as a destination where they could regain their health in the vivifying highland air. In other words, Chałubiński not only summered in Zakopane; he sent more Varsovians there—to be transported, housed, and guided by the highlanders.

News of Doctor Chałubiński's convictions as to the health-giving properties of the Tatra Mountains began to spread. Before long lowland Poles were vacationing, some even building homes for themselves, in the picturesquely situated village of Zakopane, to be used especially during the summer months. By the end of the next decade, there were more than six hundred rooms to let and around three thousand "guests"—a tenfold jump from 1873.[37]

Much recent scholarship has countered that Polish elites had been traveling to the Tatras since the early nineteenth century, that Poles from the nearby city of Kraków had already begun to summer in the vicinity prior to 1873, that even a basic guidebook or two to the Tatras had already been compiled.[38] However, these developments did not amount to a true discovery. Chałubiński's contribution should not be discounted for two reasons.

First, it needs to be understood in broader terms. This was not simply someone first setting foot in an unknown land. True discoveries are not only purposeful but also transformative. In the words of the artist, writer, and activist Stanisław Witkiewicz, Chałubiński had "discovered" the Tatras for "us"—meaning the Polish elites across the partitioned lands.[39] Following Chałubiński's popularization, Polish society became enamored of the Tatras and highland culture to an unprecedented extent. With time, the mountains would become a destination vested with an invigorated Polishness, a site of national pilgrimage, a place where Poles from all three zones of partition could interact, and a place of national experimentation.

Second, it appears that, for this discovery to have a real effect, it needed to gain advocates in the heart of the Polish lands: in Warsaw and the Russian Empire, not only in the nearby Galician lowlands or piedmont. For the Galician elites, Tatra Mountain highlanders were simply "their" local peasants.[40] By contrast, for Varsovian urbanites of a positivist bent—and this was the age of Warsaw positivism, with its "work at the foundations" motto and prioritizing of social and economic development—the self-assured highland peasants were no less a revelation.[41] This was important for national activists who sought to turn peasants, emancipated only recently, into conscious Poles, but found the peasants of the plains far less promising than the highlanders.[42]

These elites from Russian Poland also appreciated the relative freedom of nationally motivated action accorded the Poles in Austrian Galicia, who according to Article 19 of the Fundamental Laws of 1867 were allowed to "defend and nurture [their] nationality and language"; this made the Habsburg province more attractive to Poles from the Russian and German empires. Indeed, it was not until Chałubiński started convincing other Poles from the Russian Empire to visit the remote and distant Tatras instead of traveling to foreign destinations for vacation that this particular form of "domestic tourism"—or, more correctly, "national tourism" (for the tourists came from different empires, while considering themselves to belong to the same nation)—took off.[43]

Zakopane and the mountains were also remote enough as to be nearly invisible to the partitioning powers. It is altogether fitting that Chałubiński and many other lowland outsiders hailed from the Russian Empire and helped to popularize the Tatras among fellow subjects of the tsar, those who perhaps chafed the most under foreign rule—although at least one Polish priest from the German Empire made annual pilgrimages to Zakopane because there he could sing Polish patriotic songs without fear of being arrested by the police.[44] As we will see, these nationally conscious Poles availed themselves of this room for genuine independent action in the remote highland borderland.

Alpinism, Polish Style

Borderlands are often liminal places where a momentary disorientation can lead to subsequent reorientation or transformation. Zakopane and the Tatras afforded lowland Poles precisely such an environment. The very trip to Zakopane represented the first rite of initiation for Poles from abroad, who made their way first by train to Kraków, Poland's ancient capital and one of the main cities of what was now the Habsburg province of Galicia. From Kraków, the long-distance travelers would make the trek south to Zakopane. This was a slow and arduous journey, one traversed in a springless covered wagon over the space of two days, with a night spent in a bug-infested inn along the way. If the bouncing across rocky terrain had not left the travelers sore enough, the bedbugs proved more than obliging. Impatient to see and—at long last—reach the mountains, these lowland Polish urbanites were already learning that time, as they understood it in the lowlands, took on a different quality in the highlands: one had to adjust to a slower pace, one that allowed for more introspection if not always for easier observation.[45]

The same slow pace would shape the lowlanders' experience of the Tatra Mountains themselves. Here it was Tytus Chałubiński who set the tone for the late nineteenth-century encounter with the exotic highlands, not only informing the way Poles apprehended the mountains but also shaping the very nature of Polish alpinism of that age. This is visible from Chałubiński's detailed account of a hiking expedition undertaken in September 1878 and published the following year—the first piece in what would become a tradition of Polish tourist (that is, mountaineering) literature.[46] Chałubiński invented what he himself labeled an "excursion without a program" ("wycieczka bez programu").[47] This new style of mountain climbing popularized by Chałubiński speaks volumes about the way the Polish nation would come to be imagined in the Tatras, as it faced the challenges presented by the alpine environment.

In its essence, the "excursion without a program" was just as it sounds: a mountain-climbing expedition of several days or weeks without a set itinerary. Participants made spontaneous decisions about which Tatra peaks to scale and how to climb them, often based nearly as much on whim as on the often capricious weather, which Chałubiński monitored with a barometer—the weather in the mountains determining whether an excursion could take place at all. This all being part of Austria-Hungary, they hiked in the Tatras without regard to the Galician-Hungarian frontier, which they crossed back and forth with impunity.

These programless excursions were unique. One of the peculiarities of Polish alpine tourism in the Tatras at this time was its communal and interactive nature. This special form of domestic tourism, dangerous and difficult, combined the enjoyment of the wild and majestic nature in this miniature Alps—the towering peaks, with their bare summits and steep approaches, the lush green valleys and forests, the sight of cavorting chamois and other wildlife—with an encounter with the Tatra highlanders. In this they were different from German- or Swiss-style excursions in the Alps or elsewhere.[48] Elaborate and extensive affairs, Chałubiński's excursions generally included a number of invited guests as well as thirty to forty highlanders. On the sole trip about which Chałubiński himself wrote, the group was relatively small. This resulted from the fact that the expedition was made in the autumn, once most Poles had already returned home. The weather nonetheless was so perfect for an excursion that Chałubiński invited a mountain-climbing colleague (a *taternik*, in the doctor's neologism, the label describing "those who hike a lot in the Tatras") and some ten highlanders.[49] As Chałubiński put it, this many were invited not out of need but so that they that might have a good time: "We could have taken more, but we lacked a pretext for that."[50]

These highlanders came outfitted as befitted true men of the mountains. They were known for their distinctive garb: a sheepskin jerkin, a white felt jacket, and distinctive, formfitting woolen pants, with an embroidered emblem on each leg and stripe up the sides. Highland men also wore black felt hats, in many instances improbably embellished with little seashells (imported from the Adriatic—a sign that the highlander had more contact with the rest of the world than is sometimes thought). Shod in moccasins (*kierpce*), highlanders moved with a graceful sureness of foot, much like the chamois that they sometimes hunted in the mountains. They were generally to be found with hatchet (*ciupaga*) in hand, the highlander's first line of defense. Yet, despite this commanding presence, the Zakopane highlander was no longer threatening, in part thanks to the efforts of Father Stolarczyk. The highlanders were "very polite and loquacious," according to Chałubiński, although the doctor also noted that they could quickly take the measure of a man and treat him accordingly; for example, a negative assessment could result in a lowlander, unprepared but wanting to hike to the Tatra's most famous destination, Morskie Oko (Eye of the Sea) Lake, being led to a different pond and told by their highland guide that it was the famous one.[51]

The highlanders were to be marveled at for more than their looks, fearlessness, and cleverness. They were the lifeblood of the excursion, serving as porters as well as guides, during Chałubiński's excursions also carrying musical instruments as well as numerous containers into which the doctor, an avid botanist and bryologist, placed samples of highland mosses—the science a pretense for the trip.[52]

Views as well as scientific samples were collected on the "excursions without a program," as seen from this one six-day expedition.[53] Clad as always in the sheepskin jerkin of the highlanders and his own straw hat, Chałubiński with his entourage reached the summit of three of the highest Tatra peaks: the Gerlach (Gerlachovský štít), at 8,707 feet; the Wysoka (Vysoká), at 8,399 feet; and the Rysy, at 8,212 feet above sea level—whence the best panoramas. The first two were not to be found in Galicia but rather lay on the Hungarian side of the border, while the nearby Rysy was on the Galician side—the highest mountain there. Some of these peaks had only recently been "conquered" by the Poles, the first of whom—Father Józef Stolarczyk, with highlanders Wojciech Roj, Szymon Tatar, Wojciech Kościelny, and

FIGURE 1.1. Sketch of a grand-style hiking excursion in the Tatras by Stanisław Witkiewicz. Published in Stanisław Witkiewicz, *Na przełęczy: Wrażenia i obrazy z Tatr* (Warsaw: 1891), 127. Image in the public domain.

Wojciech Gewont—attained the summit of the highest of the Tatra peaks, the Gerlach, in 1874.[54]

Another important feature of this novel kind of Polish alpinism, modeled by Chałubiński in his travelogue, was illustrated by the climbers' openness during an excursion to seeking new routes as well as new descents down these highest peaks—risky climbing in the days before ropes were used or chains or metal holds affixed to the most dangerous and exposed parts of the climb. Yet on this occasion the descent down the Gerlach went smoothly, and the group made it down from the rocky inhospitable heights to the realm of the dwarf mountain pine in time to eat and rest.

Evening rest in the liminal highland borderland took on a peculiar form unique to the excursion without a program—perhaps its most characteristic feature. Chałubiński astutely equipped his excursion with a "tent, supplies, band, and singers."[55] Add to that a roaring campfire, and magic happened. A meal was prepared and beds constructed of dwarf pine branches, and the highlanders would sing and dance around the campfire. Highland music—raw and full of dissonances—was uniquely suited to the mountains, according to one observer who could not understand the attraction it held for Chałubiński until he heard it during such a Tatra expedition.[56] During this trip in 1878 Jan Krzeptowski-Sabała (1809–94) played his squeaky and ancient fiddle for the group.[57] The tales and music of this "last old-fashioned highlander" seemed to transport all present back in time, with some longing for the primeval past that Sabała brought to life.[58] Chałubiński himself wrote that he regretted that he and Sabała had not been born a hundred years earlier. Were they alive then, he suggested to the highlander, they would have been brigands together.[59]

There truly was something special about the improbable camaraderie between the illiterate septuagenarian Sabała and the refined Warsaw doctor who helped turn him into a legendary figure during his lifetime. Special, too, was Chałubiński's unique rapport with the highlanders in general. It opened the door for the coming together of two segments of what we would now call the Polish national community but which were still hardly of a piece at this time. These were the Polish upper classes—here more precisely, the intelligentsia, defined as doctors, lawyers, writers, journalists, and other professionals—and the so-called Polish peasants, Polish in that they spoke a Polish dialect but generally lacked a Polish national identity.

And there was more to the "excursion without a program" than just improved relations between highland peasants and lowland guests. The doctor, a Russian subject, did not mention in his anonymously published account that he was advocating this Polish alpinism as a means of restoring health to the Polish nation on Polish (here: Galician) soil. Why should Polish elites travel to spas and resorts abroad when they had a curative environment within the boundaries of the old Polish state? Lowland Poles were to place themselves in the liminal environment of the mountains, put their trust in the highland guides, and in the process of mountaineering gain a new lease on life.

Chałubiński claimed that he returned from the six-day trip fresher than he set off, life amid the "sleeping granite giants" proving more restful than stressful.[60] His metaphor recalls to mind the tale of medieval King Bolesław's knights, asleep under the Tatras, who at the right moment would come to life to rescue the fatherland (a story that has parallels elsewhere in Europe). At the same time, these excursions were one of the few opportunities offered lowland Poles during this period of imperial domination to feel fully free. Instead of crowded city life, under the control, even surveillance, of the imperial authorities, here they had breathing room, literally and figuratively. Perhaps it should come as no surprise that the freewheeling "excursion without a program" became the model for this classical age of Polish alpinism.

This might also explain why the lowlanders were fascinated by aspects of highland culture that had already died out, such as brigandage. Lowland Poles came to romanticize the brigands of yore more than the highlanders, who nonetheless sang of their own Robin Hood of the eighteenth century, Juraj Jánošík.[61] Were not Chałubiński and the others, in a way, playing at brigandage—traipsing across the mountains in their merry group? The Polish physician liked to think that his band of alpinists, gentlemen and peasants alike, roaming across the highlands with their jaunty airs, music, and occasional shots from a pistol, might actually be taken for brigands on the other side of the border by the Germans and Hungarians they encountered.[62]

Here the parallel between brigands and warriors seems pertinent. The British alpinist Leslie Stephen maintained that mountain climbing was the nearest thing an ordinary civilian got to soldiering: "He has some of the excitements, and many of the difficulties and privations of warfare, without any of the disgusting and dreadful features."[63] Might not these excursions be imagined as the movements of a Polish army patrol, in a period when there was no Polish state? Walery Eljasz also saw something attractively "chivalric" in mountain climbing.[64] Eljasz's alpinist son Stanisław would compare Chałubiński and his band to a "detachment of errant borderland knights."[65] These expeditions appeared to be the perfect vehicle for upper-class lowlander and lower-class highlander to bond—again, something much desired by positivistic Varsovians.

The "excursion without a program" thus especially suited stateless Poles longing for genuine freedom. Polish alpinism à la Chałubiński was unique.

Taking part in these excursions, lowlanders learned to be calm in the face of danger, were restored to health, and became attuned to the natural world as never before in the helpful and inspirational company of the highland guide, the latter a reminder of the days of yore when brigands roamed freely with disregard for boundaries and authorities. Together in this highland realm, the rocky substance of which reinforced a sense of Polish national permanence despite the partitions, they were enacting freedom, as imagined by the upper-class climbers—freedom they so dearly lacked in the imperially dominated lowlands. Should it come as a surprise that the Warsaw physician, so convinced of the health-giving properties of these excursions, would henceforth spend the rest of his summers in the Tatras—and convince others to join him there?

The Birth of the Tatra Society

The year 1873 would prove significant for the Tatras, the highlanders, and Zakopane in more ways than one. That same summer, an organization was founded that would complement and expand on what Chałubiński himself was able to achieve. The Galician Tatra Society was the first tourist or hiking organization active in the lands of the former Polish-Lithuanian Commonwealth.[66] It was part of a general and growing interest in alpine clubs across Europe. Britain, with its elitist British Alpine Club, established in 1857, was the leader, to be followed before long by the Austrian, Italian, Swiss, and German alpine clubs.[67] The same year as the Galicians were deliberating, the Hungarians and the local Zipser Germans right across the border established their own Hungarian Carpathian Society. Although the year of founding is traditionally given as 1873, the Galician Tatra Society's initial statute was not approved by the provincial authorities until 1874—the same year the Club Alpin Français was founded and the Austrian and German Clubs merged.[68]

That the Galician Tatra Society did not become simply another generic alpine club was in part the work of outsiders—that is, of Chałubiński and other visiting members of the Polish intelligentsia. Indeed, the founding of the society underscored a tension between those who identified themselves first and foremost as Poles (many from abroad), and the local landowners Baron Ludwig Eichborn, Józef Szalay, and others who saw themselves as residents of Galicia, may not have spoken Polish, and who may or may not have been thinking in "Polish" terms. (Initial meetings of the society took place in German, although the minutes were written in Polish.) Even if they did, they may have been inclined to equate Polishness with being "Galician," given the dominance of the so-called Polish elites—that is, descendants of the former nobles of the Polish-Lithuanian Commonwealth—in the province.

The initial interaction between Galicians and outsiders, which one historian categorized as a "coup d'état of the democrats against the aristocrats," very quickly changed the profile of the organization, as seen from the fact that the society's statute underwent revision later that same year.[69] Some of the changes, such as the removal of the adjective "Galician" from the title of the organization, reflected the tacit acknowledgment that not only residents of Galicia took an interest in the Tatra Mountains. Implied but not stated was that the Tatra Society—which for political reasons could not easily be called Polish—was a more broadly conceived Polish organization. The Tatra Society took as its slogan an excerpt of a poem by Wincenty Pol, who had visited the region midcentury: "To the mountains, to the mountains, dear brother! There freedom awaits you."[70] And a reduction of the annual membership fee enabled numerous upper-class Poles from both Russian and German empires as well as Galician Poles—if not highlanders, as Chałubiński and the democrats had wished—to enroll in the society.[71]

The mandate of the organization also changed. Originally, the Tatra Society had three aims: to explore the Carpathians in a competent way and disseminate information gathered about them; to foster tourism by encouraging tourists—in particular members of the society but also scholars and artists—to visit as well as by improving access to the region; and to protect rare alpine animals like the chamois and marmots that were already protected in Galicia by legislation from 1868, one of the first such pieces of legislation in the world.[72] These aims were in keeping with the general mandates of alpine clubs: to improve the infrastructure and educate the population about the region while protecting the natural habitat.[73] The revised statute broadened the mandate of the society to allow for more direct influence on local and human conditions. This was done in a couple ways, one of which was to add a fourth point to the main aims that permitted (one might say, even exhorted) members to "support alpine industry." By this seemingly business-oriented statement was actually meant the "improvement of the fate of the impoverished alpine population."[74]

The basic needs of the indigenous and generally indigent highlanders, who augmented their meager finances by selling berries gathered in the forest to the summer tourists, were not neglected. Chałubiński saw to it that they were provided with clover seeds, which would help the highlanders improve their poor soil. He also established a bank of sorts that loaned the highlanders money in advance of the harvest; this helped them financially during the lean days of the sowing and preharvest seasons. With interest in the region growing, highlanders also had other employment opportunities. More highlanders were transporting lowland guests or serving as hosts to them. The talents of the highland hunters and poachers, heirs to the brigands, were channeled into more productive—and legal—activities: they took on new careers as rangers deputized to protect the endangered chamois and marmots as well as serve as guides for excursions into the highlands.[75] The mountains had been transformed into a new, and much appreciated, source of income for the highlanders.[76]

All this still did not provide employment for all young highlanders. The society took its mandate to "support alpine industry" literally. To this end—encouraged by Chałubiński and Eljasz—it founded a woodworking school in 1876.[77] Such training would help boys make a career in the construction and furnishing of guest houses for the lowland visitors. Girls were to benefit from a lacemaking school, founded by Chałubiński and the actress Helena Modrzejewska (known as Modjeska in the United States, where she performed to acclaim), who at this time was already a frequent summer vacationer in Zakopane.[78]

✷ CHAPTER 2

On the Mountain Pass

Another outsider who would contribute immensely to the popularity of Zakopane was the man who in 1889 declared that Chałubiński had "discovered the Tatras for us."[1] This was Stanisław Witkiewicz (1851–1915).[2] The artist and writer was a patient of Chałubiński's in Warsaw, although he had been born further east, in the historic Lithuanian lands. Witkiewicz first came to the Tatras in 1876 but began to visit annually after 1886 to cure his tuberculosis. His encounter with both highlands and highlanders in these years led Witkiewicz in new and original directions, completely changing his life trajectory.

Soon to become a fixture of Zakopane, Witkiewicz was arguably the greatest popularizer of Zakopane and the Tatras. Most important for Tatra tourism, Witkiewicz penned an evocative account of a journey to Zakopane and a hiking expedition that was simultaneously more literary and more programmatic than Chałubiński's of a decade earlier. This work was entitled *On the Mountain Pass: Impressions and Pictures from the Tatras* (*Na przełęczy: Wrażenia i obrazy z Tatr*). *On the Mountain Pass* was first published in serialized form in the popular Warsaw journal *Tygodnik Illustrowany* (Illustrated Weekly) in 1889–90 and contained illustrations done by the author. In 1891 it came out in book form, appearing in several editions before World War I.[3] While the turn-of-the-century Polish poet Kazimierz Przerwa-Tetmajer said it was "the most beautiful thing ever written about the Tatras," Ferdynand Hoesick touted it as "one of the most read books in the lands of the [former Polish-Lithuanian] Commonwealth," a work that elevated its author to the status of one of the "most famous and most popular Polish writers."[4]

While it has been argued that the syncretic and innovative work—part diary, memoir, essay, ethnographic sketch, novel, travelogue—helped to initiate a new form of writing about the Tatras, *On the Mountain Pass* functioned as a kind of literary Polish Baedeker, a tourist guidebook to Zakopane and the Tatras written by Witkiewicz for his lowland compatriots from the Russian Empire.[5] Witkiewicz helped to construct the "tourist gaze" for those headed for the mountains; he directed their gaze in specific ways, not only instructing the lowland philistine on what kinds of experiences he should strive for during his own pilgrimage to the highlands but literally telling him how to interpret what he encountered—for example, to note the artistry of the intricately carved highland cottage and the highlander's objects of daily use.[6] If ever there was a literary work on the Tatras that taught readers how to view the Tatra Mountains and Zakopane, this was it.

It also taught them to appreciate the Tatra highlander. In many ways, *On the Mountain Pass* is a paean to the góral. Although Witkiewicz wrote that Chałubiński's generation "fell into a boundless admiration at the sight of the highlanders," the author was clearly even more enamored of these highland peasants, so superior to the peasants back home.[7] He called the highlander an integral "part of nature, the fantastic interpreter of its beauty and force."[8] (That did not stop this quick-witted folk from perceiving the visitors as "one of the most rewarding crops to cultivate.")[9] The consumptive Witkiewicz was not only appreciative of the highlanders' assistance in the mountains; like many other visitors, he seemed to place the highlander—Sabała in particular, whom Witkiewicz called a Polish "Homer"—on a pedestal.[10] In *On the Mountain Pass* he devoted pages and pages to Sabała's tales, related in highland dialect.[11] The ancient highlander told stories of that fabled age, when brigands roamed the mountains and when highlanders engaged in life-or-death battles with their biggest enemies: bears and the Liptak highlanders across the Hungarian border. Witkiewicz also related Sabała's tales of a brigand of noble ancestry, Józef Baczyński.[12] Indeed, a nobleman could often be seen by Jánošík's side on the folk paintings on glass for which the region was known. This juxtaposition could be construed as yet another image of lowlander/highlander togetherness—an example of what happened in the liminal zone of the Tatras, where a nobleman could become a brigand.

Lowlanders of Witkiewicz's age could profit from the physical outlet that was Chałubiński-style *taternictwo*, in the author's neologism. Witkiewicz termed this Polish alpinism "the reckless games of serious people," given the danger of the endeavor.[13] Nonetheless these games were transformative: this encounter with the mountains would awaken in the participant "instincts, strengths and abilities [that were] dead or impotent" in his regular, peaceful life, making him even more like the much-admired highlander.[14] Lest my choice of pronoun suggest that this was solely a male venture: many women likewise climbed peaks, crinolines and all, with Witkiewicz claiming that anyone could be a *taternik*.[15]

But was there no limit to who could become a Polish alpinist? In part four of *On the Mountain Pass* (by far the longest section), Witkiewicz described a Chałubiński-style ("grand-style") excursion. He told of a trip taken by a motley group of thirteen guides and ten relative novices, all intelligentsia types who might well profit from an excursion into the mountains, according to both Chałubiński and Witkiewicz. However, instead of ascending the tallest peaks, as had climbers before them, they satisfied themselves with climbing mountain passes, Zawrat and the titular pass of Mięguszowiecka, which represented a challenge for the group.[16]

Witkiewicz's tale contains a brief episode that sheds light on the way the nation was being imagined in the mountains. During this excursion a rare moment of harmony seemed to have been achieved atop the mountain pass known as Zawrat, located on one of the more popular routes taken to the lake called Morskie Oko (Eye of the Sea), the ultimate destination of Witkiewicz's excursion. The climbers paused to take in the beauty of their surroundings. The mists cast an otherworldly glow, softening the impressions of the deserted wilderness. Resting atop the mountain pass, the hikers absorbed the changed atmosphere of the place, perceiving their newly attained mountain pass as less threatening than it was minutes earlier. This unusually tranquil, evocative moment was interrupted by an unexpected sight:

> Suddenly, on the background of azures and opals stands a comic figure in a jerkin atop a long paltote, in droopy, trailing trousers. He removes his hat, bows, smiles with an undertone of humbleness, fear, and desire to win affection, parades before the entire band with perpetual ogles and disappears, like a specter, leaving behind a somewhat familiar smell in the valleys.
>
> Where did that little Jew come from? With whom did he come? After whom has he gone? No one knows.
>
> This commonplace, fantastic specter, which at this precise moment populated Zawrat with entire crowds of meschures, traders, small-town troublemakers, filth, stench, the Jewish question.[17]

Visions of Polish oneness with nature, and oneness with the highlanders, dissipated: "From all sides through the clean airy expanses, dirty 'shades' flew in and occupied the imagination."[18]

The passage conveyed concluded with a more damning assessment. The "polite little Jew" was compared to a famous metaphor from Polish literature. Witkiewicz labeled him "'the shade of the enemy'" that came 'to mix blood in the wedding cups.'"[19] These lines come from Adam Mickiewicz's epic poem *Konrad Wallenrod*, a work that centered on the question of treachery. Here the Jew was seen as the deceiver: seemingly eager to ingratiate himself with the Poles, he was a potential traitor in their midst—one who seemed to be interfering with the lovely experiment of the intelligentsia in the mountains.

This particular Jew was clearly a Polish Jew: he was seen again in the hut at Morskie Oko writing paeans to the mountains in the guest book in three languages: Hebrew, German, and Polish, expressing his wish to return again to Morskie Oko the following year.[20] He was not the Jewish trader, innkeeper, or moneylender of stereotype: rather he was a tourist, an alpinist—a taternik, just like the Poles in the group he encountered up on the mountain pass. This ultimately may have been the most incredible revelation of all to those who did not see Jews as part of the Polish national community, especially as he had arrived at Morskie Oko ahead of Witkiewicz's group.

It may be wrong to base one's reading of the significance of taternictwo and this world of lowlander-highlander interaction on the basis of one text. Nonetheless, Witkiewicz's *On the Mountain Pass* was not just any literary work. Analyzing and presenting excerpts of various travelogues and writings about the Tatras around the turn of the century, Ferdynand Hoesick claimed it took Witkiewicz's work to bring throngs of not only Varsovians but other Poles from the Russian Empire to Zakopane. In his words, "The magisterial description of the Tatras in *On the Mountain Pass*, presenting these native mountains as protecting from consumption and neurasthenia, represents an epoch in the development and popularity of Zakopane as the 'summer capital of Poland.'"[21] Given its influence, *On the Mountain Pass* could not help but shape Polish lowland perceptions of the highlands, the reasons to visit, and who "belonged" there.

This was not all Witkiewicz had to say about Jews in the Tatra wilderness. He reflected on the fact that the tourists and travelers had contributed to this peculiar mix of people and division of labor now to be found in the village: "The Jew, who earlier had so little work here, who off this simple and poor life, the shepherds' life . . . could not make much money here, now becomes rich and multiplies, flocks into the village, buys up land, builds, and often paralyzes the initiative and enterprise of the highlanders."[22] If the Tatra highlands were to represent a microcosm of Polish life as it should be, then the Jew was seen by Witkiewicz as the spoiler in their midst. Yet this influx of Jews paradoxically was made possible only by the fact that tourism to the region had increased enough to give them employment as innkeepers, restaurant owners, and purveyors of many of the foodstuffs and supplies needed by lowland guests.[23] The Jewish newcomers proved more enterprising than did the generally conservative highlanders, who were not as quick to sense the full range of opportunities this windfall of tourists provided them.

The Jewish presence in Zakopane was viewed differently by various parties to the highland encounter. When many lowland Poles, a number of whom were now moving to Podhale, decried the fact that it took Jews to feed, supply, and outfit the guests, they were projecting some of their own lowland antipathies onto the region. The native highlanders, by contrast, had little reason to dislike Jews, who filled a gap in what the highlander could or would not provide, not to mention that as innkeepers they provided highlanders with their favored place for socializing: the tavern.

That the man on the mountain pass was actually an alpinist—someone intent on taking in the beauties of the mountains just like Witkiewicz—caught off guard those who did not perceive Jews (even Polish-speaking ones) as part of the national community. He had penetrated the High Tatras, the inner sanctum of this liminal world of what might now be seen as ethnic Polish lowlander-highlander communion. This man clearly was no less a taternik than the members of Witkiewicz's party. Was there to be room in the high uplands—room in this still sparsely inhabited borderland, where identities and allegiances were still being shaped—for him as well? The answer to this question would have implications for Polish nation building. This was particularly true if, to cite Witkiewicz once again, the Tatras and Zakopane were "the synonym of our vitality,"—a pair of terms that, with time, the Russian and German press reportedly came to understand as referring to "the name of some kind of forge in which weapons were being prepared for the fight for existence."[24]

For Witkiewicz there were other hindrances to the pretty Polish future noted in his *On the Mountain Pass*, some of which were the doings of other ethnic groups or nations. He blamed the Austrians for the nameless *Holzconstruction* of the hut near the lake, which should have been built in authentic highland style; and later he remarked on not being allowed to cross the nearby Hungarian border, even if there were Polish villages in Spisz (Spiš/Zips).[25] As we will see in the next two chapters, these were battles that

Witkiewicz and his compatriots would fight—not quite "Homeric" battles, but rather battles of a new age.

It is tempting to read the trip to Morskie Oko in *On the Mountain Pass* as a parable for the future trajectory of the Polish nation, perceived in ethnonationalist terms. The one German in Witkiewicz's group, although professionally outfitted, had to be led back to civilization by a highland guide, having found the climb too daunting. Then when the rest of the climbers were near their destination, Morskie Oko, they encountered two Englishmen. It turned out that they were of Polish descent (although one spoke no Polish); the men found much to praise in the Tatras and Zakopane. It was as if various elements of the Polish nation—highlanders, lowlanders, and even the former emigrants (or their descendants) to the West—were finding common ground in the highland borderland.[26] Only the Jewish presence apparently seemed incongruous.

Yet perhaps Witkiewicz changed his mind about this Jew in the Tatras. The 1906 revised edition of *On the Mountain Pass*—the final edition published during the author's lifetime—omits much of the text cited above.[27] Nonetheless, many readers of both the original serialized version and the first edition of the book may have found themselves pondering this passage.[28]

Witkiewicz was correct to credit Chałubiński with the discovery of the Tatras: it was the respected Warsaw doctor whose recommendations carried much weight among the Poles of the Russian Empire, who—as will be discussed further in chapter 3—began to come in ever increasing numbers. Chałubiński brought the upper-class lowlanders and lower-class highlanders together after centuries of tension and alienation (the lord/peasant relationship having been fraught in historic Poland). Was this new togetherness foreshadowing the future of the Polish nation? Here one might venture that, while the Carpathians served as Poland's liminal borderland, they were also its frontier, à la Frederick Jackson Turner. One can see parallels: Polish elites experiencing the wild Carpathian frontier shed the trappings of civilization, rediscovered their primitive racial energies, reinforced democratic principles, and thus reinfused themselves with a vigor, an independence, and a sense of unity across the social divide that were to characterize the modern Polish nation. At the same time, the wilderness became a place of national development, the quintessential location for feeling truly Polish.[29] It was as if the granite solidity of the Tatra Mountains reinforced a sense of Polish national permanence, even primordialism, the partitions notwithstanding. All this was fostered by Chałubiński's "excursions without a program," which ultimately amounted to much more than the carefree outings they purported to be.

It was Stanisław Witkiewicz who in 1889 so labeled him for posterity, in this way burnishing the halo that already surrounded the person of Chałubiński. As Sabała once remarked, the man who had nursed so many highlanders back to health in 1873 "is not a man of this world. He is here with his legs, but his heart is in heaven."[30] The Warsaw doctor's legendary stature was also emphasized by prominent visitors to the region. After his visit to the Tatras in 1883, the renowned Warsaw positivist Aleksander Świętochowski stated: "I looked with amazement at the Giewonts, Czerwone Wirchy [sic] and Rysy, but for me the greatest peak in the Tatras remains Chałubiński."[31] While one can speak of a "myth" of Chałubiński, propagated most consequentially by Witkiewicz, it was he more than anyone else who made a difference for the perception of both man and nature in this remote alpine borderland.[32] Men and women of Witkiewicz's generation would try to take things a step further.

🎵 Chapter 3

Transforming the Tatras

Doctor Tytus Chałubiński and his merry band had been demarcating with their feet a territory they hoped would soon be peopled by compatriots in need of a restorative climate and a breath of freedom. A new vacation destination for the Polish nation was literally taking shape: the transformation of this tiny remote piece of economically challenged Galician real estate ensued. Not only was the highland borderland transformed physically as the infrastructure to bring in increasing numbers of guests was put into place, but the Tatras would find their way onto the mental maps of Polish lowlanders. One might even venture that during the last half-century of the period of partitions (from the 1870s to the first years of the twentieth century) this highland borderland moved from the periphery of Polish consciousness to its center.

This was due to the encounter of increasing numbers of nationally self-conscious Poles, some of whom would settle in the region (and in the process become what one might term "neonatives"), with this borderland territory.[1] It turns out that the southern borderlands were perceived by the Polish elites who came into contact with both land and people as distinctive, unique, inspiring, even malleable. The remoteness, the primitive folk quality as well as the historic national connection of the region combined to lend it a particular salience. The influx of Poles from abroad would soon cause the little Galician village of Zakopane to be labeled "the Polish Athens" as well as "Poland's summer capital"—this at a time when there was no Polish state.

Polish elites of the period projected their own visions of Poland onto the southern borderlands, imagining both the land and people in ways that suited their new, socially broader sense of what constituted the Polish nation. They used the human and natural landscape of the Tatra Mountains creatively—and here I mean this literally—to recast, in a very public way, the definition of Polishness. In their encounter with the remote and wild frontier, they transformed it into a part of their heritage. In the process, the indigenous inhabitants of this region—the highlanders—found themselves not only written into the Polish national narrative: they became a repository of the core values and characteristics of the Polish nation and served as inspiration for their lowland neighbors.

Nineteenth-century Poles had no better area to carry out their own national experiments than in the alpine borderlands; the region afforded a unique opportunity for ideas about (Polish) nationhood to assume concrete form. Still, in the decades following the discovery various challenges faced the region, including questions of territoriality and ownership, which would firm up the contours of the borderland. Likewise, with development and the concomitant in-migration of numerous lowlanders who saw themselves as having a stake in the outcome—that is, the neonatives—came raised expectations; these begged the question of whose vision of Zakopane might win out. Interactions in the borderlands over the next decades would have an impact on all parties concerned, changing the configuration of identities— local, regional, national, imperial—that helped to define the various players in the discovery, appropriation, reconceptualization, and reshaping of this part of the Carpathian borderlands and their inhabitants.

Birth of a High-Altitude Resort

Over the ensuing decades the Tatra Society, with its membership of non-Galicians as well as Galicians, did much to further its proclaimed aims. The society constructed alpine huts where tourists could find shelter—the first built in 1874 near the picturesquely situated lake known as Morskie Oko. Society members marked trails for hikers and published articles of general interest, scholarly pieces, and reports of the society's activities in its yearbook, *Pamiętnik Towarzystwa Tatrzańskiego*. Brochures were prepared that advertised Zakopane and the Tatras.[2] At the same time, members wondered at the passivity of the highlanders, who took no initiative of their own to develop the hiking infrastructure (that is, huts and trails); the latter seemed content to build additional houses for summer guests in the village, from which they could make a pretty penny.[3]

Yet the village of Zakopane likewise benefited from the Tatra Society's largesse and advocacy. The remote high-altitude village was being connected with the rest of the world. The Tatra Society repeatedly—and successfully—lobbied the provincial authorities for infrastructural improvements: first, for the road from Nowy Targ to Zakopane to be brought up to provincial standard, then for the railroad to be brought to the region.[4] As of 1884, one could ride the train from Kraków all the way to Chabówka—about two-thirds of the way to Zakopane. The new railway line shortened the journey from Kraków from two days to one. As of the 1887 season, once the road (and all the necessary bridges) were ready, the last leg of the ride to Zakopane would not be so bumpy.

These improvements set the stage for the major undertaking of Chałubiński and the Tatra Society: to have Zakopane officially designated as a climatic health resort (*stacja klimatyczna*). This was necessary, Chałubiński thought, to guarantee that the interest in the mountains would not abate after the current fashion passed.[5] The lobbying of the provincial authorities, which began in 1881, finally bore fruit in the fall of 1885, when the new status of the air-cure village was approved. Zakopane would function as a recognized climatic health resort as of the 1886 season.[6] That year—the same year each Tatra Society member was sent a copy of the latest edition of Eljasz's *Guidebook*—would mark a new age for the Tatras, the highlanders, and Zakopane. The establishment of Zakopane as a high-altitude climatic health resort created a new framework for the village. In Austria-Hungary, localities designated climatic health resorts had various rights and obligations, including guaranteeing professional medical care to their guests; arriving for the season, the latter would be obliged to pay a "climatic" tax that would fund the maintenance of and improvements to the resort's infrastructure.

Zakopane's new designation as officially recognized high-altitude health resort, together with the easier access to the mountain region, had the beneficial effect of keeping at least some residents of the province from traveling abroad for their vacations as well as attracting foreign visitors (by far the largest group being Poles from outside Galicia). In 1886 2,156 registered guests vacationed in Zakopane; by 1895, that figure had more than doubled, rising to nearly 5,000.[7] As a result, more highlanders were engaged in housing guests and catering to their needs (for guides, porters), thus helping to develop the local economy. To give a sense of the demand: whereas in 1889 some 250 houses offered 600 rooms for let, by 1902 there were 589 houses with 3,320 rooms.[8] Before long, Zakopane would become the most frequented spa or health resort in Galicia.

The Nature of the Guests: The Polish Intelligentsia and Zakopane

Even before the construction of the railway, a number of Polish luminaries had come to frequent Zakopane. Individuals such as the actress Helena Modrzejewska and pianist Ignacy Jan Paderewski rubbed shoulders with playwrights and poets such as Władysław Ludwik Anczyc and Adam Asnyk, the artist Wojciech Gerson, as well as members of the artistic Kossak family. A Galician figure of note was the Kraków mayor turned provincial marshal, Mikołaj Zyblikiewicz, who mingled with these and other guests.[9] Representing the great Polish noble families at this early date was the Countess Róża née Potocka (primo voto Krasińska) Raczyńska, who came to Zakopane on account of the health of her children. The countess purchased a house in Zakopane as early as 1877. It was one of the places where members of the Polish intelligentsia gathered in the early years.

Indeed, given the dearth of (acceptable?) public spaces for sociability, salons became an important component of life in Zakopane as well as an important means of breaking down social barriers. As brilliantly demonstrated by historian Adrianna Sznapik, salon culture in the highland borderland differed from both the spa culture elsewhere and the lowland urban culture to which most of Zakopane's visitors were accustomed. These salons—in the houses of such Zakopane notables as Chałubiński, with the most famous being that of Bronisław and Maria Dembowski—were places where people did not stand on ceremony (no dress code—unless it was highlander dress, which was practically de rigueur among lowland guests at the time), where representatives of different social groups (including highlanders) mingled, and where opinions were freely exchanged and democratic ideas promoted.[10] A welcome addition—or, more likely, alternative—to the public space that was the Jewish-owned local tavern, the salons of the Polish elites, thus, were among the earliest places for Zakopane sociability, which in turn represented a novel, highland approach to social relations.

Most Zakopane guests tended to fall into a specific category: they were relatively well-off members of the Polish intelligentsia who needed a place to recoup after intense work in unhealthy urban environments. Used to taking the waters in the summer in places far removed from the Polish lands, as of 1886 they were given a choice of a new and intriguing high-altitude resort. No longer did the guests have to be as hardy or adventurous as those of the early days, the golden age of Chałubiński. This made it easier for habitues of Zakopane such as the historical novelist Henryk Sienkiewicz, who wrote intensively while "vacationing" in the highland village, to return time and again.[11]

The story of how tiny, distant, backward Zakopane increasingly became a recognizable feature on the Polish mental map, a well-frequented health resort, as well as a site of Polish pilgrimage, began with the influx of Poles from outside Galicia to this remote site, where they could interact, even network, in peace.[12] One historian has calculated that, in the year 1890, nearly three-quarters of visitors to the region were bureaucrats, lawyers, doctors, clergy, teachers of all kinds, artists, and writers.[13] Writer and artist Stanisław Witkiewicz noted the significance of this presence:

> Through Zakopane each year flows practically the entire Polish intelligentsia, . . . a thousands-strong crowd of all social positions and categories. It is a point of intersection of all the roads along which Polish life flows. There are no such strange fates and such distant countries that would prevent a Pole from at least once in his lifetime stopping by Zakopane. Castaways from Siberia, wanderers from Brazil, Africa, from all the countries of Europe and from the entire territory of former Poland flow here. . . . In the course of several years here, one can meet more interesting, illustrious, influential people . . . than elsewhere in the course of one's entire life.[14]

These were not just any Polish vacationers, of the kind to be found in other spas in the Polish lands and beyond. At least some of these Poles from Warsaw and elsewhere came to the Tatras, in Witkiewicz's words, "in a specific spiritual state . . . with the readiness to make personal and material sacrifices, with a desire to do something good and useful" for the nation—something that was harder to do under oppressive tsarist rule.[15] As of the last third of the nineteenth century, Galicia had distinct advantages. There Poles were able to avail themselves of opportunities for action as well as work. The engagement of pragmatic, positivistically inclined Warsaw intellectuals in the southern borderlands of Galicia seemed to satisfy the spirit of Alexander Świętochowski's dictum: "Only a madman would lie in a dirty peasant hut and dream of crystal palaces. Let society, rather than complain about obstacles, work wherever it has an open field."[16] Instead of stewing in the stale confines of the Russian imperial city of Warsaw during the summer, these Polish elites could work in the fresh, healthy air of what they envisaged as the Polish Tatras.

The region had more to offer Warsaw positivists than simply an "open field."[17] Their encounter with the highlanders—an integral part of the borderland landscape—convinced them that they were a particularly attractive lot. This peculiar "Polish" folk, so free and unfettered in its behavior and outlook, contrasted favorably with the peasants of the Russian zone, whose experience of serfdom had only just come to an end in 1864. This was noted by Świętochowski in 1883, who called the highlander "morally and mentally significantly superior to our [lowland] peasant."[18] The discovery of Zako- pane and the highlanders marked the beginning of the national appropria- tion of the highland borderlands.[19]

Yet not only the highlands were appropriated. Those who came to Zako- pane from the Russian Empire were captivated by the gregarious and self- assured highlanders. They found this distinct variant of Polishness—for they imagined the highlanders, despite their ethnically mixed pedigree, to be unquestionably Polish—very attractive, and they sought to place it within the Polish historical narrative. Purportedly "never bound by serfdom," the highlanders were seen as "preserv[ing] in a fresh and lively state elements of the old Polish culture in [their] customs and in [their] splendid speech, architecture, and artistry."[20]

That is, insofar as they preserved these splendid characteristics. For now came the rub: the influx of outsiders, however well intentioned, changed the environment of the Tatras and of Zakopane. The village's new status was bringing more guests to the highlands, visitors who far outnumbered the highland population. These lowlanders, mostly urbanites, brought with them attitudes, tastes, as well as consumer goods, the likes of which the average highlander had never encountered but soon would emulate or crave. Worse, out of a misguided generosity toward these attractive, clever, yet impoverished highland peasants, some wealthier Varsovians overpaid for ser- vices rendered by them, thus teaching highlanders that money came easily. More perspicacious guests began to decry the impact that their increasingly numerous presence was having on the Górale. If the highlander were to become an archetype of Polishness, it was imperative that he have the means to persist in his natural way of life and avoid the demoralization that came with increased contact with modern civilization and upper-class outsiders.

The Nature of the Highlander

One way to ensure this was by underscoring the worth of the old highland culture. A number of the Polish elites who settled in Zakopane collected what they could of the relics of the olden times.[21] Pioneering in this regard was the work of Bronisław and Maria Dembowski, who first began coming to Zakopane in 1874 and made Zakopane their home as of 1886. Their "cot- tage" (chata) became the most famous highland salon, a place where high- landers and Poles of every social stratum and political bent were made to feel welcome.[22] When the Dembowskis first arrived in this remote highland

periphery, they felt they were seeing the last of the old ways; newer generations of highlanders, those who had worked in the iron mills or mines, were
different from the shepherds, hunters, not to mention brigands of the past.

In taking an interest in the old highland culture, the countess and the
Dembowskis set an example for other visitors, a number of whom joined
them in collecting old household artifacts, compiling dictionaries of highland dialect, jotting down tales, transcribing melodies and songs, or sketching architectural details. Some visitors turned their interests into scholarly
articles or even volumes. For example, Bronisław Dembowski (1847–93)
compiled a dictionary of the highland dialect, while the Warsaw surgeon
Władysław Matlakowski (1850–95) not only researched but also painstak-
ingly drew highland decorative motifs and artifacts for his *Zdobienie i sprzęt
ludu polskiego na Podhalu* (Decoration and Equipment of the Polish Folk in
Podhale—please note the adjective "Polish"), which was published after he
succumbed to tuberculosis in 1895.[23]

These forays into the local folk culture inspired outsiders to draw connections to old Polish culture, with individuals such as Stanisław Witkiewicz
imagining the highlanders and their artistry as representing a deeper historical past, the way all Poles had once lived. It was thought that the osten-
sible isolation of the region had allowed the highlanders—in Walery Eljasz's
words—to "preserve the language of the forefathers, maintaining the memory of years long past in living tradition."[24] This image of the highlander as
ur-Pole seemed to reflect an ethnographic vision of Poland represented by
the earliest Polish kingdom under the Piast rulers, descendants of the quintessential Polish peasant, Piast himself.[25] The remote Carpathian periphery
was perceived as a precious remnant of an ideal, and idealized, past—a time
capsule of sorts, making this piece of rugged nature a part of an imagined
past primitive.

One prominent example of how the Polish highlander was included
within the Polish historical narrative can be found in the work of Henryk
Sienkiewicz. The Polish novelist, later to be the nation's first Nobel laure-
ate in literature, went so far as to embellish his own account of the Polish-
Swedish wars of the mid-seventeenth century to include a scene in which
patriotic highlanders come to the defense of Polish king Jan Kazimierz.[26]
Given the popularity of the author's historical novels, this blatant rewriting
of history in *The Deluge* (which Sienkiewicz finished writing in Zakopane in
the summer of 1886, his first summer there) was bound to leave an imprint
on the nation. Given the way so many Poles have learned their own history through Sienkiewicz's novels, doubtless many believed this rescue of
the Polish king to have had some historical basis. Yet even highlanders came

to embrace this rewriting of history, using it to justify their rights of pasture in the highland meadows, supposedly granted them by the grateful king.[27] Intent on writing the highlanders into Polish history, formerly the purview of the upper classes, the Polish intelligentsia cast the highlanders as primeval, even patriotic, Poles.[28]

The Polish writer also used the vigorous Podhale dialect to approximate medieval Polish speech in yet another historical novel, *The Teutonic Knights*. Sienkiewicz's appropriation of the highland dialect may seem quaint; but to his Polish readers it may have signified much more. The writer's choice of language for his Polish characters potentially tied the partitioned nation tighter, providing generations of readers with more reason to believe that the highlanders were authentic primeval Poles: anyone who visited the Tatra region after having read Sienkiewicz's novel would hear echoes of those old Polish heroes in the voices of the local shepherds and guides. In other words, the peripheral Tatra region was transformed into the true center of Polishness. At the same time, the "imagined community" of Poles—in which the connection between local speech patterns and the elite-dominated national history was being made—was becoming larger. It seems as though those active in shaping the way the modern Polish nation was perceived were trying to turn the Podhale highlander into an archetype "embody[ing] the highest national virtues in the minds of their . . . countrymen."[29]

That the highland peasant was elevated in this way by so many non-Galicians is no accident. The most influential Galician Poles were still traumatized by what Norman Davies has termed "the most sensational event in Galicia's history": the peasant *jacquerie* of 1846, in which an attempt at insurrection on the part of Polish noblemen (paradoxically seeking to engage the peasants in this effort) was transformed into a wholesale massacre of Galician nobles.[30] That the nobles of Galicia had not yet overcome the trauma of 1846 helps to explain why Chałubiński and his patients from Warsaw were so crucial in the discovery of the Tatras and, especially, of the highlander.

That said, in 1846 the sole ray of hope had shone in the highland region. The highlanders of the village of Chochołów and its environs had not joined their fellow lowland peasants in massacring nobles but rather joined the Polish-led fight against the Austrians.[31] That the Austrians were able to put them down quickly does not change the symbolic significance of the Chochołów uprising. Here—and not in Sienkiewicz's version of the Deluge—highlanders had really tried to come to the defense of the nation. This was yet another reason to think them special.

Sienkiewicz's use of the Podhale dialect to represent medieval Polish speech was praised by Stanisław Witkiewicz, who formulated a positivistic program of his own for the region—one which aimed to transform the Polish landscape in a new way. Witkiewicz turned his attention to the creativity of the highlanders, as seen in their native art and architecture. Highlanders were masters of wooden construction who, having an appreciation for beauty, embellished their buildings as well as household furniture and goods with fanciful carvings. Struck by the artistry, Witkiewicz wondered: "Perhaps the mountain people, locked in the depths of the valleys, cut off from the world, have preserved longer than anywhere else the most ancient general form specific to the mountainous regions of Poland?"[32] Given the mixed provenance of the Górale, this was wishful thinking—or even what we would call today the "invention of tradition."[33] The Polish activist came to maintain that this style of "architecture and decorative arts once flowered on the entire territory of Poland."[34] Witkiewicz nonetheless worried that the subsistence conditions of life in the mountains would restrict the impact these beautifully preserved ancient forms might have on broader Polish society. He sought a way to enliven and popularize this native art, this "treasury of the old culture," which otherwise was sentenced to die out.[35]

At that moment it seemed likely that the old style of architecture would indeed die out—or, rather, be pushed out by Tirolean-style or "resort"-style construction, which seemed more suitable for building houses in the high-altitude resort that were bigger than the traditional two-room highlander cottage. For, instead of simply mastering the techniques necessary for their own innate creativity to develop, highland pupils at the now state-sponsored Fachschule für Holzbearbeitung (Vocational School for Woodworking) were being taught Tirolean patterns from German textbooks by their Czech principal.[36] Witkiewicz and others decried this development and fought—successfully—to get the school to teach traditional highland (ergo Polish) motifs and methods.[37]

Yet the problem of an appropriate architectural form for the growing high-altitude resort remained. Ultimately, Witkiewicz and other architects "saved" (his words) the artistry of the highlanders by allowing it to inspire a higher form of architecture, by incorporating its decorative elements into a new artistic movement, transforming the folk forms into what came to be called "Zakopane Style"—or, as Witkiewicz preferred, "Polish Style."[38] Some construction in this new Polish Style subsequently took place in the Polish lands, mainly in Zakopane but also in other spas in eastern Galicia and even Lithuania where wooden architecture predominated; highland motifs were also incorporated into furniture and household goods, clothing, jewelry, even china.[39] The (re)introduction of this Polish Style was intended to inject a degree of Polishness into a built landscape increasingly devoid of any real Polish characteristics,

FIGURE 3.1. Koliba, the first house built in Zakopane Style (1893), designed by Stanisław Witkiewicz. Photo by Janusz Juda.

being the product of imperial-driven modernization. Building on the ethnographic research and earlier borrowings of highland motifs of Witkiewicz's lowland colleagues, Zakopane—ergo, Polish—Style represented the most significant appropriation of the highland past and attempt at disseminating the highland heritage, now seen as ur-Polish, more broadly.

Polonizing the Highland Borderland

While the Polish lowlands and lowlanders were being "highlanderized," the Tatras were coming more fully into Polish possession—literally. Recall that, after the partitions, the royal Polish demesne had been sold to private individuals. The Zakopane demesne had passed through both Hungarian and German hands before it was put up for sale once again in the late 1880s. At the time of the discovery of the Tatras, Zakopane and its environs were under German ownership. While Baron Eichborn had proved relatively cooperative—after all, he was a founding member of the Tatra Society—the egregious exploitative policies of his son-in-law Magnus Peltz, who had inherited the landholdings, were decried by Polish activists, who saw how he and other landowners in the vicinity ravaged the natural environment through overzealous logging and hunting. They were also unhappy that these private owners restricted access to various parts of the Tatras.

When it became clear that Peltz was in financial straits, Polish activists sought to find a wealthy Pole to purchase the land; but few aristocrats expressed an interest in this territory. To avoid German ownership, there was a curious attempt at putting the Zakopane demesne in Galician—or even imperial—hands: one of the original founders of the Tatra Society, Feliks Pławicki, proposed to transform the Zakopane demesne into a hunting preserve in honor of the fortieth anniversary of Emperor Franz Joseph's rule.[40] This Habsburg-flavored plan contrasted sharply with a patriotic Polish thought (also not realized) to turn the demesne into a national park, which would be named for the preeminent Polish Romantic poet Adam Mickiewicz.[41]

Ultimately Peltz's landholdings were auctioned. Bidders included the Jewish lumber merchant and mill owner Jakub Goldfinger of Nowy Targ, Henryk Kolischer (reported to be the plenipotentiary of a German prince), and the attorney Rettinger. Were there no wealthy Poles who could purchase this increasingly important—at least symbolically—piece of land? The bidding came down to two—Goldfinger and Rettinger—with the latter finally outbidding the former at 460,000 guldens. Poles were relieved to learn that the rest of the Tatras' trees would not end up as pulp: Rettinger was the plenipotentiary for a Pole, Count Władysław Zamoyski, owner of the Kórnik estate in the former Grand Duchy of Posen (at that time part of Germany).[42]

Władysław Zamoyski (1853–1924) was no typical Polish magnate. Young and energetic, he had already seen a good part of the world, having traveled as far away as Australia. His life experience had confirmed him as a hardworking Polish patriot.[43]

Not content simply to own Zakopane, after moving into the manor at Kuźnice the count sought to improve his landholdings. Among other things, he was keen to reestablish some sort of ecological equilibrium after years of the forests being fodder for Peltz's paper mill. The Pole Zamoyski took a different tack than had previous (non-Polish) owners, more intent on making a profit from the demesne's natural resources. More steward than developer, the new landowner strove to undo the damage caused by previous owners by reforesting devastated areas, in the hopes that further major flooding, such as that which took place in Zakopane in 1884, could be avoided.[44] Zamoyski also was not an avid hunter, as were so many other landowners in the area; he saw reason to support endangered wildlife and plants, including the edelweiss. The Polish count founded a Christian Mercantile Cooperative in the village, which allowed members to purchase at a reasonable price goods that otherwise would cost more in a regular store; it proved quite successful.[45] Zamoyski likewise became active in the doings of the high-altitude climatic health resort, successfully lobbying the provincial authorities to construct another railway spur, this time from Chabówka all the way to Zakopane. The completion of the railway line was finally achieved in the fall of 1899, marking yet another turning point for the village.

Yet other challenges for Zamoyski and those who cared about the Galician/Polish Tatras remained. In 1879, a German prince, Christian Kraft zu Hohenlohe-Öhringen, had acquired the Hungarian territories of Javorina, Jurgov, and Lendak in Spiš. The newcomer soon came to quarrel with his neighbors across the Galician frontier, even to dispute a portion of the border; this resulted in border skirmishes—the construction and destruction of border markers, huts, and fences, the arrests and attacks of the foresters and gendarmes.[46] Hohenlohe maintained that the rights to half of Morskie Oko and surrounding lands had been ceded in an agreement between the earlier landowners, who, upon exchanging a piece of territory, reportedly had agreed that the border between the two families' holdings would become the border between Galicia and Hungary—as if landowners were entitled to reconfigure state or provincial borders.[47]

The highland borderlands had long been a place of conflict between various political entities: Poles and Hungarians had disputed ownership of various portions of Spiš since the sixteenth century. By challenging the ownership of Morskie Oko, however, Hohenlohe was treading on Polish national toes. The lake, picturesquely situated at the base of the Rysy, the highest of the Polish Tatra peaks, had already become a Polish icon. It was traditionally the end point of Tatra excursions. The first marked trails in the Polish Tatras led to Morskie Oko.[48] Not for nothing did the Tatra Society call Morskie Oko the "Mecca for all tourists who visit the Tatras."[49]

While the decades-long dispute was a personal quarrel between landowners, it represented much more. Sensitive to the threat of denationalization of formerly Polish territories, the patriotic count took an especial interest in the dispute over Morskie Oko. As a non-German national, he had been expelled by the German authorities from his own inherited estate at Kórnik in 1886. It seems ironic that the Polish-German conflict of the German Empire should spill over into Austria-Hungary, where these two noblemen—one a German, the other (Zamoyski) a French citizen—ultimately fought in the name of Hungary and Austria/Galicia/Poland ("Poland," of course, nonexistent except in the minds of its potential citizenry, although doubtless the motivating factor behind Zamoyski's involvement).[50]

There is much more that can be said about the actions of all parties to the dispute.[51] Ultimately, a court of arbitration, which deliberated in Graz for three weeks in 1902, held up the Galician claim, which was ably defended by Lwów (Lemberg, L'viv) University's professor of legal history, Oswald Balzer. Based on Polish historic claims, all scrupulously documented, Morskie Oko would remain in the sole possession of the province of Galicia in Austria.[52]

The victory of 1902 electrified Polish society across the partitioned lands and helped to Polonize Galicia, as well as Zakopane and the Tatras. Some contemporaries cast the victory in Polish national terms, as seen from a version of Dąbrowski's Mazurka (the original of which would later become the Polish national anthem) that was sung and otherwise popularized at this time: "Jeszcze Polska nie zginęła, / Wiwat plemię lasze, / Dobra sprawa górę wzięła, / Morskie Oko nasze!"—"Poland has not yet perished, / Long live the Polish tribe, / The good cause gained the upper hand, / Morskie Oko [is] ours!"[53] Perhaps it should come as no surprise that the road to Morskie Oko would someday be named after Oswald Balzer, whose triumphal legal defense was justly feted by Poles, and that the lake would become the most popular natural feature of a national park, yet to come.

The victory over Morskie Oko also helped to Polonize the Tatra Society, where the tension between the Galician aristocratic/landowning members who dominated the administration and the more democratic, outsider faction had been palpable. Nonetheless, the Tatra Society and its members did further what others might term the Polish national interest in the highland borderland. Dedicated members such as Walery Eljasz marked and improved trails. And we know of the society's work in improving access to Zakopane and turning it into a high-altitude climatic health resort. All of this enabled more people to travel to Zakopane, turning the village into a Polish "Mecca," a place where Poles from all over congregated, socialized, networked, and basked in the light of Galicia's relative freedom while absorbing lessons from the local highlanders. But this was a Mecca where Poles did more than make a pilgrimage: many also sought to put an unquestionably Polish mark on the region.

For another dimension of the discovery of the Tatras was what might be termed the demarcation of national space. The process of naming sites within the Tatra Mountains after illustrious Polish figures or activists began early. By 1888, one can find numerous physical features—natural and man-made—that advertised the Polish presence. The first alpine hut, constructed in 1874 on the banks of Morskie Oko, was named after Stanisław Staszic. It was followed by a number of others, including a hut near the mouth of the Roztoka dedicated in honor of the multitalented Wincenty Pol, and one in the Valley of the Five Ponds named after the geologist and paleontologist Ludwik Zejszner. Forerunners to the discovery, thus, were being remembered in this very public way.[54] The Romantic poet Adam Mickiewicz was honored by the naming of three waterfalls of the Roztoka Stream after him in 1891, the year after his remains were reburied in the Wawel crypts in Kraków. Similar attempts to honor a second Romantic bard, Juliusz Słowacki, in 1909 by reburying his remains somewhere in the Tatra Mountains, remained unrealized.[55] Neither poet, incidentally, had ever been in the Tatras. The most illustrious Pole with a Tatra connection was of course Chałubiński, who after his death was honored by naming a gate (natural feature) after him; and 1903 witnessed the unveiling in Zakopane of a monument depicting the doctor-discoverer with Sabała at his feet.[56]

Less typical was the posthumous honoring of the Czech Edvard Jelínek (1855–97) with an iron tablet in Strążyska Valley. Jelínek, who took a great interest in things Polish, had been a proponent of closer relations between Czechs and Poles (and in general between Slavic nations). Not incidentally, he also published a little book in Czech about Zakopane (in the "Polish Tatras," please note), illustrated by Eljasz and Witkiewicz.[57]

The Slavic connection is worth considering here. The Tatras have been seen as the birthplace of the Slavs by those on the southern slopes of the Tatras: the Slovaks.[58] Yet Slovaks (long under Hungarian rule) never discovered or explored their Tatras as did nineteenth-century Poles. Slovaks were content to see the Tatras as a whole as their national symbol, at most considering the Kriváň—which the Liptaks, the Slovak counterpart to the Polish Górale, had believed to be the highest peak—a holy mountain. The exception would be the local Liptaks, who would accompany German and Hungarian hikers in the mountains. It was the latter two, especially the Zipser Germans, who took a real interest in what they considered to be their mountains.[59] Slovak writers and poets, who mentioned the Tatras all the time during the Romantic period, never went into detail.[60] Even Janko Matúška's song "Nad Tatrou sa blýska" (1843), later to become the Slovak national anthem, keeps the Tatras in their symbolic, holistic state—the indivisible, unquestioned symbol of both nation and fatherland.

Perhaps the Slovaks, whose national territory was dominated by mountains, simply were not as fascinated by them—by their distinctive peaks and valleys, their passes and highland meadows. By contrast, as we have seen, Poles, especially those from the Russian Empire, had to work much harder to experience—and possess—the mountains.

From Periphery to Center

But not always. Only five years after Witkiewicz's On the Mountain Pass came out in book form, the mountains were literally brought to Warsaw.[61] They arrived in the form of a panorama—an enormous painting-in-the-round, a form of art that was all the rage in the final decades of the nineteenth century. The panorama was the precursor to moving pictures: from atop a platform within a specially designed round building, visitors took in sights they would have seen had they really been present.[62] Think of it as a kind of vicarious viewing of an unfolding historical (often battle) scene or—in this less typical case—landscape.[63]

The idea for the panorama came from a Kraków attorney, Henryk Lgocki, in 1894. It did not hurt that, at that time, a very popular panorama of the Battle of Racławice was on display in Lwów, the Galician capital.[64] (Lgocki himself would prove an avid promoter of panoramas; he commissioned yet another one, "Golgotha," which was exhibited in Częstochowa.) As in the case of these other two panoramas, the Kraków lawyer exhibited this new panorama in a place far removed from the site of the depicted scene, a place furthermore where one might expect crowds to come for the novelty of it all: the former Polish capital of Warsaw. The Tatra Mountains were to be put on the mental map of Poles who could hardly fathom that their fatherland, so flat in the vicinity of Warsaw, had real, Swiss-style mountains.

A special pavilion was constructed in Warsaw for this largest of all Polish panoramas.[65] The Polish poet Kazimierz Przerwa-Tetmajer also prepared an explanatory text for visitors. From what Tetmajer wrote, the view from the thirty-feet-high platform must have been incredible. The seven-thousand-feet-plus Miedziane was ideally suited as the vantage point for the panorama. It loomed as the highest easily accessible mountain between the picturesque Valley of the Five Ponds and the Valley of Fish Stream. The latter led to Morskie Oko, which surely could not be missing from any panorama of the Polish Tatras. The entirety of the High Tatras was visible, only a small part of which were Polish. Nonetheless, the Polish Tatras had the advantage of possessing the best lakes and ponds. Beneath the Rysy lay Czarny (Black) Pond, and of course the Valley of Five Ponds had many more. Beyond the broad and jagged Mięguszowieckie peaks, the slender, unconquerable Mnich (Monk) also towered above the southwestern side of Morskie Oko. Tetmajer, a Young Poland poet who knew the Tatras since his early childhood years, praised the artists for not missing any detail.[66]

Varsovians were also impressed by the verisimilitude, according to the Warsaw press. One journalist rejoiced that they would "be able to make excursions into the mountains every day . . . and delight in the view of the Tatra peaks and valleys, gaze at the marvelous landscape of the Carpathian Switzerland without ever leaving the confines of Warsaw," Switzerland clearly proving a more familiar highland reference for residents of Poland's former capital than did the Carpathians, not to say the smaller range of the Tatras.[67] The panorama reportedly made the Tatras practically palpable. The sight of the mountains—even painted ones—made people feel healthier, freer. One could practically inhale the fresh mountain air; in the words of another journalist, "The genius of the paint l[ay] in the mass of air we seem to sense."[68] Likely being up on the thirty-foot-high viewing platform also made the experience feel more real, as if one were atop the Miedziane itself, perhaps experiencing a little vertigo.

One wonders whether this sense that what one saw and felt was real was actually aided by the inclusion of scenes of hikers scaling the peaks, led by highland guides. How realistic could they be? Yet perhaps they served another purpose. Viewers were being taught, via these scenes, how the Tatras were best experienced by Poles, women as well as men: in the company of the highlander, the freest and most attractive of all Polish peasants. One imagines that, given the presence on the canvas of Tytus Chałubiński, Father Józef Stolarczyk, and Sabała—all recently deceased—it was the classical age of taternictwo (Polish alpinism) that was being touted.[69] The freest part of the historic Polish lands, thus, had been brought to the former capital, at that time far from free.

The Tatra Panorama was exhibited in Warsaw for three years, bringing the sight of the mountains—and, perhaps, a whiff of freedom—to those who found the journey to the south to be too expensive or uncomfortable. In 1899, the time may have been right to take the panorama down. After years of lobbying by Count Władysław Zamoyski, the owner of the Zakopane demesne, the Galician provincial authorities had finally approved the extension of the railway from Chabówka to Zakopane. As of that autumn, lowlanders no longer had to disembark from the train to ride in a highlander's covered wagon the last third of the journey. The train would make three to four round trips a day from Kraków: it took the regular train six hours, the fast train just over four hours to traverse the route.[70] All this put the real Tatras within easy reach, relatively speaking, of Varsovians.

Unlike the 1852 "panorama" of Mont Blanc in Piccadilly, which made a fortune for Alfred Smith, the Tatra Panorama ultimately proved not to be a moneymaking venture for its Polish initiator. To recoup his losses, Lgocki decided to put it up for auction. The largest ever Polish panorama was cut up and sold as canvas, to the outrage of many. For those three years, however, the panorama served to remind Varsovians of not only the natural beauty of the Tatras but also the dispute over Morskie Oko, to which the German land-owner Hohenlohe laid claim.[71] No wonder, perhaps, that the public reaction of Poles to the victory over Hohenlohe and Hungary in 1902—only three years after the panorama was taken down—was so large. Morskie Oko had become a true Polish icon, a Polish "lieux de mémoire," even for those who had never traveled to the Tatras. For those three years, the mountains had come to Mohammed—the periphery to the center.

There was more vicarious viewing to be done in this period, if not while one was perched atop a viewing platform in a large round building. Not only monumental art, such as the Tatra Panorama, was produced in these decades. Many artists visited the region and took away with them sketches or paintings recording what they saw, some of these ending up in postcards toward the end of the century.[72]

One should not underestimate the impact of the picture postcard—which Werner Telesko has called "the first visual mass medium"—for the "tour-ist gaze," a concept popularized by John Urry, with the gaze referring to the ways in which prospective tourists learned how and what to see in the places they hoped to visit.[73] The first Tatra scenes on illustrated postcards appeared in 1895, the earliest in the form of a photographic reproduction; the first artistic cards began to be produced in 1899—just in time for the "golden age of the postcard."[74] This was a period when guests had the habit of writing at least one postcard a day—leading to some thirteen postal work-ers being employed in Zakopane and carrying up to two thousand missives and parcels daily.[75] Those back home or unable to make the journey would be treated to iconic images of Morskie Oko, various notable Tatra peaks, and the proud Tatra highlander, with many images, some quite patriotic, produced by Walery Eljasz.

These icons would become part of the list of sights to see or things to experience in the future. But the landscapes also provided recipients with a sense of what could be construed as their fatherland, in its various permuta-tions. While mountain scenes could be sublime, the Tatra landscapes with elements of civilization—a highland lean-to or hut, hikers—represented the mountains tamed (oswojone), made more accessible, even assimilable.

✒ CHAPTER 4

Turn-of-the-Century Innovations

Encroaching civilization could be felt in various ways, as in the establishment of public meeting spaces, such as could be found in regular European spa destinations. Members of the Tatra Society and their guests long had a place to gather, the so-called casino. Renamed the Tatra Manor, it became an important center of social life in Zakopane and a regular *cursalon* of sorts. There one could read newspapers, attend concerts and performances, have a meal, even spend the night (the clubhouse had several rooms for guests).[1]

The emergence of restaurants and (later) cafés would provide other spaces for congregating and networking—a boon when it rained (as it so often did in the summer). Sienkiewicz was famously known for his daily routine of spending certain regular hours in one such café. Artistic and intellectual life could be seen in the very rich calendar of cultural events, the literary readings, theatricals, and concerts (many for charitable purposes) that Zakopane had to offer.[2] Combined with the growing crowds of distinguished Poles representing many different fields, with time this proliferation of meeting places and events would help turn Zakopane into a veritable Polish Athens, a place for Poles from all three empires to interact.[3]

This was particularly pronounced around the fin de siècle. As of the 1890s, the centrality of the region in the minds of Poles was underscored by an outstanding new generation of writers and poets, the so-called Young Poland

(*Młoda Polska*), the preeminent fin-de-siècle Polish literary movement—
a counterpart to Vienna's Secession or Germany's Jugendstil as well as a
host of other "Young" movements.[4] These writers, artists, and architects
took a great interest in the Tatras: witness Tadeusz Boy-Żeleński's quip that
Young Poland was either "tatrzańska" or "szatańska" (that is, it occupied
itself with either Tatra or Satanic themes).[5] Young Poland poems and paintings were vividly impressionistic, evocative, and fresh. The strength of the
Tatra strand of Polish literature, including the forty highland tales that comprised Kazimierz Tetmajer's *In Rocky Podhale* (*Na skalnym Podhalu*), helped
further to popularize the region and its residents. Zakopane was becoming
truly fashionable for the artistic set, who increasingly accepted as a given
that Zakopane was Polish—and soon even poked fun at the place and its
paradoxical popularity. Take for example, satirical pieces such as Andrzej
Strug's *Zakopanoptikon, or The Chronicle of Forty Rainy Days in Zakopane*,
penned in 1913 and 1914, which wrote of mud that had not dried since
Chałubiński's time.[6]

Likewise, around the fin de siècle, a new and different sensation of freedom was increasingly felt. A new kind of taternictwo was taking shape in the
Tatras.[7] No longer were Polish visitors to the Tatras interested in scaling the
highest peaks. They all had been conquered earlier, which meant that what
remained for the tourist who sought novelty was not the traditional seeking
of awe-inspiring views but rather the thrill of something new. The younger
generation took a sporting interest in less exposed peaks, in ridges and crags
that had never been climbed before. Given the difficulty of these ridges and
smaller, irregular peaks, climbing became more technical (or assisted with
ladders and chains, which is how the dangerous, three-mile-long trail known
as Eagle's Path was equipped).

Yet another important dimension of Polish alpinism à la Chałubiński was
on the wane. Climbers began to climb solo, without highland guides, something made easier as of 1903, when the first Polish map of the Tatras for
hikers was distributed to Tatra Society members. Founded that same year,
the Tourist (that is, Mountaineering) Section of the Tatra Society became the
haven of these new technical climbers, men such as Janusz Chmielowski and
Karol Englisch; they publicized their exploits and developed the sporting side
of Polish alpinism further.[8] A notable first: in 1902 Englisch summited Ostry
Peak (Ostrý štít) in the Hungarian Tatras, brazenly mounting a Polish flag
atop it—this, when there was no Polish state (and still several weeks before
the Morskie Oko verdict).[9] Taternictwo was being redefined. Once it became
clear that Poles could climb yet unconquered terrain by themselves, the tide
turned and solo climbing became the rule, not the exception.

This was in part related to the new demographics of the climbing community. Whereas taternictwo had originally been practiced by established members of the intelligentsia, mainly well-to-do, middle-aged men, the new technical climbing became accessible to youth, in particular, to the college student. These young people could not afford to hire a guide, let alone organize "grand-style" excursions with numerous highlanders. The new Tourist Section furthermore provided them with instruction on how to use mountaineering equipment, the ropes and ice-axes that had already been in use in the Alps. In this, modern taternictwo was taking its cues from the rest of Europe.[10]

And a new kind of mass Tatra tourism also appeared on the horizon. During one summer month in 1904, a summer school of sorts was held in Zakopane, the so-called Higher Vacation Courses, taught by Polish luminaries. More than five hundred persons signed up, the overwhelming majority of whom were Poles from the Russian Empire, and over half of whom were women. Hiking excursions were part of this ad hoc university.[11] Given the phenomenal weather that summer, these proved popular: two hundred individuals joined one excursion to Czarny and Zmarzły Ponds in Gąsienicowa Valley alone; not all of them could satisfy their thirst at the little hut en route. Think of these excursions as enormous "grand-style" excursions that were lacking in style . . . and in highland guides. Despite the trial-and-error method of the excursion leaders (including a young Mieczysław Orłowicz, later to become the doyen of Polish tourism), more than one student-hiker was captivated by the Tatras.[12] More proof that Zakopane was the "summer capital of Poland."

These new twentieth-century developments (for, before long, with the advent of skiing, Zakopane quickly became the "winter capital of Poland" as well) changed the very experience of the mountains—this of course beginning with the much shortened journey to Zakopane. With the extension of the railway all the way to Zakopane in 1899, the hardships of travel had disappeared. No longer did guests have the suspense of the seemingly endless journey, the discomforts of the ride in the covered wagon that nonetheless eased them into a new world, one in which the driver spoke in a barely comprehensible dialect (again, perhaps more comprehensible if one had read Sienkiewicz's *Teutonic Knights*). Guests were deposited directly at their destination, at the Zakopane train station. Highlanders would still whisk guests off to their accommodations, increasingly less likely to be a primitive highland cottage. Zakopane was beginning to be much more like any other spa town, if clearly one in which Poles could be Poles.

The decline of the Chałubiński-style expedition brought further changes. The new generation of climbers had much less contact with the highlander in his element. There were fewer opportunities to become acquainted with highland culture, with tales of the old times. Where were the wild, hatchet-swinging dances around the campfire that had brought home to an earlier generation the wildness in its own subconscious? There were fewer and fewer reasons to see the highlander as that primitive ur-Pole.

The Zakopane Experiment

The advent of the railway in Zakopane in 1899 portended other changes. Zamoyski's victory was, or rather seemed to be, a defeat for the highland-ers. Many had opposed the railway. After all, plenty of highlanders made a living as wagon drivers who shuttled back and forth between Zakopane and Chabówka. They greeted the first train arriving in Zakopane by mooning it.[13]

Yet the highlanders quickly adapted to the new conditions. When wagon rides from Chabówka no longer were needed, they came to realize that they could transport guests to Morskie Oko or Kościeliska Valley. Demand for a ride to Morskie Oko was reportedly so high that several hundred highlanders could not keep up with it.[14] Highlanders likewise became hoteliers, building and running their own hotels and boardinghouses, demonstrating that they could adjust to the new Zakopane that was springing up around them.

At least, up to a point. Some of the Polish transplants from the lowlands had also come to believe that Zakopane and the Tatras provided the perfect field for social experimentation. Among them were Stanisław Witkiewicz, who saw his lowland compatriots as "c[oming] here to Zakopane . . . contrib-uting to the existence of this previously forlorn, out-of-the-way . . . commune their thought and work, assum[ing] that on this ground, in such extraordi-nary conditions, one will be able to create a higher, more perfect type of human relations. . . . that here one will be able to create an environment of higher aspirations and forms of life that will radiate out to the rest of soci-ety."[15] Witkiewicz believed that Zakopane had "exceptional conditions" for this, given its healthfulness and its "perfect human material"—by which he meant the Tatra highlanders, "an amazing [genialny] folk, wonderfully suited for civilization"—that is, the civilization imagined by the Polish activist.[16] In other words, Zakopane was the microcosm that, if developed correctly, could influence, even serve as a model for, the rest of the Polish lands.

This was a powerful vision, but was it realizable? During this heyday of spa going in Europe, medical professionals in the resort would play a key role.[17] A number of physicians had begun to treat patients in Zakopane, among them Dr. Andrzej Chramiec (1859–1939). A Zakopane native, Chramiec was the scion of an impoverished highland family. He nonetheless managed to get an education, first in Zakopane, then in Nowy Targ, and finally at the Jagiellonian University in Kraków, where he received his medical degree. After a brief residency at another Pole's hydropathic institute in Styria (recommended to him by Chałubiński), the young doctor came home to Zakopane.[18] From 1886 to 1888 Chramiec served as the first official "climatic" doctor for the health resort, and before long he established his own sanatorium.

At the turn of the century, the sanatorium of this enterprising highlander dominated the health resort landscape. From a single building with fewer than twenty guest rooms it had grown to three buildings containing more than one hundred rooms as well as treatment pavilions, a private chapel, and the necessary administrative buildings—with central heating and electricity to boot.[19] But it could not itself care for all the patients—for all those who needed medical supervision—especially as it did not treat patients with tuberculosis.[20]

A proposal to create a "Zakopane Berghof" (avant la lettre) in nearby Kościelisko came from Dr. Kazimierz Dłuski, the brother-in-law of the scientist Maria Skłodowska-Curie.[21] As the refugee physician did not have the funds to do this himself, Polish literary figures who congregated in Zakopane initiated a campaign in Zakopane and elsewhere for financial support and donated the proceeds from literary readings. The internationally renowned pianist Ignacy Jan Paderewski turned out to be largest shareholder in the sanatorium, which opened in 1902.[22]

Chramiec's and Dłuski's sanatoria would end up representing two different visions of Zakopane: natives and neonatives. A native son of the region, Chramiec had demonstrated his understanding of the highlander mentality during his two-year stint as Zakopane's first climatic doctor, finding ingenious ways to get his highland brethren to do what he required of them. He also served as the delegate to the climatic commission of the Provincial Executive in Lwów from its beginnings in 1885.[23] And in 1902 Chramiec was elected head of the communal council.[24]

Despite his efforts on behalf of the village and resort during his tenure, Chramiec would end up on the wrong side of the biggest internal conflict the village was to witness—a sign that all was not well in the "experimental workshop" of the Tatras and Zakopane.[25] The conflict arose between Chramiec and Dr. Tomasz Janiszewski. A refugee from the Russian Empire, Janiszewski had his positions as climatic and communal doctor thanks to Chramiec. Yet the two quickly clashed over various matters. Janiszewski was convinced that Chramiec and the highlanders (meaning the communal council) did not appreciate his vision of Zakopane; and he rallied his friends, including the influential Witkiewicz, to take up his cause.

The doctors' styles as well as alliances were quite different. Chramiec was a pragmatic, self-made man, on good terms not only with the highlanders but also with Count Zamoyski and various levels of Galician officialdom. The left-leaning Janiszewski subscribed to the idealism of men like Witkiewicz, who hoped to create a new social environment in Zakopane. Janiszewski furthermore was leery of the Habsburg-loyal Galician authorities and did not wish to have anything to do with them.

Beginning in the last years of the nineteenth century, the clash between the neonative idealists and the realists grew palpable. The two men quarreled over a number of matters—the question of how to prioritize the projects of giving Zakopane running water, a sewage system, an isolation house, and communal hospital; whether one could sufficiently disinfect highland cottages after a tubercular patient's stay there; and whether the commune should gain control over the climatic commission (as was true at other spas), and not the other way around. Janiszewski appealed to like-minded visionaries, a handful of other doctors, as well as public opinion, in particular through the local media.[26] Chramiec's most vocal critic would be the influential Stanisław Witkiewicz.

Witkiewicz already then was changing his mind about the Zakopane highlanders: they had rejected his idea of building the new parish church in Zakopane Style, which to them did not seem sublime enough for sacral construction. This lack of support led the energetic neonative to believe that something was wrong with intelligentsia-highlander relations.[27] Witkiewicz wrote a scathing, booklet-length critique directed at Chramiec entitled *Quagmire (Bagno)*. According to Witkiewicz, the noble, disinterested intelligentsia, which dedicated itself to the improvement of this remote highland locality with its perfect conditions for social work, had found itself stuck in the muck. And a quagmire did not provide an appropriate foundation for the beautifully conceived building of the future, which was to turn Zakopane into "one of the greatest environments of Polish life."[28] Witkiewicz declared that clean water needed to be introduced into the quagmire to flush it out, so that Zakopane could move forward.

Although Chramiec and the communal council published a (shorter) sixteen-page booklet debunking some of the accusations in 1903, the matter continued to fester.[29] Ultimately Chramiec resigned as head of the communal council and a more pliant highlander was installed in his place.

We thus have a situation in which men with different visions of Zakopane, and the future, clashed.[30] Chramiec represented the pragmatic, conservative view associated with the highlanders—the natives—from the very beginnings of the high-altitude climatic health resort. They were worried that the village would be overrun with tubercular patients and thus scare away the healthy. Chramiec worked well with the Galician authorities, another conservative institution that did not wish to annoy the imperial center. His ideological counterpart held more radical, nationalistic—even utopian— views centered on a Poland of the mind. Change in Zakopane was both necessary and salutary, according to Janiszewski and Witkiewicz, especially if directed by the disinterested Polish intelligentsia—by the outsiders turned neonatives in Zakopane. Anti-Habsburg, anti-Austria, these neonatives were out to make Poland in the mountains.

That Chramiec in a way straddled two worlds—that of the highland- ers, into which he was born, and that of the intelligentsia, in which he was educated—seems to have sharpened the conflict. In a way, the neonatives would have been happier with an uneducated highlander at the helm of Zako- pane, a man who could be persuaded to follow the advice of the intelligentsia activists, who were convinced that they knew what was best for Zakopane, and—by extension—for Poland.

In the face of all this discord, the outsider or guest's view of highlanders was changing. This is seen in Witkiewicz's own evolution. He saw the high- landers through rose-colored glasses when writing *On the Mountain Pass* before the turn of the century. Upon his return from a trip abroad (taken for health reasons), and observing that his Zakopane or Polish Style of architecture had not made the inroads he expected in the village, he finally saw the highlander as he was, a less romantic vision, one that did not fit in with his plans.

So much for the great social experiment. Its failure must have hurt those who had hope for the future, a future that transcended the village: "Zako- pane is not a parish, it is all of Poland . . . under the conditions that it has, it could become a crystal, a germ of a new social system, based on brother- hood, justice and love for one's neighbor, it could become in this way a model and example for all of Poland, as if its experimental station."[31] If Zakopane were indeed an example for all of Poland, it demonstrated that differences— highlander/lowlander, native/neonative, Galician/non-Galician, peasant/ intelligentsia, conservative/progressive—remained all too palpable.

Despite this disappointment, the discovery of the Tatras and Zakopane did help to bring the highlanders of Podhale closer together. A sense of high- lander distinctiveness was fostered in the early twentieth century, when Pol- ish elites encouraged the highlanders to organize themselves in order better to protect and buttress their native heritage, of which they were more and more cognizant, having come into contact with more and more lowland vacationers.[32] Their first association—the Union of Highlanders (Związek Górali), founded in 1904—sought, among other things, to develop Zakopane

Style as well as preserve authentic highland dress, both something that the intelligentsia also supported.[33] The union was behind the idea of the first Congress of Podhalans, held in 1911, at which members and other interested individuals could discuss burning issues concerning the region, their own lives and livelihoods, as well as aspects of highland culture and their cultivation. Further congresses were held in 1912 and 1913.[34]

During this period, thus, a corporate identity was emerging among Tatra highlanders, bringing them together across the various villages of the highland region to see themselves as a distinct group: they were Podhalanie (Podhalans) or Górale (now understood with a capital G). Under the influence of neonatives, the union assumed a Polish patriotic stance. Indeed, its first congress—attended by members of the intelligentsia such as Kazimierz Przerwa-Tetmajer and Władysław Orkan, of highland descent—had both Polish national and Tatra highlander regional components. These two components would continue to shape the organization. Under the influence of the intelligentsia, the participating highlanders were coming to consider themselves part of the Polish nation. Surely they had their differences, as seen in the *Quagmire* debacle, with those who thought they were doing what was best for the highlanders, the region, and Poland; yet at least some highlanders were being encouraged to consider themselves part of a larger Polish whole. As has been argued in the case of other European nations, a regional identity could potentially lead to or reinforce a national identity.[35] "The walls of this communal-parochial little world" (Witkiewicz's words) were being burst asunder by well-intentioned outsiders and neonatives.[36] As Ferdynand Hoesick later assessed, these disinterested lowland activists "nonetheless were not always conscious of all the ramifications of their initiative." As a result, he added, "Zakopane is still in a state of the chaotic crossing of various influences and the opposing of very conflicting interests and egoisms."[37]

Zakopane ultimately meant different things to different people. There were those who increasingly behaved as though Zakopane was just another Central European health resort, if undeniably a Polish one, a place where one could take the cure while enjoying a degree of comfort and social interaction (here, between the guests themselves, not with the highlanders). These people stayed in the sanatoria or in Zakopane with its eight hotels and twenty-two boardinghouses in the center of town alone and would be counted among the thirteen thousand registered guests in 1911.[38] Then there were those for whom Zakopane was merely the gateway to the Tatras—to the world of mountaineering and skiing.

Nikodem Bończa-Tomaszewski has theorized that the Poles' "fascination with the mountains grew in parallel with the birth of national consciousness."[39] Highland experiences were part of the intelligentsia's coming of age. Each generation took the mountains on its own terms, which reflected the spirit of the times. Whereas the classical period was one of Warsaw positivism, with its outreach to the highland peasant, the modern period had a much more self-focused, internalized, fin-de-siècle character, one hinted at already in Witkiewicz's evocative *On the Mountain Pass* and even more obvious in the thrill of the technical challenge that faced the next generation's individual alpinists and skiers. Either way, generations of the Polish intelligentsia came to the mountains to push the limits of their capabilities, to explore the wilderness, and in the process find themselves and perhaps their place in the world.

Walery Eljasz once wrote, "For the *kulturtreger* [sic] this world [of the Tatras] is a backwards land, progress enters here extremely slowly"; he added, however, that it was heaven for artists and poets, for those "who sought impressions of a higher order."[40] It was the Poles, and not the Habsburg overlords of Galicia, who truly appreciated, and appropriated, the mountains. In a sense it was Poland writ small. Although Varsovians and other Russian subjects figured prominently in the undertakings, ultimately Poles hailing from all three zones took inspiration from the highlands and concocted their own visions of its future. Some imagined increasing progress and economic development; yet others saw the region as a springboard for national development. All sought to incorporate the territory more fully into the larger picture, whether provincial or national. Poles recolonized the Tatras and purchased Zakopane, refusing to give way to Hungarian or German claims. They likewise integrated the indigenous folk into a Polish historical narrative. The once nebulous frontier was becoming sharper, its inhabitants, permanent residents and visitors alike, more clearly defined relative to each other. Residents of Galicia—some highlanders included—were feeling themselves more Polish, thanks to the contributions of Poles from outside the province. As Eljasz also remarked, "One cannot imagine Poland without the Tatras."[41] This statement, paradoxical though it may seem, proves how far both nation and nature had come since the discovery of 1873.

✎ PART II

The Eastern Carpathians of Galicia and the Second Polish Republic

❧ CHAPTER 5

The Hutsul Region and the Hand of Civilization

In the last decades of the nineteenth century, it was not only the Tatra Mountain segment of the Carpathian Mountains that began to draw the interest of more than the occasional visitor or traveler. The area known as the Eastern Carpathians—Czarnohora (Chornohora) and its environs—also gained the attention of lowlanders, although there was no expressed claim of discovery, which sets this encounter off from that of the Tatras. Now part of Ukraine, at the time this region was the south-westernmost part of eastern Galicia. Arguably the most ethnically hetero-geneous part of all Galicia, this remote corner has often been referred to as the Hutsul region, a name associated with its most distinctive inhabitants: the highly original, horseback-riding, rugged highland people known as the Hutsuls.[1]

If the identity of the Hutsuls was a quintessentially local one, tied to the unforgiving yet sublime terrain that over the centuries had shaped the life patterns of this pastoral people, the attention turned toward the Hutsuls at this time raised the national question. It did so by offering membership in nations that were both stateless and still very much works-in-progress: the Polish and the Ruthenian/Ukrainian.[2] Further complicating matters, the battle for influence over the Hutsul region took place on Habsburg imperial land and under Habsburg imperial policy that permitted the nurturing of one's "nationality, national tradition and national past."[3]

In the course of the popularization of this segment of the Carpathian Mountains, relations between national groups and the as yet nationally uncommitted Hutsul highlanders were reordered. This remote space was integrated into the lowlands in specific ways—in part the work of individuals, in part the result of technological developments. In particular, the railway would play a key role in the discovery of the Hutsuls and in the discovery and subsequent popularization of the Hutsul region. Both highlands and, to a lesser extent, highlanders would be transformed by the "hand of civilization" at the fin de siècle, when vacationing in the Eastern Carpathians suddenly became fashionable.

Before the "Orderly Hand of Civilization"

The Hutsul region may be thought of as the mountainous terrain located in the southeast corner of the Galician Carpathians and lying between the Prut and Czeremosz (Cheremosh) rivers, which flow into the Dniestr (Dnister) in the Podolian lowland. This territory—including the alpine river valleys and the human settlements along them—fell within the East Galician districts of Kosów (vel Kossów; Ukrainian Kosiv), Kołomyja (Kolomyia), and Nadwórna (Nadvirna). The mountain range served as the frontier between Galicia and Hungary to the west, while the swiftly flowing White Czeremosz separated Galicia and the Habsburg province of Bukowina (Bukovyna) to the south.

This region of Galicia was one of the most impoverished and isolated parts of one of the most impoverished and isolated Habsburg provinces. Still, it abounded in natural beauty: dense primeval forests, chiseled cliffs, cascading waterfalls, and fast flowing streams leading into the lowlands where orchards and vineyards grew in this sun-kissed corner of Galicia. But the high uplands were best known for the verdant pastures that fed countless sheep (as well as cattle); both Hutsul shepherds and their animals spent the summer months moving from one grassy *połonina* (polonyna), or highland meadow, to another.[4]

The highland meadows where sheep grazed attracted some visitors who sought to avail themselves of the curative properties of the whey of ewe's milk: drunk warm, it was the treatment of choice for nineteenth-century consumptives. Yet the region also had a wilder reputation, related to the Hutsul brigands, or *opryszki* (opryshky), who had preyed on travelers until the Habsburgs' harsh reprisals against them made brigandage less attractive. Much as the Tatra Górale saw Jánošík and other brigands as highland heroes, brigands such as Oleksa Dovbush (in Polish: Dobosz or Dowboszczuk) served as Hutsul heroes and were celebrated in songs and stories.

MAP 4. The Hutsul region of the Eastern Carpathians (pre-1939). Map by Daniel P. Huffman.

The region also abounded in natural resources: salt deposits, sources of water containing minerals deemed curative, as well as signs that metal ores—lead, iron, and silver—were once mined there.[5] The Habsburgs, who acquired the territory in 1772, quickly sought to exploit these resources, nationalizing the great salt deposits and retaining much of the territory as property of the state treasury. They sent the Frenchman Balthasar Hacquet to study the province's mineral wealth; he is generally credited with the first scholarly treatment of the region.[6] To improve transport, the Habsburgs sought to make the Prut River navigable—but in vain: they only managed to lower the Prut waterfall somewhat before abandoning the project as both impossible and impossibly expensive.[7]

The region was also ethnically diverse, on a scale seen perhaps nowhere else in Galicia. Long before Hacquet and various early nineteenth-century ethnographers visited the region, the area had been penetrated by a dizzying array of different peoples, Slavs and non-Slavs alike. Some of them coursed through the region, like the invading Tatars. Others, such as Wallachian shepherds, Ruthenian farmers, Jewish traders, Polish soldiers, and miscellaneous renegades/deserters, ended up settling there. These in turn mingled and created both the distinctive people known as the Hutsuls as well as the extraordinarily heterogeneous and interdependent population that called this remote end of eastern Galicia its home.[8]

This unusual diversity and mobility uncovered a hidden feature of the mountain region. Armenians engaged in the cattle trade long frequented one of its natural blessings: the spring (also place) known as Burkut. Burkut was the Hungarian word for the carbonated acidulous mineral water (in Polish, *szczawa*) found there.[9] The curative properties of this rich mineral spring made it the watering hole of choice for the lowland nobility in the vicinity already around the beginning of the seventeenth century.[10] However, getting to this tiny remote hamlet not far from the Hungarian border proved difficult, both then as in later centuries.

An anecdote related by the Polish poet, geographer, and ethnographer Wincenty Pol conveys a sense of this near-inaccessible idyll, which he came to visit by accident. Pol and several dozen companions had been traveling on horseback through the highlands on a narrow and dangerous road when they encountered a caravan three times their size coming up the same road—a caravan not unlike the noble parties of old, with their women blindfolded so as not to see the precipice below. Something had to give, and it was Pol's smaller caravan. Graciously invited to join the others at Burkut, the explorers nonetheless had the harrowing experience of reversing direction on that narrow path before continuing their journey.

This encounter nonetheless afforded Pol the pleasure of visiting the spring as well as seeing what "civilization" could do to it. Burkut could hardly compete with the fancier, and more luxurious, type of spa common on the Continent. At midcentury, this remote and near-inaccessible backwater offered at most some small cabins where visitors could stay and benches near the spring, where one could drink one's fill for free.[11] This particular summer, however, the barebones "resort" (if one dare call it that) had been transformed into a whimsical summer idyll: the love of a lady had prompted a certain gentleman to have arranged for all manner of comforts, including a piano, to be shipped there, as well as to have the locals construct one-of-a-kind benches and chairs out of tree branches and stumps, to grace both the buildings and the vicinity of the spring itself. Leaving the specially prepared dwellings to the other party, Pol had some Hutsuls build a more rustic camp on the hill above the spring, in that way adding a bit of native charm to the summer haven.[12] His overall reaction is nonetheless telling: "Still, what could this wilderness not become, if civilization were to put her orderly hand here?!"[13]

This anecdote conveys a sense of both the promise and problems of the region. Rich in minerals and breathtakingly beautiful views, but with few passable roads and no convenient means of provisioning, the Eastern Carpathians ultimately bewitched only the hardiest travelers—or those able to approximate the conditions of home wherever they roamed. Still, these encounters were fairly isolated incidents, having little resonance at the time among broader swaths of society.

The Uncredited Discoverer of the Hutsul Region

Two events, one interwoven with the other, set the process of the undeclared discovery of *Huculszczyzna* in motion. The first was the establishment of the Tatra Society, Galicia's first alpine club, and its subsequent activities in the Carpathians farther to the east. The second event turned out to be Emperor Franz Joseph's 1880 tour of Galicia, which included a brief stop in the East Galician city of Kołomyja to visit an exhibition.[14]

As was demonstrated in chapter 1, the Tatra Society was Galicia's answer to the alpine clubs that were springing up across Central and Eastern Europe. Established by a group of wealthy landowners in the region, the organization also attracted interest from the Polish intelligentsia, especially Chałubiński and his Warsaw friends. With pressure from these "outsiders," several modifications were made to the society's statute, which originally set as its main aims the exploration and popularization of the Carpathians, the fostering of tourism, and the protection of endangered alpine animals. Two new points were added. First, members were exhorted to "support alpine industry." Second, members were now permitted to establish branches of the society to care for the alpine regions closest to them. In other words, it was possible for other segments of the vast Carpathian Mountain range within the province of Galicia to be discovered, just as the Tatras had been in 1873.

The popularization of the Eastern Carpathians in the last third of the nineteenth century did not mean that no Pole or lowland Ruthene had been there previously. The sentimental writer Franciszek Karpiński (1741–1825), in modern times considered the "literary discoverer of the Hutsul region and people," had experienced the age of brigandage firsthand, having survived a visit of Oleksa Dovbush to his home in the vicinity of Kołomyja on the day he was born.[15] In the first half of the nineteenth century, various individuals came to the region to study it and its people or collect folk songs; these included Karol Milewski, Ivan Vahylevych, August Bielowski, Kazimierz Władysław Wójcicki, Wacław z Oleska (vel Zaleski), and Żegota Pauli.[16] In an interesting twist, Ruthenian writers Iakiv Holovats'kyi and Ivan Vahylevych published about the Hutsuls and their region in . . . Czech.[17] Shades of the Tatras: all these lowland outsiders seemed to see the Hutsul region as a unique reservoir of the past that had somehow avoided detection, and thus had been preserved to modern times.[18]

But the fortunes of the Hutsuls had declined since the first half of the century. Syphilis, brought to the region by troops and workers constructing the Kratter Road linking Galicia and Hungary, disfigured their ranks. Even emancipation paradoxically led to the impoverishment, not the enrichment, of the Hutsuls. They engaged in lengthy, expensive, and often unsuccessful legal battles over ownership or access to forests and grazing lands, the two staples of the Hutsul economy—this at a time when the area increasingly was being denuded of its timber by outsiders.[19] The increasingly impoverished highlanders desperately needed help.

As in the case of the Tatras, which required the services of a Warsaw physician to get Polish society to visit the hardscrabble region in droves, the Eastern Carpathians had their own, if homegrown, discoverer of sorts. No Varsovian, and not even an ethnic Pole, this discoverer was a Greek Catholic priest named Sofron Witwicki (1819–79).[20] Beginning in 1855 he served as a parish priest in Żabie (today's Verkhovyna), an enormous if sparsely inhabited village—home to Hutsuls, Jews, and the occasional German, Pole, Armenian, or Roma—that has been called the capital of the Hutsul region.[21] Witwicki's early contributions to the discovery of this remote region came in written form. Penned for a Polish audience, *A Historical Sketch on the Hutsuls*

(*Rys historyczny o Hucułach*), the first scholarly, book-length treatment of the subject in any language, was completed in 1862 and republished in 1873.[22]

The timing of its second edition surely played a role in what was to transpire. In October 1875, Witwicki received a letter from Maksymilian Nowicki, vice president of the still young Tatra Society, inviting him to become a member and seeking information on how to bring the Hutsul region under the society's mandate. Witwicki responded positively and poetically, keen to engage in "joint brotherly work," which would bring Ruthenes and Poles together.[23] Not your typical Ruthene (as if such existed during this period!), Witwicki was an individual who styled himself, using the old Latin formula, "gente Ruthenus natione Polonus"—a Ruthene by birth, a Pole by nationality.[24] He was sympathetic to the causes of the Tatra Society and eager to make them his own, publishing articles in the brand new yearbook of the Tatra Society and in this way joining the ranks of priests like Father Stolarczyk of Zakopane.[25] And it would take someone who could transcend ethnic and social differences to discover the Eastern Carpathians for the Poles of the Tatra Society.

In addition to advice on how and where to build a tourist hut and whom to involve in the doings of the society (for example, the wealthy Germans of the Göz & Comp. lumber business), Witwicki embraced the fourth aim of the Tatra Society, to support alpine industry. He advocated the reactivation of a silver mine on Czywczyn połonina and the improvement and construction of spas (at distant Szybene as well as Burkut, perhaps also in Żabie, which had good spring water as well), endeavors that would require significant capital. Of Hutsul handicrafts, he promoted gunmaking, an art that these highland peasants had not been allowed to practice since 1848.[26]

The Tatra Society made Witwicki a special delegate and charged him with working toward the society's next goal: to form an affiliated but distinct regional branch for the Eastern Carpathians. To this end, a three-man exploratory commission, led by Witwicki, was founded and set to work.[27]

The resultant Czarnohora Branch of the Tatra Society was officially sanctioned by the Galician authorities in 1877. Yet this important milestone was ultimately reached without Witwicki. His pioneering work done and goal nearly attained, the clergyman resigned from his post in June 1876. Witwicki would never play an active role in the organization he had done so much to create—not because he was not interested in the fate of the branch: rather his health was failing.[28] Before three years had passed, the Greek Catholic priest was dead.[29]

Although little known today, let alone credited with discovering the Hutsul region, Witwicki was conscious of the role he had played in popularizing the Eastern Carpathians and his Hutsuls.[30] The Greek Catholic priest ended his farewell letter to the Tatra Society with a poem, part of which reads: "With scanty powers, I showed the way, / and united Czarnohora with the Tatras; / I roused life . . . You [must] lead further; / And if [you be so] kind— do not forget me."[31]

His contributions, if inexplicably forgotten or unacknowledged, were undeniable. Witwicki had set into motion the makings of a particularly vital branch of the Tatra Society, in existence until the outbreak of World War II. Worthy of note, he had helped to assemble a particularly well rounded, ethnically and socially mixed membership. Of the ninety-one members enrolled in the Czarnohora Branch in early 1878, there were Poles, Ruthenes, Armenians, Germans—and Hutsuls. The first Hutsul member of the Tatra Society was Athanasyj Ursedzuk, a "first-rate farmer," according to the minutes of the second session of the Czarnohora Branch, in January 1876.[32] But he was not the only one to pay his dues and join.

With the accession of Hutsuls to the Tatra Society, the Czarnohora Branch was proving itself to be more democratic as well as more diverse than the main organization. In this distant branch, titled nobles, university professors, and oilmen (for there were other riches in the foothills) mingled with Hutsul homesteaders.[33] The existence of the organization was also advertised in the local Ukrainian press.[34] Thus, although the Tatra Society historically has been associated with the Polish intelligentsia, thanks to this literary, energetic, engaged Greek Catholic priest its Czarnohora Branch reflected greater ethnic and social diversity.

The branch began to popularize the mountains. A noteworthy endeavor was the 1878 trip to the Rokieta, near Berezów Wyżny (Vyzhnii Bereziv), for the two-day Pentecost holiday. A hundred lowlanders from Kołomyja alone signed up; they were met by others on the way, as well as joined by a substantial number of Hutsuls, bringing the total participants to four hundred. More a semiofficial gathering than a regular hiking excursion, the lowlanders were greeted with triumphal arches in several localities and even had their photograph taken.[35] The excursion would have been impossible without the cooperation of local government officials and foresters (some of them also branch members), who supplied Hutsul horses and guides and saw to it that rafts for the thrilling ride down the Czeremosz back to "civilization"—the reservoir's sluice gates further upstream having been opened especially for them—would be ready.[36]

Having learned firsthand how difficult it was to travel through this challenging wilderness (scarred in places by logging), the two branches initiated a series of projects designed to improve access and accommodations. The first alpine hut (on the Gadżyna połonina at the foot of the Szpyci) was ready already in 1878, soon to be followed by three more. In 1884 some preliminary trails were marked; in this way, the Czarnohora Branch was ahead of its parent organization, which began to mark trails in the Tatras only as of 1887. And an alpine base camp of sorts—the Dworek Czarnohorski—was established in Żabie.[37] Members also published accounts of their trips and any scientific findings gleaned from them.[38]

They also took seriously the mandate to support alpine industry, as it became clear how impoverished a people the Hutsuls were. However, instead of doing something as costly as reopen the Czywczyn silver mine, they focused on finding a market for Hutsul handicrafts. Thus, in 1879, Czarnohora Branch members began to plan for an ethnographic exhibition, to be held in Kołomyja the following year, which would educate a broader public about the Hutsul region.[39]

The Tatra Society's Ethnographic Exhibition

This ethnographic exhibition—the first ever organized in Galicia—would mark the true public début of the Hutsuls.[40] Whereas an influential Warsaw doctor popularized the Tatras and the Górale far and wide, the Hutsul region got a boost of sorts from none other than Emperor Franz Joseph, who accepted an invitation to attend the ethnographic exhibition in conjunction with his September 1880 tour of Galicia.[41] The committee members timed the opening of the exhibition to coincide with Franz Joseph's stop in Kołomyja on September 15: the emperor would be their first, and most illustrious, guest. With him would come the attention of the broader world, far beyond this tiny provincial corner, as the accompanying journalists and imperial entourage would thrust Kołomyja and the adjacent Hutsul region into the limelight.

It only remained to make the ethnographic exhibition an event to remember. The promised presence of the emperor galvanized the Galician public. Ethnographer Oskar Kolberg was able to instruct committee members and other volunteers to complete the collections of textiles and clothing, haberdashery, household utensils, ceramics, musical instruments, and the like without regard to cost, for suddenly money was forthcoming from municipal, county, and provincial offices across Galicia as well as from wealthy individuals.[42] Special buildings were constructed to house the exhibition, which itself was expanded to include materials from beyond the Hutsul region. Indeed, the projected presence of the emperor initiated the transformation of what essentially had been a small-town Tatra Society affair to an all-Galician (or, as we shall see, all-Polish) one.

FIGURE 5.1.   1880 Ethnographic Exhibition poster, showing the exhibition site in Kołomyja as well as Hutsuls (on the left) and other peoples of the region (on the right). Published in *Kłosy* 32, no. 831 (1881): 341. Image in the public domain.

Despite its independent origins, the ethnographic exhibition was seamlessly woven into the fabric of the emperor's Galician tour. Early on, it had been decided that Franz Joseph would be treated to what was unique in this poor province: its native traditions.[43] Noblemen everywhere were decked out in traditional noble dress, and peasants sporting their Sunday best had been on display in every Galician locale.[44] There were even more than the usual "live" ethnographic items displaying traditional dress and demonstrating facets of folk life in Kołomyja. Indeed, an imposing sight greeted the emperor at the Kołomyja railway station, that of a three-hundred-strong banderya of Hutsuls on horseback, which escorted him to the exhibition site.[45] With their wild countenance and colorful traditional garb, the Hutsuls inspired much gushing on the part of journalists: "It was a genuinely extraordinary sight, to look at rows of these beautiful highlanders with cocky expressions, galloping gracefully on their agile little horses, with their capes blowing in the breeze, gutsily shouting in honor of the Monarch, waving shiny hatchets or banners."[46] They were "the great attraction" for those visiting from elsewhere, according to Count Stanisław Tarnowski.[47]

But the real revelation—certainly the one the Tatra Society sought to promote—was Hutsul artistry. At the exhibition this was manifest, for example, in extensive displays of Hutsul homespun: from delicate and fancifully embroidered linens to substantial, brightly colored woolens, some of which hung from the walls like rich tapestries. Even more incredible were the elaborately decorated Hutsul weapons (rifles, pistols, and the ubiquitous hatchet, the Hutsul's "favorite tool"), smoking paraphernalia (a pipe also being a Hutsul necessity, even for women), and riding tack on display.[48] The exhibition's patrons led the emperor through the exhibition, with Kolberg and others explaining the significance of various items. The emperor took a genuine interest in the collection of Tatra Society member Bohdan Bohosiewicz, who contributed a wardrobe full of Hutsul accouterments of leather, wood, and metal.[49] The decorated wooden stirrups, richly embellished hatchets, pistols, canes, tobacco pouches, and the like so enchanted the emperor that he ordered the artist, Jurko Shkribliak of Jaworów (Javoriv), to make copies of some of the items for him.[50]

The emperor's positive reaction, as well as its reverberations—many other visitors placed orders or paid for items, to be given to them after the

Banderya huculska towarzyszące pociągowi Cesarza Franciszka Józefa.
Kopia z akwareli T. Rybkowskiego.

FIGURE 5.2. Hutsul *banderya* accompanying the train of Emperor Franz Joseph, copy of a watercolor by Tadeusz Rybkowski. Published in *Kłosy* 36, no. 929 (1883): 256. Image in the public domain.

exhibition was closed—was precisely what the exhibitions' sponsors wanted. This interest in Hutsul handicrafts suggested a future for Hutsul cottage industry at a time when the highlanders were struggling.

One wonders, however, what form the Galician Polish lowlanders imagined Hutsul cottage industry would assume. Was the Hutsul merely to increase his traditional production of household goods in the winter months or make his living not as a shepherd in the high uplands but as a craftsman? And would demand for traditional objects be great enough to allow him to do the latter? Indeed, would the encounter between lowlander and highlander lead to traditional Hutsul output becoming "commodified" or transformed, perhaps beyond recognition?[51]

Even at this early stage, one sees the effects of highlander-lowlander interaction. It turns out that some of the most notable examples of Hutsul handiwork had already been adjusted, with the help of lowlanders, to appeal to more bourgeois tastes. Reportedly Bohosiewicz had "order[ed], encourage[d] and look[ed] after Skriblak [Shkribliak]," to ensure that the Hutsul artisan properly executed the Pole's orders, and he was not above having the items polished or varnished on his own afterward.[52] In other words, these most celebrated items of Hutsul applied arts—those the emperor deemed worthy to add to his own collection—were not as "authentic" as may have been imagined.[53] Could the Hutsuls maintain their uniqueness, as some argued, while assimilating new models, methods, or motifs?[54]

Another threat to whatever might be termed "authentic" Hutsul craftsmanship came, paradoxically, in a project designed to help them. This is signaled by Count Tarnowski's campaign to drum up business in this corner of Galicia for Kołomyja's new ceramics school; it, however, produced utterly common items, devoid of any connection to Hutsul shapes and ornament—their greatest attraction being that they were dirt cheap.[55] The school was not fostering genuine Hutsul craftsmanship, the kind that might interest true connoisseurs of folk art. It seems that there was little confidence that there was or could be a demand for such items in provincial Galicia at this time.[56] Perhaps it was still difficult to imagine, in poor, provincial Galicia, that tourists might someday come en masse and purchase Hutsul souvenirs for sentimental reasons—hence the safer marketing of goods with a greater, albeit commonplace, utility. These were still the days before Poles became more sophisticated in their assessment of highland culture, less willing to allow some foreigner—for the directors of both the ceramics school in Kołomyja and the woodworking school in Zakopane were Germans or Czechs—to impose his own (inferior) models on the impressionable highlanders, who had no sense of what made their own style unique.

Still, what kinds of options faced the Hutsul in an increasingly modern world—a world he ignored only at his peril? Would the Hutsul still be a Hutsul if he stopped spending his summers on the alpine meadows and instead devoted his time to producing wares not only for his own household's use (work usually done in the winter) but also for broader consumption? Or if he let rooms to guests for the summer, led excursions, or served as a porter for a living? To what extent was that preferable to his going to work in the new industry of oil production, which was about to take off, thanks to Czarnohora Branch member Stanisław Szczepanowski, right in the middle of the Hutsul region, thus juxtaposing primeval forests with "forests of oil rigs"?[57] Indeed, the Kołomyja exhibition also contained samples of crude oil from Słoboda Rungurska.[58]

Dueling Exhibitions

The encroachments of modern life might have another effect: on the Hutsuls' identity. Those who left the mountains to work elsewhere might well assimilate into the Ruthenian population, with which it shared a religion— Greek Catholicism—and similarities of language. That this was a genuine possibility is suggested by yet another facet of the emperor's trip. Franz Joseph visited not one, but two exhibitions in Kołomyja. Indeed, one might think of September 1880 as the month of dueling exhibitions, the "Polish" "ethnographic" exhibition and the "Ruthenian" "agricultural" exhibition.

Behind the second exhibition stood an organization that was a contemporary of the Tatra Society: the Kachkovs'kyi Society (Obshchestvo im. Mykhaila Kachkovs'koho).[59] According to its statute, the society was allowed to set up an exhibit at its annual convention "to display tools and agricultural products."[60] In 1880, visitors to Kołomyja, including the emperor, found a modest display of vegetables, some farm equipment, and—along the lines of the Tatra Society's event—some ethnographic goods and a number of artistic works.[61] Two parallel events, it would seem—but not without a sense of rivalry. Galician Poles clearly feared that the Hutsuls might be brainwashed into supporting Ruthenian separatism. Given the poorer impression made by the smaller exhibition, they were happy to label it the "real Ruthenian" one, reserving the label "Polish" for the more impressive exhibition.[62]

Here it should be noted that the moniker "Polish" referred to more than the fact that Poles were in charge. It represented a particular political view of what it meant to be Polish, one with echoes of the glorious multinational commonwealth past. News that the emperor was to attend had resulted in an infusion of elements into the exhibition that allowed for some to place the word *ethnographic* in quotation marks while making the modifier "Polish" all the more appropriate. For example, the more generous outpouring of financial and material support facilitated the expansion of the project to other (neighboring) regions and other peoples. The Hutsuls were now but the most outstanding people of a richly multicultural region—dating from the times of the Polish-Lithuanian Commonwealth—in which Hutsuls, Ruthenes, Armenians, even Roma coexisted. (That the region's Jews were overlooked suggests that attitudes in eastern Galicia were not far removed from those found in the Tatras.)

Another reminder of the old commonwealth was a Turkish tent, to which the emperor retired before gazing on the two Hutsul wedding parties that rode in on horseback and subsequently danced for him. Influential Galician Poles went to great lengths to secure it for the exhibition, as it could be used to remind the emperor of a historic fact of world-historical significance: the defeat of the Turks at the gates of Vienna in 1683 by Christian forces under the leadership of the Polish king, Jan Sobieski.[63] Poles, in the broadest definition of the term—that is, the forces of that multiethnic commonwealth, which could now be imagined in the brightly dressed Hutsul "cavalry" that had escorted the emperor to the exhibition site—had defended the empire, and it was hinted, would and could do so again.[64]

The so-called ethnographic exhibition had become a vehicle to buttress the position of the Poles in Galicia. A comparison of the two dueling exhibitions sufficed to show Emperor Franz Joseph that the Poles put on the better show: they were able to rally to "their" exhibition representatives of all the peoples of eastern Galicia, including an impressively chivalric Hutsul host. The fact that so many participated in the "Polish" ethnographic exhibition was indeed a coup for the Galician authorities, who nonetheless spared no expense to see that it was a success.[65] This allowed the authorities, perhaps, to buy the participation or cooperation of some of the Hutsuls and other participants: sources mention that the two wedding parties received some kind of compensation from (or were even "outfitted" by) the nobles Dzieduszycki and Przybyłowski, in addition to receiving a gift from the emperor.[66]

One can only intuit what may have motivated the Hutsuls to participate and what they got out of the event. Given the traditional peasant enthusiasm for the person of the emperor, doubtless his visit is what brought them en masse to Kołomyja and, perhaps, emboldened them to sell their handicrafts to the Polish exhibition committee members. It may also have induced those hundreds of Hutsul men to participate in the escort. These, after all, were Hutsul *lehini* (knights), men with the greatest status in Hutsul society.[67] The Hutsuls had cause to ponder their reception and, indeed, their access to the emperor. Their exalted status as prime ethnographic exhibit must have conveyed some of the interest of the emperor and the broader public in them, their attire, their handicrafts, their traditions. They also learned that the emperor and his entourage were impressed enough with some of the Hutsul wares to purchase or order copies for themselves. These may have been powerful messages for an impoverished and struggling people.

There was yet one more message the Poles sought to impress on the Hutsuls and others present in Kołomyja. It was hoped that some of the emperor's popularity among the folk would rub off on the Polish nobility that ran Galicia. In a way, thus, the exhibition and the emperor's visit to Kołomyja were "hijacked" by the Galician Polish political elites for their own purposes. What began as a modest exhibition became a Galician Polish-run show, the cast of characters the diverse population of this part of the province. While there clearly were important imperial dimensions to the visit, there were no less important domestic ones. Ultimately, what was at stake was control and influence over an attractive yet struggling highland population that could choose to work together, and identify itself, either with the Poles or with the Ruthenes. Here we have identities in the making: Polish, Ruthenian/Ukrainian, and Hutsul being only some of the possibilities.

Yet, did the Galician Poles manage to transform these relations, as befits a true discovery? Recall that, in the case of the discovery of the Tatra Mountains, the Warsaw Poles not only saw the Polish past reflected in the Górale but came to accept the highlanders as their equals, as part of a modern Polish nation. By the turn of the century, their forays into ethnographic research even led to the propagation of the Zakopane Style of architecture throughout all the Polish lands as something quintessentially Polish. Did anything similar transpire in the Eastern Carpathians? After all, the Hutsuls appeared to have much to offer to a modernizing Polish nation. With the stock they placed in freedom, their artistic abilities, bravery, hardiness, and willingness to bear arms and possibly defend a country, they might well have become the Eastern Carpathian counterpart to the beloved Górale of the Tatras.

Yet were Galician Poles ready to embrace them in this way? We have seen how the Hutsuls were presented as part of the fabric of the old Polish commonwealth as well as the Habsburg province of Galicia. Such peasants were the raw materials out of which Poles could be made, much as, at the same time elsewhere in Europe, peasants in a "country of savages" in which "the reality was diversity" were being turned into Frenchmen.[68] That this vocabulary was not being used yet—turning Hutsuls into Poles—doubtless reflects the fact that the Polish Galician elites, unlike their Warsaw counterparts, were not thinking in terms of the modern nation as yet.

What transpired after the 1880 exhibition and visit confirms a sense that this discovery of the Hutsuls, if judged by modern nation-building standards, was incomplete. To be sure, not long after the event, the dramatic scene of armed Hutsuls on horseback escorting the emperor made its way onto canvas, courtesy of painter Tadeusz Rybkowski.[69] Other artists such as Teodor Axentowicz began to frequent the region, helping to shape what one art historian has called the "cult of the Hutsuls."[70] This would develop further in the first years of the twentieth century, when artists of the caliber of Piotr Jarocki, Władysław Sichulski, and Fryderyk Pautsch began to make sketching pilgrimages to the region. The fruits of these trips were exhibited in Galicia, Austria-Hungary, and in the West.[71]

As to making the mountains accessible for tourists, the Czarnohora Branch tried to live up to its mandate. The need for huts was greater in the Eastern Carpathians than in the Tatras, as the distances from civilization were significantly greater. The Czarnohora Branch opened and operated various huts as well as two alpine base camps in the more easily accessible Hutsul villages of Żabie and Worochta. It lobbied for discounts on military maps, railway discounts on the return trip as well as a favorable timetable for the trains. The branch produced stereoscopic slides for Galician peep-shows, while members Henryk Gąsiorowski and Juliusz Dutkiewicz published picture postcards.[72] Henryk Hoffbauer penned two slim, inexpensive guidebooks covering important as well as easy excursions.[73] That the branch did not establish a group of certified Hutsul guides, such as was done in the Tatras, can likely be blamed on the small number of tourists to the region and the fact that, again, not all Hutsuls knew the mountains intimately—this despite Witwicki having listed names of some in one of his letters to the Tatra Society executive early on.[74] There was no East Carpathian Chałubiński to foster this knowledge, let alone highlander-lowlander rapport. That tourists did not come in greater numbers reflects the fact that only the Kołomyjan members of the Czarnohora Branch seemed to have a real stake in the region; and even these respectable yet provincial middle-aged men and women lacked a tradition of mountain climbing.

For a long time, most traveling in the Hutsul region had been done by horseback, and with the help of highland guides. Yet parallel to developments in the Tatras there were some new initiatives in the Eastern Carpathians: most notably, young people began to hike on their own, and on foot. The first independent student tourist organization in the Polish lands, the Academic Tourist Club, was founded in Lwów in 1906. Its members predominately came from Lwów University and Lwów Polytechnic (most of the latter were refugees from the Russian Empire).[75] As impoverished students they wrangled discounts for train travel for their excursions, purchased not only Henryk Hoffbauer's guidebooks but also a complete set of Austrian military maps, and set about exploring the mountains by themselves.[76]

Within two months of its founding, the Academic Tourist Club sponsored its first four-day trip to Czarnohora over the Pentecost holiday. The only one properly outfitted amid a group of complete novices, the trip leader Mieczysław Orłowicz called it a comedy of errors. Some students carried their gear not in backpacks but in suitcases; those fellows lasted only two days, although somehow they made it up the region's highest peak, the Howerla. Participants were shod in a wild array of leather footwear, most of it not suitable for hiking. Their shoes got soggy in the rain, and the Hutsul manager of one hut put them near the fire to dry out—too near the fire: the shoes were essentially cooked, making for stiff walking the following day. A ragtag group made it back to Lwów and had its picture taken as a memento.[77] Undaunted, the Academic Tourist Club managed three more trips in the Eastern Carpathians that year. A sign that Tatra Society members were not doing much hiking: as it had been vacant for so long, the hut on the Poliwny had been turned by local Hutsuls into a barn for their sheep, and its door and windows had been removed. When the Czarnohora Branch was notified of this development, members remarked that they had not been there themselves, as it was far from the railway.[78]

❧ CHAPTER 6

The Advent of the Railway

The rapid rise of the Eastern Carpathians as a more popular vacation destination came on the heels of a quintessentially nineteenth-century development: the advent of the railway. Already the Lwów-Czernowitz (L'viv-Chernivtsi) railway had made it possible in 1880 for Emperor Franz Joseph to visit the provincial town of Kołomyja, and other provincial towns in Galicia and Bukowina, with relative ease. But Kołomyja was hardly in the Carpathians itself, although of the larger Galician cities it lay nearest to the mountains of the Eastern Carpathians. New railway lines would provide fast access to this remote region, in the process helping to transform the traditional landscape. According to Laurence Cole, who has written about Austrian Tirol, "Tourism is one of the main conduits in bringing modernity—and its attendant benefits and problems—to Alpine regions."[1] In the form of spa going and summer holidays, tourism would bring aspects of modernity—or certainly what passed for it in the Galician backwater—to the remote highland wilderness that was the Hutsul region.

Early on, the only means of penetrating the Eastern Carpathians was to travel as far as was possible by carriage or wagon. One route into the mountains was provided by the Kratter highroad, which stretched all the way from the highland town of Delatyn to the Hungarian border. Lowlanders who traveled this leisurely route through the highland villages in the Prut River Valley were struck by the distinctive pattern of settlement. For, although these were among the largest villages in Galicia, they hardly resembled villages, so sparsely were they settled. In contrast to the linear layout of lowland villages, the East Carpathian villages had no genuine village center—at least, not one in which Hutsul homesteads would be clustered.[2] If there was any density of settlement in the village center, the settlers were likely to be Jews or other non-Hutsul "outsiders" (including the occasional Polish or German official as well as clergymen of different faiths). To complicate things further, the Hutsul residents of villages tended to identify not with a village in its entirety but rather with their own hamlet. This centripetal pull reflected the way the villages had grown in the past, in bits and spurts, as further lands were settled or used as pasture. Historically this pattern had also led to the creation of new villages, as settlements coalesced.[3]

The coming of the Stanisławów-Woronienka railway to this distant corner of eastern Galicia in 1894 led to the reconfiguration of this lightly populated space. The railway was also sometimes referred to as the Stanislau-Körösmezö line, as it linked Stanislau/Stanisławów/Stanïslaviv (today's Ivano-Frankivs'k, in Ukraine), Galicia's third largest city, with the Hungarian city of Körösmezö (today's Yasinia, in Ukraine). This sixty-mile route through some of the region's most stunning terrain had paradoxically not been set with any tourist purposes in mind. Rather it was to facilitate the quick supply of troops from the Hungarian lands to the Russian border in the case of war.[4]

This change in accessibility nonetheless opened the region to new possibilities. The railway journey from Stanisławów, especially after the thirty-sixth mile and the town of Delatyn, where the railway entered the Prut River Valley, provided an "amazing panorama of romantic mountain vistas": magnificent valleys and dense forests, towering mountains, and gigantic rocks as one traveled higher and higher the length of the valley.[5] An Austrian official present at the opening of the railway compared the picturesque region to the Salzkammergut, one of Austria's most scenic destinations.[6]

Yet it was the juxtaposition of natural and man-made wonders that created this new, and newly appreciated, landscape. Perhaps overshadowing the natural beauty of the Prut River Valley in the eyes of some guests to the region was the technical feat of the railway. Its calling card was the aesthetically pleasing stone bridge across the Prut at Jaremcze. Unique in the world at that time, the central feature of this "masterpiece of the new railway" was the imposing arch spanning the river, 92 feet above the Prut. Together with the viaducts connecting the bridge on both sides, the entirety was 672 feet long.[7] Poles took especial pride in the fact that the line—finished on schedule despite an outbreak of cholera—was the work of Polish engineers, among them Stanisław Nikodem Rawicz Kosiński, inspector of the Austrian railways before he took on this job.[8]

The engineering feats contributed to the transformation of both the landscape and the experience of it. This smoothing and leveling of the terrain traversed by the trains, as well as the train ride itself, would have consequences for the tourists who would descend on the region after 1894. Here one surely can speak—as has Wolfgang Schivelbusch—of the "annihilation of time and space."[9] Unlike travel in a horse-drawn carriage, in the railway car there would be no palpable sense of the undulations of the terrain; and while the train would speed on past the rest of the landscape, railway stops and stations would break up the space into discrete, identifiable localities, where travelers could be deposited—and which were now ripe for development of various kinds.

The Stanisławów-Woronienka railway revolutionized the settlement pattern of what had been sleepy, sparsely settled villages through which the Kratter Road meandered.[10] This was facilitated further by the construction of another railway line in 1899, a *Lokalbahn* connecting the city of Kołomyja

FIGURE 6.1.   Bridge over the Prut at Jaremcze. Drawing by Karl Jeczmieniowski, published in *Die österreichisch-ungarische Monarchie in Wort und Bild*, vol. "Galizien" 1898 (Vienna: 1886–1902), 887. Image in the public domain.

with the Prut River Valley destination of Delatyn. Little Delatyn, an East Galician shtetl, metamorphosed into a railroad hub of sorts, something that increased its potential to develop as a resort as well as be a destination for the Hutsuls of the region, for whom it was the closest town.[11]

Yet as a town in the mountains, Delatyn—which with its saline baths also had pretensions to being a spa destination—was a bit of an exception. Together, both railway lines facilitated the growth (in density, not in area) of a series of villages situated along the railway line. These were localities such as, in order of elevation, Dora, Jamna, Mikuliczyn, Tatarów, and Worochta, with Worochta at 2,625 feet above sea level.

The Polish Switzerland

The most striking changes came to the hamlet of the village of Dora known as Jaremcze (Yaremche). The hamlet would soon assume the monikers "The Zakopane of the Eastern Carpathians" and "The Polish Switzerland."[12] One could say without a doubt that the Stanisławów-Woronienka railway made Jaremcze—and in a "fairy-tale-like, American" fashion, with parallels to New York's discovery of the Catskills or the making of the White Mountains of New Hampshire.[13]

Prior to the 1890s, much of Jaremcze had been pastureland and forest, let by the village of Dora to a Jewish tenant, who raised cattle and exploited the grove, for a mere 100 guldens per annum. The advent of the railroad in 1894—and with it the construction of the iconic railway bridge—put an end to that arrangement and land usage. Early construction in Jaremcze housed workers engaged in building the railroad. Local Jews began to build, followed by a handful of outsiders: the head of the directorate of demesnes and forests in Lwów, a school principal from Kołomyja, and a whole series of engineers from Stanisławów.[14] Jaremcze was quickly inundated by tourists and summer guests, mainly from eastern Galicia, who swarmed the region, happy to have quick and easy access to vivifying highland air and bathing in the Prut River.[15] Other outsiders found investing in land to be a moneymaking venture, as did the pharmacist Dr. Beill, who bought a large parcel and sold off lots at a nice profit. Soon on that very same territory where cattle had once grazed stood dozens of new villas as well as a billboard advertising one of Dr. Beill's concoctions—a further sign of the entrepreneurial capitalism that was the gift of Western civilization (in its Galician idiom) to the East Carpathian wilderness.[16]

A visitor from Warsaw saw this development as the first move in the right direction. In an article that reached Polish audiences in all three empires the writer Tadeusz Smarzewski pleaded for even more entrepreneurship: "What do all these localities, strewn along the length of the railway between Delatyn and the Hungarian border, need? They need above all what all of Galicia needs: faith in their own strength, entrepreneurship, a grain of optimism." He suggested that "tens of thousands of guests should already be swarming along this valley" and in order to "attract these crowds, one must not fear investments, one must establish hotels, stores, bathhouses, bakeries, slaughterhouses, one must ensure the supply of milk and vegetables, one must awaken in oneself the merchant's spirit of profit-making." He concluded: "It's obvious that it will happen someday, but why delay? Why deny oneself the earnings, which themselves press into one's hand? The Prut valley can become a wealthy corner of the country; for this to happen, shrewd, bold, ingenious people full of ideas must settle there."[17]

And indeed: the entrepreneurial spirit, seemingly so rare in impoverished Galicia, was awakened by the sight of the Prut River Valley destinations and their potential to become first-rate "European"-level spas and high-altitude resorts. Jaremcze—essentially built from scratch—was but the biggest success story, representing the biggest makeover of the highland landscape.

As befitted a place with European aspirations, accommodations in the hotels or villas did not come cheaply: a single room soon cost 100 guldens for the season.[18] By 1902, there were eighteen taverns where there had been just one in the hamlet before.[19] Development continued to come in true "American" (Wild West) style, as entrepreneurs sought to make a fast buck off the summer guests and day-trippers. As one anecdote had it, the rich of Stanisławów spent their summer vacations in Jaremcze and the poor in Switzerland—where the cost of the trip was amortized by the less expensive cost of living.[20] And a thousand people took the train to Jaremcze on summer Sundays, three-quarters of whom came from Stanisławów.[21]

To make Jaremcze the most European, most developed, and most ambitious of the Prut River Valley localities, someone had to shape the landscape and deal with the elements. Several years after the railway came to what had previously been empty space, the newcomers established an organization of like-minded people who wished to further Jaremcze's development. Initially led by Kołomyja high school principal Józef Skupniewicz and representing the owners of the new properties, many of whom were Galician civil servants, the Jaremcze Club showed much initiative. Hailing mainly from Stanisławów and Kołomyja, these new property owners were already transforming the landscape of Jaremcze with villas standing in close proximity to each other, hotels and restaurants near the railway station, and an increasing number of streets.[22] The Jaremcze Club subsequently sought to beautify the public spaces: the walking route to the nearby gloriette gained benches and a boardwalk was constructed along the entire, streetlight-lit, main road.[23] Their efforts were needed time and again: the flooding of the Prut in 1899 and 1911 wiped out wooden bridges, inundated roads and houses, and caused the trains to stop running, as did landslides in 1896, 1907, and 1908.[24] And club members fought to stop a rock quarry from operating within the hamlet's limits, which would undo everything they had fought so hard to achieve.[25]

On the whole this new Jaremcze had a multiethnic Galician feel to it, mirroring the composition of the East Galician towns. That said, there were a handful of elements that referenced a broader Polish sensibility; these included the Roman Catholic Church of Our Lady of Częstochowa, built partly in Zakopane Style.[26] Yet the budding resort was quite different from Zakopane. To be sure, the Czarnohora Branch of the Tatra Society, the region's first alpine club, was also involved in Jaremcze, marking trails to the nearby peaks. It also organized special excursions from Kołomyja to Jaremcze for the two-day Pentecost holiday, making good use of the Kołomyja-Delatyn line.[27] Still, despite such excursions, one gets the sense that relatively few East Galicians knew the Eastern Carpathians at all well. Witness this description of the annual day trip to Jaremcze sponsored by the Union of Railway Employees in Lwów: instead of climbing the nearby peaks, the three thousand or so visitors contented themselves with having a large picnic near the train station, feasting on their chickens, cakes, and beer while dancing to music played by the band of the Thirtieth Infantry Regiment, all the while inhaling the fresh mountain air.[28] The urban lifestyle—the "loud bourgeois crowd" of the Lwów/Stanisławów/Kołomyja street—was transplanted to this little oasis of civilization in the Carpathian wilderness.[29]

Most visitors to the Prut River Valley were of the spa-going, not mountain-climbing, kind. Like spa goers elsewhere in Europe (think of Thomas Mann's *Magic Mountain*) or even in Galicia (the most [in]famous example being Leopold von Sacher-Masoch's *Venus in Furs*), the guests-cum-patients tended to be preoccupied with their own health, amusement, and affairs—anything to stave off boredom.[30] And what could one do when it rained—a frequent occurrence in the summer months? Given the hamlet's lack of a *Kurhaus* or casino where people could congregate and get to know each other, the social life that lay at the center of "genuine" spas was reportedly much missed.[31]

It was not that the Jaremcze Club did not want to build a Kurhaus or transform the hamlet into a real European-style spa. For this it needed to obtain health resort status officially, such as Zakopane was awarded in 1885. Yet, despite the efforts of the Jaremcze Club, for fifteen years Jaremcze could not even apply for this status: it remained administratively a part of the village of Dora, where Hutsuls, engaged in their traditional pursuits, were loath to invest in infrastructure of the spa sort to make the hamlet more attractive.[32]

According to a petition sent to the Galician authorities, the contrast between Dora, which essentially remained the sleepy little village it had been, and its hamlet Jaremcze, an already bustling if unofficial health resort, was striking. By 1906 Jaremcze had seventy villas. A sum of 500,000 crowns of capital had been invested in the hamlet. No longer an "impoverished highland village" with ramshackle cottages, the hamlet "had a European look." Jaremcze strove to make a name for itself as well as to lobby for health resort status, which is why it wished to be independent from Dora. Jaremczans averred that in asking for separation "they ha[d] in mind only the general good, and the slogan of Jaremcze [wa]s the creation of a health resort, which would be for this part of the crownland a second Zakopane." The Jaremcze Club claimed that Jaremcze would be a model commune, given that the property owners in the hamlet belonged to the intelligentsia, many of them occupying high positions in the province.[33]

Although the comparison here was with Zakopane, their attitudes toward the indigenous Hutsuls again prove quite a contrast. Whereas the Tatra highlanders were embraced by the Polish intelligentsia, the entrepreneurs of Jaremcze seemed to take little notice of the ethnographic curiosity that was the Hutsul population, emphasizing instead the imported "European" aspects of this oasis of civilization in the East Carpathian wilderness. Nowhere in the advertising materials on Jaremcze were the Hutsuls and their culture touted as an attraction.[34] Could this have been because the elemental folk might scare off guests? Or that the Hutsuls in the Prut River Valley were already becoming deracinated? For it appears the Hutsuls were relegated to being part of the scenic backdrop to the resort, marginalized as mere purveyors of dairy products and meat, or being brought into the modern world, for better or for worse.[35]

Stanisławów's Poles reported that the local population had become accustomed to the guests in Jaremcze, longed for them, and even eagerly awaited them as summer guests, suggesting that Hutsuls also got involved in the hospitality business.[36] All this alarmed members of the Ruthenian/Ukrainian intelligentsia resident in Stanisławów, who came to take an interest in their highland brethren. A number of newspaper articles decried the move of Poles and their Jewish allies into Hutsul space, claiming that "all kinds of speculators demoralize and take advantage of the Hutsuls every step of the way."[37]

By 1912 lowland Ukrainians had given up on Jaremcze, which, having finally separated from Dora two years before, was witnessing a flurry of investment and played host to nearly four thousand paying guests annually—still significantly fewer than the thirteen thousand who summered in Zakopane.[38] Nonetheless, that same year Jaremcze was visited by the Habsburg archduke Charles, later to be the last emperor of Austria-Hungary.[39] This "Interlaken of the Eastern Carpathians" was thus the place for those demanding visitors who wanted a European-level spa in their (provincial) backyard.[40] Eschewing such ambitious comparisons, the region's Ukrainians referred to Jaremcze simply as a "pol's'ke misto" (Polish city)—perhaps aptly so, as the locality had seen its Polish (i.e., Roman Catholic) resident population rise twentyfold, not counting the huge seasonal influx of guests from Lwów, Stanisławów, and Kołomyja.[41] It was suggested that Ukrainians, instead of spending their summers abroad at foreign rivieras, should vacation in their own mountains, to keep them from falling into the hands of Poles and Jews. They should vacation in Dora.[42]

Apparently some took this admonition to heart. Civil servants of various kinds—that is, the most well-to-do Ukrainians—came to spend their summers there: directors of Ukrainian high schools/gymnasia, schoolteachers, catechists, judicial councilors, lawyers, doctors, and the like. Reportedly Sundays in Dora were filled with lectures, readings, and concerts, which took place in the local reading room. Indeed, so many of these were scheduled that "one could speak of a Hutsul university."[43]

The groups of activists active in Dora and Jaremcze were claiming these Prut River Valley destinations for their own use and shaping them to their own purposes. In the case of Dora, national issues proved paramount, at least in the minds of the well-to-do Ukrainians of Stanisławów. Although apparently few would invest in or move permanently to Dora, these national activists sought to maintain the East Slavic majority characteristic of the Carpathian piedmont, perhaps even to turn the Hutsuls into nationally conscious Ukrainians. That is, if Hutsuls actually attended the Sunday enrichment events in the village.[44]

In the case of Jaremcze, entrepreneurs of varied provenance created an East Galician resort, one that aspired to be the region's Zakopane or Interlaken.[45] At the same time, it brought an influx of Poles and Jews, tipping the ethnic balance away from the Hutsuls, although the Galician Poles seemed to wear their nationality lightly.[46] In this Galician iteration of "Europe," there appeared to be little room for the Hutsul highlanders, who were demoralized and deracinated by their contact with the guests. Jaremcze was turned into a vacation destination for spa goers and resort guests *not* by nationally conscious Poles from Warsaw but rather by East Galician civil servants and small business owners with essentially an anational agenda of entrepreneurial capitalism, happy to entertain all visitors and uninterested in the fate of the highland peasants whom they were displacing. In this case, the moniker "pearl of the Eastern Carpathians" seems to suit Jaremcze best. For what was Jaremcze supposed to be but an island of genteel urbanity in a wild and perhaps dangerous sea?

The Polish Meran

A different oasis in the East Carpathian wilderness ultimately proved more similar to Zakopane: the sanatorium of Doctor Apolinary Tarnawski in Kosów (vel Kossów; Ukrainian Kosiv).[47] It was unusual in that, unlike the more conventional Galician resorts and sanatoria springing up along the Prut River Valley, it neither lay on the railway line nor was given impetus by improvements in infrastructure.

Tarnawski chose out-of-the-way Kosów for its climate, unique for Galicia. The dell where the little town lay was the warmest part of the Hutsul region, with long summers and ample sunshine, even in the winter.[48] The clean and lightly moist air of Kosów recalled the Moravian spa of Rožnov (German: Rosenau) or Bad Gleichenberg in Styria. Important for Tarnawski and the nature of his sanatorium, all kinds of fruit—including apricots, peaches, and grapes—grew in the dell, and cornfields were plentiful. Kosów was referred to as the Galician Meran, after the famous resort in the south Tirol.[49]

Despite the comparisons to resorts elsewhere, which helped prospective guests imagine what they might encounter in Kosów, in Tarnawski's sanatorium nature and nation went hand in hand in a truly sui generis way, in the process transforming what might have been just another oasis of health into a real utopia of sorts.[50] A contemporary of Doctor Andrzej Chramiec in Zakopane, Tarnawski proved to be a man with a mission. He was out to cure his compatriots, whose health had been compromised by the ills of civilization: air pollution, gluttony/overeating, a sedentary lifestyle. These he saw as the root cause of all illness. Having served as a district doctor in Kosów before opening his sanatorium there, Tarnawski took inspiration from his Hutsul patients, whose simple lifestyle made them much healthier than their urban counterparts: this was due to their near-meatless diet, lots of fresh air, and physical work outdoors. Not medicines, thus, but rather natural means were to cure what ailed society.[51] The Hutsuls, then, seemed to have served as inspiration for the doctor's back-to-nature focus.

Despite the anticivilizational thrust of Tarnawski's program, it was hardly antimodern. One might consider Tarnawski's sanatorium ahead of its time. Witness the mirrored contraption of his own design for indoor sunbathing, a sign of his interest in innovation.[52] Other elements of his sanatorium were likewise especially contrived to complement his program. Tarnawski profited from the cutting-edge ideas of various doctors abroad (most notably Heinrich Lahmann and Sebastian Kneipp); however, he used them as raw materials from which he created a simple program of hygiene (understood as how to live a healthy life), one that his patients could return home with and implement.[53] Shades of Stanisław Witkiewicz's ambitions for the new Zakopane Style of architecture, Tarnawski wanted to call his treatment the "Polish method," which, radiating outward from his sanatorium, would restore health to the nation.[54]

The relative isolation of the sanatorium—it lay a mile outside the town and was essentially a village unto itself—worked to his advantage. Insulated from the ills of civilization on the grounds of the sanatorium, Tarnawski's patients were to break old habits and acquire new, healthier ones during their six-week stay. In the process, patients would reportedly be transformed from degenerate urban sybarites beset by various ills into healthy, strong, and strong-minded people unafraid of work.

Strict discipline was enforced at the spa, the better to break bad habits. The very first sign that this was not a typical spa was the motto hanging over the entrance gate: "Control thyself!" (władaj sobą)—which was also to be the motto for life. Patients would rise and go to bed early, sleeping with the windows opened to maximize their intake of fresh highland air. First thing in the morning all the patients at the sanatorium would exercise together on the dewy uncut lawn. Barefoot or shod in sandals, they were clad in special, light-colored, loose, and loose-weave garments, reminiscent of what the ancient Greeks wore, designed to let the air and sunlight penetrate.[55] Twice a week the entire sanatorium exercised in unison to music. Elements of the exercise program, including special breathing exercises, came also from Hatha yoga.[56] Tarnawski likewise exhorted his patients to pick up a shovel or hoe and spend an hour working outdoors—in the cornfields, prize-winning gardens, or orchards that the doctor had planted, brimming with a wide variety of produce that would make its way to the kitchen.

The sanatorium was a farm-to-table establishment, with proper diet an important part of the treatment. Tarnawski's wife Romualda was renowned for her creativity with fruits and vegetables; her recipes would later be published in a trailblazing cookbook entitled *Kosów Vegetarian Cuisine*, with an extensive explanation by Doctor Tarnawski of the virtues of the style of eating taught at the sanatorium.[57] Alcohol consumption was forbidden. In accordance with the sanatorium's motto, many patients were encouraged to fast or reduce their food intake.[58] While that could help with weight loss, it was also a way to exercise self-control.[59]

Despite some of the similarities to trailblazing spas abroad, Tarnawski's sanatorium was perceived as undeniably Polish. As the author of one newspaper article gushed, "This [institute] is . . . the first and only one that arose from our national spirit and is conducted in that spirit."[60] That may be wishful thinking for a nation of undisciplined individualists. But the goal was certainly one that had the fate of the nation uppermost. Given the no-nonsense, positivistic, antiromantic thrust of Tarnawski, perhaps the last clause of the citation is most apt here. Tarnawski and his wife, both great originals, were pushing unconventional, reformist, innovative ideas with the intent of winning patients over to a healthier, new, modern way of life that furthermore would allow them to serve the Polish national cause. In this the doctor was no less ambitious than Witkiewicz—although temperamentally quite different. The small and wiry Tarnawski, with his shock of white hair and beard, seemed to have the energy of several persons in one. The doctor was not above pulling guests out of their beds to go exercise on the grassy field; opening windows in their rooms or increasing the force of the showers; and sentencing the overweight to strict diets of radishes, black bread, and soured milk. He confiscated hidden supplies of canned hams and sardines and weighed fasting patients daily to make sure they were not sneaking downtown to Truhanowicz's saloon.[61]

Tarnawski was not one to mince words, coming across to some as brusque. Not all patients understood his exhortations to dig in the vegetable garden or pick their own supper, as is seen from the reaction of the writer Gabriela Zapolska, who responded to one such exhortation during her 1905 stay in Kosów by calling the doctor a "common brute, a man lacking in imagination."[62] Zapolska would later pen a play, *The Assistant*, that poked fun at the sanatorium.[63] A contrast in personalities, his ruddy, rotund and genial wife was always busy in the kitchen, known for her excellent tortes as well as vegetarian dishes.

It was said that under the somewhat despotic (if always well-intentioned) care of these two, men lost weight and gained endurance, women lost their flightiness—as well as their pale complexions in the bright sunshine—and children gained strong bodies. For those who came from abroad, Tarnawski's sanatorium truly was an oasis of Polishness, one furthermore where social differences were effaced by the "Grecian" garb they wore—shades of Zakopane's salons. It also had a distinct intellectual side—daily lectures and the like—that presented a marked contrast to many other spas in the Polish lands and abroad, where flirting and matchmaking and other self-centered pursuits were the order of the day.

While the sanatorium may have been an oasis for Poles (paradoxically, in the suburbs of a Jewish shtetl), the local Hutsuls referred to the patients as the "crazy people from Tarnawski's." That they were also labeled the "Warsaw fasters" suggests that at least some patients were the kinds of outsiders who frequented Zakopane.[64] Many came to "drink their fill of Polishness" as well as take in regular spa treatments, which as we know were all the fashion among Polish society during this period.[65]

The politics of the sanatorium were clearly nationally oriented, if not exclusively partisan.[66] That said, Doctor Apolinary Tarnawski was himself a National Democrat, and many of that ilk—including the party's leader, Roman Dmowski—were patients. However, Poles of all political inclinations were welcome not only to be treated but also to be employed at the sanatorium—assistant doctors Emil Bobrowski and Stanisław Kelles-Krauz were socialists.[67] Patients of varying political and intellectual persuasions— for there were also mystics and sectarians present—all seemed able not only to coexist but to flourish in the rarefied intellectual and curative air of Kosów.[68] In the words of one memoirist, Tarnawski's sanatorium was not your average spa: "It was a brick in the building of national culture—beautiful, valuable, original and very Polish."[69] In this way it resembled Zakopane.

Things seemed to be going well for the sanatorium and this corner of eastern Galicia, as a look at developments in 1911 and 1912 attests. A joint stock company was being founded with a capital of 500,000 crowns, with Galicians as well as Poles from the across the Russian border investing.[70] This influx of capital would enable the sanatorium—which reportedly was operating at capacity, with an overflow of patients residing in the nearby suburbs—to operate all year round, for, since the sun shone often in the winter, just like in the south Tirol, one could take sunbaths and be outside all day long.[71] Improvements in travel also seemed to be forthcoming: the idea of building a railway spur from Kołomyja to Kosów resurfaced.[72] It was clearer in 1912 than it had been in the 1890s, when the idea was first bandied about, that the line would help with the development of tourism and spas.[73] This time the authorities were supportive, despite the line's lack of strategic significance. Construction of the railway spur was anticipated to begin not earlier than 1914.[74]

The Subaltern Speaks

As in the case of Jaremcze, Hutsuls were all but absent from Tarnawski's sanatorium, although at one point the doctor complained about dogs barking so insistently that he had to buy off their owners to silence them—the dogs perhaps serving as "weapons of the weak"?[75] To see Hutsuls appreciated for who they were, and for the closest thing to discovery, one had to travel to yet another East Carpathian village, the village of Krzyworównia/Kryvorivnia, where the literary and scholarly Galician Ukrainian elites vacationed.

Kryvorivnia (the Ukrainian name for the village) was picturesque if remote, located on the Black Czeremosz, downstream from the Hutsul "capital" of Żabie. That there was no spa infrastructure to speak of in the Hutsul village did not deter this elite group of Ukrainians. While guests such as the ethnographer Volodymyr Hnatiuk and writer Ivan Franko stayed in Hutsul homesteads, the historian and Lwów University professor Mykhailo Hrushevs'kyi had a summer house built for himself and lavishly furnished it in Hutsul style.[76]

For these elites, the fashion for things Hutsul doubtless followed the publication in 1899 of the first volume of a multivolume work on the Hutsuls, *Hutsul'shchyna* (Hutsul Region and People), by Volodymyr Shukhevych. An active member of the ethnographic commission of the Shevchenko Scientific Society in Lemberg/Lwów/L'viv, Shukhevych published his oeuvre both in Ukrainian and Polish.[77] The valuable multivolume work doubtless turned the attention of Ukrainian circles toward the Hutsuls, helping them to discover the highlanders and their region at the turn of the century and turn Kryvorivnia into a "Ukrainian Athens."

While the Galician elites did engage in ethnographic as well as work on their own writing projects while on vacation in the mountains, as in the case of Zakopane it took a catalyst from outside of Galicia to tap the innate talents of the Hutsul population and present them to the broader world.[78] Two Ukrainians from the Russian Empire figured most prominently. After summering in Kryvorivnia on Hnatiuk's invitation, writer Mykhailo Kotsiubyns'kyi published the evocative *Shadows of Forgotten Ancestors*, which in Soviet times was made into an iconic film by Sergei Paradzhanov—a film that popularized the Hutsuls, their region, and culture globally. The second was Hnat Khotkevych.[79] A railwayman, bandurist, and writer who directed a workers' theater in Kharkiv, Khotkevych first encountered the Hutsuls in the mountains of eastern Galicia in 1906, also as a guest of Hnatiuk's. With that vacation began Khotkevych's fascination with this proud highland folk, among whom he would live for the next six years, learning their dialect and otherwise absorbing their culture.

Enthralled by the larger-than-life Hutsuls' "insane, enraptured, carried-away energy," the former thespian ultimately decided to found a Hutsul Theater in nearby Krasnoila so they could put to good use their ability to act, to perform in public.[80] But what does theater mean to an illiterate peasant who has never seen a play? And what on earth could the Hutsuls perform? Khotkevych cleverly decided to put on a Hutsul-dialect translation of the

Polish play *Carpathian Highlanders*, thus most of the dozen or so Hutsuls were able to play themselves: Hutsuls (albeit after much rehearsing).[81] One of the actors remarked on the "turbulent" first performance in the fall of 1910, the Hutsul audience unsure how to react to what was taking place on the stage.[82] But ultimately the performance in Krasnoila was considered a success, as was the one following it in Żabie, where members of the local multiethnic intelligentsia were present.

The Hutsul Theater would prove even more of an eye-opening experience for the Hutsul actors. For Khotkevych wanted to show off his Hutsul troupe to the world.[83] He began with the province of Galicia, where in the spring of 1911 the Hutsuls took their play on the road. They headed north, then west, ultimately making their way to Kraków, where their performances were particularly well received. It did not hurt that the colorfully dressed Hutsuls attracted the attention of curious onlookers upon their arrival—perhaps the best way to advertise their performances.

The Hutsul Theater in some ways functioned like the Tatra Panorama in Warsaw—a moving and speaking, true-to-life *tableau vivant* that brought the mountains and their inhabitants to the attention of lowlanders, who came for the "songs and dances that were not learned but rather were practically

FIGURE 6.2.   Photo of the Hutsul Theater, with Petro Shekeryk-Donykiv (third from right). Published in *Nowości Illustrowane* 8, no. 13 (1911): 13. Image in the public domain.

sucked in with mother's milk," for the glimpse it gave into real Hutsul life.[84] As one scholar concluded, "The Hutsuls came to know the world, and the world came to know the Hutsuls."[85] The tour broadened the horizons of the Hutsul troupe, which was exposed to train travel, urban life, as well as different constellations of the multiethnic life that were seen in various parts of Galicia. Even if it ultimately was not a moneymaking venture, that first tour proved to be a "practical school of life" for them, admitted Petro Shekeryk-Donykiv, one of the actors.[86]

This experiment in folk theater was all the more amazing, as Galicia had no permanent Ukrainian theater. In fact, some Ukrainians in the province had discouraged Khotkevych from the very outset.[87] That did not stop him from being ambitious for his troupe. The Ukrainian writer decided to take them further out into the world, into the Russian Empire, whence he had come. That was a trickier business. This time, the handful of Hutsuls who came to Kharkiv had to work for a living, making Hutsul handicrafts, while honing their theatrical skills. Khotkevych took great pains with this tiny troupe, adjusting their performances, even their costumes, for greater theatrical effect.[88] In other words, these were no longer the same, raw, natural songs and dances so admired by the Cracovians but rather self-conscious reinterpretations of the same. The troupe performed in various parts of today's Ukraine—Kharkiv, Kyiv, Odesa, Mykolaiiv, Kherson[89]—as well as in Moscow, where they were touted as "perhaps the only Slavic tribe that had preserved the patriarchal way of life and even pagan rites."[90]

The Hutsul Theater was met with interest, including from none other than the famous Russian actor and director Constantine Stanislavsky, which led to plans being laid for the future: a larger troupe and bigger tour. Khotkevych imagined that the Hutsul Theater might have a good career ahead of it. He averred, "Put on a certain path, with the requisite resources and special repertoire, the Hutsul theater could create, in the bosom of the Ukrainian theater, a unique and colorful phenomenon, no less interesting than the Sicilian theater in Italy or the Tirolean theater on the German stage."[91] This was a story of what might have been, for the outbreak of World War I put an end to such dreams. Not only did the full troupe never travel to the Russian Empire; some of the Hutsuls who had performed there never made it back home to Galicia.

What does this little episode tell us about perceptions of this mountain folk? Petro Shekeryk-Donykiv, a rare literate Hutsul who wrote an account of his experience, claimed the folk theater as a moral victory: it changed perceptions of the Hutsul as someone inclined to drink and fight. The Hutsuls had shown how mature they were as a people.[92] Yet another Hutsul thespian remarked that they proved to everyone that the Hutsuls "are talented and cultured people, that they can perform on the stage dramatic pieces, that they know how to behave among people better than some civilized Europeans."[93]

Such observations came from their tours, which were extremely important for this highland people. In the words of Khotkevych, "The Hutsuls have seen the world, seen people, become acquainted with the life of not only their own village but also the entire province." The Hutsul Theater's founder and director thought it made them more nationally conscious—more Ukrainian (although he does not use the term here). Khotkevych wrote that "national life" was now as clear as day to the Hutsul, and he was well oriented in it.[94]

This Ukrainian orientation is better illustrated by one of the later plays, *Dovbush*, named after the most famous of Hutsul brigands. In the version of the Dovbush story penned by Khotkevych, there is a scene in which a Cossack comes to the Carpathians, claiming that the brigand's fame had reached the vicinity of the Dnieper River. Played by a real Ukrainian from the Russian Empire, the Cossack in the play said that Hutsuls and Cossacks were brothers, and that they needed to both play and work together.[95] This was a new, broader casting of the Dovbush story, one with potential implications for a broader Ukrainian nation.

Regardless of the level of development of the vacation destination of Kryvorivnia, it would have broader repercussions for the Hutsul highlanders who came into contact with Ukrainian lowlanders, from Galicia but especially from the Ukrainian heartland across the border. It was the latter who were most captivated by the Hutsuls, seeing in them a relic of a deeper Slavic past. Here one finds parallels between perceptions of the Hutsuls and the Tatra highlanders, both by individuals—be they Poles or Ukrainians—hailing from the Russian Empire. Khotkevych became an advocate for these highland Ukrainians, whom he showed off to the broader world, broadening their horizons in the process. At the same time, the motley group of Hutsuls representing different villages and hamlets acquired a distinct corporate identity: as self-conscious, and self-respecting, Hutsuls.

By 1914, the Eastern Carpathians represented a changed world. The railroad had brought with it much development, which began the transformation of the Prut Valley from a region of lightly populated Hutsul settlements and Jewish shtetls to a place where "practically every station or stop has several, a dozen, or several dozen villas or houses in which summer guests reside."[96] These stations and stops on the Stanisławów-Woronienka line helped to turn hamlets into high-altitude climatic health resorts, which in turn transformed the landscape of those parts beyond recognition—although the occasional

flood or landslide would connive to undo the transformation. The new summer high-altitude resorts and sanatoria developed in different ways: Jaremcze
as a particularly picturesque, commercialized, anational, Galician/Habsburg
spa, projecting an image of itself as no less European than the spas of Switzerland. Kosów by contrast was a self-consciously Polish enactment of a better, healthier, national future. Although both destinations were indebted to
both highlands and highlanders, it was the more barebones summer destination of Kryvorivnia that would lead to a broader recognition of the Hutsuls. Still, even those vacationing Ukrainians did not proclaim discovery in
so many words, likely assuming already—in good primordialist form—that
Hutsuls were an intrinsic part of their nation.[97]

For the latter, participation in the Hutsul Theater was a route to a route
to self-awareness: as Hutsuls most certainly, perhaps also self-awareness as
Ukrainians. At the same time, the encounter with the Hutsuls brought this
highland folk to the attention of Ukrainians, Poles, and Russians. Each of
these groups could vie for the Hutsuls' allegiance, consider the Hutsuls a
part of their larger nation. These developments and developmental options
would make the next wave of interest in the Eastern Carpathians and the
Hutsuls, one that would be labeled a discovery, that much more complicated.

A New Alpine Club

The year 1934 marked the beginnings of a busy period of activity for a new, regionally focused, "nongovernmental" organization in the still young Second Polish Republic, a successor state to the empires that collapsed in World War I.[1] A new group of activists sought to convince the general public that they were no less engaged in "discovering" the Hutsul region than was Tytus Chałubiński in his popularization of the Tatra Mountains as a destination for Poles in the previous century.[2] To be sure, there were some similarities. The impetus for both highland discoveries came not from the surrounding lowlands but from outside the region, from Warsaw. The highlands were viewed as a place where the nation's health might be restored; and the indigenous highlanders garnered no less attention than did the natural environment. Once again the mountains would serve as an experimental realm, one designed to solve a burning question of the day. Yet, as we will see, there were many differences as well, which reflected the new political reality that was the Second Polish Republic, one of the new states of East-Central Europe.

The Hutsul region in the remotest corner of eastern Galicia had been discovered only partially before the war, and then mainly by Galicians. During that period relatively few Poles and Ukrainians from the Russian Empire seem to have encountered the highlands and highlanders. The First World War, the Russian Revolution, the Polish-Ukrainian War, and the Polish-Soviet

War of 1920 firmed up the border between the new Polish state and its neighbors, including the Union of Soviet Socialist Republics. With few—but important—exceptions, Ukrainians from the Ukrainian heartland would have little opportunity after 1914 to discover the Hutsuls and their land.[3]

Life in the Eastern Carpathians was transformed by these developments. The very concept of the region as borderland had now changed. What earlier had been a soft, porous, internal Habsburg borderland solidified into a sharply delineated frontier separating independent states. Hungary and Bukowina had been supplanted, on the border, by the new state of Czechoslovakia and an expanded Romania. In addition to having suffered the privation and destruction of multiple wars, the Hutsuls of Galicia found themselves hemmed in. The frontier cut them off from their traditional source of corn (Bukowina) and various metals and leather goods (Hungary). Citizens of the new Polish Republic who wished to cross the border—or in some cases, spend time in the mountains—had to apply for proper papers and permissions in advance. Smugglers, bandits, and those who sought to overthrow the new order hid in or made their way through the mountains. Border guards patrolled all sides.

Thus reoriented, the region slowly rebounded after years of war and destruction. (During World War I, resorts such as Jaremcze had been rendered into ashes, the beautiful Jaremcze bridge blown up by retreating Russian forces; both would be rebuilt in the 1920s.)[4] The (re)discovery of the Hutsul region in the interwar period was to a great extent a Polish story, for the reasons cited above as well as because ethnic Poles were the dominant nationality in the Second Republic, politically as well as demographically (nearly 70 percent of the population).[5] After the Great Depression hit the country in the early 1930s, Polish officialdom in the heart of the country took an interest in this remote yet strategic corner of the Second Republic and its indigenous inhabitants. But first, it would have to learn more about the place and people.

The government during this period—that is, after the coup d'état of Marshal Józef Piłsudski in 1926 (the "Sanacja" government)—was not ill inclined toward Poland's minority populations. Unlike the politicians behind the center-right governments that preceded him, Piłsudski had a more inclusive vision of the Polish state, one that emphasized not a homogeneous Polish nation as a separate people but rather Polish *raison d'état*. His Sanacja regime wanted not a nationally homogeneous Poland: it simply wanted the entirety of the population to be loyal to the Second Polish Republic—something that minority as well as majority populations were asked to embrace.[6]

The danger of Hutsul indifference was brought home to a certain intrepid journalist from the central Polish city of Łódź, who visited the Hutsul region in 1927.[7] Jadwiga Sawicka's investigation turned up remnants of the multi-ethnic Galician heritage, with a population of mixed provenance, further complicated by intermarriage. Certain phrases uttered by people she encountered sounded quite foreign: the Hutsul-German phrase "svizhy Luft" for "fresh air," interjected into a Polish sentence, was particularly noteworthy.[8]

But where did the Hutsuls stand nationally? At least one equivocated: asked whether he would raise his children as Poles or Ruthenes—Sawicka's choice of terms—her guide Dmytro, who was married to a Polish woman, shrugged and replied, "Is it not all the same, my lady benefactress? Is there not one God over all people? They have devised politics to make children of one land fly at each other!"[9] Dmytro's equivocating response could have been a polite way of deflecting what was *the* burning issue for many Poles interested in the Eastern Carpathians. It was hardly "all the same" to many in the Second Polish Republic circa 1927 whether children in this remote borderland region were brought up as Poles or "Ruthenes," the preferred term for Ukrainians in interwar Poland, whether of the highland (Hutsul) or lowland (Ukrainian) variety.

Surveying the State of the Eastern Carpathians: Discovering America?

Many in the country—even in the provincial capital, Stanisławów—had much to learn about this corner of the young Polish state, as witnessed by the holding of a formal survey (*ankieta*) of the state of the Eastern Carpathians in the spring of 1931. The survey conference involved specialists or experts in the respective fields as well as delegates of institutions active in the region, who had been asked to address a broad array of issues affecting the mountain's human and natural dimensions. Nature preservation as well as hunting and fishing were discussed; also tourism, spas, and health resorts; transportation within the region; and matters concerning the indigenous Hutsul population. These assessments offered enlightenment to anyone interested in the state of the region circa 1930, including a variety of governmental ministries and local and provincial authorities, who also sent representatives to the conference.[10]

The timing of the survey and conference seems directly related to the events of 1930, an annus horribilis for southeastern Poland. That spring, hostility toward the state erupted among the non-Polish population referred to as Ruthenes (Ukrainians). Poles were attacked; barns, haystacks, and cottages burned down; and telegraph and telephone wires cut. Both the police and the military—a thousand policemen plus a regional cavalry regiment—were sent in to "pacify" (with the use of armed force) the region, to put an end to the disturbances. Unrest did not reach the Hutsul region, however.[11] Could the Hutsuls have been unmoved by Ukrainian national calls for sabotage against local Poles and the Polish state? All the more reason for Poles to take an interest in the Eastern Carpathians, the one place in southeastern Poland that remained unperturbed. A blank slate for so many Poles, the Hutsul region seemingly held promise as an attractive primeval highland realm in which everyone lived in harmony.

The presentations and discussions at the survey conference tell us much about the way the Hutsul region and its indigenous inhabitants were marked as primordial yet problematic circa 1931. Consider the survey's focus on the intersection of man and nature in the region. Following the example of many other countries in Europe and elsewhere (the United States in particular), members of the State Council of Nature Preservation sought to establish national parks. They praised the current plan of the Ministry of Agriculture to form a national park in Czarnohora out of the state forests near the Howerla. National parks and nature reserves were proposed for other areas, including the Czywczyn Mountains in the very tip of the Polish Republic, all to protect the "first-rate qualities that already are lacking in many parts of Europe"—in other words, the seemingly primeval wilderness that was characteristic of the eastern Beskids.[12] Yet the same wilderness, with its rich and rare fauna and flora, was paradoxically threatened by the lumber industry, the reach of which extended along waterways and railways, including the privately owned narrow-gauge ones of the various sawmills. The endangered dwarf mountain pine (Pinus mugo) was fast disappearing due to the existence and reconstruction of a turpentine factory; before the war it had already devastated the ravine beneath Dancerz, an area frequented by tourists.[13]

While helping to preserve the wilderness, the creation of a national park in the Hutsul region could have a deleterious effect on the Hutsuls, who both owned hundreds of hectares of land there and worked as lumberjacks and *kermanychi* (helmsmen) transporting rafts of logs down the Czeremosz.[14] At the survey it was suggested that Hutsuls could profit by organizing river rafting for tourists instead, like the highlanders on the Dunajec River in the Pieniny Mountains, where such rafting is practiced to this day to the delight of tourists. Yet when confronted with the economic interests of the Hutsuls in the region by the chief forester of the state forests in Worochta, Professor Walery Goetel, a member of the State Council of Nature Preservation, ignored the human implications of this potential displacement and remarked instead that the state would have to purchase these enclaves carefully so that their prices would not rise.[15] So much for the Hutsul's transhumant way of life.

Tensions between development and conservation persisted. Those present at the conference were not above imagining the region as primeval: representatives of the Polish Tatra Society, the Carpathian Ski Society, and the Polish travel bureau Orbis all touted the Eastern Carpathians as unique in Central Europe and as yet unspoiled by the cupidity of man, and thus of potential interest not only domestically but also to jaded foreigners for whom regular tourist destinations had lost their luster.[16] Nonetheless, they wanted greater accessibility to a seemingly primeval region that could also serve as a site of hiking, skiing, and tourism. The great distances in the Eastern Carpathians posed a problem for many tourists who wished to penetrate these more remote Carpathian destinations: more and better roads were needed. The region's minimal network of extant roads, subject to the elements and ruined by logs being dragged along them in winter, left much to be desired, making it impossible (for example) for a bus to make the journey from Worochta (on the railway line) to Żabie. Without that important connection, any dreams of Żabie becoming the Polish Davos would remain just that.[17]

Doctor Apolinary Tarnawski touted the central Hutsul village of Żabie as a Hutsul Zakopane, one that awaited "enterprising people who would make it the *premier health resort* in all of Poland."[18] A drawback for Poles was that Żabie lacked a Roman Catholic priest (there were several Greek Catholic ones). Plenty of rooms for tourists were available in Jewish establishments, such as the inns of Gertner and Szuster, and the Polish Tatra Society's Czarnohora Manor in Żabie likewise provided short-term accommodations. The village was also the starting point for the exciting river rafting trips down the Czeremosz to the Armenian settlement of Kuty, near the Romanian border.

Those present at the survey conference saw promise in this largest of the Hutsul villages. Żabie was ideally situated, according to yet another doctor present, as a climatic station for people with respiratory ailments. This was because it, like Worochta—which had surpassed Jaremcze as the most popular of Prut River Valley destinations—lay in the transverse valleys with southern exposures yet was protected from the cold by mountains to the north. Its only problem concerned how to get there: one had to spend hours traversing rough, bumpy, or boggy roads to reach Żabie.[19] Without a doubt that kept it from "beat[ing] Worochta as a summer resort" and retarded its development.[20] Not only enterprising outsiders but also assistance with road repair and construction were needed if it was to attract some of the 300,000 Poles who availed themselves of spas annually.[21]

Huculszczyzna Гуцульщина   Widok z Żabiego na Czornohore Вид з Жабя на Чорногору

FIGURE 7.1. View of Czarnohora from Żabie, postcard by N. Sen'kovs'kyi. From the collection of Henryk Gąsiorowski.

Not only the high-altitude resorts and spas but also the Hutsuls and their traditional way of life were a draw. The survey approached the subject from a particular angle, emphasizing what was termed "ochrona swojszczyzny"—a phrase that appeared not only in the survey but also in many works in the interwar period dealing with the peculiarities of Poland's regions. The Polish "ochrona swojszczyzny" may be rendered as the "protection of nativeness." Czarnohora Branch vice president Henryk Gąsiorowski defined the phrase as akin to the German term *Heimatschutz, Heimat* referring to the homeland, with the root *-schutz* meaning protection. He described it as a state of responsibility for "preserving in its entirety everything that characterizes the fatherland, and in smaller parts of territory, a given region, area or locality."[22] The protection of nativeness encompassed above all the conservation of nature, that is, those features that are characteristic of a given region; the protection of the landscape against the destruction of its peculiar features and against its disfigurement; and the maintenance of traditional local customs and ethnographic characteristics, primarily of the village folk.

What motivated this interest in the protection of nativeness was the fact that not only nature but also man contributed to the distinct character of a given region. And, when it came to the preservation of the landscape of the

Eastern Carpathians, there was no way to separate the two.[23] These observers of interwar society were conscious of the disappearance of folk culture not only in the Second Republic, but also in all of Europe—more prevalent doubtless in the West rather than in overwhelmingly agrarian Poland.

The speakers addressed the specific ethnography of the Eastern Carpathians by considering how the presence of the indigenous folk would be experienced by tourists, mountaineers, and vacationers.[24] Recall that in the period prior to World War I the Hutsul was not always truly visible to vacationers. Many Hutsuls in the Prut River Valley destinations were relegated to the background: some provided labor within the boardinghouses, hotels, and curative institutes or supplied spa towns with dairy products or produce. In the most visible cases, Hutsuls themselves served as hosts, opening their homes or other properties to the guests. Nor did map-bearing tourists of the mountaineering kind find much need of Hutsuls as guides in the interwar period. At best, the latter served as porters.

In the interwar period, the indigenous folk began to be acknowledged as an intrinsic part of the spectacular primeval highland landscape, putting it too on display. The Hutsul was perceived as a tourist attraction, one that might appeal to foreign guest as well as lowlander Pole—a foreigner such as the Swedish traveler and adventurer Gustaf Bolinder, who had recently written about what he saw in the Hutsul and neighboring Boiko regions.[25] Members of the survey saw a need to ensure that the nature *and* human "preserve" be as attractive as possible.

Yet the Hutsuls were an endangered folk, one capable of losing its unique qualities and properties. This was already seen in the Prut River Valley, where the men were employed as workers in the lumber industry, the women as maids or kitchen help in the hotels and boardinghouses. Such jobs tended to move Hutsuls out of the traditional sphere into direct contact with the industrialized world, aspects of which they unconsciously assimilated.

Given this state of affairs, the preservation of native material culture was seen as a crucial element in the defense of Hutsul nativeness. Speaking at the survey conference, Professor Adam Fischer emphasized that unique aspects of Hutsul material culture such as its architecture—also part of the native landscape—were no less endangered than parts of the natural world. It was being contaminated with foreign elements imported from the Swiss Alps or the Polish Tatras, as Hutsuls strove to reconfigure their homesteads (*grazhdy*) into summerhouses for the *liuftnyky* (a Hutsul neologism based on the German word *Luft*, or air, meaning those who came to take the air cure).[26]

Hutsul wooden implements and furniture had long been famous for their ornamentation, whether carved, burned, or incrusted. Each Hutsul home had its set of wooden furniture, a fancifully carved wooden chest, table, benches, to complement the similarly adorned beams, entryways, and windows. Many articles of daily use—the ubiquitous Hutsul hatchets, shotguns, pistols, powder horns, not to mention various moneybags and purses—were traditionally suspended from the walls, providing aesthetically pleasing decoration within the home. Yet this ideal picture was reportedly seen less and less in the region. Already one could find certain wooden items left unadorned in some homes. The best exhibits often ended up in museums, leaving Hutsuls to decorate their walls with the cheap ware sold at fairs.[27]

Other folk industries and customs, including pottery making and metalworking, also appeared to be on the decline. Even one of the most iconic aspects of Hutsul folk art, their colorful traditional attire—which, not incidentally, was designed for horseback riding—was not what it once was. The inimitable Hutsul embroidery, for example, "went astray," in Fischer's words, by using only blue and yellow threads instead of combining those with other traditional colors.[28]

The professor's complaints were not prompted solely by aesthetics or questions of historical veracity. The Hutsuls' choice of blue and yellow threads was not aesthetic but political. Although national or ethnic politics were not acknowledged by those taking part in the survey (at least, not published in the survey proceedings), those present without a doubt recognized this pairing as the Ukrainian national colors, just as red and white were the Polish ones. The use of yellow and blue, to the exclusion of traditional Hutsul colors, sent a political message: some Hutsuls chose to identify themselves as Ukrainians. If Hutsuls were now becoming conscious members of a Ukrainian nation that was seeking its independence, then that was a frightening prospect indeed. Was it so frightening that it was censored out of the proceedings? Or were the survey participants unusually circumspect? Perhaps such considerations are what caused Professor Adam Fischer to opine that the fate of the Hutsuls was at that time the "most burning question."[29] He nonetheless maintained that the Hutsuls were of a "completely distinct ethnic countenance" than the neighboring Boikos, many of whom already felt themselves to be Ukrainians.[30] This suggests that he was among the interwar scholars who saw the Hutsuls as not entirely Slavic/Ruthenian, and thus—it was hoped—less susceptible to claims of Ukrainianness made by lowland Ukrainians. All this was another reason for taking especial interest in this segment of the Carpathians.

A motion made by Fischer at the survey conference suggests a special Polish approach to the "Hutsul question": "The Polish state must cordon off with studious care the regional characteristics of the Hutsul region. By this we will give proof that German methods are foreign to us, [methods which] always obliterated the Slavic-ness of the regions occupied by them. We should care for the preservation of the old characteristics of this folk culture and protect that which even the Ruthenian nation itself does not always adequately value."[31] Poles were not to treat their minorities as the Germans had treated the Poles within the German Empire. That is, they were not to be like the famous chancellor Otto von Bismarck, who had persecuted the Polish minority, for example, in his so-called *Kulturkampf.* Instead, Poles were to set a better example and serve as caretakers of the various peasant peoples within the Second Republic. For, as was true of many indigenous peoples, the Hutsuls were oblivious to the value of their native folk culture. All told, Fischer's motion sounded a note of patriotic paternalism.

It was argued that Poles needed to help the Hutsuls by fostering adherence to and respect for the old, traditional ways. For this, one needed to know this indigenous culture, what it was as well as what threatened its existence as a distinct highland people. That meant understanding the pastoral and equestrian lifestyle of the Hutsuls, which, according to Gąsiorowski, was perfectly suited for the natural environment of the Eastern Carpathians.[32] Their well-being was threatened by the increasingly poor state of the grasses and soil, as they could not afford fertilizer; likewise much could be done to improve the quality and quantity of the milk and cheeses, especially *bryndza* (a soft cheese), which—it was thought—could be produced on a much greater scale for domestic consumption.[33]

A greater threat to that culture came from Hutsul impoverishment, and the transfer of many Hutsul landholdings into the hands of local Jews—referred to euphemistically as the "different [from tourists and summer guests] alien element that had settle[d] there permanently."[34] The abuse of alcohol in the Hutsul region was apparently at record levels within Poland, a country not known for temperance.[35] Because of Hutsul impoverishment, "beautiful but . . . expensive" customs were dying out: the sewing of traditional clothing—the flowing capes, even the leather *postoly*, or moccasins—as well as the adornment of stoves with traditional hand-painted ceramic tiles, each a work of art in its own right yet increasingly left undecorated in poorer households.[36]

Of course, yet other ills had been caused by the Great War or predated the second half of the nineteenth century. For example, syphilis—passed down generation to generation—continued to plague the region.[37] The Hutsul horse was more of a rarity, its numbers having been decimated during the war, when the animals were pressed into service pulling machine guns. Yet they, too, were no longer a necessity in regions such as the Prut River Valley, where the highroad and railway had penetrated. One had to press deeper into the Hutsul region to encounter the Hutsul astride his horse, making his way down the rugged terrain from his homestead into the valleys or headed to the high upland pastures. The postwar borders also affected the grazing lands of the Eastern Carpathians. When the Hutsuls had been cut off from their traditional source of corn (now in Romania), they were forced to plow some of their grasslands in order to produce food for themselves. This changed landscape reflected a change in Hutsul attitudes toward agriculture. Hutsuls had historically considered it a sin to pierce the skin of Mother Nature, to plow and sow, something they had not done as seminomadic shepherds.

Given this endangered status, Gąsiorowski suggested that someone should make sure that the new tourists and summer guests, through the efforts of the institutions that promoted tourism and seasonal stays in the Eastern Carpathians, were instructed as to how to deal with the Hutsuls, how not to spoil them, as had been done with the Górale in the Tatras. Already—he maintained—Hutsuls were on the verge of demoralization in places such as Jaremcze and Kosów.[38]

No one at the survey conference spoke of the spiritual culture of the Hutsuls, their rich mix of paganism and Christianity, or their storytelling. They did, however, provide a plethora of suggestions for new pursuits for the Hutsuls, ranging from expanding their woodworking to sewing shearling jerkins, as was done in the Tatras, or even imitating the Swiss or German model of making cuckoo clocks. In many ways, the primeval yet simultaneously commodified region imagined by the experts and officials at the conference seemed rather out of touch with reality. Then again, this was a period when the Polish Ministry of Internal Affairs, regarding its own holdings in Burkut, knew nothing about the chemical composition of the spring or whether one could reach it by car or cart.[39]

The time was ripe to discover the Hutsul region. In a Poland that was becoming grayer by the day, in the economic crisis of the 1930s, here was an explosion of color and a lively, musical folk. One writer for a major Polish newspaper gushed about the vivid embroidery, "Each shearling jacket is an epic poem, [each] bodice and shirtsleeve a palette of the broadest scale." Men's hats were dripping with ribbons and spangles; and the risk-taking of the color composition seemed to have paid off. "This is a folk of artists! They don't acknowledge ugly things and don't have any at all. Each cottage . . . is a small ethnographic museum. But a living museum!" The article in the *Illustrated Daily Courier* (*Illustrowany Kurier Codzienny*, or *IKC*) was a ringing endorsement for the Hutsul region, where such lovely items could be purchased so inexpensively. "Of course," the journalist admitted, "I am discovering America."[40]

"America" was still being discovered in interwar Poland. Despite efforts to rebuild on the part of the locals and the Polish Tatra Society after peace returned to the region, the Eastern Carpathians still remained to a great extent a terra incognita for many Poles—including Poles in the government. But not for long.

The Hutsul Region Holiday

At the survey conference, Mieczysław Orłowicz suggested that the Poles "suitably arrange" and advertise Hutsul folk celebrations during the summer season in Jaremcze, Worochta, and Żabie. The Polish tourism official was taking his cues from across the border, in Czechoslovakia: folk celebrations in the Slovak cities of Trenčín and Turčiansky Sväty Martin had become popular, with the republic's officialdom and even the Czechoslovak president in attendance.[41] Might not these events have been designed as a way to strengthen the Slovaks' sense of belonging to the state, still dominated by the Czechs?—in which case they surely could serve as examples for the Poles.

Not long after the results of the survey conference, published the following year, were available, Orłowicz's suggestion took hold. At yet another conference held in Stanisławów in the fall of 1932, the provincial authorities decided to organize, on the territory of the Hutsul region, a special tourist event, a "Hutsul Holiday" (Święto Huculszczyzny). The holiday was devised as a way to acquaint broad swaths of the population—regular tourists as well as hikers—with the beauty of the Eastern Carpathians, and the Hutsul region in particular, as well as to help the indigenous highlanders.[42]

The members of the Provincial Social Committee, representing all the most important positions and organizations in the province, ambitiously (foolheartedly?) decided that the three-day Hutsul Holiday scheduled for June 15–17, 1933, would encompass much of the Hutsul region, not only the easily accessible Prut River Valley.[43] All three districts in which Hutsuls could be found would be responsible for providing accommodation for the visitors, providing transportation to the various events, even determining and planning a schedule of events that would entice visitors to come, while volunteers from the Polish Tatra Society would staff the planned excursions.[44] Expecting large crowds, even the tiniest and most remote of villages prepared for hundreds of guests.[45]

The expected crowds never arrived. The special excursion train that was to bring guests from Warsaw did not depart until the second day of the festival, bringing only several hundred Varsovians in time for the final day of the Hutsul Holiday.[46] As a result, most of them opted not for Kosów or Żabie but rather the more easily reachable resorts.

Yet parts of the Hutsul Holiday seem to have turned out all right. Some guests did make it all the way to the town of Kuty, the starting point of the first "tourist route," where an exhibition consisting of some ten thousand items representing the range of Hutsul artisanry had been prepared.[47] Shades of the first ethnographic exhibition of 1880: many of the handicrafts—by masters such as woodworkers Wasyl and Mikołaj Dewdiuk, potter Piotr Koszak, and the latest protoplast of the now famous Shkribliak family—were sold at the exhibition, while the artists took orders for more.[48] Another sign that the Hutsul Holiday might gain resonance among the Polish public was the radio broadcast from the town of Kosów on June 15. Transmitted by all the Polish radio stations, it included speeches by a parliamentarian from Kołomyja as well as the Hutsul mayor of Żabie, Petro Shekeryk-Donykiv (of Hutsul Theater fame), followed by a program of Hutsul songs, dances, and regional music.[49]

That the Hutsul Holiday did not live up to expectations was not the fault of either the local authorities or the Hutsuls, both of whom put great efforts into the event. The Hutsuls who came into contact with the public during the Hutsul Holiday reportedly were very well disposed to their guests, this despite the underground Organization of Ukrainian Nationalists (OUN) agitating for Hutsuls to sabotage it.[50] For such Ukrainian lowlanders, the Hutsul Holiday was setting a dangerous precedent: Hutsuls engaging positively with the Polish authorities. The fear was that Hutsuls would be won over by the chance of earning some money, something that the Ukrainian intelligentsia was not able to offer the Hutsuls. A secret military report on the festivities concluded that efforts to popularize the Hutsul region should continue, but that interests would be better served if the Polish Tatra Society, and not the government, were responsible for the events.[51]

Ukrainian perceptions of the Hutsul Holiday of summer 1933 were less positive. An anonymous piece in the still relatively new *Polish-Ukrainian Bulletin* (*Biuletyn Polsko-Ukraiński*) saw administrative promptings to erect triumphal arches and greet guests with music as redolent rather of the old days before the war, when representatives of the partitioning powers were similarly greeted. The author implied that Poles should be particularly sensitive to such situations and certainly not treat its minorities this way. Issue was also taken with the press release circulated by the Ministry of Communication to Polish newspapers, in which the Hutsuls were presented as "a tribe, which, thanks to its having been cut off from the world, for centuries preserved many archaic and highly distinct characteristics." The lack of references to the Ukrainianness of the Hutsuls apparently rankled. According to the author of the article in the *Polish-Ukrainian Bulletin*, the Hutsuls were hardly "clay to be shaped." Rather, they had already demonstrated their allegiance as Ukrainians: "They had taken active part in the Polish-Ukrainian battles as Ukrainians as well as are a regional part of the Ukrainian body today."[52]

This recent militant past was never mentioned—certainly not in public—in Polish discussions of the Hutsuls, either in the 1931 survey or in 1933. Yet there had been Hutsuls in the Ukrainian Sich Sharpshooters that, just like the Polish Legions, fought on the side of the Central Powers. Volunteers from the Hutsul region had enlisted early on.[53] In October 1916, a Hutsul company of about a hundred soldiers was established; at the end of the war, the Hutsul soldiers made their way to Bukowina, where they joined the fight for Ukrainian independence. Some Hutsuls were instrumental in helping to establish Ukrainian rule in the Kosów district.[54]

This brought them into armed conflict with the Poles, who wanted eastern Galicia for their new country. The Hutsuls proved to be formidable foes. The Ukrainian regiments from the Hutsul region were reportedly among the most ardent fighters in the Polish-Ukrainian War of 1918–19.[55]

For this they seem to have been punished, once Polish rule came to the region in late August 1919. Being of the opinion that the new Poland was the rightful property of ethnic Poles, those in positions of power there antagonized the indigenous population of the region with their searches, requisitions, arrests, even beatings and torture of the "Ukrainian haidamaks" (rebels).[56] A punitive expedition was additionally sent to the region after two policemen were murdered in Żabie-Zełene. Accused of being Bolsheviks (a genuine fear at that moment), the Hutsuls in the vicinity of Żabie—the very heart of the Hutsul region—were collectively mistreated in what seems to have been random fashion: Hutsul men, women, and children were beaten and imprisoned, their property stolen or burned, even entire homesteads set ablaze as the expedition searched for the murderers.[57]

The population of the Hutsul region was not subdued but rather remained uncooperative. At the same time, remnants of the Ukrainian army as well as other Ukrainians drifted into the highlands and tried to foment boycotts or passive resistance against the newly established Polish state.[58] Yet another murder—this time, of a judicial functionary in Żabie—reportedly took place in 1920, but the Hutsuls did not heed the call to rebel.[59]

A decade made even more of a difference. By the time of the 1930 unrest among the Ukrainian population of the lowlands, Hutsuls seemed reconciled to Polish rule; there was no sabotage in the region—one reason why they were not "pacified" like other regions of southeastern Poland.[60] It was doubtless this quietude in 1930 that encouraged Poles to persist in seeing—or rather prefer to see—the Hutsuls as utterly distinct from the Ukrainians of the lowlands. They preferred to forget (insofar as they may have known) that the Hutsuls, many of whom considered themselves part of the Ukrainian nation, had from the outset been upset at the loss of their Western Ukrainian People's Republic and what they saw as Polish occupation.[61] Nonetheless, in the 1930s the highlanders were presented to the masses of Poles for whom the region was terra incognita as a fascinating indigenous people of an exotic provenance. Some posited that the Hutsuls originally came from Egypt via the Balkans, or hailed from Iran, or were descended from the ancient Goths.[62] Few, however, labeled them highland Ukrainians, this despite the Hutsuls' sense of being brothers-in-arms with the lowland Ukrainians.

In the early 1930s, this most heavily "Ruthenian" (in Polish interwar parlance) region of interwar Poland was not a region that the government wished to alienate. Nor could it afford to do so. Czarnohora was also a frontier region, and as such subject to the potential threat posed by the East Slavs of Subcarpathian Rus'—the territory that had produced a short-lived Hutsul Republic in the first half of 1919 before being incorporated into Czechoslovakia.[63]

The development of high-altitude resorts and tourism in the Eastern Carpathians was seen as potentially having a number of positive effects. In addition to providing income to the Hutsuls and offering the Poles from throughout the country a better, healthier, and less expensive alternative to the perennially popular but overcrowded Tatras, a "stronger summer movement in the direction of the Eastern Carpathians would tie [the Hutsuls], with stronger knots, to the rest of Poland."[64] The indigenous population would become conscious of the economic advantages of being an integral part of the Polish state. Hutsuls might also thus become more positively inclined toward the Second Republic, the country in which they lived. After all, the highland folk were still among the least antagonistic of the minority populations of the Second Polish Republic. It was also thought that, since they needed help so badly, they would be appreciative of all efforts.[65]

Piłsudski's Sanacja government did not wish to apply a heavy hand to the Hutsul region. One lesson from the Hutsul Holiday was that a government-driven approach to the Hutsuls needed to be presented in nongovernmental form.[66] The benefits would be twofold. First, it would make state policy—the development of the Hutsul region in ways that would benefit the Polish public—somewhat less visible on the ground. Likewise, if anything went wrong, as had been the case with the Hutsul Holiday, the state could not be blamed for it. In other words, someone else had to take a formal and sustained interest in the Hutsul region and people. The stakes were high: the state was engaged in battle for the hearts and minds of this highland population in the strategic borderland region.

To remedy the situation, a new alpine organization was established that, as we shall see, functioned rather differently from the Tatra Society, the region's first alpine club. Its birth and evolution shed light on the conditions prevailing in the Second Polish Republic in the 1930s.

The Society of Friends of the Hutsul Region

The Society of Friends of the Hutsul Region (Towarzystwo Przyjaciół Hucul-szczyzny) proved to be an institution sui generis: an ostensibly "social" (non-governmental) organization with very strong governmental/military backing.[67] It would take the credit for discovering the Hutsul region and people in the interwar period.[68]

The main force behind the society appears to have been Brigadier General Tadeusz Kasprzycki (1891–1978). Kasprzycki's interest in the region predated the founding of the society, for it was to him that the secret military report on the Hutsul Holiday of 1933 had been sent. A born-and-bred Varsovian, before World War I Kasprzycki had been active in the secret Union of Active Struggle established by Józef Piłsudski: he even led the First Cadre Company, the original core of what would become Piłsudski's Polish Legions, on its trek from Kraków into tsarist Russia on August 5–6, 1914—the first military incursion of the war.[69] Not long after becoming president of the Society of Friends of the Hutsul Region, Kasprzycki was promoted to first deputy minister for military affairs (in July 1934). Thus, he was about as close to Piłsudski, who was minister for military affairs, as anyone within the military and governmental hierarchy could be.[70]

Kasprzycki's prominent role in the organization as well as in the government made Warsaw a logical choice for the seat of the Society of Friends of the Hutsul Region. While somewhat atypical for a regional organization, the choice both reflected and amplified its proximity to the seat of power in the highly centralized interwar state.[71] This proximity would prove important for the marshalling of resources to support the activities of the society as well as for the publicizing of events that were designed to attract a broader public. In all this, Kasprzycki and his military colleagues in the society would play an important role.[72]

How these not so casual "friends" intended to support the Hutsul region and people says much about their vision of Czarnohora. The main aims of the society were four: to coordinate the methodical economic and cultural development of the Hutsul region; to protect those characteristics of the region that comprised its distinctiveness; to utilize rationally the "climatic values" of the Hutsul region in improving the "social hygiene" of the state; and to oversee and develop rationally the Hutsul region as a center for tourism, summer, and health resorts.[73] Emphasized was the organization's role as a coordinator and facilitator of various activities in the field.[74] The wording of the society's statute makes clear Czarnohora's perceived importance for the interwar Polish state: the Hutsul region was termed a "valuable component in the sum of the natural and spiritual riches of the Polish Republic."[75] In other words, its peculiar distinctiveness provided a reservoir of values—physical, climatic, even spiritual—that were to be made available to the Polish state more generally.

Even before its official founding, the society engaged with the highlands and highlanders, mainly through special sections, which gathered together specialists in specific fields who could bring their expertise to bear on the challenges that faced this remote region.[76] The doctors and specialists of the Hygiene Section conducted basic research on the region's potential as a land of spas and health resorts, scouting out the best spots for development; they also concerned themselves with the restoration of the health of the indigenous people, the improvement of the hygiene of existing villages (with competitions for the cleanest cottage), and the health of mothers and children.[77] Mieczysław Orłowicz headed the Tourism and Health Resort Section, the existence and importance of which underscored the society's vision of the region, so eminently suited for recreational physical activity as well as recuperation; it would be aided by the Propaganda Section—to advertise the region's health-promoting qualities—and Economic Section—to assist with the improvement of the region's transportation infrastructure.[78] And a Section for the Protection of Nativeness would prove key in dealings with the Hutsul population, since preserving the authentic distinctiveness of the region was seen as something that had to be done so as to avoid the spread of foreign influences that had distorted the Tatra region's unique highland style.

A no less important reason concerned the Hutsuls' own identity and position within the Polish state. If multiethnic Poland was to be a composite of little homelands, a mosaic of peoples who acknowledged Polish statehood while maintaining their own distinct identity, then peoples like the Hutsuls would have to maintain their traditional ways. To this end, over the next years the society underscored the value of Hutsul distinctiveness by mandating that participants in the various contests and festivals appear in proper Hutsul attire and on purebred Hutsul horses and did what it could to reinforce the Hutsuls' pride in being Hutsuls. The society taught the Hutsuls that their way of life was unique and exotic, and that only by maintaining the old ways could they expect to attract tourists to the region.

In addition to the sections, two affiliated clubs were able to carry out some of the work of the Society of Friends of the Hutsul Region in the field: the Scout Club and the Legionnaires' Club. The scouts were disciplined, hardy, and active—a fresh source of energy, labor, and Polish influence, one that could engage in educational-cultural and charitable activity in the region during school vacations and establish relationships with individual Hutsul families.[79] The Legionnaires' Club consisted of former soldiers of the Second Brigade, part of the Polish Legions that fought on the side of Austria-Hungary—and in the Hutsul region—during World War I. The history of the Second Brigade of the Polish Legions would prove a lynchpin in Polish-Hutsul relations during the 1930s.

The Second Legionnaire Brigade and the Hutsuls

The Second Brigade of the Polish Legions was part of the Pflanzer-Baltin Army Group, which in the fall of 1914 was assigned the unenviable task of chasing the Russians out of Hungary and back into Galicia; from November to early December the troops would do battle in the Eastern Carpathians under unusually harsh winter conditions—a reason why the Second Brigade was also known as the "Iron" or "Carpathian" brigade.[80]

Although ostensibly part of the Austro-Hungarian army, the Polish Legions were marking the terrain as Polish, even as they were building a military road from Hungary across Pantyr Pass (just to the north of the Hutsul region, in the Gorgany Mountains) to Rafajłowa.[81] Atop what would soon be known as the Legions' Pass they erected a large wooden cross, at the foot of which was placed a tablet with the following verse: "Polish youth, look at this cross! / The Polish Legions raised it up, / Crossing through mountains, forests, and hills, / To You, Poland, and for your glory."[82] This self-conscious, patriotic sentiment makes clear what the Polish Legions under Habsburg command believed: the territory they had just reached—that is, Galicia—was Poland; and they had come to fight for the glory of Poland, not just defend Austria-Hungary.

After the last of a series of battles in October and November, the Second Brigade was forced to retreat into the Eastern Carpathians, defending the high mountain passes against the enemy.[83] The soldiers' presence did not go unnoticed by the Hutsuls, seven of whom spontaneously approached the recently arrived Poles to enlist as soldiers. Learning of this, the Command of the Legions quickly appointed one of its officers, Captain Edward Szer-auc, to undertake recruitment. By December 9, the end of the brief Hutsul campaign, Szerauc had assembled more recruits: the assembled group of 143 Hutsuls became the first Hutsul company with the Polish Legions, which was dispatched to fight in Hungary.[84] Hutsuls also fed the Second Brigade information on the whereabouts of enemy detachments, with others serving as couriers or porters.[85]

Szerauc subsequently recruited another four hundred or so Hutsuls—half a battalion's worth, whom he trained in Żabie. However, after members of the Ukrainian intelligentsia got word that Hutsuls had been joining the Polish Legions, most of the Hutsuls, although originally loath to leave, were transferred by the Austrian authorities to the Ukrainian Sich Sharpshoot-ers (which did not create a Hutsul company for them until the autumn of 1916).[86] Twenty or so Hutsuls decided to stay with Szerauc and were trans-formed into a Hutsul platoon.[87]

This brief episode during World War I demonstrates that Poles and Hut-suls had once cooperated, even fought together, in the mountains against their common foe. To be sure, both groups were subjects of Austria-Hungary, which was battling Russia. There was no reason to see anything amiss in them fighting on the same side, even under the same command—or was there? Having Hutsuls directly under the Poles nonetheless outraged lowland Ukrainians, for whom such close cooperation with the Poles was anathema; they wanted the Hutsuls to join their own military formation, the Ukrainian Sich Sharpshooters. Yet, no matter how one looked at it, there was some basis to claim at least a wee bit of Polish-Hutsul brotherhood in the not so distant past—although one should remember that the Polish-Ukrainian War of 1918–19, in which Hutsuls took the side of the Ukrainians, had taken place in the interim.[88]

The founders of the Society of Friends of the Hutsul Region made much of this Hutsul-Polish cooperation. That Hutsuls had actually been part of the fight for Polish independence—for that is how the Poles interpreted their presence in the Second Brigade—made it easier for the authorities as well as organizations like the society to see them as potentially part of the solu-tion. Shaped by the mountains, Hutsuls were to be distinguished from the lowland Ukrainians of southeastern Poland, encouraged to see themselves as a distinct people with their own separate history—a history that could be connected to the fight for Polish independence. In short, room was made for the Hutsuls in the master narrative of the Second Polish Republic (in its Sanacja idiom), which emphasized the extensive freedom-fighting pedigree of the Poles.

In the 1930s, the government and the society tried to reinforce this somewhat tenuous relationship of Poles and Hutsuls while capitalizing on the qualities to be found in the mountains. The result was the main annual event of the region, a three-day competitive cross-country ski march that referred back to the Hutsul-Polish cooperation during World War I. It was officially known as the March along the Hutsul Route of the Second Legionnaire Brigade.[89]

Sponsored by Piłsudski, the march from Rafajłowa to Worochta utilized the natural environment of the Carpathians to good effect. The competition was viewed as a "valuable pedagogical means propagating the idea of collective effort in overcoming difficulties created by the severe nature of the mountains."[90] Teams of the more than three hundred competitors—military, civilian, and Hutsul, each in their own division—were to traverse a marked route in three stages, with their times recorded. There would also be a shooting component. Between the teamwork and various skills required, the participants would demonstrate their hardiness and discipline in the Carpathian proving ground while providing a sporting event for bystanders to enjoy and appreciate.[91]

That the Hutsul Route March was a success can be chalked up to cooperative nature and competent organization as well as plausible justification for holding the event in the first place. One advantage of a winter event was that the pockmarked roads were covered with forgiving snow, in this way smoothing out the travel routes. The military organizers sought to emphasize the wartime connection with a photographic exhibition to show images of the Second Brigade.[92] Various Legionnaires' Clubs took part in the event, and one of the Hutsul veterans, Jan (vel Ivan) Kitleruk, also addressed the assembled crowd.[93]

The participation of Hutsul teams, in traditional attire, had been greatly desired.[94] To that end, the society had sought to gain more skiers by offering courses that winter not only in skiing but also in ski making. Forty pairs of skis were distributed to Hutsul children in Żabie during the Hutsul Route March that first year.[95] The courses apparently were popular among Hutsul youth, if not among pro-Ukrainian forces.[96] The latter were not happy to see how well the former Hutsul Legionnaires were treated, how their efforts were acknowledged, how they were provided for (with pensions and schooling for their children). Nor may they have been happy to see the new developments in the Hutsul region, courtesy of the Polish state: improvements to

FIGURE 7.2. The Hutsul team from Jabłonica at the finish line of the Hutsul Route March (with General Tadeusz Kasprzycki among the dignitaries present). Photo by Witold Pikiel, published in *Światowid*, no. 10/499 (3 March 1934). From the Narodowe Archiwum Cyfrowe collection, image in the public domain.

the transportation infrastructure; the establishment of sports clubs to handle events; better advertising of ski competitions and excursions (such as the prize-winning but pricey "Skis, Dancing, Bridge" vacation train that appealed to foreign tourists as well); the production of films, radio programs, articles, and exhibitions touting the region, all of which brought an influx of Poles.[97]

The Society of Friends of the Hutsul Region also organized a major annual summer counterpart to the Hutsul Route March—the Hutsul Holiday. With this second large annual event, the society had come full circle. Organizationally streamlined and better advertised than the first Hutsul Holiday in the summer of 1933, it was attended by some ten thousand to fourteen thousand guests this time around.[98]

The Society of Friends of the Hutsul Region had done its utmost to prepare the Hutsul population and encourage it to participate in the Hutsul Holiday. The first two issues of a Hutsul newspaper, *Nowiny*, written partly in Hutsul dialect, partly in Polish, appeared in the weeks preceding the holiday. These informed their Hutsul readers why people were coming to the region—to see the Hutsuls—and exhorted them to maintain their folk customs and attire—there would be a competition for best dressed—as well as keep clean cottages.[99] The society also strove to organize events that would appeal to Hutsuls, such as shooting competitions in various villages. Kasprzycki himself was keen on seeing a Hutsul win one of the events, thinking it would have a positive influence on their becoming loyal citizens of Poland.[100]

Guests were not the kinds of tourists who packed the nightclubs of what was now the city of Zakopane or sought the creature comforts of spas and resorts elsewhere. The society's brochure of 1934 appealed to those visitors interested in physical fitness and the challenge that mountains presented (Henryk Gąsiorowski's newly published guidebook to the region had a more extensive list of excursions).[101] Other tourists sought a different kind of challenge in coming to know the Hutsuls and contribute to their well-being. Visitors were encouraged to leave behind the Prut River Valley, where Hutsuls had to a great extent lost their distinctiveness, to penetrate territories where the old ways persisted.[102] Poles were advised to hike to the very tip of the Second Republic, the vicinity of the legendary "Rozrogi" immortalized by Wincenty Pol in the mid-nineteenth century. (Pol had come across a stone atop one of the peaks marked with the letters "FR" [Finis Reipublicae]: the

FIGURE 7.3. Winners of the best-dressed Hutsul competition at the Hutsul Holiday of 1933. Left to right: Fedor Dyto, Ołena Medweczuk, railway director Józef Wołkanowski, Maria Ołeksiuk, Michał Moczerniak. From the Narodowe Archiwum Cyfrowe collection, image in the public domain.

end of the commonwealth.) The Society of Friends of the Hutsul Region clearly wished for Polish boots to traverse this distant, and heavily Ruthenian, corner of the Polish Republic, which they wanted to remain firmly and securely within the Polish state.

In organizing the Hutsul Holiday, the society sought to ensure that the region would be visited by the type of Poles that might make a good impression on the Hutsuls: interested citizens from the center of the country, scouts, and Legionnaires, even well-disposed regional bureaucrats. In turn, the visitors were exposed to a hardy and attractive folk, one that seemingly had lent its skills to the Polish fight for independence. As such, it was considered to be one of the brighter pieces of the ethnic mosaic that was the Second Republic.

It was hoped that, with time, the Hutsul region would "attract thousands of Polish and foreign tourists as well as become a valuable health resort center for the entire country."[103] Unlike the Tatra Mountain region, the development of which had been chaotic and compromised by foreign influences, the Hutsul region still had a chance to be developed with a greater respect for native style, architecture, and traditions. The Society of Friends of the Hutsul Region would also ensure that development was powered by a Polish, not Ukrainian, engine—a matter of extreme importance in this borderland region, for reasons of state security as well as national politics. That this was one part of the *kresy* (borderland) where Poles and the indigenous peoples had once—briefly—worked together made the task of the society somewhat easier.

✿ CHAPTER 8

A Poland of Regions

The Hutsul Holiday appeared to inspire yet another highland holiday that soon would reshape general attitudes toward highlanders and the highlands as well as the attitudes of the highlanders toward the Carpathian Mountain region, and by its extension, the rest of Poland.[1] The aptly named Highland or Mountain Holiday (Święto Gór), held in 1935, was originally slated to take place in Zakopane in the summer of 1934, but destructive floods in the highlands undid those plans. Behind the event stood two groups: the Tatra Mountain highlanders and the Society of Friends of the Hutsul Region. Brigadier General Tadeusz Kasprzycki headed the organizational committee, and the military was of assistance during the event as well.

Featured at the Highland Holiday was a much anticipated folk song and dance competition—the first ever in the Polish lands—with highlanders from throughout the Carpathian Mountain region of Poland taking part. Among the various highland "tribes" were Tatra Mountain highlanders, Silesian highlanders, Lemkos, and Boikos, not to mention several groups of Hutsuls, whose dancing was considered most impressive. Indeed, one of the Hutsul troupes won the competition.[2]

The event had several aims. The organizers encouraged the highlanders to maintain their colorful manner of dress and their highland traditions. By bringing representatives of the various highland peoples together at one event, the organizers hoped to foster a sense of brotherhood across the Carpathian region. They also sought to strengthen the highlanders' sense of belonging to the Polish state; all highlanders participating in the Highland Holiday were rewarded with a free trip to the major Polish cities of Kraków, Gdynia, and Warsaw after the event. In this regard, the Highland Holiday seemed to have been a success. While still present in Zakopane, leaders of the regional groups resolved to create an organization that would work toward the "unification [zespolenie] and elevation—ideologically, culturally, and economically—of all the highland areas of Poland."[3]

This resolution would result in the establishment of the Union of Mountain Lands (Związek Ziem Górskich) the following year at the Highland Congress in Sanok.[4] At its head stood the by now familiar figure of Brigadier General Tadeusz Kasprzycki. While its main preoccupations were to be tourism, nature preservation, animal husbandry, and dairy production, the goal of the Union of Mountain Lands, in the words of one of the organization's leaders, Walery Goetel, was to "connect the Carpathians with the rest of Poland economically and culturally." To be sure, the territory of over eleven thousand square miles—about 8 percent of the territory of the Second Republic—differed in manifold ways from the rest of Poland, the quintessential lowland, as did the various groups of highlanders. Yet—Goetel averred—the highland congresses in Zakopane and Sanok had demonstrated that the various highlanders had much in common with each other, and that they saw that Poland had their best interests at heart.[5]

The Union of Mountain Lands also underscored an important fact: diversity reflected the very nature of interwar Poland. The country was to be no regular nation-state but rather a state of regions, each potentially with its own distinct profile and making unique contributions to the whole. According to those present at a Union of Mountain Lands conference, the southern borderlands—which, despite its great diversity, was conceived of as a unitary region—held promise as a producer of waterpower, which would contribute to the country's electrification. Likewise the vivifying climate, curative mineral springs, and the beauty of the landscape would contribute to the regeneration of the citizenry, including its workers (unlike the intelligentsia, members of the working class were yet unaccustomed to taking vacations).[6] The vast swath of territory between the already discovered Tatras and Czarnohora—the Sącz Beskids, Low Beskids, Bieszczady, even the Gorgany; that is, the lands inhabited by Lemkos and Boikos, two other groups of East Slavic highlanders, previously ignored—also needed to be integrated

into this touristic whole. This also explains the decision to hold the Highland Congress of 1936 in Sanok, that is, in the Low Beskids. The integration
of these parts of the Carpathians was to have "a great significance from a
nationalities point of view."[7] It was hoped that Poland's Carpathian Mountain borderland would become a unified entity, its inhabitants uniformly
loyal to the Polish state that did so much to promote it.

In the interwar period, thus, Poles addressed the question of the highlanders' allegiance to the state. Building on the work done in the experimental
realm that was the Hutsul region, various Polish organizations strove to turn
the seemingly nationally indifferent highlanders across the length of the Carpathians (Górale, Lemkos, Boikos, Hutsuls) into loyal Polish citizens while
at the same time making room for continued or even increased ethnic, local,
and regional distinctiveness. This move toward a Poland of regions, with a
slogan of "unity in diversity"—perhaps not coincidentally, the slogan of the
defunct multiethnic Habsburg Empire—gives the lie to views of the new Polish state as striving above all to become a pure nation-state.[8] Yet the push for
a civic understanding of Polishness was doubtless less benign, and less long
lasting, than it may seem at first glance.[9]

Under the rule of first Piłsudski, then the colonels who took over after
the death of Piłsudski in May 1935, Poles redoubled their efforts in the Carpathian borderlands, which they sought to make secure as well as integrate
into a well-functioning, rational, and modern (technocratic) state. Early
on they not only acknowledged but appeared to value the diversity of the
borderland—indeed, to foster it through the varied projects of organizations
such as those initiated by the Society of Friends of the Hutsul Region and the
Union of Mountain Lands. Of course, this appreciation of diversity (or was
it a mere folklorization of the highlanders?) was likewise colored by the fact
that the maintenance of traditional local and regional identities might keep
highland populations such as the Hutsuls, Lemkos, and Boikos from becoming "national"—that is, from becoming nationally conscious Ukrainians.[10]

To what extent this pretty picture of a "Poland of regions" would be
realized in the years to come lies outside the scope of this book. The post-
Piłsudski regime—certainly at the outset—appeared intent on turning what
could be considered a liability (the multiethnic nature of the state) into an
advantage. Whether it took its cues from the experience of the now defunct
multiethnic Habsburg state or even from the Soviet Union, which historian
Terry Martin has labeled the "Affirmative Action Empire," remains unclear.[11]
Nonetheless, one might see this Polish strategy as "highlander in form, Polish in content"—especially if by Polish is meant loyalty to the state.

The Hutsul Museum, the "White Elephant," and Other Projects

This brief look at the beginnings of the Society of Friends of the Hutsul Region and ancillary activities suggests a level of ambition on the part of the post-Piłsudski regime and Kasprzycki in particular. The discovery of Czarno-hora proceeded apace. Not only was Kasprzycki full of ideas for the Hutsul region; he and his associates were able to realize many of his pet projects over the next years.[12]

The flagship project was the Hutsul Museum, the cornerstone for which was blessed at the Hutsul Holiday in 1934.[13] The idea for such a museum surfaced early in the life of the society. This is reflected in both the importance of the Section for the Preservation of Nativeness and the desire to highlight Polish-Hutsul brotherhood, as well as the need for a place where scientific research could be conducted and disseminated. The design of the project reflected these varied needs. The large, modern three-story brick building housed museum halls, a library, an ethnographic archive, rooms for scientific work, a dark room, housing for visiting scholars, as well as a huge lecture hall. Part of the building served as a hut for tourists. The Hutsul Museum also boasted an astronomical/meteorological tower.

Located in Żabie-Ilci, the museum proper was to be composed of various sections. The historical section would highlight the World War I experience of Hutsul-Polish cooperation. The nature section would feature the flora and fauna, geology, and paleontology of the Eastern Carpathians. The especially elaborate ethnographic section, containing more than five thousand items, would exhibit the material culture of the Hutsuls, informing visitors and reminding Hutsuls of their rich and colorful culture. The organizers wanted to transport a real Hutsul homestead to the property as well as provide an outlet where Hutsul wares could be purchased, thus giving the local popula-tion a chance to earn money. Also projected was a botanical garden and alpi-narium.[14] Depicting an idealized brotherly and primeval past, the museum set the Hutsuls firmly within this particular Polish vision of the region.

Although officially opened in February 1938, not all the rooms were yet finished. On account of its great expense, the completion of the Hutsul Museum dragged on: over half a million zloty, and this not including the ninety thousand zloty paid for the plot of land.[15] Yet the expense and effort were seen as justified. In a letter, Kasprzycki underscored the special nature of the museum: "The entire operation is being conducted in a strictly non-governmental dimension with marked support on the part of practically all state ministries, for it is a fragment of a creative national [państwowej] and economic endeavor [*pracy*], conceived on a wide scale, on the territory of the Hutsul region."[16]

Nowhere else in the extant correspondence of the Society of Friends of the Hutsul Region was this special nature of the Hutsul region made so explicit. The public face of the Society of Friends of the Hutsul Region masked a hidden dimension, found in a fascinating document amid the papers of the Department of General Command of the Ministry of Military Affairs that clearly dated from the early 1930s.[17] The anonymous author— perhaps Kasprzycki himself or someone close to him—presented a plan for a sustained and in part secret program of work in the Hutsul region designed to counter the efforts of Ukrainians in southeastern Poland.

The author of this document claimed that the territory of the Hutsul region was "open to the influences of him who first arrives," since the Hut- suls were distinct from the rest of the Ruthenes / Ukrainians, lacking in ideo- logical conviction, and thus "easy to bind to the state" (being easily won over with money). Thus, action on the part of both state and society had to "on the one hand paralyze the anti-state movement in the very Ukrainian cen- ter with all possible legal means," while on the other hand "strengthen the Polish element" in these territories. Given the natural riches of the Eastern Carpathians and their suitability for spas and tourism, it was thought that the "state will achieve vis-à-vis the Hutsuls a *quick and dazzling effect*, and in improving their lives via this easiest of roads would connect them indissolu- bly with Polish statehood."[18] The author concluded that this Hutsul experi- ment would allow those carrying out the project to gain experience that would be helpful when engaging in similar projects in more difficult regions within the country.

To further the region economically and especially to increase the pen- etration and strengthening of the Polish element in the region, this "plan of work in the Hutsul region" required "more complicated, indirect, often con- spiratorial work." The overall plan had to remain secret. There would need to be two channels of work: one, the official work of governmental circles, and the second, "an unofficial, social work of extragovernmental circles, but one strictly inspired by the government, whence arises the need to create a *Society of Friends of the Hutsul Region*."[19] Thus, from this military point of view, the Society of Friends of the Hutsul Region had been posited as an important, government-inspired, and in part conspiratorial organization.

This multilayered nature of the Society of Friends of the Hutsul Region raises numerous questions. Despite the statement above, the only conspira- torial part of the society would turn out to be colonization: that is, helping Legionnaires purchase plots in the region of Żabie known as Kraśnik, where they would build specially designed vacation homes with rooms to rent out to guests.[20] There were many members of the society—scholars as well as people in the field—who were not involved in, or cognizant of, the conspiratorial side. They are what enabled the society to be seen as a nongovernmental organization, albeit one with governmental support. Nonetheless, it took little imagination to see the Society of Friends of the Hutsul Region as a government front organization.

Given the existence of the secret plan, we should not be surprised to see more of a military involvement in the activities of the Society of Friends of the Hutsul Region than the name of the organization might suggest. Take the brand new high-altitude agricultural school in Żabie, where Polish teachers would instruct the Hutsuls in agriculture, the growing of vegetables and fruit trees, beekeeping, animal husbandry, and the use of meadows. The military brass came out in full force for the festive opening, in the form of three generals and a group of former officers of the Second Brigade. They joined the governor of southeastern Poland and other officials for the opening ceremonies. The carefully choreographed event began with a Hutsul banderya escort, after which dignitaries were greeted with bread and salt (traditional East Slavic hospitality) by the mayor of Żabie, Petro Shekeryk-Donykiv. "Long live the Republic and the President of the Republic!" resounded in Hutsul dialect, and a youth choir sang the national anthem. Was the military's plan for the Hutsul region working? Unable to be present, Minister of Military Affairs Tadeusz Kasprzycki sent a telegram, in which he mistakenly called the state agricultural school a "military agricultural school."[21] A slip on his part that nonetheless must have reminded those present who was behind the effort.

The military seemed to be behind yet another enormous investment, one that demonstrated Polish domination of nature: the construction of a high-altitude meteorological/astronomical observatory atop the 6,647-foot mountain of Pop Iwan, begun in summer 1936.[22] The location of the imposing three-story, L-shaped building was terribly remote, with neither of two possible travel routes easy—not for man or beast, let alone the eight hundred tons of material and equipment (not counting the locally quarried sandstone) that had to be brought to the peak—and no easily accessible source of water, the spring lying nearly five hundred feet below the observatory.[23] Could the Pop Iwan have been chosen because it had special, sacral meaning for the Hutsuls—meaning (perhaps) that they would stay away? Or because the mountain, on the Polish-Czechoslovak border, was on the route taken by smugglers and members of the radical Ukrainian nationalist organization, the OUN? Regardless of its exact location, this was to be the easternmost meteorological station/observatory in Europe (before the Urals).[24] It also was in a strategic corner of the Second Polish Republic, lying a dozen miles from the mountain Stoh, atop which Poland, Romania, and Czechoslovakia intersected.[25]

The location of the observatory as well as a sense of its being of strategic value may also have been part of the reason why the Hutsuls came to believe that the enormous building, built in the style of the stone Tatra huts, was a cover for an underground airport, and that the huge housing for the triple-lens telescope special-ordered from England hid a big gun that could fire on the neighboring countries.[26] The observatory's director, Władysław Mido-wicz, made no effort to correct such rumors, so as to keep outsiders away from the "White Elephant," the nickname of this million-zloty project.[27] The attitude of at least some Hutsuls to the building may be suggested by the following anecdote: on the day of its opening in July 1937, Hutsuls who had been assigned to carry dinner upstairs to the dignitaries present instead diverted part of it to their friends waiting a little lower down the mountain. Only the sudden need for the guests to depart in the face of an approaching storm saved the day for Midowicz.[28]

Hutsul and Ukrainian Reactions

Were Hutsuls living up to the expectations that a little economic assistance would win them over to Polish statehood and turn them into loyal citizens of the Second Republic?[29] That Hutsuls sabotaged the dinner of the dignitaries in the observatory suggests that local bonds were stronger than any loyalty to the state or sense of responsibility to one's employer. Did that mean that the Hutsuls were becoming, or had become, nationally conscious Ukraini-ans? Or were they simply intent on "sharing the wealth" with fellow Hutsuls?

Lowland Ukrainians—who took an interest in the Hutsuls in 1933, after the latter had participated in the first Hutsul Holiday—thought Hutsul alle-giance to the Ukrainian national cause was far from certain. So, when it came to attempts to ameliorate hunger in the Hutsul region, these lowland Ukrainians wanted to convince the Hutsul that "the sincerest (helping) hand for the brother-Hutsul was the hand of the brother-Ukrainian" by being the ones to distribute aid given by the Polish government.[30] During prepara-tions for the Hutsul Holiday of 1934, a group of Ukrainians from the city of Kołomyja founded a new biweekly newspaper, Hutsul Word (Hutsul's'ke Slovo) to counter the work of the Society of Friends of the Hutsul Region.[31] Not directed at the Hutsuls, despite their growing literacy, this nonpartisan newspaper encouraged all Ukrainian political and economic organizations to support Hutsul craftsmanship and employment.[32] It also painted a bleak picture of the region's future, were lowland Ukrainians not to get involved: Poles would buy up the heavily mortgaged land, erect villas in Zakopane Style, and push the increasingly deracinated Hutsuls out of their villages and higher up into the mountains. The only sign of the latter's existence—it averred—would be found in highland-garbed mannequins in Żabie's Hutsul Museum.[33]

Lowland Ukrainians were concerned about the Hutsuls morally as well as economically. They saw their lightly churched brethren as demoralized by the Polish presence, learning that money came easy (which they then squandered) and succumbing to the temptations presented by tan and scantily clad bodies.[34] Furthermore, in their benightedness Hutsuls hardly acted like (nationally conscious) Ukrainians. In one example, Hutsuls in Żabie requested that a certain fervently nationalistic priest be transferred out of their parish—in this way rejecting the guidance of the most significant member of the Ukrainian intelligentsia to work in the village.[35] Instead of demanding Ukrainian language instruction in school, the majority of Hutsuls in Kosmacz wanted their children to learn Polish and German as well as Ukrainian, saying that each already spoke Ukrainian at home.[36] Such linguistic indifferentism was anathema to nationally conscious Ukrainians. And Hutsuls generally would not lend a helping hand at any Ukrainian national events in the region, as they were "not obligated" (that is, paid) to do so.[37] Thus, many demonstrated what lowland Ukrainians saw as a lack of commitment to the Ukrainian national cause and a maddingly nonchalant acceptance of what the Polish authorities had to offer. This appeared to be an example less of national indifference than of what historian Brendan Karch has called "instrumental nationalism."[38]

That is not to say there was no opposition to Polish moves in the region or to Hutsul cooperation. Mockery (calling collaborators "traitors" and "pigs" fed rotten sausage by the Poles) and ostracism (for example, from the rich Ukrainian associational life that was developing in the region) both worked to incline some Hutsuls to the Ukrainian side or at least keep them from collaborating with the Poles.[39] While members of the various Ukrainian political parties, including the illegal Organization of Ukrainian Nationalists, exerted pressure on the Hutsuls in various ways (local ski clubs were thought to be OUN breeding grounds), Hutsuls also demonstrated their own independence.[40] There was a year when several teams of Hutsul participants in the Hutsul Route March abandoned the competition just as it started, perhaps intimating that they had been coerced into participating by the Polish authorities.[41] Hutsuls did not necessarily feel any obligation vis-à-vis the Poles, even when being paid. These last two examples—of desertion and pilfering—demonstrate the Hutsuls' use of James C. Scott's "weapons of the weak."[42]

Still, there were also good reasons to take what the Poles were willing to give. Living perennially on the edge of poverty surely encouraged some Hutsuls to react opportunistically when offered a chance to make a livelihood through tourism. Not to mention that any infrastructural improvements wrought by the Society of Friends of the Hutsul Region could be seen as investments in their future—a future perhaps without Polish rule.[43]

Nor did all Hutsuls turn down the opportunity to travel and perform aspects of their rich culture elsewhere in Poland, where they were admired—not criticized—for being Hutsuls. Here one sees a difference between the Ukrainian and Polish approaches to the Hutsuls. The lowland Ukrainian focus was on nation building above all, with little concern for Hutsul traditional culture, while the Polish was on the protection of nativeness and state building. Poles preferred the Hutsuls retain their distinct identity to them becoming Ukrainian nationalists.

This difference notwithstanding, how loyal were the Hutsuls—even those who worked together with the Poles? A look at the behavior of the village mayors and Hutsul notables is instructive.[44] The mayors of Jabłonica, Jaremcze, and Żabie attended meetings of the Society of Friends of the Hutsul Region and represented their constituencies as well as accompanied the Hutsul participants in the various Hutsul and Highland Holidays.[45] They availed themselves of the opportunity to travel, with meals, accommodations, and other expenses covered. These local leaders and their constituencies were encouraged to nurture their Hutsul culture in all its dimensions and even were paid on occasion for doing so.

However, if the Polish writer Jalu Kurek is correct, this favored treatment touched only the top layer of the highland population—the most prominent or well-connected individuals, who could afford to outfit themselves or their relatives in proper traditional folk style (much more expensive than store-bought clothes), folk costume being the synecdoche of the highlander. It was these individuals, he maintained, who traveled to the various holidays and about the country representing their region.[46] Any signs of loyalty, then, emanated at most from a narrow top layer, the masses of highlanders—still impoverished and untouched by developments—remaining oblivious.

Let us listen to the one of the few Hutsul voices we have, that of the mayor of Żabie, Petro Shekeryk-Donykiv (1889–1940?).[47] He was unusual in that he was a highly literate Hutsul, already as a young man corresponding with Ukrainian ethnographers and even starring in Hnat Khotkevych's

Hutsul Theater. A member of the Radical Party, Shekeryk did what he could, after the collapse of Austria-Hungary, to help create an independent Ukrainian state, whether in Stanisławów or Kyiv. He ended up for a spell in exile in Czechoslovakia, where he escaped the first harsh months of Polish rule in the Hutsul region. In the interwar period he made a stir by becoming a deputy to the Polish parliament in 1928.[48] Yet soon enough he returned to his little homeland to serve as village mayor, in which capacity he cooperated with the Society of Friends of the Hutsul Region. Shekeryk also happened to be a good friend of the Polish writer Stanisław Vincenz, who in these years penned the first book of his tetralogy On the High Uplands. On the sixteenth anniversary of Polish independence, the mayor of Żabie gave a carefully worded speech in his village. In it he called all present to unity, brotherhood, and cooperation, while also stating that whatever Ukrainians did well for the Polish state they also did for their nation, for when Poland would be rich so too would the Ukrainians.[49]

That very public statement, in which the mayor justified cooperation with interwar Poles, made its way into the secret monthly reports to the Stanisławów governor. Yet this was the man whose cooperation was all the same stigmatized as the "Żabie comedy" by his lowland Ukrainian detractors, and thanks to whom at least one Greek Catholic priest forbade his parishioners from meeting with residents of Żabie.[50]

Hutsuls could be more candid in private, and in conversation with some lowland Ukrainians en route to a religious feast, one Hutsul reportedly declared, "Hutsuls aren't stupid. Hungry, they take what is given. . . . However, Hutsuls will never sell their nation and faith for bread. We know that our brother Ukrainians from the lowlands would rather help us, but they still are not able to." This was hardly the frivolity or indifference imputed to the Hutsuls by so many lowland Ukrainians. Perhaps it is better to think of them, in Brendan Karch's terms, as instrumentally rational: choosing what made sense at a given moment.[51] Of course, en route to the same event, the same Ukrainians encountered a Hutsul who offered two hundred sheep for . . . the "lass in the blue sweater."[52]

The post-Piłsudski state—or military—was hardly secure in its assessment of Hutsul loyalty, as seen from an event of late summer 1937. Hutsuls were featured in a major Polish newspaper announcing that they had contributed funds for the purchase of an airplane, to be named "the Hutsul."[53] This purportedly was yet another sign of the Hutsuls' attachment to the Polish armed forces. In post-Piłsudski Poland, essentially run by a coterie of colonels, this "donation" (of thirty-seven thousand zlotys) was even more telling. If only it were made by the Hutsuls. The money actually appears to have been collected (extorted?) from the region's Jews, although that information was not made public.[54] It was the Hutsuls' sign of devotion and colorful appearance in Warsaw that made the news. Consummate actors, Hutsuls such as the master woodworker Wasyl Dewdiuk, accompanied by the Kosów district captain, performed loyalty in the Polish capital. Surely such Hutsuls—or at least their leaders—knew that they were being used as props in an effort to demonstrate broad social support for the Polish military, the organization responsible for the ultimate security of the country.

Stanisław Vincenz and Other Hutsul Region Activists

Not all men and women who had the best interests of the Hutsuls at heart got involved in the region through the Society of Friends of the Hutsul Region. A number of Poles who lived or worked in the region were not primarily motivated by *raison d'état*, even if some of them cooperated with the society, a source of funding for some of their projects. These activists too brought the Hutsul region to the attention of a broader constituency.

The most famous of the Hutsul region promoters, if at the same time a man who was skeptical about some of the efforts of the society, was Stanisław Vincenz. The author of the tetralogy *On the High Uplands*, which has been called the Kalèvale of the Hutsuls, was born and raised in the region.[55] Vincenz's first language was the Hutsul dialect, which he learned from his nanny, Palachna Slipenchuk-Rybenchuk. Although his magnum opus was published in Polish, Vincenz had taken to heart his nanny's admonition never to forget the language of the people—a language he would later make his wife learn so as not to Polonize the Hutsuls, which suggests his particular respect and care for Hutsul heritage.[56]

It was the multicultural nature of the region that Vincenz sought to promote, not only in his writings but also by bringing guests to visit. These included the rabbi Marcus Ehrenpreis, who came to do research on the Baal Shem Tov, the founder of Hassidism, who had once lived in the Hutsul region; the Italian anthropologist and ethnographer Lidio Cipriani, who took measurements of the Hutsuls and penned some popular articles about his research subjects; and the Swiss writer Hans Zbinden, a good friend, who visited repeatedly and wrote extensively of his impressions of the Hutsuls.[57] Vincenz turned their gaze, as well as the gaze of those behind the society, toward the multicultural world that he knew and loved, a world where Hutsul and Jew, Pole and Armenian lived in relative harmony.[58]

In a valuable article-cum-interview with Vincenz, this independent popularizer of the Hutsul region cleverly underscored, by reporting the reactions of the consul general of Great Britain to what he saw in his company, the respectability and even nobility of the Hutsuls and Jews of Żabie (the latter including Lejzor/Eliezer Gertner, restaurateur, hotelier, and connoisseur and collector of Hutsul handicrafts) and their fascinating cultures and unique community.[59] But he also provided some candid thoughts on the society. Vincenz noted the breadth and ambition of the enterprise and its numerous projects, not all of which were in harmony with each other. In particular, he feared what would happen to Hutsul culture if a mass tourist movement into the region took place. Vincenz was conscious of the fragility of such unself-conscious traditional cultures like that of the Hutsuls. Suffice it, he wrote elsewhere, that some small break with the past would take place or foreign influences would encroach on them, and they would cease to exist.[60] That said, he was very much for research on the Hutsuls and their region, the creation of a Hutsul Museum in Żabie, while ensuring that the culture continued on in lived form—and he stated that he would support the society as it worked in these spheres.[61]

Vincenz intimated that it would take a careful hand not to do more harm than good, especially given the first—unsuccessful—Hutsul Holiday, and suggested it best that people already working in the field have a say. He likewise thought it important that Ukrainian intellectuals be involved in the project. This demonstrated Vincenz's belief, shared by other individual regional activists, that interwar Poland would do better to model itself after the old multiethnic Jagiellonian state, that Poland was not simply for ethnic Poles (as the integral nationalists in the country would have it), and that the various peoples in the Second Republic needed to live together in harmony.[62]

Such was the idealized world that Vincenz sought to bring alive in his four-volume epic, On the High Uplands, the first volume of which was published in 1936. In it, he painted a picture of the Hutsul region of his youth, the "last island of a Slavic Atlantis," a multicultural world par excellence, one with a palpable sense of community and common bonds. Even the form of the work—a seemingly endless rambling narrative—helped to convey a sense of the Hutsuls' own love of storytelling as well as the timelessness of that world. At least one reader expected On the High Uplands, labeled the "Bible of the Hutsul region," to play the same role in the discovery of the Hutsul region that Witkiewicz's On the Mountain Pass had for the Tatras.[63]

While still writing the first volume, Vincenz became involved with the Society of Friends of the Hutsul Region.[64] His opinions were sought out by the society's administration, in the hopes that his knowledge of the Hutsuls would shed light on what was of particular value in their culture and community, how to preserve it, and how best to approach the Hutsuls. In this way, the "bard of the Hutsul region" was able to teach Poles such as Kasprzycki how to see the region as well as what to see, making his function akin to that of Stanisław Witkiewicz in the Tatras.[65] Vincenz, too, could take advantage of the Society of Friends of the Hutsul Region to push for his own pet projects. These included publications in the Hutsul dialect: Vincenz's suggestion led to the biennial publishing of Hutsul almanacs from 1935 to 1939.[66] The texts and stories in the almanacs were largely the work of Petro Shekeryk-Donykiv, mayor of Żabie, who was a talented writer and author of the novel *Dido Yvanchik*—a work, like the almanacs, written in the Hutsul dialect.

Vincenz understood the predicament of those Hutsuls who cooperated with the Polish authorities. He thought that hiring Shekeryk to write for the almanacs had a "good moral side" in that it "engage[d] his very positive abilities."[67] Producing these texts in Hutsul dialect would be socially acceptable work for his own people—work that might actually strengthen the mayor's position among the Hutsul population.

It also could have positive repercussions for a common Polish-Hutsul future. In the future Shekeryk would have "much more of a chance," claimed Vincenz, to affect the political views of his people, acquainting them with "a state policy independent of radical Ukrainian strivings."[68] What this meant was that the Hutsuls might indeed be eventually won for the Polish cause: they might learn to think of themselves as loyal citizens of the interwar Polish state, while still retaining their identity as Hutsuls or Ukrainians.

What was at stake was bigger than Poland. For men like Stanisław Vincenz, Hutsul culture was one of the sole remnants in Europe of a primordial past, one the reasons why they sought to conserve and protect it, while at the same time opening the region to visitors who would respect that culture.[69] Another burning question in the first half of the twentieth century was whether the Hutsuls would lose their connection to their traditional world and values, instead feasting indiscriminately on what Western civilization brought to the region. Would the world of progress and cultural homogenization displace the unique, still enchanted world of the Hutsuls?

At least some Hutsuls were becoming more conscious of the value of their traditional highland culture and ways. As Shekeryk wrote in one of his many pieces for the almanacs, "Only by valuing our old customs, language, and construction can we be confident that we will fulfill our task . . . for the development and elevation of our corner of the country." He maintained that only then could Hutsuls "be sure that the new European mechanical and leveling civilization will not flood us and not destroy us, and not wipe us from the face of the earth." "Respecting and loving what is our own,"

Shekeryk concluded, "let us go bravely into the world to encounter what is new!"[70]

Clearly some regional activists, Hutsuls and Poles alike, considered this uniquely preserved Hutsul culture as part of the spiritual riches of not only the interwar Polish state but also humanity in general. They encouraged the Hutsuls to maintain or even buttress their distinctiveness—that is, not to jettison their old ways and to partake only selectively of what the outside world had to offer. That in itself was some achievement.

Despite a lack of memory on the part of many residents of the Second Polish Republic, for whom the remote Eastern Carpathians were terra incognita, Poles ultimately came to know and appreciate the Hutsul region. On the surface, it seemed that the Society of Friends of the Hutsul Region grew from life itself, that inspiration for the organization and its doings came from the field and from those dedicated individuals who were working there or who found the Hutsul region to be of special interest. It may have grown out of the near disastrous first Hutsul Holiday of summer 1933, envisaged as a way to lift this fascinating yet impoverished region out of its perennial hunger and want. Yet percolating not far below the surface, there was another, secret dimension—one based on a sense of the strategic importance of the Hutsul region and the need to introduce more Poles (in)to it.

The region's borderland position was unique in interwar Poland. This remote corner of the Eastern Carpathians cut a wedge southward into Romanian territory while lying adjacent to Czechoslovakia and not far from the Soviet Union. In both Romania and Czechoslovakia dwelled populations of highlanders also known as Hutsuls, while in the Soviet Union was the Ukrainian heartland. And one should not forget the lowland Ukrainians of southeastern Poland. It seemed to be this last group—the country's own nationally conscious and mobilized Ukrainians—that the Polish authorities found most threatening. They sought to keep the Hutsuls from seeing themselves as simply highland Ukrainians.

The allegiance of the Hutsuls to the Second Republic was much desired. It was important enough for those behind the society to seek to camouflage top-down state policy as a bottom-up, organic development. Money somehow could be found to support most anything—whether history or economy, tourism or the preservation of regional distinctiveness—that could be seen as bringing the Hutsuls, as Hutsuls, into closer contact with the right kinds of Poles (those who saw the value of Hutsul distinctiveness), who would embrace their highland brothers and help them to feel a welcome and valued part of the Second Republic. This was an uphill battle, although the author of the secret report seemed to think that allegiance could be easily purchased. Poles of a certain sort persisted in seeing the Hutsuls as malleable enough to be turned into loyal citizens of the Polish state. On the other hand, Hutsuls seemed to accept what was being done for them in their region, pleased to have investment and even happier to gain employment in the course of construction.

Yet the Zeitgeist was increasingly against this multiethnic vision of Poland. A whiff of inevitability was in the air. By 1939, Lejzor Gertner was not sanguine about the activities of either the Ministry of Military Affairs or the Society of Friends of the Hutsul Region in the Eastern Carpathians. In private conversation he maintained that it was only a question of time before all Hutsuls would feel themselves Ukrainian—their leaders already did, even if they did not say so publicly. The latter were simply happy to take advantage of this protection from above in order to achieve their own goals.[71]

The Hutsuls as well as lowland Ukrainians had no illusions as to the source of interest in the Hutsul region—this despite the Ministry of Military Affairs' desire to keep parts of the program secret. One such Ukrainian later claimed that the Hutsul region was under the "stern control" of the society, which was run by the military; furthermore, he averred that some of the publications it financed—including the almanacs—were not worth reading, given their bias.[72]

Here he clearly differed with Stanisław Vincenz. Vincenz thought that, if done properly, the almanacs would be of value—culturally, linguistically, but also politically. As products primarily of the pen of Petro Shekeryk-Donykiv, the inveterate Hutsul author, they also have literary value. Shekeryk would not live to see his own magnum opus in print: repressed by the Soviets after the latter invaded Poland in mid-September 1939, he died in Siberia. His family buried his manuscript somewhere in the Hutsul region. Only after Ukraine gained its independence was it dug up and published, allowing the post-Soviet generation to see Petro Shekeryk-Donykiv as yet another "bard of the Hutsul region."[73]

Such things could not be foreseen in the early days of 1939. To be sure, the new astronomical observatory on Pop Iwan gave wonderful views of the planet Mars, looming as large as it ever had. The god of war was already stirring in Hitler in the west. Yet Poland continued on its previous course, not oblivious to the danger, but continuing to live, work, and play.

By this point, countless Poles had become enamored of the exotic, wild, fascinating Hutsul region, now perceived as a "native landscape"—perhaps on the way to becoming a "national landscape" like the Tatras.[74] The mountains had an entire network of huts where climbers could stay, and there were more and more vacation homes for military officers and others.[75] Polish hiking, ski, and scouting organizations across the board had taken responsibility for the huts, as had the very active and still quite new Kosów branch of the Polish Tatra Society, which proved more active than its parent organization, the Czarnohora Branch in Kołomyja.[76] It is worth noting that, from 1937 on, specially trained Hutsuls (among others) served in the newly established volunteer rescuer corps in Czarnohora.[77]

Żabie was turning into a lively place, with automobiles parked in front of tourist lodgings, music playing in the various restaurants. The Hutsuls rendered the village picturesque in the eyes of visitors, while the vistas continued to impress.[78] The doyen of Polish tourism, Mieczysław Orłowicz continued his practice of organizing an annual excursion into the region. These were elaborate events involving a "cavalcade" of tourists, numerous Hutsuls, who on occasion performed for the group—the interwar equivalent of Chałubiński "grand-style" excursions.[79]

The sole problem for tourists and others was the increasing concern with the security of the border zone, which was being defined larger and larger. One had to gain permission to travel in the border zone, and the sale of real estate apparently also required the approval of the authorities.[80] The implementation of this legislation was to ensure that only the "right" people traveled or purchased land. The region became a military frontier. Perhaps this was appropriate, given the militarization of so much of interwar Poland.

Nor was a military air lacking from the preparations for yet another annual highland holiday. The 1939 festivities, at which the fiftieth anniversary of the death of Tytus Chałubiński was to be commemorated, were scheduled for the first days of September. That year the event, already earlier renamed Highland Week, was to be a "great patriotic demonstration of the highland people" of the Polish Carpathians, one in which they showed that they were ready to serve as a "highland Maginot Line."[81] The Hutsul experiment seemed to have borne fruit. Yet even that seeming support from the country's highlanders could not save the country in September 1939, which witnessed the double partition of the country, this time at the hands of Hitler and Stalin. The attack by Nazi Germany on the Second Polish Republic on September 1 ensured this final highland holiday would not take place, ultimately putting an end to this new Polish regionalism as well as to the interwar Polish state. After the invasion of Poland's easternmost lands by Soviet troops on September 17, the Poles' "Hutsul Experiment" in the Eastern Carpathians came to an end. What would emerge from this conflagration remained to be seen.

PART III

The Bieszczady Mountains of the Polish People's Republic

CHAPTER 9

A Novel Wilderness

The Soviet invasion of September 17, 1939, was but the beginning of a new period in the history of Polish statehood and the Carpathian Mountain region. The Galician-turned-Polish Carpathians had been partitioned. Now under Soviet rule, the Hutsul region would forever be lost to Poles and Polish statehood. After the war, Polish attention would shift westward, to a part of the central Carpathians previously known as the Western Bieszczady. Extending from Komańcza in the west to the San River in the east, this range would henceforth be termed, simply, the Bieszczady— no mention of the missing eastern half, firmly ensconced, along with most of what prior to the war had been the Second Polish Republic's eastern borderlands, within the Union of Soviet Socialist Republics.

Territory Transformed

One of the transformations concerned population density and diversity. Before World War II the western Bieszczady Mountains were rather densely settled, if not in the main by ethnic Poles but rather by East Slavs and Jews.[1] Jews—mostly traders, shopkeepers, and artisans—tended to live in the towns and larger settlements, as did many Poles, who also dominated localities further north in the foothills.[2] Agricultural and pastoral folk, the region's East Slavs were composed of two highland "tribes," Lemkos and Boikos.[3] Boikos

POLISH PEOPLE'S REPUBLIC

Arłamów

Sanok

Zagórz

Lesko

Krościenko

Ustianowa

Ustrzyki Dolne

Solina

Rzepedź

Polańczyk

Lake Solina

USSR

Komańcza

Baligród

Wołkowyja

Czarna

Łupków

Jabłonki

Terka

Łopienka

Lutowiska

Smolnik

Cisna

Solinka

San

Stuposiany

Wetlina

Berehy
Górne

Muczne

Bieszczady

Ustrzyki Górne

CZECHOSLOVAKIA

x Halicz

Wołosate

POLAND

Mapped
Area

MAP 5. The Bieszczady Mountains (post-1945). Map by Daniel P. Huffman.

were found in the east across much of the Bieszczady, and Lemkos in the
west of the region from Komańcza into the Low Beskid. These two highland
peoples were claimed by Ukrainians as part of their nation, although in the
interwar period Poles likewise claimed them, as they had the Hutsuls, as
"Polish tribes"—their Polishness understood not in ethnic terms but rather
in broader, civic terms.

The heterogeneous population of the Bieszczady region lived together in
relative harmony before the war.[4] A sign of this was the number of mixed
marriages, the offspring of which would be baptized in the religion of the
parent of the same sex. However, already during this period various Greek
Catholic priests of a Ukrainian nationalist bent had begun to agitate on
behalf of the Ukrainian nation, which left relations between East Slavs and
Poles somewhat cooler than in an earlier period.[5]

The conflict between these competing assessments of the highland folk of
the Central Carpathians came to a head during World War II and its immedi-
ate aftermath. In the early days of the war, the territory was divided between
the Soviets and the Nazis at the San River—the dividing line between the
western and eastern Bieszczady. The first major change in the composition
of the population came with the Holocaust, which struck the Bieszczady in
1942. Although 650 Jews were shot on the spot in Lutowiska, most Jews were
transferred to an intermediary camp near Nowy Zagórz, whence they were
shipped to the extermination camp at Bełżec to meet the fate of so many
other Polish Jews. A group of Roma camped in the Bieszczady region was
also murdered.[6]

Murderous intent also motivated the Ukrainian nationalist partisan groups
that were forming in the Bieszczady region toward the end of the war.[7] The
radical nationalist Organization of Ukrainian Nationalists (OUN), illegal in
Poland before the war, had not changed its thoughts about the Polish "occupation" of territories that were claimed by the Ukrainian nation. Together
with its military arm, the Ukrainian Insurgent Army (UPA), these integral
nationalists sought to cleanse the Polish population from territories they
claimed for Ukrainians. Coming from the east, the UPA entered the Bieszczady in the summer of 1944. At that time, the ranks of the underground
force swelled with deserters from the SS "Galizien" Division—Ukrainians
had placed their hopes with Nazi Germany, thinking they might create an
independent Ukraine—with other Ukrainian collaborators, and with those
fleeing from Soviet rule. They resolved to rid the Bieszczady region of the Polish presence, to which end they murdered a number of Poles, with Baligród
and Muczne witnessing the greatest numbers. The seventy-four Poles killed
in Muczne proved to be Poles who had escaped from the east, from Volhynia,
where violent ethnic cleansing had already taken place.[8] Still, the numbers

of Poles killed by the UPA in the Bieszczady were only a tiny fraction of the bloodbath that was Volhynia.

Soon a new development would lead to a change of focus of the Ukrainian underground forces in the mountains. This was the planned emptying of the Bieszczady region (and other parts of Poland) of its East Slavic population via population transfers and resettlement, per an agreement between the Polish Committee of National Liberation and the Ukrainian Soviet Socialist Republic of September 9, 1944. Poles and Jews were to be transferred to Poland, "Ukrainians" (including Boikos and Lemkos) to the USSR. This "voluntary" population transfer was meant to serve as a fait accompli before the Big Three met at Yalta to determine the postwar borders of the region's countries.[9]

While Poles and Jews of the territories taken over by Stalin were to some extent happy to escape the USSR and be "repatriated" to Poland, the reverse did not hold true for the generally conservative Boikos and Lemkos of the western Bieszczady—the part that remained in the new communist-run Polish state. Not all of them identified with the Ukrainian nation to which they supposedly belonged, and many of them simply did not wish to leave their ancestral lands. So few volunteered to be repatriated that, in the fall of 1945, the Polish army was sent in to facilitate the population transfer. Its methods resulted in great destruction and loss of life, and many a family hid in the forests to escape deportation.[10]

There were other people in the forests, most notably members of the UPA. Anticipating a third world war that would create a free Ukraine, Ukrainian nationalists were adamant that the East Slavs within Poland remain where they were, to reinforce Ukrainian claims to the region. The UPA literally fought to keep the region's East Slavs of this southeastern corner of the newly drawn Polish state from being repatriated to the USSR, terrorizing villagers, East Slavic as well as Polish, in the process. Those Boikos and Lemkos who agreed to be repatriated were targeted as traitors to the Ukrainian nation, and some of them were killed. The villages the deportees left behind were burned down by the UPA to keep Poles from settling there. The Polish army also burned down the occasional village in its attempts to convince the highlanders to leave for the USSR and deny the UPA further support. In addition, the UPA targeted infrastructure: they tore up railroad tracks, cut telephone lines, and bombed bridges so as to make it hard for the population transfer, which came to an end in July 1946, to take place.

The truncated southeastern border of the Polish People's Republic (PRL) proved hard to subdue. The presence of the UPA was all too palpable, and the Polish army seemed unable to root out this Ukrainian underground, especially given the latter's better knowledge of the terrain and its hidden bunkers. It also had some support, willing or not, from the local population. Throughout this period, young Boiko and Lemko men were being drafted into the UPA and their home villages pressed to give support to the Ukrainian underground, which continued to attack Polish military outposts and border guard stations.

The Polish communists who, with Stalin's assistance, had come to power in the summer of 1944 knew they had to rid themselves of this problem. The central authorities sent the Polish deputy minister of defense, General Karol Świerczewski, to the mountains in the spring of 1947 to assess the situation.[11] After visiting troops in Lesko and Baligród, Świerczewski spontaneously decided to add a trip to a border guard outpost, despite being warned about the danger. He and an escort of forty-six officers and soldiers set out the next morning for Cisna. They were met by gunfire from two UPA companies near the village of Jabłonki, at a place where the road wound its way between brush-covered hills—a perfect place for an ambush. The chaotic Polish counterattack could not save the general: Świerczewski perished on the spot. Whether this was an attack directed specifically toward the general—that is, an assassination—or only a lucky coincidence for the UPA has yet to be settled definitively, although the latter seems more likely.[12]

Whether accidental or planned, the death of Świerczewski served as a rallying point for the Polish authorities. It gave them an excuse to enact plans to remove from the southeastern territories the rest of the East Slav population, now unequivocally labeled Ukrainian, under the assumption that at least some of them had sympathized with and lent support to the UPA. Thus, those who had not already been repatriated to the Ukrainian Soviet Socialist Republic were dispersed in the west and north of Poland in the course of Operation Vistula (Akcja Wisła), initiated in 1947. The East Slav highlanders found themselves transported to the faraway flatlands gained by Poland at Germany's expense—a small compensation for the loss of the vast eastern territories that had represented 47 percent of the territory of interwar Poland but now were retained by the USSR.[13] In other words, highland populations that the interwar state had sought to assimilate in the 1930s were now labeled as being of a different nationality—Ukrainian—and collectively punished by association with the UPA, which the Polish army proceeded to root out. Ironically, someone drew parallels with an earlier period, as seen in a commemorative tablet on a cross at the military cemetery in Baligród, the words of which echo those on the Legions' Cross in the Eastern Carpathians from World War I: "Passerby! / Look at this cross / Polish soldiers raised it up / Chasing fascists / Through forests mountains and hills / For you, Poland / And for your glory."[14]

Nothing was to remain of the East Slavic communities in Poland, although interestingly some qualified workers in the strategically important oil industry, as well as some foresters and railway engineers, were allowed to remain.[15] In Operation Vistula, the rest of the highlanders were dispersed about the country in such a way that, it was hoped, they would soon assimilate to Polishness. Stalin and the communists made it clear: postwar Poland was to be a nation-state, not a state of nationalities, as it had been in the interwar period.

The forced movement of the East Slavic populations from 1944 to 1947 affected a large number of individuals and their families: close to 483,000 Ukrainians and Ruthenes were deported to the USSR in the population exchanges, while another 140,000–150,000 (of which Lemkos amounted to 25,000–35,000) were resettled in the north and west of Poland.[16] (The not insignificant numbers of people who perished in the process are harder to calculate.) Others found their lives changed without moving from their ancestral homes. The inhabitants of places such as Lwów and the Hutsul region—formerly citizens of Poland—who had not already been transferred to the new postwar Poland now found themselves residents of the Ukrainian Soviet Socialist Republic.

Yet that was not quite the end of adjustments. Poland's eastern border was revised in 1951, when Poland exchanged a piece of territory in the Lublin province for a section of the Bieszczady, a territory amounting to some 185 square miles. Poland gained the region of Ustrzyki Dolne, which had been renamed Shevchenkovo during its short tenure under the Soviets. Although the exchange was advertised publicly as a friendly move on the part of the USSR (as in Mieczysław Orłowicz's 1954 guidebook to the Bieszczady), it was motivated by the fact that the Soviets wanted the coal mine that had been rebuilt near Sokal.[17] Both territories were emptied of their respective populations so as not to undo the ethnic cleansing that had already taken place in these borderlands. While the populations were exchanged, the natural and man-made landscape remained much as it had been.[18] While the very southeastern tip of the Polish People's Republic was now more accessible, the change ultimately resulted in a net loss of population in the Bieszczady, for most of the population from the Sokal region chose not to settle in the Bieszczady but rather to travel to the new territories Poland gained in the west.[19]

Following the war, the Holocaust, and postwar battles, deportations, and border shifts, the transformation of the Bieszczady Mountains was nearly complete. Villages had been burned down, inhabitants dispersed, leaving behind the occasional homestead or church, overgrown cemetery, orchard gone wild, half-buried tool or other remnant of past life. The Bieszczady region was a veritable no-man's land for the better part of a decade, as the last underground forces were routed from their highland lairs and a modicum of Polish control exerted over the mountains.

A Palimpsest Inscribed Anew

This part of the Carpathians had reverted to a wilderness—a veritable no-man's land transformed into "nature's wonderland."[20] Waist-high nettles and hardy aspen grew unimpeded, while endless mud covered whatever paths remained. Wildlife attracted to the dense forests included brown bears and wolves, wildcats and lynxes, as well as the magnificent Carpathian deer with their impressive antlers. Yet this wilderness was one sprinkled with relics of former human settlements. One of the first visitors to the region after it was emptied of its former inhabitants wrote movingly of an overgrown well with a bucket left as if only a moment earlier, the extensive alpine meadows and forests, canyons and ravines—a "frighteningly wild paradise." While this "land of elemental and undisciplined nature" may have been cruel and harsh for the Polish settlers whom the communists subsequently tried to lure to the region, it was—in the words of pre- and postwar tourism activist Władysław Krygowski—"beautiful and wonderful for the eye of the tourist," by which Krygowski had in mind the active, even rugged, tourist of the mountain-climbing sort.[21] This was in keeping with the way the word *tourism* (*turystyka*) had long been understood in the Polish lands, as a synonym for hiking/mountaineering/alpinism.

Unlike the Tatra Mountain region to the west, with its well-developed network of trails and longer history of mountain climbing, the Bieszczady Mountains were practically unmarked—unknown. Their densely covered, nearly inaccessible, challenging landscape nonetheless appealed to a certain category of tourist. The lush terrain with thick forests, canyon-carving streams, and grassy highland meadows would be viewed as a restorative land par excellence, a place where the vivifying highland air and spectacular views could cure whatever ailed the postwar Pole. At a time when the Tatras were finally being transformed into a national park, tourists in the Bieszczady could hike to their heart's content, with few strictures.[22] The time appeared ripe for the terra incognita of the Bieszczady Mountains to come into its own as a tourist destination within the Polish People's Republic, where they had the potential to become the country's premier highland wilderness.

The Poles' understanding of the region would be colored by images imported from abroad, from west as well as east. Before long, this wilderness found its way onto the silver screen, which cast this corner of the country in a new light. In 1959, a film entitled *Rancho Texas* made its way into the theaters of the Polish People's Republic. With their wide expanses, sparse settlements, and harsh conditions, the Polish Bieszczady stood in for the prairies of the American West a century earlier. Although critics panned this Polish Western, *Rancho Texas* did encourage Poles to view the Bieszczady Mountains—previously terra incognita—as their own "Wild West."[23]

The Polish People's Republic would seek to repopulate the territory, but not only that. The priorities of the new socialist state were to rebuild after the devastation of the war and—even more important—to build socialism along the way. The authorities sought to alter the physical space of the Bieszczady in keeping with their vision of what a socialist state would be: progressive, industrial, collectively owned. At the same time, they sought to change the human material at hand as well, to transform peasants—the most numerous part of the Polish population—into workers. The task was thus twofold: to reincorporate into the state a region that had been off limits as a result of the continued fighting, and to settle it with new socialist men.[24] It was a challenge. Early on practically the only people to be found in the region—barring some foresters—were border guards and leather-jacket-clad security police. (In the 1950s they also kept an eye on the sky, expecting American "imperialists" at any moment to drop anti-Soviet leaflets or send in balloons containing potato beetles to devastate the Polish economy.)[25]

The presence of foresters and other settlers suggests that the socialist leaders of People's Poland had a different vision of the Bieszczady than did someone like Krygowski. Given a blank slate, they sought to imprint it with modern (Soviet-style) technological progress, in this way satisfying the ideological imperative to maximize economic production.[26] Inspired by Soviet-style gigantomania, the authorities envisaged enormous lumber mills, powerful dams producing hydroelectric power, extensive state farms. For the socialists, this was a territory—like the American West—to be taken over and tamed, to be made over in their image and likeness.

Hatchet-in-Hand Hikers

The socialist authorities' vision did not stop some intrepid tourists from seeking to gain access to Poland's new wilderness. Although this border zone was not truly open until 1954, in 1952 and 1953 two experienced mountaineers led teams from the newly formed state controlled Polish Society of Tourism and Local Studies (PTTK).[27] Toting hatchets and cans of paint, the groups hacked their way through the overgrowth to clear, and mark, a trail across the Bieszczady. It took them two seasons to open a route from the spa town of Krynica in the west (in the neighboring region of the Low Beskid) to the Bieszczady mountain peak of Halicz in the east, thus preparing the region for the beginnings of tourism.[28]

These hatchet-in-hand hikers were inspired by the experience of the wild mountains—inspired enough to encourage others to come and experience the challenges presented by a region untamed.[29] The leader of one of the trailblazing groups and author of an early (1958) guidebook to the Biesz-czady, Władysław Krygowski, wrote of "the paths and roads not yet trodden, the battle with a space that summons and attracts, which allures and releases the need to battle with difficulty and with highland surprises."[30] Let tourists come to the Bieszczady, he declared: "A journey amazingly rich in new and instructive impressions and experiences" awaited them there.[31] The prewar mountain climber, who remembered a very different Bieszczady, wrote of "new, discovered anew, mountains"—perhaps the first use of the trope of discovery in conjunction with the new highland wilderness.[32] Soon to be opened to further encounters, the Bieszczady were clearly the Polish destination of choice for the rugged adventurer.

In reality, Poles seeking adventures of this kind had few options. The postwar border settlements had shifted Poland westward geographically, if eastward politically. Many took hard the loss of the Eastern Carpathians, the Hutsul region with its peaks and people. The Bieszczady Mountains thus came to serve as a substitute for that severed limb. As Jacek Kolbuszewski has written, "Bieszczady rivers and streams became a symbolic reminder of the murmur of the Prut and Czeremosz" rivers, so identified with the Eastern Carpathians; the poloninas, or grassy highland pastures, of the Bieszczady likewise reminded Poles of the beloved region that was now lost to them.[33] Although orographically not as impressive as the lost lands—the mountains were not as high, although the poloninas provided excellent panoramic views—the Bieszczady had become the new wilderness.

While the basic trail through the Bieszczady was being blazed, other tourists gained permission to hike in the region—permission given on a case-by-case basis still at this time. Among them was a thirty-two-year-old priest who in 1952 and 1953 was part of two early summer excursions in the Low Beskid as well as in the Bieszczady.[34] His younger traveling companions had agreed to call him "Uncle" instead of the usual deferential "Father" so as not to raise suspicions in this sparsely settled land, where socialist border guards and security officers seemed to outnumber settlers. Lest anyone think that a mountain-climbing priest was utterly atypical, it should be recalled that priests were among the very first Polish alpinists.[35] However, this priest, who secretly celebrated Mass during these excursions, would turn out to be more influential than most. He was Karol Wojtyła, later to become Pope John Paul II.[36]

Mountain-climbing priests like Wojtyła were nonetheless rare—doubtless thankfully so, as far as the socialist regime was concerned, which did not look favorably on the practice of religion in the Bieszczady or elsewhere. The young priest also represented an older tradition, one identified more with the historic Polish intelligentsia that dominated Polish mountaineering before World War II. It was a group that hiked to dissipate mental stress, not to recharge after physical labor.

The future saint and his young friends were not the only ones to enjoy the new wilderness. Other groups—including experienced prewar hikers from the circle of tourism activist Mieczysław Orłowicz—were able to hike, albeit with some restrictions. For example, in the mid-1950s such tourists were not allowed to pitch camps; rather, they had to sleep at the outposts of the border guard. That these were separated by a distance of more than twenty miles made for quite a long daily hike, especially with heavy backpacks, for one could not expect to buy any provisions in this out-of-the-way place. As Maria Dulęba wrote, each hiker was eager to add some of the cereals he or she was carrying to the common pot of watery gruel, which they cooked for supper at the outposts.[37]

In 1953 Dulęba's group was blessed by amazingly good, sunny weather—a real treat in the Bieszczady, where summers tended to be rainy. They located the newly marked trail, which ran along the ridges of the mountains, and were treated to the sight of colorful grasses, lush beech forests, rocky cliffs, and flowing rivers on their way to the Bieszczady's second highest peak, Halicz (4,331 feet). But what they did not see along the way also impressed the hikers, who knew that the region had been heavily populated before the war. The only signs that there had once been a village en route to the Caryńska meadow were the flowerbeds that surrounded what used to be cottages. Where the houses had stood, nettles now rose as tall as a man. Yet there were other remnants of earlier life. In Cisna the group slept in an old Greek Catholic church, which at the time was serving as a silo for hay—a sign that some settlers had made it to the village.[38] The latter must have been less taken with the gilt Byzantine interior of the church than were the hikers, who likewise found eating supper in the adjacent cemetery by the light of the moon an uncanny experience.[39] (These and other experiences in the Bieszczady also provided more than one couple with a romantic setting.)

One did not have to be a religious person or even a member of the prewar intelligentsia, let alone a young couple in love, to appreciate the mountains. The lush, barely penetrable terrain of the Bieszczady and adjacent

Low Beskid acted like a magnet on a new generation, one that had much to gain from interacting with pure untrammeled nature, even of the secondary kind. University and polytechnic students from Warsaw in particular became enamored with the Bieszczady, "their" mountains.[40] These "highlanders from the Warsaw environs" approached the region in an organized if spontaneous way, forming various student hiking clubs in the mid-1950s.[41] Early clubs went under names such as "The Great Brotherhood" and "Club of the Left Pant Leg."[42]

Hiking in, conquering this wilderness—even if it was of a relatively new vintage, and not devoid of the occasional trench, munitions, or skeletal remains—proved infectious. Their experiences trekking in the Bieszczady ultimately led a group of students, in 1957, to establish a club of hiking tour guides. This came to be called the Student Club of Beskid Guides (SKPB— Beskid being another name applied to the Carpathians), an organization in existence to this day.[43] That would lead someone to conclude, several years later, that the Bieszczady were discovered circa 1957.[44]

These Warsaw students were originally tourists bearing axes—tourists that the state authorities came to classify under the rubric of "qualified tourism" (turystyka kwalifikowana). They were fit, trained, and experienced, able to find their way where there were no marked trails, prepared to carry in all or most of the food they needed as well as their own accommodations, in the form of tents and tarps.[45] As early as 1962, some student guides were accredited as regular state guides for the Bieszczady region.[46] A couple of years later a dilapidated observation outpost with a wooden observation tower at Łopiennik with great views of the Bieszczady, rented by the Union of Polish Students for next to nothing, was transformed into a primitive student hut (no electricity, no water), giving them a base in the mountains.[47] The initial push for tourism of the qualified variety nonetheless came from the segments of society that had provided highland tourists before the socialists came to power: university students in particular, not the working classes. Furthermore, this qualified tourism in Poland's new highland wilderness tended to foster individualism—not exactly what the Stalinist regime viewed as the proper type of leisure for the new socialist man.

Demarcating Socialist—and National—Space

A more welcome type of tourism for People's Poland was what might be termed mass tourism with a socialist face. The state strove to put its own stamp on the region and the way it was perceived. For example, the provincial authorities in Rzeszów requested that the presidia of the local national councils take care of places that recalled "the martyrdom and heroic battle of the Polish people for national and social liberation."[48] This approach to the history of the region suggests an important way in which the socialist state used the Bieszczady mountain region to buttress and justify alike the role played by the Polish United Workers' Party (PZPR) in postwar Poland.

The socialist authorities preferred qualified tourism, which had more social and educative value than did "unqualified tourism" (*turystyka niekwali-fikowana*, or tourism for the uninitiated masses). The former was seen as raising the intellectual and cultural level of society while breaking down social barriers and increasing patriotism. The Subcommittee on Tourism concluded, "In all its disciplines, qualified tourism demands solidarity, fortitude and endurance. . . . becoming an ideal method for the physical and moral education of youth. Camping, marches, and *rajdy* . . . are perfect forms of the indirect preparation of youth for the defense of the country."[49] It should come as no surprise that the state should try to avail itself of such useful opportunities to uplift its young people physically, morally, and ideologically while providing them with a taste of the outdoors. One of the ways it did so was through organizing group tourist excursions called *rajdy* in Polish—clearly related to the English homonym "ride," although these were group hiking excursions.[50] Organized by the Warsaw student guides' club, branches of the PTTK, even labor unions, such excursions could have as many as a thousand or more participants.[51] The rules and regulations for participants could be extensive, with literally every detail provided regarding preparation and behavior.[52] Such rajdy could also be considered an ideologically inflected subset of qualified tourism that not only influenced the tourists' health and self-discipline but also taught them more about the region in which they were hiking or about the event being commemorated.[53]

An early example was the Friendship Rajd.[54] It took place for the first time in 1954, on the tenth anniversary of the "independence of People's Poland."[55] The slogan for that week-long excursion was "We Are Deepening Friendship with the Nations of the USSR."[56] Teams composed of three to six persons were equipped with tents, sleeping bags, backpacks, and food for a minimum of three days, thus making it a serious hiking trip. Each team was also instructed to pack a hatchet or axe, as hikers would have to cut their way through various parts of the terrain. They would also need personal documents, for they were to travel in the border zone.

That first year the Friendship Rajd boasted a total of 345 participants, including 97 women, 76 manual laborers, and 43 members of the communist-sponsored Union of Polish Youth. A full 160 participants were in the mountains for the first time.[57] The rajd consisted of both strenuous hiking and ideological elements. During the trip, Polish and Soviet songs were sung around the campfires, presaging a later student repertoire of less ideologically imbued campfire songs. On the 4,330-feet-high Halicz, delegates of the Rzeszów Province erected "friendship banners," while all teams helped erect a mound out of rocks—such mounds being traditional Polish means of commemorating significant individuals or events. They even mounted busts of Lenin and Stalin atop the mountain.[58] At the concluding festivities in Ustrzyki Dolne, the participants were called on to "manifest their common feelings for the brotherly nations [of the USSR]" at the foot of the sole Stalin monument in Poland.[59]

The Friendship Rajd became an annual event. Within a few years, advertisements for the rajd, amazingly enough, would focus on the vacation aspects, suggesting what the real attraction for Poles would be: "Beautiful, wild, attractive routes. Departures from Ustrzyki Dolne, Ustianowa, and Komańcza. Three days of rest in Ustrzyki Górne. Plan [your] vacation for September."[60] Nonetheless, it was still very much an ideologically imbued escape—what historian Dariusz Jarosz would consider one of the "ritualized political demonstrations" characteristic of much of Polish tourism in the postwar period.[61] For example, the 1959 rajd commemorated the fifteenth anniversary of People's Poland and was to lead the tourists around the "place of bloody battles with bands of Ukrainian nationalists as well as the place of death of General Walter-Świerczewski."[62]

This Friendship Rajd was far from the only tourist event that commemorated General Karol ("Walter") Świerczewski.[63] He proved to be an ideal martyr to the communist internationalist cause—People's Poland's communist martyr par excellence. The basic biography of this son of the working class reflected both the internationalist and communist qualities that the new Polish regime sought to propagate. A communist already in the interwar period, Świerczewski fought in the Spanish Civil War on the side of the communists, under the nom de guerre "Walter," and was immortalized in Hemingway's For Whom the Bell Tolls. He subsequently served in both Soviet and Polish armies.[64] Świerczewski was appointed deputy minister of defense in the new Polish socialist regime.

After his death, Świerczewski was brought into postwar Polish lives in various ways. Streets, schools, and factories were named after the general, whose cult—it was hoped—would supplant that of Marshal Józef Piłsudski from the interwar years.[65] Świerczewski's biography made it to the silver screen twice. A two-part film entitled *Soldier of Victory*, directed by Wanda

Jakubowska, was released in 1953. In 1959 one of the officers involved in the Bieszczady in the 1940s, the communist Jan Gerhard, wrote a novel, *Łuny w Bieszczadach*, that essentially shaped the Polish reading public's knowledge of the battles with the UPA in the Bieszczady. Universally read at that time as a straight historical account, the book proved so popular that it came out in a dozen editions before 1989, and only two years after its initial publication it was turned into the film *Sergeant Kaleń*.

Świerczewski perished in the Bieszczady Mountains, at Jabłonki, on March 28, 1947, felled by bullets fired by members of the UPA, fighters who in postwar Polish lore were termed alternately "bandits" and "fascists."[66] While Poles of a certain age may remember him as "a man who did not bow before bullets," he was also depicted as the internationalist "symbol of revolutionary battle for freedom in our time."[67] The communist authorities did what they could to turn the heavy-drinking and not very successful general into a model citizen of the Polish People's Republic, one who "fought for a Poland ruled by workers and peasants."[68]

The Bieszczady village of Jabłonki was henceforth connected with the person of Świerczewski. Although an obelisk was erected there already in the year he died, it was replaced by a more permanent monument, a pedestal on which rose an enormous stone topped with a stylized metal eagle, unveiled with much fanfare on July 15, 1962.[69] The fifteen hundred persons present were told, "We have gathered here at the place of the heroic death of a great patriot, the illustrious son of the Polish working class." A soldier, he gave his life "in the battle with the dark forces of fascism—in the name of the great question of the socialist future of our Fatherland."[70] Although not exactly a vacation escape of the more restful sort, this highland site would figure prominently in organized Polish mass tourism in the Bieszczady, with busloads of tourists from across the country brought to commemorate the death of Świerczewski and the triumph of People's Poland over fascism.[71] One wonders to what extent the fostering of memory of these heroics was designed to displace the memory of the Polish underground Home Army's exploits fighting the Nazis during World War II.

These fascist-fighting, socialism-building characteristics were an important component of the image of the Bieszczady—and Poland—that the regime sought to propagate. Jabłonki functioned as the ideological key, even as the proper socialist gateway, to the Bieszczady. That is why the 1960s also saw the blazing of a "freedom" trail named after Świerczewski, which ran from Wysoki Dział through Jabłonki and Łopiennik to Smerek.[72] The trailblazers notably used red and white paint—Polish national colors—in

FIGURE 9.1.   A visit to the Świerczewski monument in Jabłonki in the 1970s. Photo from the collection of the editorial board of *Wierchy*.

marking the trail. Although the color red could also be seen as communist, here the intent seemed to be to identify this communist (internationalist) martyr with the fight for Polish independence. In another combination of postwar socialism and nationalism, Świerczewski was also to become part of the daily currency—literally: the fifty-zloty bill was emblazoned with the general's likeness.

❧ CHAPTER 10

Tourism for the Masses

Bieszczady tourism with a socialist face was only one kind of tourism in People's Poland—and not the most popular kind. Once the socialist state turned its attention to tourism more broadly, it claimed tourism should be for the masses, not just for the elites—which is what the regime averred had been the only kind of tourism in Poland before the war.[1] With his finger on the pulse of the Stalinist regime—and striving to keep the his tourist yearbook *Wierchy* in line with Stalinist currents in Poland—Władysław Krygowski wrote as early as 1949 of "mountains for everyone" in People's Poland.[2] The mountains were to regenerate the strength of working-class comrades—of the new socialist man. But was the working class ready to face the challenges of the mountains?

A story related by a member of the propaganda office of the Central Committee of the Polish United Workers' Party on the new mass tourism suggests some of the pitfalls the regime faced.[3] Zbigniew Kulczycki admitted that qualified tourism was the "most advantageous, most valuable," for health, body, and mind.[4] Yet there were different ways of providing such opportunities to the masses—some better than others. Kulczycki himself had witnessed an unforgettable scene during a trip to the Bieszczady circa 1961. A tour bus from the Silesian city of Katowice (in the west of Poland) arrived in Ustrzyki Górne, one of the most remote villages of the region—a jumping-off point for serious hiking. It deposited its cargo and drove off. The tour guide then gathered the tourists together and told them that they were going to hike to the alpine meadow known as the Caryńska połonina and the village of Berehy Górne; the bus would meet them upon their return.

Kulczycki was horrified. That was a full four hours' hike. The tourists had no idea what they had got themselves into. Women were in high heels and all wore regular street clothes. It started to rain during their hike, so they were soaking wet for the all-night ride home. This was, exclaimed Kulczycki, "qualified tourism in unqualified execution."[5]

The Orbis tourist bureau, the bus driver, and tour guide had the right idea: give workers a taste of the mountains; let these Silesians from the most polluted corner of Poland breathe the fresh highland air.[6] But this particular experience was bound to discourage them from ever coming back to the Bieszczady—or from ever attempting a hike in the mountains again.

As this anecdote indicates, qualified mass tourism may have been an oxymoron in the late 1950s and early 1960s, a time when workers had not yet had any exposure to the culture of hiking or mountain tourism. Rather, the toiling masses were more immediately able to profit from unqualified tourism, given that few members of the working class had ever experienced mountains or even other less trying vacation sites. This tension between types of tourism—especially between qualified and unqualified tourism—would stretch to near breaking point in the Bieszczady in the years to come.

Projections for the future of the Bieszczady were only beginning to take shape at this time. The first major state plan for the development of the Bieszczady was presented only in 1959, half a decade after the border zone had been opened.[7] Tourism was hardly uppermost in the minds of the country's socialist planners. Dancing around in their heads were visions of modern technological progress in the highlands: gigantic lumber mills, great dams producing hydroelectric power, large state farms.[8] These would transform the Bieszczady and southeastern Poland from the most backward and lightly populated region of the state into something more in keeping with the image the authorities sought to project. Perhaps it should come as no surprise, then, that the planned investment in tourism foreseen in 1959— 15 million zloty for the construction of huts in Komańcza, Cisna, Ustrzyki Górne, and Stuposiany as well as a tourist center in Jabłonki—was not even begun during the five-year period in which it was to be completed.[9] (While that may sound like a lot of money, much more was directed toward agricultural settlements: total investment in the Bieszczady region was to amount to about 2.5 billion zloty.)[10]

Even the two biggest investment projects in the region—projects that would catapult tourism in the Bieszczady to unheard-of and unimagined heights—were designed not with tourism in mind at all. These were the construction of the dams and hydroelectric power plants at Myczkowce (completed in 1962) and Solina (120 megawatts strong, completed in 1968) as well as two highway loops that cut through the highland region (dating from 1962 and 1969).[11]

Building the Bieszczady

The way these projects were completed tells much about how the socialist state functioned, as well as how it harnessed nature for its own ends, while suggesting that it took its cues from "Big Brother" next door. This infrastructure was built at significant cost to the country but was considered worth the investment by those at the top, who clearly manifested what Loren Graham has called "gusher psychology," choosing investment in big splashy projects over a more measured and long-term approach to the utilization of the country's resources.[12] Under the slogan "building the Bieszczady," workers, laboring as well as living under extreme conditions, raced to complete the regime's mammoth projects. The workers' hotels were drafty, bug-infested barracks; the men had to make do with whatever the canteen could scrounge up for meals, there being no nearby stores; and those building roads had to clear great swaths of land while working in the ubiquitous mud and rain in the summer and often impassable snow in the winter. Shades of the "brute force technology" seen in the Soviet development in the Urals (among other places) were employed in Bieszczady: more than fifteen hundred miles of roads were to crisscross the mountain region, making it possible to exploit the region's natural resources—timber, stone—as well as build the hydroelectric power plants.[13]

These jobs were true hardship posts, as the state gave little thought to the needs of the workers. The only way to gain cadres was by promising more money—the wages were nearly double that in the lowlands. The peasants attracted to this hard physical labor sought to earn enough to buy more livestock for their farms or replace their wooden cottages with ones of brick. Their numbers had to be augmented by soldiers and inmates from local jails. The top-heavy bureaucracy sought to imbue the workers with socialist ideals as well as a sense of mission—and urgency: the construction teams were in constant competition with one another. This also led to the administration often inflating the numbers, in order to ensure that bonuses were given.[14]

The offspring of "technological hubris married to state power," the Solina dam was the biggest of the communist regime's projects in the Bieszczady.[15] Built over the space of eight years, it cost a whopping 1.5 billion zloty.

The communist authorities demonstrated little understanding for the needs of the nearly three thousand residents of the fertile San Valley being displaced by the dam and reservoir, which occupied more than eight square miles.[16] (This was part of the northernmost reaches of the Bieszczady, an area more densely settled than most of the region.) The inhabitants of the villages suffered the indignity of being required by the state to dismantle their own buildings themselves. Peremptorily sentenced to "disappear on the command of authority," a historic church in Wołkowyja was dynamited, its pastor kept under house arrest until the job could be done.[17]

As historian David Blackbourn has noted, the human domination of nature speaks volumes about the nature of human domination, so evident in the case of the Bieszczady's—and Poland's—modern transformation.[18] Nothing was to get in the way of the enormous project. It ultimately produced a reservoir that held over 600,000,000 cubic yards of water and—more importantly for the development of tourism—had nearly 100 miles of shoreline, if one featuring backwaters.[19]

Transforming Tourism

Both reservoirs and highway loops would prove important for the region's economic development and for its use by tourists. Designed to facilitate access to forests for the deficit-running lumber industry, the first highway loop marked a sea change in the Bieszczady. The new, nearly one-hundred-mile-long, road made a previously inaccessible region easier to reach, especially for persons who were not inclined to march for several days on foot from the nearest railway station.[20] Now any tourist could penetrate the heart of the region in only a day's hike from the highway, which one could traverse by bus or by car. The second, smaller highway loop encircled the Solina dam, making accessible this enormous man-made lake. The dams at Myczkowce and Solina had the unanticipated effect of producing picturesque reservoirs on the stunningly beautiful San River. These artificial lakes were places where the Polish masses longed to spend a summer's day—although originally no permission was granted by the authorities to swim, sail, approach, or photograph this new feat of engineering.[21]

The construction of the Solina and Myczkowce dams refocused some of the tourist experience of the Bieszczady from high in the mountains to the vicinity of the reservoirs. The push for highland tourism on the part of Polish citizens, as well as the authorities' grudging acceptance of the fact that tourism could be a moneymaking venture, led to the transformation of housing for construction workers near the dams into (rather ugly) vacation hotels, some of which—such as those in Polańczyk—were the property of specific Polish factories, industries, or unions. This reflected the needs of a relatively new socialist phenomenon: that of *wczasy pracownicze*, or organized, company-sponsored vacations away from home for workers.[22] This was a true form of tourism for the masses. No familiarity with hiking, its etiquette, or indeed physical conditioning was required. Given that a particular workplace owned or had access to the vacation site, no particular planning was required of the vacationers. Both room and board were provided, and vacationers could behave as had earlier generations of guests at spas or health resorts, something that Wojciech Młynarski sang about in the late 1960s (one of his hits was "Jesteśmy na wczasach"—We're on vacation). They could socialize and drink all day, or simply lie in the sun and breathe in fresh air.

Or relatively fresh. For this kind of tourism in the Bieszczady has also been dubbed "exhaust fumes- and alcohol-fueled tourism."[23] This reflects two major pillars of mass tourism: the ubiquity of alcohol consumption by the vacationing workers, and the rise of the automobile in Poland. These developments in the Bieszczady came to pass just as Poland was beginning

Figure 10.1 A group of tourists fording a Bieszczady stream (already occupied by two cars). Photo by Zbigniew Żochowski, from the collection of the editorial board of *Wierchy*.

to be motorized in the 1960s (although it was still before the mass production of that car for the masses, the Fiat 126, in the early 1970s).

Once Poles had automobiles, they were free to engage in another activity for holidays: camping. The highway loops brought tourists all the way into the mountains. A dearth of organized campsites resulted in a proliferation of "wild" camps, with deleterious results for the highland ecology: Poles parked, camped, and hiked wherever they fancied.[24] Given the lack of hiking culture among much of Polish society, this could be disastrous. Trash was a perennial problem. There were Poles who went on hiking excursions or bus tours of the region drunk, much to the disgust of their guides—or else they hiked simply to get from one tavern to the next.[25] Poles with automobiles drove inebriated along the highway loops, with the obvious results: automobile accidents and further devastation of the landscape. That this was a local problem is also reflected in the fact that, at nine bottles of spirit per resident per year, the Bieszczady region had the highest alcohol consumption in Poland.[26] Reportedly most of the truck drivers working in the Bieszczady coped with difficult working conditions by being in a constant drunken stupor.[27]

"Wild West" Tourism under State Socialism

Only in the early 1960s does one begin to find some degree of recognition of the value of tourism on the part of the state.[28] Yet, instead of putting a premium on qualified tourism, with its need for only a bare minimum of tourist infrastructure, the central authorities' vision was related to their desire to make money off foreigners with hard currency.[29] They assumed that only the proper touristic infrastructure—hotels, spas, ski lifts, etc.—would bring these foreigners to the Bieszczady or satisfy the vacation/leisure needs of the Polish masses. In the mid-1960s some tourism activists like Wilhelm Dębicki likewise imagined the Bieszczady as predisposed to become a "tourism-resort basin" (zagłębia turystyczno-uzdrowiskowego)—a phrase redolent of Poland's coal basins, if now carrying healthful connotations. More than that: what was needed, he maintained, was to transform the region into "a gigantic Swiss-style resort."[30]

Such expectations proved problematic for People's Poland. As of the mid-1960s, over a million vacationers annually were interested in what the Bieszczady had to offer.[31] Demand for highland vacations during the 1960s and first half of the 1970s, the heyday of Bieszczady tourism, was infinitely greater than the supply of hotel rooms, campsites, and provisions.[32] This resulted in even mass tourists often roughing it.[33] There was simply no way for People's

Poland, with its command economy, to catch up, let alone keep up, with the demand. In a way, tourists in the Polish Bieszczady found themselves somewhat like the pioneers of old, struggling to secure a place for themselves to spend the night or rustle up provisions. Sometimes, even when goods were within reach, the locals simply refused to sell them to outsiders.[34] Such an encounter could lead to fisticuffs, as the frustrated tourists, hot and hungry, grappled with the obstinate salesclerk in their quest for loaves of bread or bottles of lemon-flavored soda.

Romance, Respite, and Renegades

The Bieszczady were a social as well as a natural phenomenon.[35] We have already noted the presence of foresters and lumberjacks, border guards and security police. Hard-drinking peasants turned workers or lumpen proletariat who could not find work elsewhere, even boys from the Volunteer Work Detachments helped to build roads and short-gauge railways or fell trees. A steadier population included more qualified workers who built the dams or directed the road work. Farmers had to work hard to reclaim the overgrown hardscrabble land; one scholar has written that the extreme conditions under which Bieszczady homesteaders lived had turned them into a "different—that is, extremely apprehensive and uncooperative— kind of species," not easily malleable for the purposes of socialist engineering, which itself was ineptly implemented by the state authorities.[36] Bieszczady society was fragmented, diverse, economically differentiated, isolated, and recalcitrant, the regime incapable of harnessing the human element, all its efforts focused on exploiting the natural resources in this out-of-the-way place.

Off-putting to some, the wild nature of this remote corner of the country attracted more educated individuals. Some of Poland's best polytechnics and universities supplied engineers and technical experts, at least a few of whom had a deeper interest in the region. The daughter of historian Paweł Jasienica, engineer Ewa Beynar, helped to build the Solina reservoir over a period of seven years, preferring work in the Bieszczady—which she already knew as a member of the Student Club of Beskid Guides—to an office job. During this period, she and other guides would meet on their one day off a week to climb the mountains, most often gathering at the hut on Ustrzyki Górne run by Maria and Kazimierz Hartman.[37]

Among the Sunday mountaineers were Bronisław Bremer and his wife Miśka (Elżbieta Misiak-Bremer).[38] No strangers to the Bieszczady, they had been active members of the Student Club of Beskid Guides—Bronisław later elevated to the level of honorary member.[39] Upon finishing his studies in 1963, he eschewed academia to build various roads through the difficult terrain of the Bieszczady, battling nature as well as human nature in the form of hard-drinking manual laborers. The civil engineer also miraculously managed to change the course of the Hoczew-Czarna road (part of the little highway loop) to bypass the ancient linden trees in Polana—this quite an accomplishment when so few remnants of the past were spared. No less well known in tourist circles, Miśka, an electrician by training, also soon worked for the road work company and subsequently ran the decrepit former barrack that passed for a PTTK tourist hut in Wetlina.[40] Like Beynar and her husband Olgierd Czeczott, they were also active in the volunteer mountain search and rescue organization (GOPR) that operated in the Bieszczady. The Bremers' son was born in the mountain region. Their lives combined a true tourist's love of the Bieszczady with a desire to live there under the less than deluxe conditions that prevailed. Miśka once gave an interview in which she said she had no wish to exchange her rough hut in Wetlina for a four-person (M-4) apartment in Warsaw.[41] That said, the upheavals of 1968 in Poland— the same year that the Solina project was completed—brought some of them back to the country's capital, even if they continued their work with GOPR for decades to come.

Coming out of the Warsaw mountaineering milieu, the Bremers and their colleagues from the Polytechnic may have been attracted by the sublime nature and touristic possibilities of the Bieszczady. But other citizens of the Polish People's Republic (PRL) imagined the Bieszczady as a true Polish "Wild West." Not just the film *Rancho Texas* (or later films) but also Poland's "real" cowboys attracted the attention of Poles far and wide. Witness the career of Poland's most famous cowboy, Henryk Victorini, whose fame actually predated the film. Although he grew up in Krosno, his family hailed from the former eastern borderlands, perhaps making him less rooted than most. In 1957 Victorini set off with fellow veterinary student Mariusz Merski to the Bieszczady to pasture cattle for a State Agricultural Farm (PGR). That same year a photojournalistic piece on the two cowboys was published in the popular weekly *Przekrój*. It seized the imagination of many a young urban Pole, longing to "experience a real fairytale, wild, primitive, and at the same time beautiful."[42] Many of them would travel to the Bieszczady to try to emulate this attractively free lifestyle. Cementing his fame, Victorini subsequently served not only as inspiration for the screenplay but also as a stuntman for the leading man in the 1959 film *Rancho Texas*. This "first Polish cowboy," Victorini ultimately settled in the Bieszczady for good on his own ranch, becoming a legend in his own time.[43]

Not only did the lavish *Przekrój* spread advertise and romanticize the Bieszczady, there were numerous other articles, films, television programs, newsreels, and songs that over the decades contributed to the mystique of the Polish wilderness.[44] In 1966 the student hut at Łopiennik was featured in a memorable newsreel, with New Year's Eve revelers dancing the polonaise and enjoying a campfire in the snow.[45] Jerzy Hoffman's 1969 silver screen version of Henryk Sienkiewicz's swashbuckling historical novel *Pan Wołodyjowski* was filmed in the Bieszczady. Even the pop singer Wojciech Młynarski claimed to have found there the answer to every young man's problems. The gendered nature of the 1966 song "Just Head Out to the Bieszczady" reflected a place where there were always infinitely more men than women while implying that the cowboy would attract members of the opposite sex.

The Bieszczady Mountains were also a place where one could escape one's troubles—if in the process acquiring others. Many of the "romantics" who sought to make a living in the Bieszczady found its stingy nature an insurmountable challenge. Only those who could stand the distance from the comforts of civilization had an easier time. "Pioneers" is how they were known, and how they would come to think of themselves.[46] Despite the government's blessing (and, in a number of cases, loans), it was hard to make a go of it from scratch. Farmers would have to clear the brush before being able to sow, while also building their own houses and barns, there being little extant in the region. Nor did Greek communist refugees, who were settled in Krościenko and Liskowate, have it easy, although they may have been the only successful commune in the Polish People's Republic.[47] While early on there was opportunistic settling in villages with buildings still standing, few Polish farmers preferred this difficult, mountainous terrain to what was to be had in Poland's newly acquired west.

The central authorities came up with various schemes—mostly unsuccessful—designed to resettle and develop the region. Despite at one point offering incentives of long-term credits to Bieszczady settlers, the authorities ultimately favored peasants with large landholdings, leaving the smallholders without access to assistance, in the process alienating those less well off. The 1950s and 1960s, thus, were characterized by "lawlessness, reluctant local bureaucrats, intergroup rivalry and intimidation."[48] Hard-pressed to attract the "right" kind of people to the hardscrabble Bieszczady, the state never was able to repopulate the region as it wished. Even the large-scale State Agricultural Farms—the regime's pet form of agricultural enterprise—in places such as Nowy Łupków, Olszanica, Uherce, Smolnik, Stuposiany, and Średnia Wieś were staffed by inmates of local prisons.

The authorities tried other experiments as well. As historian Bianca Hoenig has demonstrated, the expulsion of the region's East Slavs from the Polish Carpathians turns out to have served yet another purpose of the socialist authorities: to populate the Bieszczady region with Tatra highlanders who were overgrazing the highland meadows further west where the future Tatra National Park (established in 1954) was to be.[49] From the early 1950s highlanders and their sheep were seasonal guests in the Bieszczady. The Tatra highlanders constructed shacks for themselves and continued their traditional way of life, milking the sheep and making the cheeses for which they were famous as well as selling some of their surplus to workers in the region, for whom dairy products were a rarity.[50] Yet, despite pressure from the authorities, these highland shepherds from Podhale could not be convinced to settle in the Bieszczady permanently, preferring life in their own mountains, the Tatras, over this wild territory they often referred to as "Ukraine."[51]

There was one tiny segment of the already tiny population of the Bieszczady that was frowned on by Polish officialdom. It consisted of what might be termed the antipioneers, those who disappeared into the remote yet expansive wilderness not to build socialist Poland but to escape its strictures. In the early days of Bieszczady tourism, the moniker for such was CHBC (pronounced hah-beh-tseh): "characteristic Bieszczady person"—the unconventional type of person attracted to, and found in, this remote region.[52] These wild men (the vast majority were men) have also been labeled "zakapiorze," essentially, bums or freeloaders, as they escaped into the wilds in part to avoid being regular, productive members of society in the Polish People's Republic.[53]

The quintessential Bieszczady bum was the hard-drinking Władek Nadobta. An orphan from the Hutsul region, after the war he ended up in Silesia but longed for mountains. Nadobta sought to live independently— that is, independently of everything but vodka. As his biographer explained, this freeloader survived by selling the riches of the Bieszczady forests, which he gathered in seasonal fashion. He went from collecting the antlers shed by stags, to catching trout in the streams, to gathering berries and mushrooms, finally in the winter hiring himself out for work in the forest, which got him temporary housing in a barrack.[54] Other bums, such as Piotr "the Frenchman," would frequent student tourist bases such as the one at Łopiennik. Some more artistically inclined Bieszczady residents carved wooden sculptures to sell. Could it be that for not holding down steady state jobs, these Bieszczady bums—renegades, misfits, some fugitives from the law, all chafing at the socialist bit—were among the freest men in Poland?

With time, such individuals became legendary. Nadobta, as well as several other Bieszczady originals, inspired Wojtek Bellon of the band Wolna Grupa Bukowina to compose a ballad in his honor. Bellon too was passionate about the Bieszczady—and other—mountains, even becoming a volunteer rescuer.[55] He and his hugely popular band won awards at various Polish competitions of tourist and student songs in the 1970s, bringing Majster Bieda (Master Poverty, his nickname for Władek Nadobta) and the mountains closer to Polish youth in particular, who sang these and other songs around countless campfires. Yet this would be even more true of the 1980s than the 1970s, to which we return.

Poland's "Wild East" was very much a place where people could go to try their luck in challenging frontier conditions or to disappear into the wild in relative anonymity. It was also a "mountain Eden" for the Polish hiking community, both of the prewar and the new (student) kind, which discovered the new wilderness for their compatriots—this at a time when the priorities of the state were not to preserve but to build the Bieszczady.[56] The desire of the authorities to imbue their favorite form of tourism, mass tourism, with a decided socialist content and purposefulness—to create, as Diane Koenker labeled it in the case of the Soviet Union, a "proletarian tourism"[57]—only resonated so far with the broader public. It was not the new monuments in concrete, the Friendship Rajdy, or commemorations of Świerczewski that excited vacationing Poles in the early postwar period, although they did undergird the foundations of the postwar regime. Rather, the vast majority of Poles who made the southeastward trek sought to avail themselves of what made the Bieszczady Mountains unique: the wildness of it all. Whether "roughing it" or relaxing, Poles sought to escape the socialist quotidian and bask in highland freedom.

The secondary wilderness that was the Bieszczady after World War II and Operation Vistula had more than its share of diversity, if not of the kind it had known prior to the war. With the encouragement of the regime, farmers, foresters, shepherds, workers, border guards, prisoners, even Greek communists peopled the Bieszczady, if only lightly, some of them coming in (many temporarily) for the higher earnings and "Bieszczady bonus." Into this crucible went other categories of Poles. Bums and dreamers, misfits and hippies, lovers of nature, poets and artists, borderland rebels and true originals, all self-reliant and above all freedom-loving, were drawn to the wild expanses of the Bieszczady—a region that seemed to serve as a relief valve for the still young state-socialist country. The remoteness and thinly settled nature of the region made it a prime destination for those who sought to escape the strictures of People's Poland.

The fate of the newly wild region in the young postwar state was far from certain. Would it serve the purposes of highland tourism, offering fresh air, refreshing waters, lush forests, and beautiful vistas to vacationing hikers, just as the Eastern Carpathians had in the interwar period? Or would the Bieszczady become increasingly tamed in accordance with the communist injunction to develop large-scale agribusiness and industry throughout the realm, to turn wilderness into productive land? Was it possible to achieve a "happy medium" in the Polish People's Republic?

§ CHAPTER 11

Battling for the Soul of the Bieszczady

The 1970s would be of crucial importance for the Bieszczady. The demand for tourism would rise exponentially: by 1977, more than 5 million vacationers would visit the greater Bieszczady region annually. The pressure on the mountains and foothills of Poland's southeastern corner, as well as on the country's tourist infrastructure, only increased. At the same time, the decade would witness the entry of the Bieszczady into the national discourse. New players would strive to direct the region's development—or lack of—in accordance with their own futuristic plans. Campaigns were waged in the public sphere on behalf of a certain vision of tourism, ecology, and modernity in the highland region. A power struggle of sorts over the nature of the Bieszczady ensued. "The embrace of tourism triggers a contest for the soul of a place," historian of the American West Hal K. Rothman has argued.[1] In a way, what transpired would be a battle for the soul not only of the Bieszczady, but of Poland itself.

At the end of the 1960s, nature conservation made the headlines. In 1969 the secretary general of the United Nations, U Thant, had initiated a global discussion about nature preservation. The world was facing an environmental crisis; mankind had to acknowledge that there were limits on the biosphere and take responsibility for nature.[2] These ideas reverberated behind the Iron Curtain as well. Poland created a committee for the protection of the natural environment, and the country's journalists and youth came to take a particular interest in this issue.[3] A sense emerged globally that there was less and less true wilderness left, especially in countries that were highly industrialized. That made the remaining untouched land all the more precious—and, thus, in need of preservation.

Poles might have sat back complacently. After all, they had the Bieszczady, a seemingly endless wilderness, one of the only wildernesses left in Europe. Yet how wild were the mountains, given the developments of the 1950s and 1960s, the roads and reservoirs? And how would the next decades affect the shape of this unusual terrain, which in the space of several decades had already undergone incredible transformation from being an overlooked and overpopulated backwater to a newly minted "wilderness" nearly devoid of human presence? The pendulum seemed to be swinging back again.

Development Dilemma?

This was not a period when Poles would sit passively and accept the arrangements made for them by the authorities. A change at the top ultimately fostered discussion of the future of the Bieszczady.[4] The Polish United Workers' Party (PZPR) gained a new leader in Edward Gierek, who came to power in the last days of 1970. Gierek had some new ideas about the future of the Polish People's Republic and at any rate had promised to improve the material conditions of his compatriots. During his stint as first secretary, Gierek began to provide more much-needed consumer goods. He also initiated a propaganda of success. A more charismatic leader than his predecessor, Gierek famously claimed that "Poland was to grow in strength and [its] people live in prosperity," and he came up with the slogan "A Pole Can Do It."

Gierek had spent much of his early years in Western Europe, an experience that shaped him in some ways. It may have inclined him as new head of the PZPR to change the state's policy of closed borders. Within a year, the Polish People's Republic allowed its citizens to travel out of the country, to the West (if they could get visas) as well as to the East. Some set off with backpacks to explore the natural beauty of the countries they visited. This opening of the border proved eye-opening. Experiences hiking abroad provided Polish trekkers with different models of development, which affected the way they thought about their own Bieszczady. These travelers were formulating a critical, more informed, stance toward what they saw happening back at home. In the process, they had to contend with a certain fuzziness of concepts in use in socialist Poland.

From the outset, varied conceptions abounded of the highland region, Poland's wildest, even as a tourist destination. These ultimately depended on the type of "tourism" (*turystyka*) envisaged—of which there were many, given the ambiguity of the word in Polish. On one end of the spectrum, tourism reflected the historic use of the term to connote those traveling on foot—in this case, genuine hard-core hikers/trekkers who carried all they needed on their backs and sought to escape civilization.[5] On the other, tourism was equated with the comforts of full room and board for the duration of a cherished break from the socialist quotidian. As we have seen, tourism could be socialist, qualified, or unqualified. Yet the most significant type of tourism during this period was mass tourism, the opportunity for Poland's workers to take a much-needed break from their jobs. This was part of the promise of the regime to its citizens, a concept that for many was originally quite foreign—the masses had not been accustomed to vacationing—but with time became an expected aspect of their lives in the Polish People's Republic. The question of how to indulge this universal desire for a restful break in the lap of nature without exerting undue pressure on the natural landscape was increasingly more pertinent.

The way the regime sought to cope was through what in Polish was termed *zagospodarowanie*, a hard-to-translate word conveying a sense of bringing land into cultivation or use, or of bringing order to or establishing a household. One might render it as the "reclaiming" or "developing" of the highland region: for what purpose and to what extent remained to be determined. The need for zagospodarowanie was something that the postwar regime as well as many advocates of tourism in the Bieszczady agreed on. The latter thought the Bieszczady needed to be "(re)claimed" (or perhaps even "developed," to a limited extent) for tourism. While the communist authorities preferred to create from this wilderness a much tamer, more economically productive entity, with time they too wrote rather awkwardly of its "reclamation/development for the purpose of the regeneration of the strengths of the human being" ("zagospodarowanie dla celów odnowy sił człowieka").[6]

The communist authorities saw nothing oxymoronic in the phrase "touristic zagospodarowanie." And there need not have been, not even for the most die-hard conservationists, if the type of reclamation or development were limited to the construction of the occasional hut or trail. Yet that was not how the regime understood the phrase. Indeed, in an earlier project of a law on that very subject, the authorities responsible for tourism in Poland defined it as composed of two parts. First, it encompassed "the protection and the correct utilization of the scenic [*krajoznawczych*] and rest facilities, localities, land and water routes as well as regions in which tourist movement is concentrated." Yet it also concerned "the correct equipping of tourist localities and territories as well as the roads [*arterii komunikacyjnych*] leading to them" with the proper accommodations, restaurants, forms of transportation and other facilities connected with tourism.[7] Much hinged on the adjective *correct*. What was right for the Bieszczady? Given the special nature of this corner of the Polish People's Republic, it need not have been what was "correct" for other parts of the country.

"We Are Rediscovering the Bieszczady"

A unique opportunity presented itself in 1972. Before that point, no piece of the Bieszczady had been designated as park or preserve. That spring the provincial authorities in Rzeszów established the awkwardly named Eastern Beskid Area of Protected Landscape (Wschodniobeskidzki Obszar Chronionego Krajobrazu). The designated area of protected landscape reportedly comprised some 70 percent of the Bieszczady, including the region of the reservoirs—this was a broad definition of the mountain region.[8] That was not the only change forthcoming. Later that year an overhaul of the country's administrative units led to the creation of a separate Bieszczady administrative district (*powiat*), with its capital in Lesko. Extending from the Soviet border to Komańcza, this biggest district in People's Poland was reportedly established so as to create better conditions for the further economic development of the region, in particular tourism, while at the same time satisfying the economic and cultural needs of those who lived there.[9]

The promise of a greater focus on tourism and nature preservation inspired students and scholars at the Warsaw Polytechnic, who wished to ensure that the regime would take these commitments seriously. A student activist involved with the school's weekly *Politechnik* had been approached for help in the new district, even offered a responsible position there.[10] After consulting with members of the Student Club of Beskid Guides and others interested in the Bieszczady, including sounding out people in the highland periphery as well as authorities in Warsaw, the editors of *Politechnik* announced a journalistic campaign (*akcja*) under the slogan "We Are Rediscovering the Bieszczady" ("Odkrywamy powtórnie Bieszczady").[11]

From the pages of the popular paper of the country's polytechnic schools, with its weekly print run of ten thousand copies, comes a real sense of what it meant to discover—to "rediscover"—the mountains.[12] In no uncertain terms the periodical—well enough regarded by professional journalists that, in the next years, its student writers could officially train to join their ranks—was turning the attention of broader society toward the Bieszczady and advancing a campaign for action, with a distinct vision of its own for the highland realm.[13]

The editorial board, headed by editor-in-chief Andrzej Ziemski and his deputy Janusz Rygielski, sketched out a program for long-term touristic development of the mountain region, which they hoped the Bieszczady District authorities would implement. It was not "all the same" for what the Bieszczady would be earmarked: the editors voted for what they saw as the most appropriate category of tourism (here, understood, but not stated, to be individual, qualified tourism) that would allow the Bieszczady, a "unique region in Europe [whose] fame and future" depends on the "preservation and even the development" of the "primeval character of the landscape," to thrive.[14]

They saw the Bieszczady, still heavily understaffed, in the view of the authorities, as a perfect place for youth activism and work, whether during vacation time or more permanently: "The Bieszczady should not be a place of exile, a land of compulsory labor." Young, engaged, educated cadres—artists and architects, tourist guides, scientists, and more—could contribute to the region's development; they would be won over if the state would let them help to develop the plans. After all, students had been popularizing the region for nearly two decades and wished to preserve it. "Today, when the Bieszczady District has been established, and when the need to resign from misbegotten aspirations of industrializing this region in favor of the development of tourism has become clear, we want to go further." Not only should students work in the realms of scientific research and tourism: they proposed to establish a grassroots council (Społeczna Rada Programowa) under the local authorities as well as a Bieszczady Society (Towarzystwo Bieszczadzkie) or publication devoted to shaping and developing a vision for the region. The editors concluded this opening salvo by asking all those interested in this campaign/operation to publish on the pages of *Politechnik*.

Over the next months, many did.[15] Most important, the outline program was fleshed out by Jacek Mazur and his colleague Rygielski, who was not only deputy editor but also an op-ed columnist of *Politechnik* as well as a true mover-and-shaker in the campaign.[16] Hitting on themes sounded by earlier writers, the authors of "A Moment of Justified Fantasy" proposed to develop the region in a "maverick way" and "with a long-term perspective, understanding that an area lacking certain elements of civilization can become a great attraction on our urbanized continent." While speaking, as did the communists, of the "regeneration of the strengths of the working people," Mazur and Rygielski maintained that much of the region would be for those "desiring to rest and prepared for rest in direct contact with nature." To that end they proposed what Rygielski would later term a "functional division of the mountains"—separate zones for the individual tourist and mass tourist.[17]

The former zone, the main focus of the article, was what the authors called a Tourist/Trekking Preserve (Rezerwat Turystyczny), an idea that had first surfaced in the interwar period in the Eastern Carpathians but which now was applied to the Bieszczady.[18] Reserved for the individual tourist who would traverse the region on foot, bicycle, or horse, the preserve would contain a handful of tourist bases, huts, and shelters and only one marked, main Carpathian trail, hikers free to trek and camp as they saw fit—with an eye to nature conservation. Justifying their vision, the authors of the project saw themselves as having a "unique, unrepeatable chance to create . . . a testing ground [poligon] for scientific research on nature and tourism, to give a place of physical and psychological rest to hundreds of thousands of people exhausted by civilization."[19]

Mazur and Rygielski delineated a closed-off territory for the tourist preserve—access to which would be accorded those in possession of an annual entrance card, which would be given to members of the Bieszczady Society, scientists, doctors, and militia—running south of a line drawn from Komańcza through Terka and Stuposiany to the Soviet border. These were the mountains proper, in a territory also containing a number of settlements (including Wetlina and Cisna), part of the large highway loop, and the Bieszczady National Park. (The project for the last of these—a tiny, twenty-three-square mile park—had already been submitted to the Council of Ministers).

The preserve was to be a region free of cars—or, more precisely, of tourists in cars. The Politechnik plan would allow a shuttle bus from Jabłonki to Stuposiany on the piece of the highway loop that found itself within the bounds of the preserve. According to this "fantasy," the inhabitants of the preserve would foresightedly be given special credits to purchase automobiles so that they could easily exit the region to satisfy their needs: "Thanks to the model means of treating the south of the Bieszczady, the program of scientific investigation, and culture-creating function of the region, the average education and living standard of the locals must rise."[20] These, in turn, should keep the locals from demanding more "civilization" in the mountains.

From the accompanying map, one can see that the border of the tourist preserve was cleverly—carefully—drawn to satisfy various constituencies. While the overall shape of the preserve was that of a broad rectangle, there were places where the northern, developed region projected into the rectangle. For example, the road to Jabłonki and its environs would remain open to development—a good thing for those interested in keeping the memory of General Karol Świerczewski alive. The stretch of the large highway loop that ran from Ustrzyki Dolne to Stuposiany would likewise be accessible to all; one imagines that a bus would course along that north-south route, bringing

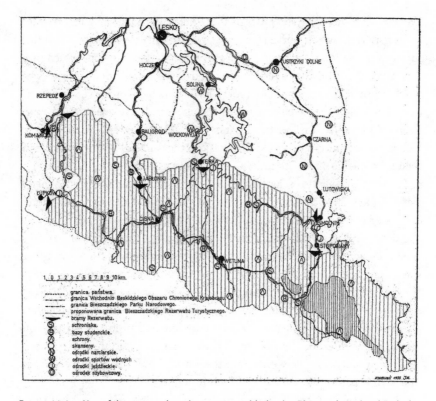

FIGURE 11.1. Map of the proposed tourist preserve, with the tiny Bieszczady National Park also marked. First published in Jacek Mazur and Janusz Rygielski, "Chwila uzasadnionej fantazji," *Politechnik* 18 (6 May 1973): 3. From the collection of Janusz Rygielski.

hikers to one of the seven projected entrance gates and vacationers to other destinations. With a border running from Komańcza eastward, the tourist preserve nonetheless covered the entire extent of what might be termed the upper Bieszczady—the heart of the mountain region.

The existence of the tourist preserve was expected to cause an increase in value of the regions located on its borders (including Solina, Komańcza, Baligród, Ustrzyki Dolne, and Lesko, as well as the entire region of the reservoirs), making them more attractive locations for European-level health resorts, hotels, and the type of tourist infrastructure that would appeal to the more sedate vacationer. The authors of the project also expected more and more people—foreigners as well as Poles—to seek direct contact with nature in the tourist preserve as an antidote to an increasingly industrialized world. Some aspects of the plan were downright futuristic for People's

Poland. All the localities near the entrances to the preserve were expected to have the types of stores and facilities that would make the preparation of the individual qualified tourists much easier. In addition, the designers of this project thought there should be the option for hikers to rent equipment at one site and return it at another. All told, the proximity of the two zones, the wild south and developed north, would be "an experiment that will allow us to avoid the standard type of development of recreational territories and go to a future-oriented model, anticipating the needs of twenty-first-century man."[21]

Parallels to the era of Tytus Chałubiński and Stanisław Witkiewicz a century earlier were drawn. This was not just about discovering a peaceful corner for those desirous of rest, a place where the landscape and fresh air would be the sole attractions. With its beauty and uniqueness, the Bieszczady region was envisaged as becoming a "source of cultural values" for the Polish nation, the existence of this fascinating nature and atypical sociological phenomenon awakening an intellectual current such as the one "connected with the Tatras, Zakopane folklore, and the Tatra region (Podtatrzem)." Echoing the opening salvo of "We Are Rediscovering the Bieszczady," with its mention of the mountains' "culture-creating role," the article's emphasis on the potential for human creativity was unmistakable. Might not the Bieszczady inspire a new, modern Polish intelligentsia to create a new intellectual current, much as the discovery of the Tatras had a century earlier?

There were other ideas connected to culture that suggested a leading role for the Poles in the realm of individual tourism. The authors of the article declared, "The means of treating the Bieszczady region should be an example of Polish culture mattering on an international scale." They also launched the ambitious idea of the tourist preserve connecting with similar preserves on the Soviet and Slovak sides of the border to facilitate transnational trekking. This idea was perhaps not so farfetched: during the interwar period there had existed such an arrangement in the Hutsul region, with zones of both Poland and Czechoslovakia open to the individual tourist. Yet in the postwar period, the borders between the "brotherly socialist nations" had become less porous, more "alienated" (to use the parlance of US borderlands scholar Oscar J. Martinez), than in the interwar period.[22]

Where things also differed in case of the Bieszczady is that mountain activists proclaimed not a discovery but rather a "rediscovery." Those behind the rediscovery did not clarify which earlier discovery or discoveries might be the students' point of departure. Was the campaign meant to be a response to the still coagulating plans of the authorities for the region, the first—and never realized—iteration of which had emerged in 1959? Or to the earlier generation that thought that the Bieszczady should become "a basin of health" or even "a gigantic Swiss-style resort"?[23] Or, possibly, to the still earlier work of Krygowski and Moskała, who had blazed the first postwar trail through the newly discovered wilderness in 1952–53? Or might this be a reference to the students' own forebears, who had founded the various hiking clubs?[24] After all, one group of guides from the Student Club of Beskid Guides responded to the campaign by declaring, "We students were the pioneers of the discovery of the Bieszczady and today we have the civic responsibility to save them."[25] Theirs was a different take on "pioneers" than the regime's: those who had settled in the region and sought to develop it. Yet another student mountain activist would say that they had proposed a "'repeated discovery of the Bieszczady,'" so that those who traveled there in a decade or so might still discover them.[26]

The campaign quickly extended beyond the world of the polytechnics. Many nonacademics published on the pages of *Politechnik*, underscoring that the idea of a tourist preserve as well as the special needs of the Bieszczady had resonance. These included individuals such as hiking activist Władysław Krygowski, who eloquently seconded (firsted?) the notion: "When I tore my way—literally—through thickets and pits, flowering hillsides and clouds of birds springing up out from under my feet, captivated by this paradise on earth, I dreamed of creating a real nature park, without the counterproductive administration and interference of man, in which one could backpack in completely primeval, paradisiacal conditions, camp in a difficult and dangerous, masculine, trek."[27] Krygowski labeled the call to preserve the Bieszczady not conservative or elitist (which is what the regime had maintained individual tourism was) but rather progressive—as, he argued, had been the case of the Tatras, now a national park. In this same vein Janusz Rygielski also fleshed out the idea, presented in earlier *Politechnik* pieces, that they needed to create a "countermovement" to the pressure to subdivide the Bieszczady into plots on which various factories would build vacation centers for their workers. The Bieszczady were not to be parceled out into "manors" that would echo the old serf economy, but rather should remain accessible to anyone who respected nature.[28]

Many of the articles that first came out in *Politechnik* were republished in the periodical *Połoniny* (*vel Połonina*). The student mountain guides behind that publication seconded the idea of creating a Society of Friends of the Bieszczady (Towarzystwo Przyjaciół Bieszczadów, called simply the Bieszczady Society in *Politechnik*'s opening salvo), with a seat in either Lesko or Sanok. It would help to educate the population about the Bieszczady as well as raise the level of hiking culture in the country, in this way cultivating what was best in the tradition of prewar Polish alpine clubs and local studies associations. The guides likewise proposed that the yearbook *Połoniny*, published since 1971 by the Student Club of Beskid Guides, become, with the proper financial support, the official newspaper of the proposed society.[29]

And students had experiences in the field on which they could build. It was thought that the Association of Polish Students should become "patrons" of various Bieszczady localities, as they had become for Komańcza already in 1971. There they had been allowed to engage in scientific research, create an inventory of springs, blaze trails, and work on other projects the locals suggested, while also turning a former pearling mill into a student tourist hut for themselves and holding a summer fair.[30] The respected mountain guide Witold St. Michałowski, who had been a moving force behind this arrangement with Komańcza, furthermore argued that student architects should create for the Bieszczady a unique style based on existing folk style, much as Witkiewicz had done for the Tatras, a reference he himself made.[31] Student artists and architects were already being asked to submit designs for bus stops in the Bieszczady—a chance to engage in the culture creation so near and dear to the hearts of those behind the rediscovery.[32]

The year of the centennial of Polish highland tourism—the centennial of the discovery of the Tatras by Doctor Tytus Chałubiński—appeared to be a good moment for a new generation of Poles to reflect on the state of the country's highland wilderness. The students and their allies were excited by the opportunity the blank slate of the Bieszczady presented. Janusz Rygielski underscored that it was not only the sole place where youth could work and relax; it also presented the sole opportunity in Poland to shape the vision of a region from zero.[33] Well, almost from zero, the region still being imagined as pristine wilderness despite all the evidence to the contrary. Yet, with the project of what one enthusiast called a "super-strict ultra-reserve of peace and quiet, protecting nature and man," the preserve's advocates demonstrated that they were ahead of their time.[34]

Counterproposals

Perhaps it should come as no surprise that, even in Gierek's Poland, this independently formulated plan, this "justified fantasizing," was met with indirect opprobrium on the part of the central authorities.[35] The official put-down came in the form of an article written by three journalists associated with the major Polish weekly *Polityka*. They saw fit to label those in support of the tourist preserve "the Bieszczady radical left, a (luckily) unorganized group of fanatics."[36] Doubtless the fact that young scholars were the first to raise the issue made it easier for such invective to be employed. That the advocates of the tourist preserve had the support of some serious personages, including Krygowski, did not seem to make any difference.

Instead, the triumvirate of journalists proceeded to present their own modernistic project for the Bieszczady—their own "justified fantasizing." The region would become an "experimental plot [*poletko*] for a new, dynamic, and well-functioning social policy."[37] By this they meant creating a system to ensure that all existing and future accommodations in the Bieszczady were used to the full. The triumvirate fantasized about a computerized system run by the Workers' Vacation Fund to keep track of places in the various vacation houses so that individuals throughout Poland could choose where to stay and would not be limited to the choice offered by their place of employment.[38] The *Polityka* triumvirate was against restrictions being placed on who could vacation in the Bieszczady, while agreeing that the southernmost part should be protected. The central part of the Bieszczady was to be open to development, suggesting that the borders drawn by the "radical left" were too generous to qualified tourists.

A similarly cavalier attitude toward nature preservation was forthcoming in a major Warsaw newspaper. The mocking tone of a series of articles in *Życie Warszawy* (Warsaw Life)—"Schopenhauer on Ordynacka Street," "Babbling about the Bieszczady," and "Cows Don't Bother Butterflies"—suggests that the students' initiative was not taken seriously by their elders.[39] That said, the dispute over the fate of the Bieszczady played itself out over the next year or so on the pages of countless periodicals, even on radio and television, where a number of advocates of the tourist preserve appeared.[40] A heated and well-attended meeting of participants to the discussion took place in Warsaw, with those on the students' side convinced they had won the debate.[41]

Ultimately both sides ended up unmoved. Each side saw in the Bieszczady its own projection of the future that it was loath to relinquish. The difference, as reflected in the initial dispute, boiled down to one of access to the mountains. While the students and their allies wished to ensure that only qualified tourists had access to the upper reaches of the Bieszczady, the *Polityka* journalists and their allies were more concerned about the organization and rationalization of mass tourism or the economic zagospodarowanie of the Bieszczady.

Such was the reaction on the part of those two Warsaw papers. An early, semiofficial response from the Bieszczady region itself was the hurried creation of a counterorganization to the as yet not established Bieszczady Society. A Society of Bieszczady Development (Towarzystwo Rozwoju Bieszczadów) was reportedly founded on March 5–6, 1973, precisely when the

"Moment of Justified Fantasizing" article came out.[42] Here the word *development* was key, as this vision saw room for continued logging, expanded animal husbandry, and the pouring of concrete wherever settlers dwelled. The organizers hoped to co-opt students, suggested that only then would they pass from the world of ideas into the concrete world (no pun intended) of the Bieszczady; yet this new organization did not seem very active on the ground.[43] Still, it claimed the credit for organizing a competition for Bieszczady settlers to write their reminiscences of life in the Bieszczady, under the telling rubric "My Part in the Development of the Bieszczady." The winners were published in a volume no less tellingly entitled *Pioneers.*[44]

Local Voices

Who had the right to determine the fate of the Bieszczady region? Whose voices amid society—if, under state socialism, any—should be given preference? Tensions rose between the advocates of the tourist preserve and those living in the southeast of the country. Some of the Rzeszów (provincial) press thought that advocates of the tourist preserve were interfering in something that they had no right to disturb. They bristled at the claims of discovery of part of the region where they lived and worked. And what about the actual residents of the Bieszczady, those living in settlements such as Wetlina and Cisna: did not their opinions count for more than those of occasional visitors? What of their efforts, and the efforts of the socialist regime, over the years to "build the Bieszczady," to settle and try to tame the wild terrain?

What was needed, thought some locals interviewed by journalists from *Kultura*, was to bring the various localities up to the national norm, complete with restaurants and movie theaters. As one farmer put it, "Could one live one's whole life like a tourist?"[45] By the word *tourist* Maria Tetera of Michniowiec clearly had in mind the no-frills, backpack-wearing kind, not the kind of vacationer that frequented Polańczyk and Solina. Other residents of the Bieszczady were ambitious for their region and thought locals should have a say in how it was to develop. Militia sergeant Henryk Suszek of Lutowiska averred, "All of Poland will vacation here in the future." He envisaged a hotel in Ustrzyki like the gigantic Hotel Forum in Warsaw and lots of big parking lots. An advocate of group tourism, the sergeant saw no place for the tourist who wanted to hike in the Bieszczady by himself (and make trouble, in his view): "No entrance for the individual tourist."[46] So much for the efforts of the tourist preserve planners, who had foreseen private automobiles for the local population—not that any local voices remarked on that. (It is unlikely that many—if any—of them read *Politechnik.*)

Of course, residents of the Bieszczady were not all against the project or something like it. Some had come to the region for its beauty and wildness and wanted it to stay that way. They deplored the higgledy-piggledy construction that had taken place there. If new vacation houses had to be built, they opined, let it be in Solina, which was already made ugly by the vacation houses on the perimeter of the reservoir.[47] More than one expected Ustrzyki Dolne or Lesko might turn into a Zakopane, which by this time was frequented by millions of tourists annually. That of course would not have been out of keeping with the students' plan for a tourist preserve: developers would have carte blanche to develop the region north of the preserve, which is where these towns, the reservoirs, and the small highway loop lay. But again, the term *Bieszczady* was all-encompassing and undifferentiated for some, for whom the region began as far north as Sanok—well out of the frame of the map of the tourist preserve.

Not all locals appreciated the uniqueness of the Bieszczady, although those who had traveled abroad seemed to.[48] For many, life remained hard and primitive. Some did not see the region's beauty. "There are no vistas here," claimed a resident of Wołosate—right in the wildest part of the Bieszczady.[49] They thought the Bieszczady needed to be turned into a civilized place. Some did not expect that enough tourists would come to the tourist preserve. As one resident of Stuposiany observed, one of her neighbors went hiking every weekend and had yet to see a tourist.[50] This was yet another argument for development that would bring this corner of Poland up to the level of the rest of the country.

Could students and their allies affect the development of an entire, if remote, district in a country where decisions tended to be dictated (not to mention financed) from on high, where additionally many locals—the pioneers—did not see eye to eye with them? Control over the fate of the Bieszczady seemed to be in the thrall of those who still thought in terms of the 1950s' push for development at all costs. The local authorities, with whom some of the editors met, did not seem interested in earmarking a corner of the Bieszczady for the qualified tourist. Reaching out to a different readership, Rygielski emphasized however that this was not a generational matter, of youth against their elders: "There exists a united front of those who know what is good tourism, healthy and formative, particularly necessary in an age of intense industrialization and environmental threat—against the advocates of building up recreational territories, intent on transmogrifying cultural values into profits from the sale of services."[51] At the same time, he sought more allies among Polish youth, while reminding his readers that, according to the VII Plenum of the Central Committee of the PZPR, environmental protection was a task allotted them.[52] He and his allies found some among the Socialist Union of Polish Students (SZSP), who began working out a program for its members in the development of the Bieszczady.[53]

With dozens of articles and op-eds in a number of periodicals, the "We Are Rediscovering the Bieszczady" campaign initiated what without a doubt was the biggest spontaneous journalistic undertaking of that period. Despite an early tone of disinterested—if enthusiastic—engagement, criticism of what was being done in the Bieszczady by the regime also made its way onto the pages of *Politechnik*. Writers criticized the Bieszczady style of (concrete) construction, the relentless logging of the region, even declared the Bieszczady to be a "nightmare"—the last a photo reportage on the disaster that was the Eastern Beskid Area of Protected Landscape, an area protected only on paper.[54]

Had the students gone too far? Even before these critical pieces came out, the "student republic" in the Bieszczady came under question. In late March 1973, the students' hut in Komańcza (where all their hiking equipment was stored) burned down under suspicious circumstances, suggesting that not everyone found such student involvement in the Bieszczady palatable.[55] Could it have been also because they disapproved of the students' concern for what traces remained of Lemko material culture, even to the extent of purchasing and renovating a Lemko cottage as a little museum of sorts?[56] Their relationship with the local Lemko population (such as it was at that time) might not have set well with the authorities, who had hoped to Polonize the highland borderland.

Although the fire did not stop students from being involved in the Bieszczady, it did limit what they could do: construct an occasional shelter or take on projects desired by the local authorities.[57] Most other projects forthcoming from the students and their allies would be hamstrung by the authorities. This included art historian Olgierd Łotoczko's fascinating, (paradoxically) award-winning project of renovating the Greek Catholic church at Łopienka, together with a collection of East Slavic cottages, to be part of a tourist village and center for tourism. For his pains Łotoczko was put under surveillance by the security service, his idée-fixe not realized during the period of state socialism.[58]

It is worth noting that the advocates of the tourist preserve were in no way a political opposition: at least some of its advocates were, or would become, members of the PZPR.[59] All were working, as they saw fit, within the system, to shape the Poland of the future—their future. In this, the Bieszczady Mountain region was the lynchpin, much as the Tatras had been for Stanisław Witkiewicz some seventy years earlier. The Bieszczady were the "experimental laboratory" that would demonstrate what kind of a Poland the still young postwar state was to be.[60] Was it to be a country that put stock in preserving the inimitable natural beauty of the former Lemko and Boiko territory, that demonstrated understanding of the uniqueness that was the Bieszczady and knew how to preserve and nurture it in keeping with modern ideas of nature conservation? Or was it to be one that sought to make a backward region modern in a different way, to transform "Poland B" (second-class Poland) by creating all the trappings of Soviet-style industrialism and development—gigantic factories, large state farms, and a tourist infrastructure that penetrated all but the tiniest scrap of wilderness? At stake was the very nature of the state.

State-Socialist Experiments in the Bieszczady

With the exception of the inspired (from on high) responses in the Warsaw press, the central authorities did not deign to respond to the students' initiative, nor, likely, did they care what the local population—the pioneers—thought. Perhaps they were too busy developing counterprojects, their own hubristic highland experiments. In March 1973 the communist authorities had passed further legislation regarding the development of the Bieszczady for the next five-year plan, in which the construction of a gigantic lumber mill complex in Ustianowa, to the northeast of the Solina reservoir, figured.[61] The highland region already had a sizeable lumber mill at Rzepedź, on the western edge of the Bieszczady, named after General Karol Świerczewski.[62] But the communist authorities determined that the Bieszczady needed another lumber mill—a bigger and better one. Located on the site of a prewar hangar for glider planes, the mammoth lumber mill complex in Ustianowa would house a number of separate factories, all united by the need for the same raw material: it was to process more than 3.5 million square feet of wood annually.[63] This was the regime's biggest, most ambitious project of this kind in the Bieszczady—if one that would prove ill thought out and ill-suited to its localization, which lacked a reliable source of water, ultimately to be pumped in from Solina. Furthermore, its appetite for lumber would make continued, aggressive logging in the Bieszczady a priority—and with it, the construction of additional roads, with more asphalt crisscrossing the wilderness. Despite the flaws of this grandiose plan—among other things, water runoff would pollute the area's source of drinking water—construction at Ustianowa began almost immediately.

A different Bieszczady experiment of the central authorities paid at least lip service to nature preservation. Five months after making public their plans for Ustianowa, the communist authorities announced the creation of the Bieszczady National Park (on August 4, 1973).[64] The name sounded more impressive than the park was in actuality. The tiny, twenty-three-square-mile park encompassed both forested terrain—land belonging to the forest district administrations of Stuposiany and Lutowiska—and poloninas (highland meadows), the latter coming from several mountain groups: Szeroki Wierch, Tarnica, Halicz, Rozsypaniec, Krzemień, Bukowe Berdo, and the Caryńska meadow, as well as the meadows on the mountain ridges from Rozsypaniec to Kińczyk Bukowski.[65] The oddly configured park was assembled piecemeal in a very stingy way, with the borders in places (as on the highland meadows) drawn above the tree line. Did that mean that the state reserved to itself the right to chop down those trees, right on the edge of the park? Furthermore, the territorial integrity of the park was broken by the large highway loop, the traffic along which would foul the air. All this made for a miniscule, irregularly shaped and somewhat senseless park, its shape and size proof of the authorities' reluctance to relinquish control of any patch of land that might have potential productive use. To add insult to injury, the authorities dragged their feet as to the official opening, claiming that certain organizational matters had to be taken care of first (including the construction of administrative buildings). In the meantime, a rock quarry functioned within the borders of the future park.[66] The socialist authorities seemed congenitally incapable of relinquishing anything that smacked of economic development. Such was the amount of attention paid to nature conservation by the highest authorities of the Polish People's Republic.

CHAPTER 12

Power, Ecology, and the Public Sphere

The authorities continued to realize their own vision in the region—not without help, being chronically low on manpower and short on funds. The help would come from a new quarter: the communist-inflected Union of Polish Scouting. The scouts were exhorted in summer 1973 by Prime Minister Piotr Jaroszewicz to take on the Bieszczady over the next decade in an operation entitled "Bieszczady-40," the "40" a reference to the end point of the endeavor: the fortieth anniversary of the Polish People's Republic in 1984.[1] The regime's answer to the less pliant, more independently minded university students, the scouts would build the Bieszczady according to specification.

The regime thought that the Bieszczady should be reclaimed, developed, and (re)populated. This meant that scouts would be put to work on the types of projects favored by the regime—forestry, agriculture, construction—with some room for tourism as well.[2] Concrete was poured at each of the twenty-three scout campsites, an adjacent twenty- to thirty-person tourist "hotel," and a tent camp for one hundred, complete with parking lot.[3] "Bieszczady-40" was essentially an opportunity for the state to add much-needed hands to the Bieszczady labor force while turning the country's older teenagers into new socialist men and women who saw and understood the importance of a developed Bieszczady for the state. Once again, the authorities sought to mold men as well as the mountains to their own liking. Scouts would get a taste of the Bieszczady—a heady taste of freedom for many, despite the hours of compulsory labor and the conditions of endless mud and rain—while contributing to the development of the region and learning about past Bieszczady heroics.[4]

The program turned out to have been subsidized at the local level, as the cost of the scouts' tours was greater than the effects of their labor.[5] One of the main goals of "Bieszczady-40"—which rarely fulfilled the "plan" of projected work-hours—was to produce cadres for the Bieszczady down the line and bring the region fully into the modern world.[6] In the course of participating in the operation, scouts would come to see that they were needed in the Bieszczady, while helping to build "the Socialist Poland of the future."[7] The tens of thousands of scouts who would come to work in the Bieszczady over the next years were treated as muddy miniature members of the socialist working class, "young shock workers" who might return there permanently.[8] And, for sure, some were bitten by the Bieszczady bug, given a whiff of freedom (and perhaps romance) as well as fresh air, which made the stay in the mountains more attractive and induced some to sign up for future tours—this despite the ideological side of the camps. Any lip service paid to scout self-government in the mountains, which was touted as an important component of the program, was belied by fact that the entire operation was dictated from above by the central authorities of the PZPR.[9]

"Bieszczady-40" was yet another component of the regime's approach to the country. It knew best what Poland was to be: a modern, socialist Poland. Doubtless all Poles wanted their state to be a full-fledged part of the modern world. The problem lay in the definition of modernity that prevailed in the Polish People's Republic. Modernity meant standardized, steel-and-concrete, oversized construction. This Poland in some ways seemed futuristic, in the sense that it moved entirely away from the nature-based regionalism of the interwar period, a regionalism that was grounded in the landscape and assumed that man was shaped by his environment. Here the land was seen as offering only territory for construction. Nature, insofar as it was noticed, was perceived as natural resources to be utilized fully by the new socialist regime.

Privatizing the Periphery

Given this overwhelming focus on "building the Bieszczady," one might be surprised to learn that not everyone at the top devalued the mountains' natural beauty. It turns out that the regime did understand the special nature of the Bieszczady, with its dense forests and plentiful wildlife. Furthermore, the regime apparently warmed to the idea of a closed-off preserve in the wildest part of the mountains. However, it was not to be made accessible to the individual tourist, as the student-proposed tourist preserve would have been, but rather reserved for the regime's own pleasure. All the other dachas and company-owned vacation homes paled by comparison with what was secretly done at Arłamów, Trójca, and—most crucial for the mountain region proper—Muczne.

In the early 1970s, the leaders of the party established a secret vacation center in Arłamów, a heavily forested region teeming with wildlife. (Not hikers, the communist leaders of Poland preferred to hunt on their vacations.) Called by the locals the "Red Principate," this was a place where Edward Gierek and those like him could go on "bison hunts such as have not been seen since the days of the Tarnowskis and the Potockis" (grand Polish noble families), according to Timothy Garton Ash.[10] No expenses were barred in the mammoth building's construction; even foreign specialists were brought in to ensure that the vacation house for the Council of Ministers contained the best that could be had. To ensure privacy, the government unceremoniously dispossessed the villagers in that area and sealed off access to the preserve, which amounted to nearly ninety square miles. Nor did they have respect for previous residents: Prime Minister Piotr Jaroszewicz commanded that a Greek Catholic church dating from 1763 be razed, together with its cemetery.[11]

Arłamów was run by the formidable and fearsome Colonel Kazimierz Doskoczyński.[12] It was he who conscripted Tatra highlanders to build four deluxe two-story villas at nearby Trójca for the private use of the communist bigwigs, and made sure the job was done in record time. No need to wait for supplies when the object under construction belonged to the Council of Ministers—although it should be noted that funds for the construction came out of the budget of the State Forests.[13] The first of many foreign guests to be entertained at the new facility, opened in 1973, was France's president, Valéry Giscard d'Estaing.[14]

Arłamów and Trójca lay near the northern reaches of the greater Bieszczady region. Squarely within the territory of the Bieszczady Mountains was a second secret vacation complex. The village of Muczne was located in the southeastern tip of the Bieszczady known as the "Pouch," which hugged the upper reaches of the San. Reportedly an official from the construction industry had boasted to Doskoczyński of the beauty of that area, leading the colonel to take a helicopter ride over it. In 1975, the Council of Ministers expropriated a workers' hotel that had just been built in Muczne, leaving the workers to find other accommodations, as the entire area would likewise be off limits. The hotel would be gutted and redone in a style befitting the communist elites, outfitted with top-of-the-line imported fixtures and hunting lodge accouterments. Few beyond the communist bigwigs and their guests would gain entrance or even learn of the existence of the secret vacation center, known by its codename "W-3." (It was the third such vacation spot for the Council of Ministers, behind Arłamów and a location in the Baltic region).[15] The communist leaders could fly in by helicopter or even airplane (an airstrip and helicopter pad were built expressly for that purpose).[16]

Foresters were instructed to take care of the wildlife in what was to become Europe's most exclusive hunting grounds.[17] Even the wooden architecture was in harmony with nature, unlike the concrete construction so prevalent in the region. It was as if the communist leadership had suddenly become the old Polish nobility or even royalty, known for its keen interest in hunting—although Hungary's nomenklatura was no less keen.[18] Prime Minister Piotr Jaroszewicz—the same man who had sent the scouts to work in the Bieszczady—was a particularly avid hunter. The party leadership entertained heads of state in Muczne as well as Arłamów. They came to shoot deer, foxes, wolves, bison (which had been reintroduced into the Bieszczady in 1963) and even bears, despite the latter being protected under law. While most of the hunters were Polish communist bigwigs and foreign heads of state, in the 1970s the occasional wealthy foreigner could also pay lavishly in hard currency for the right to shoot the animal of his choice—most often the exotic bison.[19]

Emboldened by the success of their private little fiefdom—paradoxically, about the size of the tourist preserve proposed by the students—the cream of the communist elites continued making over the Bieszczady region in their socialist-inflected, Polish nationalist likeness and image. In 1977 they changed the names of some 120 localities in southeastern Poland—names that suspiciously sounded Ruthenian/Ukrainian, Wallachian, Tatar, or Hungarian—to something that sounded more Polish.[20] Of these localities, some fifty were in the Bieszczady.

The decision appears to have come from the avid hunter Jaroszewicz, who marveled at the name Muczne, a locality where he spent a good deal of time. Having been told that there were other odd names in the Bieszczady, he reportedly told his interlocutors to "take care of it."[21] The regional officials took on the task to show that society desired the change and found some scholars to help them think up new monikers. Thus, some names were etymologically Polonized: Berezka became Brzózka, Smerek became Swierków. Others were replaced with unrelated Polish words or forms: Chrewt became Przystań, Dwerniczek became Jodłówka, Wołosate became Roztoka. Still others are harder to explain, as with Stuposiany, which inexplicably turned into Łukaszewicze. None, incidentally, seemed designed to commemorate the battles that had taken place in the Bieszczady, the type of renaming that Jan Gerhard had once advocated.[22] In an ironically personal twist, Muczne was transformed into Kazimierzowo—it was suspected, after the iron-fisted Kazimierz Doskoczyński, who ran the place.[23]

The toponymic overhaul did not, could not, pass unnoticed. Indeed, the outcry in opposition to this brazen abuse of power was loud, clear, and differentiated. The locals—who had not been consulted—hated to have to abandon names to which they had grown accustomed and bemoaned the outlay in new signage and stationery. Hikers and cartographers considered all the changes that would have to be introduced into maps and guidebooks. And Poland's literary, scholarly, and cultural elites, as well as other Poles who were sensitive to such things, decried the wiping away of these traces of the historical, colorful, and multiethnic past.[24] All to no avail: the name changes went into effect on October 1, 1977. The communists would not be moved.

The Dispute over the Bieszczady

The change in names did not take place in time for two proponents of the tourist preserve to discuss it in the first edition of their forthcoming book, which revisited the rediscovery of the Bieszczady of the earlier part of the decade.[25] Penned by Witold Michałowski and Janusz Rygielski, both Warsaw Polytechnic graduates, members of the Student Club of Beskid Guides, and experienced trekkers who had long advocated the tourist preserve, it was aptly entitled *The Dispute over the Bieszczady*. Michałowski and Rygielski had not given up hope that something might still be done in the region to protect the natural landscape and open a broad swath of the admittedly derivate wilderness to qualified tourists, while keeping more sedentary vacationers from planting themselves in the protected region. One motivation to write the book was the fact that, in 1975, the Bieszczady District had been abolished and a new administrative unit, the Krosno Province, created—the latter supposed to put a premium on tourism. Was the time ripe for a change in tack from the anything but harmonious "everything goes" approach that so far had prevailed?

Michałowski and Rygielski, who finished writing *The Dispute over the Bieszczady* in late 1976, laid out their arguments clearly and dispassionately. They continued to endorse what they now termed the "absolutely necessary functional division of the mountains" while underscoring that the piece of wilderness under consideration amounted to but 2 parts-per-thousand of the Polish People's Republic, a piece of territory that could never contribute much to the overall economy of the country.[26] Less idealistic than in 1973, Michałowski and Rygielski noted that the tourist preserve in the Bieszczady was not elitist or exclusionary: anyone who wanted to become a genuine qualified tourist could do so, but it required an expenditure of love, effort, and solicitude on their part. The mountains were not going to be fenced off—no more talk of access through a passport system—but rather needed to be developed (zagospodarowane), if in a profound and consequential way. In words echoed by many reviewers, the Bieszczady had to be "rescued so that there might still be in our country, on our earth a place where one can stand face to face with Nature."[27] Given the level of development in much of the rest of the Polish Carpathians, with their motels and parking lots, taverns and ski lifts, Michałowski and Rygielski hoped that the Bieszczady might not meet that fate.

Its singlemindedness and relevance praised in numerous reviews, The Dispute over the Bieszczady was called one of the most valuable books to come out that publishing season.[28] Many reviews cited longish excerpts of the book with approbation. These ringing endorsements conveyed the danger of continued development, whether haphazard or planned, in what was left of the Bieszczady wilderness. Also noted was that the book importantly continued the broader dispute over how to develop the country as well as over the model form of rest and relaxation.[29]

If only one could get a copy of it. Despite an initial release in the spring of 1979, the distribution of the book suddenly ceased. It turned out that seven thousand copies of the print run of ten thousand had been impounded in a warehouse on the orders of the first secretary of the Krosno Province.[30] Somehow the authors learned their book's fate, and news spread to reviewers, some of whom alluded to the difficulties with obtaining a copy of this "'stick stuck into an anthill.'"[31]

Yet the book's resonance was not limited to those who could get their hands on it. At the end of November 1979, a public discussion of The Dispute over the Bieszczady took place at a Warsaw bookstore (KMPiK na Ścianie Wschodniej). The Polish Radio's second station covered the discussion, its story subsequently rebroadcast, repeatedly, by student radio in Rzeszów.[32] One of the conclusions drawn from the Warsaw discussion was, paradoxically, that there is no dispute over the Bieszczady—clearly those present were convinced of the correctness of the authors' approach—but there is a dispute over whether a group of people can affect a decision of state bureaucrats.[33] Again, it was a brave book to publish at this time.

Third Time a Charm?

In Warsaw, creativity made the contents of *The Dispute over the Bieszczady* available: page after page had been plastered on the walls of the Warsaw Polytechnic so anyone could read it.[34] This may help to explain the next development in our saga of discovery: yet another journalistic campaign by a new generation of editors of *Politechnik*. Announced in February 1980, it was called "We Are Discovering the Bieszczady for a Third Time." This time around, the focus would be more ecological, pragmatic, and even more working class (that is, with a greater reach) than in previous iterations of discovery.

Laid out in several articles, the February arguments for reengaging with the mountains reviewed the history of interest in the Bieszczady and the initial 1972–74 discovery/dispute, which they proceeded to place in universal terms.[35] Eight years earlier they had sought visionary solutions to the Bieszczady's problems, when it became clear that the authorities were moving in a direction different from the global trend, which dictated that such remaining swaths of wilderness needed to be more protected than civilized. A consensus was forming that the natural world was shrinking, and that man increasingly wished to gain access to what remained. Since the dispute, the Geneva Convention, Helsinki Accords, and nature preservation had made the global news, while on a local level the Krosno Province was supposed to be a haven for tourism, a word still understood by students as a synonym for hiking. The latter wished to cooperate with the authorities in the Krosno Province in developing a farsighted program for the region.

Times had changed since the first secretary of the Bieszczady District Committee of the PZPR had said he was personally for the tourist preserve, but then prioritized other things.[36] The Society of Bieszczady Development and the regime's experiments, including the "Bieszczady-40" scouting operation, ultimately set the tone. But was the second discovery of the Bieszczady a failure? Certainly the book that immortalized it appeared to be having an effect. In a debate in the Sejm (parliament) over a projected law on environmental protection and formation at the beginning of December 1979, one of the parliamentarians spoke of the need for a functional division of the mountains, in this way echoing Michałowski and Rygielski. In this time of national belt tightening, given the country's economic straits, perhaps the slogan now proposed by Andrzej Ziemski, longtime editor-in-chief of *Politechnik*, could catch on: "A Lack of Investment Is the Best Investment."[37]

That the Bieszczady, nature conservation, and the model of tourism in the country were in the news was also due to the continued work of Rygielski in the public sphere.[38] He published article on article during this period, taking first prize for his publications in the area of "environmental formation and protection" (1979), later to be followed by one for tourism and local studies (1980).[39] Since his days as deputy editor of *Politechnik*, Rygielski had laid the groundwork for an authentic social movement. He decried the limitations placed on the individual tourist, the doing away with the tourist stations that enabled independent hikers to traverse the Carpathians, the forbidding of camping anywhere but the approved campgrounds along the large highway loop, the allowing (until 1977) of automobiles to drive into the forests where there were no roads.[40] A gadfly of sorts, in numerous op-ed columns he turned the readers' attention to fraud or senselessness within his country, to the paradoxes that characterized the coexistence of man and technology. Even before the dispute Rygielski understood the challenges presented, quipping that mountains are perhaps the best example of how man's fantasy and his knowledge of technology often do not serve progress and culture, instead giving birth to ideas and their implementation that not only were out of keeping with humanity but also simultaneously undermined the reason why their author was in the mountains in the first place.[41] In the spring of 1980, at the Polish Academy of Sciences in the Staszic Palace, Rygielski gave a public lecture on the provocative topic of whether there existed an overall conception for the development of the Bieszczady. Attended by more than sixty people, including many inhabitants of southeastern Poland, the lecture was followed by a question-and-answer period that lasted for well over three hours, such was the interest in the topic.[42]

Students and academics seemed to understand better than their elders the pitfalls and potential of state socialism. The authorities seemed to privilege short-term and particularistic gain while relegating to the background "the less quantifiable . . . higher values," which, in the words of Philippe Saint Marc quoted in one of the "third discovery" articles, had been counted among "the main tasks of the objectives of socialism."[43]

Those in power with their hands on the purse strings truly ruled, their whims turned into orders, with little thought about the long-term consequences. So many experiments had been tried in this challenging mountain region: the transhumance of the Tatra highlanders with their flocks, who preferred not to settle in the Bieszczady; the establishment of the Eastern Beskid Area of Protected Landscape that functioned only on paper and was increasingly covered in concrete; the "successful" lumber industry, which ravaged the region; the use of prisoners as a compulsory labor force on state agricultural farms; and the off-limits military-run secret hunting preserve in Muczne—about which hikers knew all too well (it even bravely received oblique mention in a letter to the editor). One writer bemoaned that the experimenters had not had to affix their signatures publicly to these mainly infelicitous ideas.[44]

Comeuppance

In mid-summer 1980 the "We Are Discovering the Bieszczady for the Third Time" campaign was very much ongoing. Consciousness had been raised among the *Politechnik* readership and beyond, with Janusz Rygielski even publishing an article on "being a tourist" in the influential weekly *Polityka*—the same periodical where his project of a tourist preserve had once been criticized.[45] Were times changing? Then came the August strikes along the seacoast, bringing in their wake the establishment of the independent and self-governing trade unions known as Solidarity.[46] The situation was so incredible that the publication of *Politechnik* ceased, not to resume until October—and then with a vengeance. The age of new possibilities was dawning, and the students and their allies were poised to take advantage. One could speak even more eloquently—as did literary scholar Jacek Kolbuszewski—about the fact that destroying individual tourism was destroying one of society's biggest achievements, that the cult of the native landscape had been a traditional value of Polish culture, and that stripping away the primeval quality of the Bieszczady would strip Polish culture of values that were created by the Poles themselves.[47] One could also speak more plainly about Doskoczyński and the fact that he could do anything with impunity.[48]

The same direct, even confident, tone on the part of Bieszczady activists could be detected at a public event that took place at the end of November in a Warsaw bookstore, with representatives from the region present. Earlier that month the impounded copies of *The Dispute over the Bieszczady* had finally been released for sale and evidently read. Instead of discussing the book at the event, the advocates of the tourist preserve confronted the provincial representatives. Rygielski declared that those present wished to create a Bieszczady Society as a pressure group within the ranks of the new Polish Ecology Club. He and his allies came with demands as well as questions. The nonplussed Krosno deputy governor, Wiesław Skałkowski, tried to mollify those present, announcing that the Krosno authorities wanted to award Rygielski and Michałowski a distinction for their service to the Krosno District (!). Yet the crowd of more than one hundred had not come to exchange niceties but rather to push the authorities, who had brutally put down their earlier campaign of 1972–74, to change their act. The activists demanded the right to rest and relaxation given in Article 69 of the Polish constitution, the right to do so in the form of individual tourism; they wanted to increase the Bieszczady National Park by a factor of ten and transform the regime's not so secret hunting preserve, which they noted was actually larger than the proposed tourist preserve, into such. On the defensive, but reluctantly admitting mistakes had been made, the authorities—some of whom ended up joining the new Bieszczady Society, founded that day—nonetheless claimed to have clean consciences.[49]

Despite both sides not seeing entirely eye to eye, the situation appeared to be changing—as was Polish society, emboldened by the Solidarity movement. Those at the head of the Polish United Workers' Party felt compelled to listen to workers now. Within several months even the central authorities, in the person of the deputy chair of the Main Tourism Committee in Warsaw, were instructing the local Krosno authorities to come up with a plan that would make room for qualified tourism and implement ideas taken from Michałowski and Rygielski.[50] By the end of July 1981 a plan for the Krosno Province had been formulated. It would be subdivided into zones (zespoły), the last of these being the Cisna-Lutowiska zone, which contained the Bieszczady National Park, its buffer zone, and the swath of territory long desired for the tourist preserve. That entire zone would be for tourism of the two-legged kind. In his letter to the Warsaw authorities the author of the project offered assurance that "the creation of this Zone liquidates the famous 'Dispute over the Bieszczady'—meeting the postulates of the tourist and ecological milieux and nature preservation."[51] The work of the past eight-plus years seemed to have paid off.

The response of the central authorities followed not only the Warsaw meeting but also another important development in the Bieszczady region: the creation of Rural Solidarity, a trade union for individual farmers in which Bieszczady village activists played a key role. In addition to advocating for the legalization of Rural Solidarity, these representatives of the community produced a list of demands of a more local nature. Among them was the restoration of the former names of Bieszczady villages and the publicizing of the Council of Minister's secret landholdings in Arłamów, Muczne, Caryńskie, and Wołosate.[52] Bieszczady residents had been outraged that funds earmarked for the improvement of the Bieszczady had been funneled into the government's vacation haven. Nor had they been happy to have foresters feed the wild animals, some of which—like wolves—wreaked havoc with their flocks. (Although they were to be given compensation for each lost animal, the money was often long in coming.)

The government was not eager to satisfy these demands and even wished to keep some of them secret. (While Bieszczady residents knew of the existence of Arłamów and Muczne, the entire country did not.) This led to the farmers organizing a strike: they occupied the town hall in Ustrzyki Dolne.[53] Things got so serious that, after fifteen days, the militia, secret police, and the feared motorized militia known as ZOMO were brought in to disperse the strikers, who nonetheless ended up leaving peacefully.[54]

That next month Rural Solidarity was legalized. In the interim, the strikers continued to hone and expand their demands, which would have repercussions for the fate of the Bieszczady. They sought to make their own lives, as farmers, easier and more comfortable. The strikers and their allies demanded that Arłamów be transformed into a sanatorium for the tubercular, that the Trójca buildings become vacation houses for invalids and retirees, that the workers' hotel in Muczne—that super-deluxe hotel for the cream of the communist elites—be returned to the foresters, and that lands under the control of the Council of Ministers be made available to farmers for acquisition.[55] In addition, the signed agreement freed farmers on land above 1,150 feet above sea level from paying the land tax, indirectly encouraging them build summerhouses rather than make a living from farming or animal husbandry.[56] The villagers sought to nix two planned museums—the Regional Museum in Hoczew and the Bieszczady Nature Museum in Ustrzyki Dolne—and transform the buildings into cultural centers.

Were these the best usages for the buildings and the land? The museums would have enriched the nation as a whole, while cultural centers provided only for the needs of the locals.[57] After the foresters moved into Muczne later that year, the luxurious building, with its fireplaces, chandeliers, and platinum wall sconces, which might have served as an exclusive vacation destination for a broader swath of Poles or hard-currency-paying foreign guests, was trashed during drunken brawls. Nor was there any talk of restoring the land formerly controlled by the Council of Ministers—much of it still pristine—to its former state or including it in the Bieszczady National Park. Had the campaigns of the previous decade had no resonance in the Bieszczady region?

Rural Solidarity was not good to the Bieszczady—the bieszczady with a small "b," the wild terrain that made the region so special.[58] To be sure, the region's toponyms were restored to their original form. But other salutary changes were not made. In essence, Rural Solidarity preempted any moves in the direction of nature conservation that might have been forthcoming from the broader Solidarity movement—efforts that might have considered the value of the Bieszczady and these landholdings for the nation as a whole.[59]

Could it be that the student activists, who had for so long fought to change things in the region, had won the battle but lost the war? No one representing their views had been on the ground in Ustrzyki Dolne during the negotiations. That surely is one main reason why their campaigns had not succeeded to date: they had lacked allies in the Bieszczady region itself, either among the "pioneers" or the authorities. These facts were not lost on one of *Politechnik*'s editors, Jan Bazyl Lipszyc, who analyzed the agreement to create Rural Solidarity. Entirely missing were any questions of nature preservation or the correct model and organization of tourism.

Not knowing that the authorities were beginning to think along these lines already that spring, Lipszyc said that he and the other activists would have to impress the importance of such matters on the local authorities, through means of the Bieszczady Society, which perforce must include locals as well. There would be compromises, he added, on what he saw as only the beginning of the road they would all have to travel; but tourism activists and conservationists needed to convince those in the periphery as well as the center of the uniqueness of the mountain region that was the Bieszczady, that it was not, nor should it become, just another piece of the country like the Kielce or Elbląg regions.[60]

That, unfortunately, is how the locals treated it—as just another inter-changeable piece of Polish real estate. A lack of the hiking culture so dear to the hearts of its Polish aficionados was all too palpable in the Bieszczady. Krygowski had once placed the onus on the Poles themselves: they needed "wisdom, in order to subjugate this land, love, in order to save its one-of-a-kind beauty."[61] Yet wisdom and love seemed to be in short supply—this despite the salutary return of the PTTK. Under socialism, it had devolved from a hiking and local studies society to a consumption-oriented provider of mammoth rajdy and sedentary vacations, but now returned to its origi-nal mandate, to take care of the needs of its 700,000 members, those recal-citrant individual tourists. In a letter to the Sejm of November 14, 1981, the PTTK leadership, including Janusz Rygielski who had just been elected deputy president, emphasized that the mountains were "an environment of uncommon natural and cultural qualities [*walory*], the protection of which serves the preservation of the identity of our nation and has an influence on the correct development of tourism."[62] These activists, too, were fighting for the soul of the nation.

These changes were part of the overhaul of Polish organizations and soci-ety during what turned out to be a mere fifteen months of at times exhaust-ing euphoria. One month after the PTTK meeting, Martial Law was declared by Wojciech Jaruzelski, in one person general secretary of the PZPR, head of state, and head of the military. What proceeded was a clampdown on society and its accouterments, including the flourishing free press. This sounded the death knell for *Politechnik* and countless other periodicals. Doubtless when

Lech Wałęsa came to the Bieszczady at the beginning of 1981 and tried to gain access to Muczne (his car was turned back) he did not expect that he would soon enough see these secret and exclusive properties. When Martial Law was declared, the Polish symbol of Solidarity was interned in Arłamów.[63]

The short period of Solidarity was too little for the changes in the Bieszczady, fought for so long in the process of discovering, to be implemented. How ironic that Rygielski's next book—memorably titled *By Fiat Up the Rysy* (Poland's highest mountain)—should come out the day after Martial Law was declared. His dream of Poland creating in the Bieszczady a "unique area in all of Europe for natural tourism" had not been realized.[64] During the Solidarity period he had already learned of one reason why. For there had been yet another, no less key reason to withhold the rest of the print run of a book promoting a tourist preserve in the Bieszczady: the central authorities had feared that a large uninhabited territory on the border with the Soviet Union could be a splendid spot for NATO parachutists.[65]

After the imposition of Martial Law, all talk of consolidating the functional division of the Bieszczady ceased. Indeed, although this topic cannot be developed here, the hare-brained megalomanic schemes of the Ustianowa lumber mill complex and the stinky pork- and mutton-producing industrial-agricultural conglomeration that was IGLOOPOL in the 1980s—truly shepherding on steroids—would continue to pollute the formerly pristine rivers and transform the landscape. Even scouting activities puttered on, despite the striking farmers' concerns about their activities, the regime refusing to resign from any of its pet projects/experiments. An additional edition of *The Dispute over the Bieszczady*, more necessary than ever, would be published in 1986. Yet, only after yet another important milestone, the heady year of 1989, would the fate of the Bieszczady take a different turn.

Whereas the Tatras had been "altars of freedom" several generations back, and the Hutsul region a wild and exotic land, the Bieszczady were all raw untrammeled nature, "a place"—as Jacek Kolbuszewski has written—"free from the inundation of cultural junk."[66] At least, so it had been in the early years after the war. The Bieszczady had been the place where modern hiking of the qualified type evolved—a place where modern man could traipse about, fully free. In the Gierek era, a new generation sought to create in the Bieszczady the kind of tourist infrastructure that would best serve a modern Poland. How could Poland "grow in strength and [its] people live in prosperity" if the air they breathed was polluted and even the most pristine corner of the country, the Bieszczady, could not escape concrete-and-steel development? Yet the regime turned a deaf ear on the well-intentioned projects of dedicated young cadres, those who "rediscovered the Bieszczady," who sought to protect the mountains from too much civilization.

While this disregard for nature preservation and sustainable tourism could be felt already earlier, it was especially true in the 1970s under the author of that slogan promising prosperity, Edward Gierek. His attempts at providing for scatterbrained hard-currency investments in heavy industry while simultaneously endeavoring to raise the Polish standard of living took the Polish economy to the brink. This while providing a little fiefdom for himself and the communist leadership in a part of the Bieszczady off limits to other citizens of the Polish People's Republic.

As the 1970s wore on, the nature of the postwar Polish state became all too clear. Nature counted for little. The multiethnic past counted for less. While lip service was paid to nature preservation and the healthier kinds of tourism, in practice the communist authorities clung to their outmoded Stalinist-era definitions of modernity. The only sign that they appreciated the natural beauty of the Bieszczady was evinced by their investment—misappropriating monies that had been earmarked for Bieszczady development—in places such as Arłamów and Muczne. Even then, the nature they most appreciated came in the form of trophies and rugs made of animal hides.

The "We Are Discovering the Bieszczady for a Third Time" campaign, sparked by the publication of The Dispute over the Bieszczady, anticipated the changes that could be wrought during the Solidarity period. For a brief moment, it seemed that the tourist preserve would be created, after all. Yet all hopes of transforming the Bieszczady into a haven for the individual tourist, defined as a genuine trekker, were lost after the declaration of Martial Law. Without Politechnik, there was no chance of another generation of students picking up the standard. Without Rygielski, who soon found himself with a one-way ticket to Australia, the war had lost a key general. In the 1981 yearbook Wierchy, the ever cautious Krygowski would publish a review of The Dispute in which the veteran hiking activist wrote that it was a "half-measure and, at that, a tardy" one.[67] Time had indeed been wasted, not to mention money: all this ultimately left the residents of the Bieszczady unsatisfied, the region's hiking enthusiasts disappointed, and much of the natural environment destroyed.

Within the decade, Poland would shed its socialist attire for a more avowedly capitalistic one in which private property claims, and not the public good, would gain precedence. New priorities turned Poles' attention elsewhere. That prompted Witold Michałowski to publish, by himself, what essentially was a third, expanded edition of The Dispute over the Bieszczady in 1993, with a foreword entitled "Against Stupidity."[68]

Conclusion

> In what is rooted the secret of these green hills,
> middling-old forests, and miserable weather? Why is
> it so easy to get the involvement of society in matters
> pertaining to them?
>
> —*Politechnik* editorial board

The questions posed by the *Politechnik* editors behind the "We Are Discovering the Bieszczady for the Third Time" campaign have not only accompanied us throughout this work of scholarship but also motivated it.[1] How has it been that so many Poles as well as some Ukrainians, both quintessentially lowland populations, have come to be captivated by the Carpathians? Here in these pages we have shown how various mountain ranges were discovered by a number of generations of lowlanders for their conationals. Some established and propagated a specific mode of mountain climbing or vacationing. Others presented the region and its people to the outside world in the form of exhibitions, excursions, events, and entertainment. In the wake of the discoveries, the challenging highland landscape became fashionable as well as familiar. More than that, since the days of Tytus Chałubiński, our first discoverer, mountains have become a peculiar Polish preoccupation.

A multifaceted approach to the Carpathians—the result of a unique blend of environmental history, borderland studies, tourism and leisure studies, together with aspects of political, social, and cultural history—has illuminated larger questions that transcend the mountains. How to construct a modern nation in the absence of independent state existence? How to shore up the frontiers of a new, fragile, and undeniably heterogeneous state in a world in which national self-determination was supposed to be the norm?

How to modernize in such a way so that places on this planet that provide respite from an increasingly industrialized world will be preserved for posterity?

This is foremost a story about how the remote, unfamiliar, and peripheral highland borderland moved to the center of attention for each generation of lowlanders, in the process becoming a recognizable and prized native landscape and major tourist destination, with many lowland tourists taking inspiration from the mountains to the extent that highland culture became an intrinsic part of national culture. Although on the margins, the mountains and their indigenous mountain peoples ultimately proved to be of interest to each ensuing regime, with responses ranging from curiosity to concern about how to control them. The Carpathians meant even more to the discoverers responsible for spreading word of the mountains. Uniquely utilized, these distant and relatively inaccessible mountain ranges of the Carpathians have been seen time and again as a workshop, field, or region where one could experiment, with the hopes that lessons learned could be extrapolated elsewhere. The experiments in the highland borderland were to help shape the future and resolve problems facing the generation of the discoverers and their allies. Each was sui generis, reflecting the different situations in which our protagonists found themselves.

In the final decades of the nineteenth century, after the failed insurrection of 1863–64 and the emancipation of the peasantry, Polish elites were concerned with not only the fate of their nation but the shape it was assuming during a period when there was no Polish state. The discovery of the Tatras and Zakopane was as if an answer to their prayers, both highlands and highlanders providing inspiration in numerous ways. Amid the "sleeping granite giants" that seemed to portend a brighter future for the nation, they could work out the parameters of the modern nation-in-the-making, one with room for lower-class highlanders as well as members of the lowland intelligentsia.[2] This encounter subsequently led Stanisław Witkiewicz to opine that there one would "be able to create an environment of higher aspirations and forms of life that will radiate out to the rest of [Polish] society."[3] The summer, and, later, winter, capital of a Poland of the mind held promise. It brought Poles from across the partitioned lands together, and gave hope that even lowland peasants might eventually rise to the level of their self-assured highland counterparts, thus helping to flesh out and reinforce not only a modern Polish nation but also a modern Polish culture in which the Tatras figured prominently.

Although less ambitious, Ukrainians, especially those from the Russian Empire, also sought to profit from what they found in "their" Carpathians, beautiful, remote, if prone to flooding. They were captivated and inspired by the Hutsuls, enough to write about them and even, in the case of Hnat Khotkevych, work with them. Although close to declaring discovery, albeit never in those words, during the various tours of the Hutsul Theater before the war broke out, Khotkevych did opine that "the Hutsul theater could create on the bosom of the Ukrainian theater an original and colorful phenomenon, no less interesting than the Sicilian theater in Italy or the Tirolean theater on the German stage."[4] For the most part, their strivings were limited to the cultural sphere, with the exception of the Ukrainian elites of Stanisławów/Stanïslaviv, who seemed to engage with the Hutsuls of Dora in order to turn them into nationally conscious Ukrainians, to keep them from what they saw as the pernicious influence of Galicia's non-Ukrainian elites, who created their own highland vacation destinations in places such as Jaremcze and Kosów.

In the interwar period, an overarching concern was for the integrity and security of the borders of the young and undeniably heterogeneous Second Polish Republic. Recall that Poles prior to the war had not embraced the Hutsuls in the same way as the Górale, retaining an old-fashioned approach in which the Polish elites of the Galician piedmont dominated the rest of the inhabitants of eastern Galicia, which remained quite pro-Habsburg in outlook. Now a new approach would be tried that involved outreach to the Hutsuls, investing in their region, and otherwise trying to put the Hutsuls into a larger Polish narrative via the World War I military connection that had brought Poles and Hutsuls together, ostensibly fighting for a common goal. Tadeusz Kasprzycki and his military colleagues expected that their (seemingly successful) engagement with the Hutsuls would gain them experience in dealing with Poland's minorities, which then could be put to use elsewhere in the state. The authorities strove to strengthen the sense of distinctiveness of the country's highlanders across the board in order to keep the Hutsuls, Boikos, and Lemkos from being Ukrainianized (and Silesian highlanders from being Germanized, although that aspect lies outside the scope of this book). A Poland of regions, with regions defined functionally rather than historically (again to keep highlanders in their place), was in the works. Those behind the Society of Friends of the Hutsul Region emphasized loyalty to the Polish state over nation, although under the rule of the Colonels, after the death of Marshal Józef Piłsudski, the tight skin of the nation was increasingly stretched over the unwieldy multiethnic state, which it was hoped would become more Polish over time. Others engaged in the discovery of the Hutsuls, such as Stanisław Vincenz, were much more faithful proponents of a Jagiellonian—a multiethnic and multidenominational—Poland, where all might live in harmony.

Those visions of past and future were lost to the post–World War II generation, which could only marvel at their elders' tales about the exotic wilderness of the Hutsul region. They had to make the best of the new, more homogeneous, nature of a state-socialist Poland, a country desperately trying to modernize after the fashion of the country's "Big Brother," the Soviet Union, and the derivate wilderness that was the Bieszczady Mountains. As interpreted by Poland's communists, modernization meant industrialization across the board. In the early 1970s, the younger generation became more attuned to questions of receding nature and the need to preserve and protect it, while not rejecting the idea of modernity. Intent on preserving a piece of the Bieszczady wilderness for posterity as well as for his and others' own trekking pleasure, Janusz Rygielski described the project of a tourist preserve in the Bieszczady as "an experiment that would permit us to avoid the standard type of development of recreational territories and to move toward a futuristic model, anticipating the needs of twenty-first-century man."[5] The Warsaw Polytechnic students and their supporters sought to create a Poland of the future in which there would be room for the natural as well as human environment, in which modern man could commune with nature. That their independent social movement that preceded the birth of Solidarity did not ultimately succeed—they came tantalizingly close—was due to the declaration of Martial Law and the return to the status quo ante (or worse) afterward. The window of opportunity in People's Poland seemingly had passed. What is clear is that, in the 1970s and early 1980s, Poles could find ways to promote their own interests in the public sphere and come up with their own visions of the future, even if they were at odds with those of the authorities—hardly the picture of a totalitarian state.

These episodes demonstrate that mountains could be discovered repeatedly, both in different ways and at different times, and later discoverers sometimes were oblivious to what had transpired earlier in the region. Each generation of discoverers was captivated by its own, still (or newly) wild segment of the mountains, so different from the familiar lowlands. What also emerges is that each discovery was meant to be a two-way street, bringing the highlands to the lowlands and the lowlands to the highlands—the periphery to the center and the center to the periphery. The highlands inspired each generation to think more creatively about that other, real life in the lowlands, to enrich it with elements of highland life. The fascination with the mountains led not only to the construction of a native-national landscape but also to much culture creation, as witnessed by all the literary and artistic works inspired by the encounter with highlands and highlanders.

Let us not forget the importance of the highlanders. Their very existence had been shaped by the harsh mountain conditions to such an extent that they pined for the highlands when forced to be in the lowlands, exhibiting an enviable oneness with nature. We have seen how, in the age of territoriality, their "primitiveness" could be praised, even idealized, as well as put to use culturally. This was obvious in the case of the Tatra highlanders, thought to be ur-Poles by, among others, Witkiewicz, who posited that "the mountain people, locked in the depths of the valleys, cut off from the world, ha[d] preserved longer than anywhere else the most ancient general form specific to the mountainous regions of Poland."[6] Their highland culture inspired his Zakopane Style, which was to spread throughout the Polish lands. The Hutsuls similarly became for Khotkevych "perhaps the only Slavic tribe that had preserved the patriarchal way of life and even pagan rites," which the writer sought to share with the world.[7] And no less a promoter than Vincenz considered the Hutsul region to be "the last island of a Slavic Atlantis." While this idealization of the highland peasant and highland ways was less obvious for the depopulated Bieszczady region, some students clearly were fascinated by Lemko and Boiko culture, as seen from their regional publications, Połoniny included. And one could argue that Olgierd Łotoczko's planned renovation and use of preexisting Lemko and Boiko buildings also would have presented them in idealized—sanitized—fashion.[8] The students and their allies were more open to the historical heterogeneity of the Polish lands than was the regime, which did much to erase signs of previous highland culture in the Bieszczady.

We have also seen how the highlanders were not as isolated as had been thought by many discoverers: they existed in a borderland realm where the two ideal-type worlds, "primitive" and "civilized," intersected. In other words, from the very outset the highland landscape was a mix of nature and culture. This was a world in which the wealth of the highlands—timber, ores, stone, oil, mineral water, fresh air—were at various times supplied to the lowlands, often thanks to the labor of the highlanders. In other words, while people maintained they were discovering the Carpathians, the highlands were already known: to the owners of highland demesnes, mines, and sawmills, and even to nobles more broadly who frequented these places in an earlier age. Recall how Vincenz's "Slavic Atlantis" as presented in his magnum opus, On the High Uplands, was peopled by his noble forebears, Jews, the occasional Armenian or Roma, as well as by Hutsuls.

This is why we need to consider what is meant by "discovering," a term used in each case, barring that of the Habsburg-inflected episodes in the Eastern Carpathians prior to 1914. The second and subsequent iterations of discovery were clearly informed by what had transpired in the Tatras, the discoverers wishing for similar success in their mountains of choice. The Tatras, thus, were the model to which each subsequent discovery related.

So, what was meant by "discovery," here in the nineteenth and twentieth centuries? In each case, what transpired was the purposeful popularizing of a region among like-minded or similarly inclined contemporaries (or those who might become similarly inclined). Discoveries were not made in a vacuum, just for the fun of it, but rather with a certain clientele in mind. The episodes of discovering discussed in this book were deliberate, public attempts on the part of engaged individuals and institutions to appropriate and reshape the region in question (imagined as part of their patrimony) as well as (re)populate it, at least seasonally, with sympathetic individuals, those who understood the value of the mountains for society or even humankind. We have seen how the intelligentsia of various nations, those for whom a certain vision of the nation and state was dear, the community of tater-niks, and qualified tourists all figured in this process. The discovery of the mountains inspired them in different ways as generation after generation adjusted its own outlook on life—past, present, and future—in response to the extraordinary qualities it found in the highlands and highlanders, shaped by an unforgiving climate and challenging conditions.

Having faced the challenges presented by the mountains, generations of discoverers were inspired to turn to the challenges of their lowland lives. Each generation of lowland discoverers had a different agenda for these mountain ranges of the Carpathians, conditioned by the times. Both challenged and enthralled by the terrain, Tatra discoverers sought to utilize the highlands as a place where they could convalesce, congregate, and create a Poland of the future. Many in the Eastern Carpathians who discovered the multiethnic highland borderland saw it to be a microcosm of "their" Poland—a Jagiellonian vision, if one in ways adjusted to fit the modern world. And various imaginative projects vied for ascendance in the Bieszczady, some with futuristic dimensions, all seeking to put a stamp on the Poland of the twenty-first century. Throughout the period of discovering and beyond, the highlands would remain a tantalizing space of modernizing experiments.

These modernizing experiments also had an effect on those who peopled the highlands. With the discovery, the indigenous folk truly began to move into the modern world—or, rather, the modern world began to move into their habitat. Somehow, however, the highlanders managed to hold their own, and partake selectively—if unevenly—of the modern. Tatra highlanders proved resistant to the most radical of Polish projects in the highlands, leaving the ideologically motivated intelligentsia to bemoan their conservative nature, although many Poles still remained fascinated by them. Hutsul highlanders—at least the members of the Hutsul Theater—would come to view themselves as no-less-civilized Europeans, while retaining a sense of distinctiveness that would allow them room for maneuver in interwar Poland. Even the Bieszczady settlers, those "neonatives" who took the place of the expelled Lemkos and Boikos, came to defend their own local interests, which were sometimes at odds with the interests of the natural realm or country at large. At times the clash of visions resulted in messy battles in which no one—including the highland landscape—came out unscathed. The imagined outcome of a special kind of ambitious, ideologically imbued development (as projected by Witkiewicz, Kasprzycki, Edward Gierek, and others) often proved unachievable in the face of highland realities. Things did not always go as planned—or stay that way for long, given the vagaries of the highlands and their history, full of natural and man-made disasters. This was one reason why discoveries, as in the case of the Eastern Carpathians, could be serial. Still, development made itself felt, sometimes too much so, insofar as the preservation of the natural environment was concerned. The paradox is this: "tourism destroys tourism," by which is meant that it destroys the natural beauty of the region in question—the rationale for tourism in the first place.[9] But is this mainly a declensionist story, a story of decline?

Surely the significance of mountains for Poles—their fascination with and love of them—amounts to far more than their tiny territorial footprint within any country that could be considered Polish. Interest in mountains remains considerable, as witnessed from the proliferation of publications on the subject, including yearbooks and almanacs such as *Wierchy*, *Połoniny*, and *Płaj*, and the general popularity of the highland tourist and mountaineering organizations connected with them. Polish scholars at Wrocław University have a thriving Workshop of Humanistic Research on Mountain Issues, which hosts an annual international conference and publishes its proceedings.

And then there are Poland's climbers. Members of this quintessentially lowland nation have gone on to conquer all the world's highest peaks, vying with the world's best climbers representing indisputably alpine countries in setting records. Poland's Jerzy Kukuczka was the second man, after South Tirolean Reinhold Messner, ever to complete the Himalayan Crown—the summiting of all fourteen of the eight-thousand-meter-plus peaks—and he did this in half the time it took Messner, while also climbing new routes, and in winter.[10]

It was the discovery of the Carpathians and the Polish tradition of mountaineering that opened the way to the summit for these and other climbers. Their love of freedom and unfettered movement continues to keep Poles in thrall of the mountains, their own Carpathians as well as other peaks across the globe.

❧ NOTES

Introduction

1. Fernand Braudel, *The Mediterranean and the Mediterranean World in the Age of Philip II* (New York: Harper & Row, 1972), 29.

2. Jon Mathieu, *The Third Dimension: A Comparative History of Mountains in the Modern Era* (Knapwell, UK: White Horse Press, 2011). Some stimulating recent works dealing with the Alps include Andrew Denning, *Skiing into Modernity: A Cultural and Environmental History* (Berkeley: University of California Press, 2015); Peter H. Hansen, *The Summits of Modern Man: Mountaineering after the Enlightenment* (Cambridge, MA: Harvard University Press, 2013); and Tait Keller, *Apostles of the Alps: Mountaineering and Nation Building in Germany and Austria, 1860–1939* (Chapel Hill: University of North Carolina Press, 2015).

3. Anonymous, "The Carpathians," in the *Saturday Review* (1867), reprinted in *Littell's Living Age*, 4th series, 4 (January–March 1867), 427–29, here 428–29, cited on 69 of Lily Ford, "Relocating an Idyll: How British Travel Writers Presented the Carpathians, 1862–1912," *Journeys: The International Journal of Travel and Travel Writing* 2, no. 2 (2002): 50–78.

4. See the entry for "Łaska Beata," in Zofia Radwańska-Paryska and Witold Henryk Paryski, *Wielka Encyklopedia Tatrzańska* (Poronin: Wydawnictwo Gorskie, 1995) (henceforth *Wielka Encyklopedia Tatrzańska*), 684–85.

5. Some of the highest Tatra peaks had already been climbed in 1793 by the English traveler Robert Townson: see his *Travels in Hungary* (London: 1797). A thorough look at the earliest discoverers of the Carpathians is Frank Michael Schuster, "Die Entdeckung der Karpaten zwischen dem späten 17. und dem 19. Jahrhundert," *Zeitschrift für Siebenbürgische Landeskunde*, no. 1 (2015): 55–80, who writes of the nineteenth-century "mystification" of the mountains (75).

6. Alexander Hadden Hutchinson, *Try Cracow and the Carpathians* (New York: Dodd and Mead, 1872). The British alpinist Leslie Stephen also traveled to the Carpathians—the Eastern Carpathians (reached via Hungary), if not the Tatras. See his *Playground of Europe* (London: Longmans, Green, 1871), 228–62.

7. Keller, *Apostles of the Alps*, 9–10; Ewa Roszkowska, *Taternictwo polskie: Geneza i rozwój do 1914 roku*, Monografie no. 11 (Kraków: Akademia Wychowania Fizycznego im. Bronisława Czecha w Krakowie, 2013), 29–45.

8. The sense of ownership of the landscape—its perceived nativeness—is key. On the creation of national landscapes, see especially the stimulating work of Thomas M. Lekan, *Imagining the Nation in Nature: Landscape Preservation and German Identity, 1885–1945* (Cambridge, MA: Harvard University Press, 2004); Marco Armiero, *Rugged Nation: Mountains and the Making of Modern Italy: The Nineteenth and Twentieth*

Centuries (Knapwell, UK: White Horse Press, 2011); and Alexander Maxwell, "From Wild Carpathians to the Puszta: The Evolution of Hungarian National Landscapes," in *Mythical Landscapes Then and Now: The Mystification of Landscapes in Search for National Identity*, ed. Ruth Büttner and Judith Peltz (Yerevan: Antares, 2006), 53–77.

9. Even Marco Armiero, in his book on Italy and its mountains, felt the need to justify his juxtaposition of the two—this when the Alps and the Apennines alone make up some 35 percent of the surface of the country. See Armiero, *Rugged Nation*, 1. Only 3 percent of today's Poland is higher than five hundred meters. Perhaps more difficult to believe: it was hardly self-evident that the Alpine landscape would become the defining factor for the Swiss, according to Oliver Zimmer, "In Search of Natural Identity: Alpine Landscape and the Reconstruction of the Swiss Nation," *Comparative Studies in Society and History* 40, no. 4 (October 1998): 637–65.

10. For more on the Hungarian case, see Maxwell, "From Wild Carpathians"; and Alexander Vari, "From Friends of Nature to Tourist-Soldiers: Nation Building and Tourism in Hungary, 1873–1914," in *Turizm: The Russian and East European Tourist under Capitalism and Socialism*, ed. Anne E. Gorsuch and Diane P. Koenker (Ithaca: Cornell University Press, 2006), 64–81. For the Slovak case, see L'ubomír Lipták, "Die Tatra im slowakischen Bewusstsein," in *Heroen, Mythen, Identitäten: Die Slowakei und Österreich im Vergleich*, ed. Hannes Stekl and Elena Mannová (Vienna: WUV, 2003), 261–88.

11. Hal Rothman has argued that tourism is the "most colonial of colonial economies"; Hal K. Rothman, *Devil's Bargains: Tourism in the Twentieth-Century American West* (Lawrence: University of Kansas Press, 1998), 11. On (post)colonialism, see the articles in a special volume of the online historical journal *Historyka* entitled "Postcolonial Galicia: Prospects and Possibilities," *Historyka* 52 (2012), http://journals.pan.pl/hsm/125555#tabs, last accessed 19 August 2020.

12. Yuri Slezkine, *Arctic Mirrors: Russia and the Small Peoples of the North* (Ithaca: Cornell University Press, 1994); Larry Wolff, *Venice and the Slavs: The Discovery of Dalmatia in the Age of Enlightenment* (Stanford: Stanford University Press, 2001).

13. Rothman, *Devil's Bargains*, 11.

14. An early work of environmental history touching on the region of East Central Europe is Simon Schama, *Landscape and Memory* (New York: Alfred A. Knopf, 1995), esp. chap. 1.

15. On the felicitous combination of environmental history and histories of leisure and sport, see Andrew Denning, "From Sublime Landscapes to 'White Gold': How Skiing Transformed the Alps after 1930," *Environmental History* 19 (January 2014): 78–108.

16. Concepts such as wilderness are both relative and problematic, as William Cronon has pointed out in his article "The Trouble with Wilderness: or, Getting Back to the Wrong Nature," in *Uncommon Ground: Rethinking the Human Place in Nature*, ed. William Cronon (New York: W. W. Norton, 1995), 61–90.

17. Laurence Cole, "The Emergence and Impact of Modern Tourism in an Alpine Region: Tirol c. 1880–1914," *Annali di San Michele* 15 (2012): 31–40, 31.

18. Peter Sahlins, *Boundaries: The Making of France and Spain in the Pyrenees* (Berkeley: University of California Press, 1989), 271.

19. David J. Weber and Jane M. Rausch, "Introduction," in *Where Cultures Meet: Frontiers in Latin American History*, ed. Weber and Rausch (Wilmington, DE: Scholarly

Resources, 1994), xiv. This definition is echoed in Paul Readman, Cynthia Radding, and Chad Bryant, "Introduction: Borderlands in a Global Perspective," in *Borderlands in World History, 1700–1914*, ed. Readman, Radding, and Bryant (New York: Palgrave Macmillan, 2014), 3.

20. The definition presented in this paragraph comes from Omer Bartov and Eric D. Weitz, "Introduction: Coexistence and Violence in the German, Habsburg, Russian, and Ottoman Borderlands," in *Shatterzone of Empires: Coexistence and Violence in the German, Habsburg, Russian, and Ottoman Borderlands*, ed. Bartov and Weitz (Bloomington: Indiana University Press, 2013), 1.

21. Here I am paraphrasing Richard White, *The Organic Machine* (New York: Hill and Wang, 1995), 15.

22. Following customary practice, I use the term *Austria* as shorthand for the "Kingdoms and Lands represented in the Imperial Council."

23. Charles S. Maier, "Consigning the Twentieth Century to History: Alternative Narratives for the Modern Era," *American Historical Review* 105, no. 3 (June 2000): 807–31.

24. Maier, "Consigning the Twentieth Century to History," 816.

25. James C. Scott, *The Art of Not Being Governed: An Anarchist History of Upland Southeast Asia* (New Haven: Yale University Press, 2009), 27.

Chapter 1. Where Freedom Awaits

1. Although in the last decades prehistoric artifacts have been found, it is hard to say whether these settlements were of any lasting nature. See Antoni Kroh, *Tatry i Podhale* (Wrocław: Wydawnictwo Dolnośląskie, 2002), 16. There is a huge frontier literature in the American context, which dates from Frederick Jackson Turner's famous "frontier thesis" of 1893.

2. The term *Podhale* did not become commonly used until the second half of the nineteenth century. Kroh, *Tatry i Podhale*, 11.

3. Witold Piksa, *Spojrzenie na Tatry poprzez wieki: Od pierwszych wzmianek do oświecenia* (Kraków: Polskie Towarzystwo Ludoznawcze, 1995), 101 and elsewhere; entries "Górale" and "historia" in Zofia Radwańska-Paryska and Witold H. Paryski, *Wielka Encyklopedia Tatrzańska* (Poronin: Wydawnictwo Górskie, 1995), 356–57, 409–13, respectively (henceforth *Wielka Encyklopedia Tatrzańska*).

4. See, for example, Mieczysław Adamczyk, "Zakopane-wieś," in *Zakopane: Czterysta lat dziejów*, ed. Renata Dutkowa (Kraków: Krajowa Agencja Wydawnicza, 1991), 1:114.

5. On the "invention" of Galicia, see Larry Wolff, *The Idea of Galicia: History and Fantasy in Habsburg Political Culture* (Stanford: Stanford University Press, 2010), 1 and passim.

6. For more on Tatra tourism prior to 1873, see Jan Kwak, "Szkice z dziejów turystyki w Tatry i na Podhale od końca XVII do lat 70. XIX w.," in *Galicyjskie drogi i bezdroża: Studium infrastruktury, organizacji i kultury podróżowania*, ed. Zdzisław Budziński and Jolanta Kamińska-Kwak (Przemyśl-Rzeszów: Uniwersytet Rzeszowski, 2016), 2:163–74.

7. Stanisław Staszic, *O ziemiorodztwie Karpatow i innych gor i rownin Polski* (Warsaw: Wydawnictwa geologiczne, 1955) (facsimile of 1815 edition), 187.

8. Per "Łomnica, szczyt," in *Wielka Encyklopedia Tatrzańska*, 690–91.

9. Other Poles likewise contributed to the scientific and scholarly understanding of the region. Ferdinand Hoesick surveyed the literature on the Tatras from its beginnings in his four-volume *Tatry i Zakopane* (Poznań: Księgarnia Św. Wojciecha, 1900), volumes published between 1900 and 1931 (the third volume is entitled *Legendowe postacie zakopiańskie*). For a briefer review, see Jacek Kolbuszewski, "Odkrycie Tatr: Turystyka, nauka, literatura i sztuka," in *Tatry: czas odkrywców* (Zakopane: Muzeum Tatrzańskie im. Dra Tytusa Chałubińskiego, 2009), 15–50; and Jolanta Kamińska-Kwak, "'Górami oczarowani': Rozwój turystyki górskiej w Galicji (XIX w. i początek XX stulecia)," in *Galicyjskie drogi i bezdroża: Studium infrastruktury, organizacji i kultury podróżowania*, ed. Zdzisław Budziński and Jolanta Kamińska-Kwak (Przemyśl-Rzeszów: Uniwersytet Rzeszowski, 2016), 2: 131–61.

10. Balthasar Hacquet, *Neueste physikalisch-politische Reisen durch die Dacischen und Sarmatischen oder Nördlichen Karpathen* (Nuremberg, 1790 and later); information on the Galician Tatras and the highlanders ("Guralen") can be found in part 4, chap. 15. See also Wolff, *The Idea of Galicia*, 52; Georg Jakob, *Belsazar Hacquet und die Erforschung der Ostalpen und Karpaten* (Munich: Theodor Ackermann, 1913); the full text can be found in *Die Karpaten: Balthasar Hacquet und das "vergessene" Gebirge in Europa; Neueste physikalisch-politische Reisen durch die Dacischen und Sarmatischen oder Nördlichen Karpathen*, ed. Kurt Scharr (Innsbruck: Studien-Verlag, 2004).

11. See, for example, "Homolacs (rodzina)," *Wielka Encyklopedia Tatrzańska*, 417–18.

12. A little unstaffed hut was also erected by the family by the picturesquely situated lake known as Morskie Oko already during this period. Franz Karl and Karl Ludwig visited in 1823 and 1854, respectively, events of enough note for the Homolacs family to erect monuments to the visitors on their property. Adamczyk, "Zakopane-wieś,"161.

13. See also the previous note.

14. These included books: Łucja Rautenstrauchowa, *Miasta, góry i doliny*, vols. 1–5 (Poznań: Nowa Księgarnia, 1844), and the more valuable account of Maria Steczkowska, *Obrazki z podróży do Tatrów i Pienin* (1858; 2nd rev. ed. Kraków: n.p., 1872). Deotyma authored feuilletons in the newspaper *Gazeta Warszawska* under the rubric "Wrażenia z Karpat" (Impressions from the Carpathians) in the winter of 1860.

15. From the sonnet "The Tatras" by Young Poland poet Franciszek Nowicki.

16. On Stolarczyk, see Ferdynand Hoesick, *Legendowe postacie zakopiańskie* (Warsaw: nakładem Księgarni F. Hoesicka, 1922), 92–173.

17. On marmot fat, see, for example, Kroh, *Tatry i Podhale*, 51, who claims that in the second half of the nineteenth century even some visitors thought it good for chest ailments.

18. Zejszner, cited in Ferdynand Hoesick, *Tatry i Zakopane: Przeszłość i teraźniejszość* (Poznań: nakład księgarni Św. Wojciecha, [n.d.]), 2:15–16.

19. On Stolarczyk, see Hoesick, *Legendowe postacie*.

20. On Stolarczyk's exploits, see Wojciech Szatkowski, "Z dziejów turystyki, taternictwa i narciarstwa," in *Tatry: czas odkrywców* (Zakopane: Muzeum Tatrzańskie im. Dra Tytusa Chałubińskiego, 2009), 136–37.

21. Wojciech Brzega, *Żywot górala poczciwego: Wspomnienia* (Kraków: Wydawnictwo Literackie, 1969), 30–31.

22. "Bałucki Michał" in *Wielka Encyklopedia Tatrzańska*, 48–49. The refrain begins, "Góralu, czy ci nie żal?"—Highlander, don't you regret?

23. A family of four or five could get by on 130 to 150 guldens for six weeks, according to Władysław Ludwik Anczyc, "Zakopane i lud podhalski," *Tygodnik Illustrowany*, no. 341 (11 July 1874): 28.

24. On the Alps, see the brilliant article by Alison F. Frank, "The Air Cure Town: Commodifying Mountain Air in Alpine Central Europe," *Central European History* 45, no. 2 (2012): 185–207.

25. Walery Eljasz, *Illustrowany przewodnik do Tatr, Pienin i Szczawnic* (Poznań: nakładem I.K. Żupańskiego, 1870).

26. First was Eugeniusz Janota, *Przewodnik w wycieczkach na Babią Górę, do Tatr i Pienin* (Kraków: Juliusz Wildt, 1860).

27. Józef Stolarczyk, *Kronika parafii zakopiańskiej (1848–1890)* (Kraków: nakład Adama Wroszka, 1915).

28. Biographical information from Barbara Petrozolin-Skowrońska, *Król Tatr z Mokotowskiej 8: Portret doktora Tytusa Chałubińskiego* (Warsaw: Iskry, 2005).

29. It was rumored that Chałubiński had secretly served as an ambulance physician during the Hungarian revolution of 1848–49, during which the Magyars fought valiantly but unsuccessfully for freedom from Habsburg rule. He most certainly visited the Tatras in 1852 and 1857. See Hoesick, *Legendowe postacie*, 3–4; Petrozolin-Skowrońska, *Król Tatr*, 41–44, 51, 68.

30. For details, see Petrozolin-Skowrońska, *Król Tatr*, 151–52. See also his letter to Aleksander Balicki of 10 August 1873, in Tytus Chałubiński, *Listy (1840–1889)*, ed. Aniela Szwejcerowa (Wrocław: Zakład Narodowy im. Ossolińskich Wydawnictwo, 1970), 107.

31. This was part of a cholera pandemic that began in the Russian Empire in 1871 and continued to spread in various directions in Europe and beyond through 1874. R. Pollitzer, *Cholera* (Geneva: World Health Organization, 1959), 36–37.

32. Contrary to what David Crowley writes, the doctor did not come specially to Zakopane to fight the outbreak of cholera there. David Crowley, *National Style and Nation-State: Design in Poland from the Vernacular Revival to the International Style* (Manchester: Manchester University Press, 1992), 17.

33. Petrozolin-Skowrońska, *Król Tatr*, 153. In this he was assisted by Dr. Witold Urbanowicz of Samogitia (in Lithuania). Irena Homola, "Od wsi do uzdrowiska: Zakopane w okresie autonomii galicyjskiej 1867–1914," in *Zakopane: Czterysta lat dziejów*, ed. Renata Dutkowa (Kraków: Krajowa Agencja Wydawnicza, 1991), 1:176. Chałubiński later wrote briefly about practical aspects of the treatment of cholera: *O cholerze ze stanowiska praktycznego* (Warsaw: n.p., 1885).

34. Hoesick, *Legendowe postacie*, 5.

35. Hoesick, *Legendowe postacie*, 8–9.

36. Brzega, *Żywot górala poczciwego*, 35.

37. Petrozolin-Skowrońska, *Król Tatr*, 155; Stolarczyk, *Kronika*, 23.

38. See for example, Jacek Kolbuszewski's introduction ("Wstęp") to Tytus Chałubiński, *Sześć dni w Tatrach: Wycieczka bez programu* (Kraków: Wydawnictwo Literackie, 1988), 23. The same had been noted already by Kazimierz Tetmajer in 1894 in *Kurjer Warszawski*; see excerpts in Hoesick, *Legendowe postacie*, 81–85.

Kolbuszewski's article about the discovery begins with the earliest mentions of the Tatras: Jacek Kolbuszewski, "Odkrycie Tatr," 15–50.

39. Stanisław Witkiewicz, *Na przełęczy: Wrażenia i obrazy z Tatr* (Warsaw: nakład Gebethnera i Wolffa, 1891), 38, 122. The second citation on Chałubiński's contribution reads: "Jest to człowiek, który dla nas odkrył Tatry." ("He is the person who discovered the Tatras for us."). More on Witkiewicz in the next chapter. The Polish verb "to discover" can also be rendered "to reveal" or "to unveil," conveying a sense of making something visible or known.

40. The obverse held as well: for the highlanders, the Galician elites were their (former) lords—and the peasants feared the return of serfdom if Poles were to regain their independence, which meant they kept their distance (Stolarczyk, *Kronika*, 11).

41. The classic work on positivism in English is Stanislaus Blejwas, *Realism in Polish Politics: Warsaw Positivism and National Survival in Nineteenth Century Poland* (New Haven: Yale Concilium on International and Area Studies, 1984). David Crowley, who has written about the Warsaw-Tatras connection, reminds us how connected that movement was with the Main School, where Chałubiński had taught; see David Crowley, "Pragmatism and Fantasy in the Making of the Zakopane Style," *Centropa* 2, no. 1 (September 2002): 182–96, esp. 186. That the "discovery" was a revelation to those from the Russian Empire is noted by Jan Reychman, *Peleryna, ciupaga i znak tajemny*, 2d ed. (Kraków: Wydawnictwo Literackie, 1976), 42–47, whose words are also cited in Kuba Szpilka, "Przełęcze," in Maciej Krupa, Piotr Mazik, and Kuba Szpilka, *Ślady, szlaki, ścieżki: Pośród tatrzańskich i zakopiańskich wyobrażeń* (Zakopane: Wydawnictwa Tatrzańskiego Parku Narodowego, Muzeum Tatrzańskie im. Dra Tytusa Chałubińskiego, 2013), 164–67.

42. In Galicia peasants had been emancipated as early as 1848. Still, the highland peasants were distinct from the lowland ones, as noted by Anczyc, "Zakopane i lud podhalski," *Tygodnik Illustrowany*, no. 342 (18 July 1874): 41.

43. For a discussion of "domestic tourism" at more or less the same time in Russia, see Christopher Ely, "The Origins of Russian Scenery: Volga River Tourism and Russian Landscape Aesthetics," *Slavic Review* 62, no. 4 (winter 2003): 666–82. One qualification: "domestic" in the case of the Tatras obviously means Polish, as Polish lowlanders came from the three empires and beyond (although the Russian Empire supplied a particularly notable group of individuals).

44. Kolbuszewski, "Odkrycie Tatr," 34.

45. The discomforts of the journey are laid out in detail in Jozef Rostafiński, "Jechać czy nie jechać w Tatry?" *Czas*, nos. 149–50 (5–6 July 1883).

46. According to Jacek Kolbuszewski; Jacek Kolbuszewski, "W stulecie 'Pamiętnika Towarzystwa Tatrzańskiego." *Wierchy* 46 (1977): 8–9; Wójcik, "Tytus Chałubiński."

47. Citations from Tytus Chałubiński, *Sześć dni w Tatrach: Wycieczka bez programu* (Kraków: Wydawnictwo Literackie, 1988). Originally it was published anonymously (as ". . . ! . . .") in the Warsaw periodical *Niwa* 7 [1879], 15, no. 105: 682–95; no. 106: 766–73; no. 108: 915–32; 8 [1879], 16, no. 109: 58–69); as well as the Tatra Society's Yearbook: . . . ! . . ., "Sześć dni w Tatrach: Wycieczka bez programu," *Pamiętnik Towarzystwa Tatrzańskiego* 4 (1879): 47–78. Excerpts can be found in Hoesick, *Legendowe postacie*, 37–59.

48. This is emphasized by the highlander Brzega, *Żywot górala poczciwego*, 36–37.

49. Chałubiński, *Sześć dni*, 34. For more on the term and its meaning, see Ewa Roszkowska, *Taternictwo polskie: Geneza i rozwój do 1914 roku* (Kraków: Akademia Wychowania Fizycznego im. Bronisława Czecha w Krakowie, 2013), 121ff.

50. Chałubiński, *Sześć dni*, 34–5.

51. Chałubiński, *Sześć dni*, 73–74.

52. Yet he did take bryology seriously: in 1879 the doctor published an article about Tatra mosses. See Tytus Chałubiński, "Spis mchów, zebranych i oznaczonych z wycieczek w Tatry z r. 1876," *Pamiętnik Towarzystwa Tatrzańskiego* 3 (1878): 28–31 and 4 (1879): 35–36. In 1882 Chałubiński published an illustrated opus on the Tatra leafy mosses in, as he put it, the language of mammoths: Latin (Grimmieae Tatrenses ex autopsia descripsit et adumbravit). Petrozolin-Skowrońska, *Król Tatr*, 230.

53. This is underscored by Jacek Kolbuszewski, "Tytus Chałubiński i jego Sześć dni w Tatrach," in Kolbuszewski, *Literatura i Tatry: Studia i szkice* (Zakopane: Wydawnictwa Tatrzańskiego Parku Narodowego, 2016): 353–73, especially 362ff.

54. Stolarczyk published an account of this achievement in a Kraków newspaper, bursting with pride that he and his highland guides from Zakopane had managed to find the way to the top of the highest Tatra peak without the help of guides from Hungary, on whose territory Gerlach lay. (Members of the Hungarian Carpathian Society had been incredulous at his claim of reaching the top, but Stolarczyk was able to convince them from his description that he and his guides had actually attained the true summit.) See Józef Stolarczyk, "Wycieczka na szczyt Gerlachu," *Czas*, nos. 235–37 (14–16 October 1875).

55. Chałubiński, *Sześć dni*, 37.

56. Rejchman, "Wycieczka do Morskiego Oka," 491.

57. Hoesick devotes a chapter to Sabała in his book on legendary figures from Zakopane: Hoesick, *Legendowe postacie*, 174–281. See also Wiesław A. Wójcik, *Sabała*, 2nd corrected ed. (Zakopane: Tatrzański Park Narodowy, 2010).

58. Chałubiński, *Sześć dni*, 60.

59. Chałubiński, *Sześć dni*, 40. Both became larger-than-life figures, the highlander thanks in part to the Warsaw doctor, who did "discover" him (per Stanisław Barabasz, cited in Roszkowska, *Taternictwo polskie*, 71).

60. Chałubiński, *Sześć dni*, 41.

61. That Jánošík was a Slovak highlander did not seem to bother the Górale—or their audience. For more on the brigand and his myth, see Martin Votruba, "Hang Him High: The Elevation of Jánošík to an Ethnic Icon," *Slavic Review* 65, no. 1 (spring 2006): 24–44. However, highlander Wojciech Brzega says that the highlanders of his youth saw little romance in the brigands, seeing them as regular thieves. Brzega, *Żywot górala poczciwego*, 31.

62. Chałubiński, *Sześć dni*, 44. Not everyone, it should be noted, was enamored of this sometimes loud form of Polish alpinism. See, for example, the colorful comments in Roszkowska, *Taternictwo polskie*, 97.

63. Leslie Stephen, "Alpine Dangers," *Alpine Journal* 2 (1866): 273–81, 281, cited from Arthur Burns, "Accidents Will Happen: Risk, Climbing, and Pedestrianism in the 'Golden Age' of English Mountaineering, 1850–1865," in *Borderlands in World History, 1700–1914*, ed. Paul Readman, Cynthia Radding, and Chad Bryant (New York: Palgrave Macmillan, 2014), 165–94, quotation from 174.

64. This was how he marketed the Tatras to potential summer guests, especially—interestingly—the youth of both sexes. Walery Eljasz, "Obrazek z podróży w Tatry," *Zdrojowiska: Tygodnik Kąpielowy* (8 August 1874).

65. From the speech of Stanisław Eljasz-Radzikowski in Zakopane on 26 August 1901, cited in Jacek Kolbuszewski, "Tytus Chałubiński," 370.

66. Reportedly as early as 1871 Adolf Tetmajer, the owner of Ludźmierz and the marshal of the Nowy Targ District Council, with his colleague Karol Rogawski, were thinking in this direction. Jan Reyman, " 'Powstanie i ideologia Polskiego Towarzystwa Tatrzańskiego,' Z kart 'Wierchów.'" ed. Artur Rotter and Janusz Zdebski (Warsaw: Wydawnictwo PTTK "Kraj," 1984), 7; for the correct name of Tetmajer's colleague, see Roszkowska, *Taternictwo polskie*, 70.

67. Tait Keller, *Apostles of the Alps: Mountaineering and Nation Building in Germany and Austria, 1860–1939* (Chapel Hill: University of North Carolina Press, 2015), 9–10; Roszkowska, *Taternictwo polskie*, 29–45.

68. Homola, "Od wsi do uzdrowiska," 208; "Polskie Towarzystwo Tatrzańskie," entry in *Wielka Encyklopedia Tatrzańska*, 948; "Statut Towarzystwa Tatrzańskiego z siedzibą w Krakowie," *Pamiętnik Towarzystwa Tatrzańskiego* 1 (1876): 9–19. A work in English that mentions the Tatra Society is Timothy J. Cooley, *Making Music in the Polish Tatras: Tourists, Ethnographers, and Mountain Musicians* (Bloomington: Indiana University Press, 2005). On the French Alpine Club, see Władysław hr. Koziebrodzki, "Pierwszy rocznik Klubu alpejskiego francuzkiego," *Pamiętnik Towarzystwa Tatrzańskiego* 1 (1876): 87–94. On the German and Austrian merger, see Keller, *Apostles of the Alps*, 10 and passim.

69. Reyman, "Powstanie," 10.

70. This poem was also featured in Eljasz's guidebook.

71. Reyman, "Powstanie," 9n6, 10; Wiesław A. Wójcik, "Tytus Chałubiński a Towarzystwo Tatrzańskie," *Wierchy* 57 (1988–91): 182. See also his letter to Feliks Pławiński, one of the founders of the Tatra Society, of 21 April 1874, in Chałubiński, *Listy*, 111–12.

72. It was Father Eugeniusz Janota and Maksymilian Nowicki who had been exhorting the highlanders not to kill the chamois and marmots and lobbied the provincial authorities on the animals' behalf.

73. For more information on the scholarly output on the Carpathians, see Jan Reychman, "Udział Polskiego Towarzystwa Tatrzańskiego w badaniach naukowych Tatr, Podhala i Karpat 1873–1948," *Wierchy* 18 (1948): 105–16.

74. As explained by Leopold Świerz, "Zarys działalności Towarzystwa Tatrzańskiego w pierwszem jego dziesięcioleciu (od roku 1874 do r. 1883)," *Pamiętnik Towarzystwa Tatrzańskiego* 10 (1885): 94. The second way was to allow for the creations of branches to care for the part of the Carpathian highlands nearest to them. For more on this, see chap. 5.

75. Hoesick, *Legendowe postacie*, 88.

76. According to Brzega, *Żywot górala poczciwego*, 35–36.

77. Some lowland Poles had imagined that highlanders could be taught toymaking or even clockmaking, like the residents of the Black Forest, whose wares were popular elsewhere in Europe. See Władysław Ludwik Anczyc, "Zakopane i lud podhalski [sic]," *Tygodnik Illustrowany*, nos. 341 and 342 (11 and 13 July 1874), 27–28 and 40–41, here 41.

78. In her memoirs, Modjeska credited herself with turning Chałubiński's mind to thoughts of a return (or rather trip) to the Tatras in 1873 (his name rendered as Dr. Titus Halubinski in the 1910 English-language edition). See Helena Opid Modjeska, *Memories and Impressions of Helena Modjeska, An Autobiography* (New York: Benjamin Blom, 1910), 204–5.

Chapter 2. On the Mountain Pass

1. See the section "The Discovery of the Tatras" in the previous chapter.

2. This Witkiewicz is not to be confused with his more famous son and namesake, the avant-garde writer, playwright, artist, and philosopher Stanisław Ignacy Witkiewicz (more commonly known as Witkacy) (1885–1939).

3. The first book edition was Stanisław Witkiewicz, *Na przełęczy: Wrażenia i obrazy z Tatr* (Warsaw: nakład Gebethnera i Wolffa, 1891). Originally the piece was published (serialized) in *Tygodnik Illustrowany* 1889 and 1890 (1889, nos. 314, 315, 317, 318, 319, 320, 321, 322, 323, 324, 325, 326, 328, 330, 331, 332, 333; and 1890, nos. 18, 19, 20, 22, 23, 25, 26, 35, 36, 37, 38, 39, 40, 41, 42, 43).

4. Tetmajer quotation from his 1894 article "Tatry," in *Kurier Warszawski*, cited in Ferdynand Hoesick, *Legendowe postacie zakopiańskie: Wybór z "Tatr i Zakopanego"* (Warsaw: Państwowy Instytut Wydawniczy, 1959), 133; Hoesick quotation from Ferdynand Hoesick, *Tatry i Zakopane. Przeszłość i teraźniejszość*, vol. 2 (Poznań: Księg. Św. Wojciecha, [1923]), 117.

5. On the literary connection to "Young Poland," see Jacek Kolbuszewski, "Witkiewicz jako kolorysta: O sztuce pisarskiej autora *Na przełęczy*," in Kolbuszewski, *Literatura i Tatry: Studia i szkice* (Zakopane: Wydawnictwa Tatrzańskiego Parku Narodowego, 2016): 375–95. Kolbuszewski also notes the utter lack of intertextual references except for Chałubiński's "Wycieczka bez programu." In this regard, Witkiewicz himself was "as if the sovereign and sole discoverer" of the world of the Tatras (383).

6. John Urry, *The Tourist Gaze: Leisure and Travel in Contemporary Societies* (London: Sage, 1990).

7. Kolbuszewski, "Witkiewicz jako kolorysta," 392, maintains that Witkiewicz, who did not know highlanders well, idealized them. Chałubiński was considerably less effusive: in his letter to Aleksander Balicki of 10 August 1873, after spending two weeks in Zakopane, he characterized the peasants thus: "A good little folk, only impoverished and a bit greedy, which because of [their] poverty one forgives it." ("Ludek dobry, tylko biedny i chciwy trocha, co mu się dla biedy przebacza.") Tytus Chałubiński, *Listy (1840–1889)*, ed. Aniela Szwejcerowa (Wrocław: Zakład Narodowy im. Ossolińskich Wydawnictwo, 1970), 107.

8. Witkiewicz, *Na przełęczy*, 39.

9. Witkiewicz, *Na przełęczy*, English translation from Teresa Jabłońska, *Styl Zakopiański Stanisława Witkiewicza / The Zakopane Style of Stanisław Witkiewicz* (Olszanica: Bosz, 2008), 17.

10. Witkiewicz, *Na przełęczy*, 174.

11. Witkiewicz later would write that the highland dialect could assume a place of importance in and influence on Polish literature, not unlike Provençal songs in France, or Italian or German dialects, all of which have their own literature. Witkiewicz, cited in Kolbuszewski, "Witkiewicz jako kolorysta," 390.

12. Witkiewicz, *Na przełęczy*, 186.
13. Witkiewicz, *Na przełęczy*, 43.
14. Witkiewicz, *Na przełęczy*, 42–43. Cited also in Maciej Krupa, Piotr Mazik, and Kuba Szpilka, *Ślady, szlaki, ścieżki: Pośród tatrzańskich i zakopiańskich wyobrażeń* (Zakopane: Wydawnictwa Tatrzańskiego Parku Narodowego, Muzeum Tatrzańskie im. Dra Tytusa Chałubińskiego, 2013), 163.
15. Witkiewicz, *Na przełęczy*, 44. For fascinating detail on women tourists, see Jolanta Kamińska-Kwak, "'Górami oczarowani': Rozwój turystyki górskiej w Galicji (XIX w. i początek XX stulecia)," in *Galicyjskie drogi i bezdroża: Studium infrastruktury, organizacji i kultury podróżowania*, ed. Zdzisław Budziński and Kamińska-Kwak (Przemyśl-Rzeszów: Uniwersytet Rzeszowski, 2016), 2:151–54.
16. Although Chałubiński had once remarked that someday a cow would climb Zawrat . . .
17. Witkiewicz, *Na przełęczy*, 147. Various Polish scholars have cited and commented on this text: Michał Jagiełło, *Zbójnicka sonata: Zbójnictwo tatrzańskie w piśmiennictwie polskim XIX i początku XX wieku* (Warsaw: Biblioteka Narodowa and Wydawnictwo Iskry, 2003), 153, likewise speaking directly of the anti-Semitism of the period; Wiesław Szpilka, "O niebyciu Żydów, gruźlików, biednych w pięknym świecie pod Tatrami," *Konteksty* 1 (2016): 53–58, citation on 55; and Szpilka, "Przełęcze," in Maciej Krupa, Piotr Mazik, and Kuba Szpilka, *Ślady, szlaki, ścieżki: Pośród tatrzańskich i zakopiańskich wyobrażeń* (Zakopane: Wydawnictwa Tatrzańskiego Parku Narodowego, 2013), 158.
18. Witkiewicz, *Na przełęczy*, 147.
19. Witkiewicz, *Na przełęczy*, 147.
20. See Witkiewicz, *Na przełęczy*, 235; and Stanisław Krajewski, *Żydzi w Polsce—i w Tatrach też* (Kraków: Wyd. "Austeria," 2019), esp. 55–59. For more on the Jewish presence in the Tatra Mountains, see Patrice M. Dabrowski, "Between Highlanders and Lowlanders: Perceptions of the Jewish Presence in the Tatras in the Nineteenth Century," in *Galizien in Bewegung: Wahrnehmungen—Begegnungen—Verflechtungen*, ed. Magdalena Baran-Szołtys, Olena Dvoretska, Nino Gude, and Elisabeth Janik-Freis (Vienna: V & R unipress, 2018), 141–53; Maciej Krupa, Piotr Mazik, and Kuba Szpilka, *Nieobecne miasto: Przewodnik po nieznanym Zakopanem* (Wołowiec: Wydawnictwo Czarne, 2016), esp. 103–28. The topic of Jews in Zakopane and the Tatras was also a special theme in *Tatry* 53–55 (winter 2016): 90–113.
21. Hoesick, *Tatry i Zakopane: Przeszłość i teraźniejszość* (Warsaw: Trzaska, Evert i Michalski S.A., 1931): 4:112.
22. Witkiewicz, *Na przełęczy*, 52.
23. Witkiewicz, *Na przełęczy*, 122. Jewish musicians reportedly played at the Casino and at Andrzej Chramiec's sanatorium. See Wenanty Piasecki, "Głosy publiczne," *Gazeta Zakopiańska* 3, no. 11 (26 July 1893).
24. Stanisław Witkiewicz, *Bagno*, in Witkiewicz, *Pisma tatrzańskie* (Kraków: Wydawnictwo Literackie, 1963), 1:223; also cited in Hoesick, *Tatry*, 4:137.
25. Witkiewicz, *Na przełęczy*, 234, 245–56.
26. Witkiewicz, *Na przełęczy*, 232–34.
27. This was also true of the scholarly edition of Witkiewicz's work published in 1963, which apparently is based on the 1906 edition. Stanisław Witkiewicz, *Pisma tatrzańskie*, vols. 1 and 2, ed. Roman Hennel (Kraków: Wydawnictwo Literackie, 1963).

28. The same is true today: the most recent reprint is of the original book edition, containing the full Zawrat section. For responses, see the works by Krajewski, Krupa, Mazik, and Szpilka noted earlier in this section.

29. Here I am paraphrasing a summary of the Turner thesis in William Cronon, "The Trouble with Wilderness; or, Getting Back to the Wrong Nature," in William Cronon, ed., *Uncommon Ground: Toward Reinventing Nature* (New York: Norton, 1995), 76.

30. Sabała's words as recalled by Chałubiński's daughter, Elżbieta Bończa-Tomaszewska, cited in Petrozolin-Skowrońska, *Król Tatr*, 154.

31. Aleksander Świętochowski, *Wspomnienia* (Wrocław: Ossolineum, 1966), 223.

32. See, for example, Ewa Roszkowska, *Taternictwo polskie: Geneza i rozwój do 1914 roku* (Kraków: Akademia Wychowania Fizycznego im. Bronisława Czecha w Krakowie, 2013), 98.

Chapter 3. Transforming the Tatras

1. I take the term from Hal Rothman, *Devil's Bargains: Tourism in the Twentieth-Century American West* (Lawrence: University of Kansas Press, 1998), 11.

2. Witold H. Paryski, "Początki Towarzystwa Tatrzańskiego i Zakopane," *Wierchy* 47 (1978): 30–31.

3. Walery Goetel, "Ideologia Polskiego Towarzystwa Tatrzańskiego w przebiegu lat," *Z kart "Wierchów,"* ed. Artur Rotter and Janusz Zdebski (Warsaw: Wydawnictwo PTTK "Kraj," 1984), 14.

4. In this the southern side of the Carpathians was ahead, with railway access since 1870–71. That had allowed for an earlier development of high-end hotels, resorts, and sanatoria than in the north. L'ubomír Lipták, "Die Tatra im slowakischen Bewusstsein," in *Heroen, Mythen, Identitäten: Die Slowakei und Österreich im Vergleich,* ed. Hannes Stekl and Elena Mannová (Vienna: WUV, 2003), 261–88, esp. 266–68.

5. Per Chałubiński's letter to Walery Eljasz on 11 December 1885: this was necessary so that Zakopane would not remain wild "like among the Zulus." Tytus Chałubiński, *Listy (1840–1889),* ed. Aniela Szwejcerowa (Wrocław: Ossolineum, 1970), 232–33.

6. For the briefest of introductions in English, see Jill Steward, "The Spa Towns of the Austro-Hungarian Empire and the Growth of Tourist Culture: 1860–1914," in *New Directions in Urban History: Aspects of European Art, Health, Tourism and Leisure since the Enlightenment,* ed. Peter Borsay, Gunther Hirschfelder, and Ruth-E. Mohrmann (Münster: Waxmann, 2000), 103–4.

7. Stanisław Eljasz-Radzikowski, "Zakopane," in *Słownik geograficzny Królestwa Polskiego i innych krajów słowiańskich,* ed. Bronisław Chlebowski (Warsaw: nakładem Władysława Walewskiego, 1895), 14:310.

8. Irena Homola, "Od wsi do uzdrowiska: Zakopane w okresie autonomii galicyjskiej 1867–1914," in *Zakopane: Czterysta lat dziejów,* ed. Renata Dutkowa (Kraków: Krajowa Agencja Wydawnicza, 1991), 1:181.

9. For further names of Polish notables to visit Zakopane during this period, see Homola, "Od wsi do uzdrowiska," 182–84.

10. Adrianna Dominika Sznapik, *Tatrzańska Arkadia: Zakopane jako ośrodek artystyczno-intelektualny od około 1880 do 1914 roku* (Warsaw: Neriton, 2009), 66–68,

102–40. This lifestyle would be duly represented in the literature of the coming fin de siècle. The Dembowskis' salon was presented in only lightly veiled fashion by Tadeusz Miciński in his novel *Nietota: Księga tajemna Tatr* of 1910. Here see, for example, Ewa Paczoska, "Zakopiańskie środowisko artystyczne przełomu wieków: Poszukiwania intelektualne i duchowne," in *Wybory wartości: Inteligencja polska u schyłku XIX i na początku XX wieku*, ed. Elżbieta Rekłajtis (Lublin: Oficyna Wydawnicza EL-Press, 1996), 104–5.

11. Jacek Kolbuszewski, "Henryka Sienkiewicza fascynacje zakopiańskie," in *Literatura i Tatry: Studia i szkice*, ed. Kolbuszewski (Zakopane: Wydawnictwa Tatrzańskiego Parku Narodowego, 2016), 397–407, esp. 405.

12. The preoccupation of Polish national elites with the fashion for things alpine—the so-called *zakopiańszczyzna and góralszczyzna*—has been treated by many scholars. See, for example, chapters by Jacek Woźniakowski and Jan Majda in vol. 2 of *Zakopane: Czterysta lat dziejów*, ed. Renata Dutkowa (Kraków: Krajowa Agencja Wydawnicza, 1991); Jan Majda, *Góralszczyzna i Tatry w twórczości Stanisława Witkiewicza* (Kraków: Universitas, 1998); Jan Majda, *Tatrzańskim szlakiem literatury* (Kraków: Szkice literackie, 1982); Barbara Tondos, *Styl zakopiański i zakopiańszczyzna* (Wrocław: Zakład Narodowy im. Ossolińskich, 2004).

13. Homola, "Od wsi do uzdrowiska," 182.

14. Stanisław Witkiewicz, "Bagno," (part I) *Przegląd Zakopiański*, no. 32 (1902): 292–93, cited in Mieczysław Rokosz, "Zakopane—stolica polskiej irredenty," *Rocznik Podhalański* 5 (1992): 125.

15. Witkiewicz, "Bagno."

16. [Świętochowski], "Opinia publiczna," *Przegląd Tygodniowy*, no. 7 (26 January 1873 / 7 December 1872), 3, cited in Brian Porter, *When Nationalism Began to Hate: Imagining Modern Politics in Nineteenth-Century Poland* (New York: Oxford University Press, 2000), 49.

17. For the literary perspective, see, for example, Jacek Kolbuszewski, "Pozytywiści wobec Tatr," *Wierchy* 34 (1965): 16–40.

18. The words of Aleksander Świętochowski, "Z gór," in *Wspomnienia* (Wrocław: 1966), 220, cited in Jan Majda, *Góralszczyzna i Tatry w twórczości Stanisława Witkiewicza* (Kraków: Universitas, 1998), 11.

19. Here I agree fully with David Crowley, who has noted the connection between the Warsaw positivists and Zakopane, as well as the connection between the local and the national, in his stimulating and insightful article, "Finding Poland in the Margins: The Case of the Zakopane Style," *Journal of Design History* 14, no. 2 (2001): 105–16.

20. Stanisław Witkiewicz, *Bagno* (Lwów: 1903), 6, cited in Anna Sidorek, "Środowisko taternickie w latach 1873–1913," *Kultura i Społeczeństwo* 22, nos. 1–2 (January–June 1978): 255. The remark about serfdom, however, is simply incorrect.

21. Edyta Barucka, "Redefining Polishness: The Revival of Crafts in Galicia around 1900," *Acta Slavica Iaponica* 28 (2010): 71–99, deals with this in historical perspective.

22. The importance of Zakopane's salons for the artistic and intellectual life of the village is illustrated in Sznapik, *Tatrzańska Arkadia*, 102–40.

23. For more on ethnographic developments at this time, see Edward Manouelian, "Invented Traditions: Primitivist Narrative and Design in the Polish Fin de Siècle," *Slavic Review* 59, no. 2 (summer 2000): 391–405.

24. Cited in Manouelian, "Invented Traditions, 394. Yet one should not forget that Hungary was directly across the southern border, already on the southern slopes of some of Galicia's peaks; and hungry highlanders had traveled to work in Hungarian fields for decades, making them more, and not less, connected with the larger world.

25. This point has been emphasized by Ewelina Lesisz, *Huculszczyzna—w kręgu mitów polskich na przełomie XIX i XX wieku* (Warsaw: nakład Wydziału Polonistyki Uniwersytetu Warszawskiego, 2013).

26. That he initially wrote this account not long before his first trip to Zakopane in June 1886 suggests how the idea of the highlanders as well as that of their patriotism was already penetrating Polish society. On this, see Jacek Kolbuszewski, " 'Ciupagami psiubratów!' Jeszcze o bitwie Górali ze Szwedami w 'Potopie' Henryka Sienkiewicza," in Kolbuszewski, *Literatura i Tatry: Studia i szkice* (Zakopane: Wydawnictwa Tatrzańskiego Parku Narodowego, 2016), 409–25, esp. 418–19, 423–24.

27. Juliusz Zborowski, "Góralskie podania o Szwedach i Potop Sienkiewicza," reprinted in Zborowski, *Pisma Podhalańskie* (Kraków: Wydawnictwo Literackie, 1972): 2:53–68.

28. The trope of the patriotic highlander is well covered in Kolbuszewski, " 'Ciupagami psubratów!' " 409–25, especially 422–25.

29. *Where Cultures Meet: Frontiers in Latin American History*, ed. David J. Weber and Jane M. Rausch, Jaguar Books on Latin America 6 (Wilmington, DE: Scholarly Resources, 1994), 141.

30. Norman Davies, *God's Playground: A History of Poland* (New York: Columbia University Press, 1982), 2:147. See also the interesting assessment of the Polish reaction to the massacres in Andriy Zayarnyuk, *Framing the Ukrainian Peasantry in Habsburg Galicia, 1846–1914* (Edmonton: Canadian Institute of Ukrainian Studies Press, 2013), 1–34.

31. On Chochołów, see Franciszek Ziejka, *Złota legenda chłopów polskich* (Warsaw: Państwowy Instytut Wydawniczy, 1984), 266–95.

32. Stanisław Witkiewicz, cited in Zbigniew Moździerz, ed., *Stanisław Witkiewicz: Czlowiek—artysta—myśliciel* (Zakopane: TMT, 1997), 310, which in turn has been cited in Manouelian, "Invented Traditions," 393.

33. This has been acknowledged by various scholars, including Manouelian, "Invented Traditions;" Stefan Keym, "Kulturhauptstadt des geteilten Polen? Zum Beitrag der Musik zur Stilisierung Zakopanes und der Tatra-Region zu einem nationalen Wertezentrum," in *Im Herzen Europas: Nationale Identitäten und Erinnerungskulturen*, ed. Detlef Altenburg, Lothar Ehrlich, and Jürgen John (Cologne: Böhlau, 2008), 307–25, esp. 307–11; Janusz Barański, "Góralszczyzna i pamięć," *Konteksty*, no. 1 (2013): 38–46, esp. 38.

34. Witkiewicz, *Styl zakopiański*, 1904 or 1911, cited by Stefan Żychoń, "Rozwój przestrzenny i budownictwo," *Zakopane: Czterysta lat dziejów*, ed. Renata Dutkowa (Kraków: Krajowa Agencja Wydawnicza, 1991), 1:445. This was a "conceit," according to David Crowley, who sees this as part of a "pan-European current of interest in the revival of vernacular tradition." David Crowley, *National Style and Nation-State: Design in Poland from the Vernacular Revival to the International Style* (Manchester: Manchester University Press, 1992), 22.

35. Witkiewicz, *Styl zakopiański*, 1904 or 1911, cited by Żychoń, "Rozwój przestrzenny i budownictwo," 445.

36. Teresa Jabłońska, *Stanisława Witkiewicza Styl Zakopiański / The Zakopane Style of Stanisław Witkiewicz* (Olszanica: Bosz, 2008), 28–29.

37. David Crowley has rightly seen this as a campaign "against the authority of Vienna and the culture of the Dual Monarchy" (Crowley, *National Style*, 22).

38. Zbigniew Moździerz, "Z dziejów 'Koliby,' pierwszej willi w stylu zakopiańskim," *Wierchy* 59 (1993): 166. For a more detailed discussion, in English, of the Zakopane Style, see Crowley, "Finding Poland in the Margins."

39. Moździerz, "Z dziejów 'Koliby,'" 166; Sznapik, *Tatrzańska Arkadia*, 191–96.

40. See his brochure "Projekt do wniosku J. Ex. Pana Marszałka krajowego hr. Tarnowskiego, celem uczczenia 40-letniej rocznicy panowania Cesarza Franciszka Józefa" (Lwów: 1888), mentioned in "Pławicki Feliks," entry in *Wielka Encyklopedia Tatrzańska*, 925–26.

41. X. Wielkopolanin, "Tatry Polskie pomnikiem dla Mickiewicza," *Pamiętnik Towarzystwa Tatrzańskiego* 12 (1888): 1–8.

42. The account of the auction is based on Sienkiewicz's article, published under the pseudonym K. Dobrzyński, "Kto da więcej?," *Słowo Polskie* (22 May 1889).

43. See, for example, Walery Goetel, *Wspomnienie pośmiertne o Władysławie Zamoyskim* (Lwów: nakładem Księgarni Wydawniczej H. Altenberga we Lwowie, 1925); also published in *Wierchy* 3 (1925); more recent works include *Władysław Zamoyski 1853–1924* (Kórnik: Biblioteka Kórnicka Polskiej Akademii Nauk, 2003) and *Działalność Zamoyskich w dobrach zakopiańskich: Materiały z sesji popularnonaukowej zorganizowanej z okazji 120. rocznicy nabycia dóbr zakopiańskich przez hr. Władysława Zamoyskiego oraz 55. rocznicy powstania Tatrzańskiego Parku Narodowego, Zakopane 5 czerwca 2009* (Zakopane: Wydawnictwo Tatrzańskiego Parku Narodowego, 2009).

44. Goetel, "Ideologia," 22. It should be noted that the Tatra Society also helped plant the seeds of the stone pine and the dwarf mountain pine in the Tatras (Goetel, 24).

45. Zamoyski opined, "He who pours vodka into the glass rules the village." For more on this and the cooperative, see Mirosław Kwieciński, "Trudne początki. Aktywność gospodarcza hrabiego Władysława Zamoyskiego w pierwszych latach po nabyciu Zakopanego," in *Działalność Zamoyskich w dobrach zakopiańskich*, 49–73, quotation on 58; Andrzej Chojnowski, "Władysław Zamoyski wobec innych nacji," in *Władysław Zamoyski 1853–1924* (Kórnik: Biblioteka Kórnicka Polskiej Akademii Nauk, 2003), 89–95.

46. See the memoirs of the forester Wiesław Bieńkowski, "Spór o Morskie Oko—Wspomnienia (do druku podał Wiesław Bieńkowski)," *Studia Historyczne* 30, no. 3 (1987): 450–85.

47. Jerzy M. Roszkowski, "Towarzystwo Tatrzańskie wobec sporu o Morskie Oko w latach 1873–1902," in *Spór o Morskie Oko: Materiały z sesji naukowej poświęconej 90 rocznicy procesu w Grazu, Zakopane 12–13 września 1992 r.*, ed. Jerzy M. Roszkowski (Zakopane: Wydaw. Muzeum Tatrzańskie, 1993), 26.

48. The earliest dated from 1887.

49. Cited in Roszkowski, "Towarzystwo Tatrzańskie," 28.

50. One wonders whether the decision of the famous Polish pianist and composer Ignacy Jan Paderewski to set his 1901 opera *Manru* for the Dresden opera at Morskie Oko was not a subtle attempt at emphasizing the Polishness of that lake for a

German audience ("Paderewski Ignacy Jan," *Wielka Encyklopedia Tatrzańska*, 869). There is much more that could be said about music and the Tatras. A thorough English-language survey of the study of highland music is found in chapter 3 of Timothy J. Cooley, *Making Music in the Polish Tatras: Tourists, Ethnographers, and Mountain Musicians* (Bloomington: Indiana University Press, 2005).

51. More detail is also available in Patrice M. Dabrowski, "Constructing a Polish Landscape: The Example of the Carpathian Frontier," *Austrian History Yearbook* 39 (2008): 45–65.

52. The disputed territory of more than 628 morgs was awarded to Galicia, the one exception being a twenty-morg forested area, given to Hohenlohe.

53. Various versions of this song are cited in, among others, Jacek Kolbuszewski, "Siedem wizji Morskiego Oka," in *Spór o Morskie Oko*, 18; and Homola, "Od wsi do uzdrowiska," 211, who attributes the song to Ludwik Solski.

54. For more naming after illustrious Poles and Tatra Society activists, see Dabrowski, "Constructing a Polish Landscape," 59–60. For the naming that figured in Zakopane proper, see Maciej Krupa, "Zakopane jest szkołą tęsknoty," *Konteksty*, no. 1 (2013): 78–84.

55. On Słowacki, see Stanisław Pigoń, "Zabiegi o wzniesienie Słowackiemu grobowca w Tatrach," in *Miscellanea z pogranicza XIX i XX wieku* (Wrocław: Zakład Narodowy im. Ossolińskich Wydawnictwo PAN, 1964), 425–67; Antoni Kroh, *Tatry i Podhale* (Wrocław: Wydawnictwo Dolnosląskie, 2002), 151–52.

56. Wiesław A. Wójcik, "Tytus Chałubiński a Towarzystwo Tatrzańskie," *Wierchy* 57 (1988–91): 189.

57. Edvard Jelínek, *Zakopané v polských Tatrách* (Praha: F. Šimáček, 1893).

58. On Slavs and Slovaks, I follow Jacek Kolbuszewski, "Symbolika Tatr w słowackiej poezji romantycznej," *Przestrzenie i krajobrazy* (Wrocław: Sudety, 1994). More detail on the Slovaks' relationship with the Tatras in this period (and beyond) in L'ubomír Lipták, "Die Tatra im slowakischen Bewusstsein," in *Heroen, Mythen, Identitäten: Die Slowakei und Österreich im Vergleich*, ed. Hannes Stekl and Elena Mannová (Vienna: WUV, 2003), 261–88, esp. 261–69.

59. On the Zipser Germans, see Bianca Hoenig, *Geteilte Berge: Eine Konfliktgeschichte der Naturnutzung in der Tatra* (Göttingen: Vandenhoeck & Ruprecht, 2018), 36–40 and passim. On Hungarian tourism, see Alexander Vari, "From Friends of Nature to Tourist-Soldiers: Nation Building and Tourism in Hungary, 1873–1914," in *Turizm: The Russian and East European Tourist under Capitalism and Socialism*, ed. Anne E. Gorsuch and Diane P. Koenker (Ithaca: Cornell University Press, 2006), 64–81.

60. Jacek Kolbuszewski claims that even the neighboring Czechs had more descriptions of the Tatras in their literature than did the Slovaks (Kolbuszewski, "Symbolika Tatr," 115.)

61. Wojciech Bogusławski's *Cud mniemany, lub Krakowiacy i Górale* of 1794 was actually the first instance of highlanders being brought to Warsaw, albeit played by actors on the stage. This is noted by Larry Wolff, *The Idea of Galicia: History and Fantasy in Habsburg Political Culture* (Stanford: Stanford University Press, 2010), 55.

62. That the panorama was a type of mass medium is emphasized by Stephan Oettermann, *Das Panorama: Die Geschichte eines Massenmediums* (Frankfurt: Syndikat, 1980).

63. Mont Blanc had been the subject of an early (1852) form of panorama, comprising a series of transparent slides, which was exhibited to great acclaim in Piccadilly by Albert Smith. Peter H. Hansen, *The Summits of Modern Man: Mountaineering after the Enlightenment* (Cambridge, MA: Harvard University Press, 2013), 175; Ralph Hyde, *Panoramania! The Art and Entertainment of the "All-Embracing" View* (London: Trefoil in association with Barbican Art Gallery, 1988).

64. For more on the Racławice Panorama and its context in English, see Patrice M. Dabrowski, *Commemorations and the Shaping of Modern Poland* (Bloomington: Indiana University Press, 2004), 122–26.

65. Krystyna Jabłońska, "Tatry na Dynasach," *Stolica* 27, no. 1 (1972): 4–5; Grzegorz Niewiadomy, "Obraz, który miał przyćmić 'Racławice': Dziwna historia 'Panoramy Tatr,'" *Przekrój*, no. 2100 (1985): 18–19. The panorama is also discussed in Franciszek Ziejka, *Panorama Racławicka* (Kraków: Krajowa Agencja Wydawnicza, 1984), 61–65.

66. Kazimierz Tetmajer, "Objaśnienie do olbrzymiego obrazu 'Tatry' przez Kazimierza Tetmajera" (1896), brochure in Polish and Russian, copy in Ossolineum, Papiery Stanisława Janowskiego, 85–135.

67. Quis, "Z tygodnia na tydzień," *Tygodnik Illustrowany*, no. 47 (9/21 November 1896): 920.

68. Walerya Marréne, in *Kuryer Poranny* (clipping in the Janowski archive, 147).

69. Chałubiński, Stolarczyk, and Sabała died in 1889, 1893, and 1894, respectively.

70. Homola, "Od wsi do uzdrowiska," 191.

71. Roman Lewandowski, "Tatry," *Wędrowiec* 34, no. 47 (9/21 November 1896).

72. For more on artistic renditions of the Tatras, see Teresa Jabłońska, "Malarze odkrywają Tatry," in *Tatry: czas odkrywców* (Zakopane: Muzeum Tatrzańskie im. Dra Tytusa Chałubińskiego, 2009), 55–81.

73. John Urry, *The Tourist Gaze: Leisure and Travel in Contemporary Societies* (London: Sage, 1990); Werner Telesko, "Visualisierungsstrategien im Tourismus in der Spätphase der Habsburgermonarchie," in *Zwischen Exotik und Vertrautem. Zum Tourismus in der Habsburgermonarchie und ihren Nachfolgestaaten*, ed. Peter Stachel and Martina Thomsen (Bielefeld: transcript Verlag, 2014), 31–46, esp. 32.

74. Adam Czarnowski, "Malarstwo tatrzańskie na pocztówkach krajoznawczych," in *Góry polskie w malarstwie: Materiały z sympozjum, Kraków 4 grudnia 1999*, ed. Wiesław A. Wójcik (Kraków: Centralny Ośrodek Turystyki Górskiej PTTK, 1999), 165–82, esp. 167, 169. On photographing the Tatras, see Anna Liscar, "Cudne widoki gór naszych," in *Tatry: czas odkrywców* (Zakopane: Muzeum Tatrzańskie im. Dra Tytusa Chałubińskiego, 2009), 85–111.

75. In 1898. Even these thirteen were too few. See Homola, "Od wsi do uzdrowiska," 191.

Chapter 4. Turn-of-the-Century Innovations

1. Roman Hennel, "Komentarz," in Stanisław Witkiewicz, *Pisma zebrane* (Kraków: Wydawnictwo Literackie), 3:443–44.

2. A wonderful sense of this is given in chapter 3 of Adrianna Dominika Sznapik, *Tatrzańska Arkadia: Zakopane jako ośrodek artystyczno-intelektualny od około 1880 do 1914 roku* (Warsaw: Neriton, 2009).

NOTES TO PAGES 54-58 221

3. This topic has been covered extensively in volume 2 of *Zakopane: Czterysta lat dziejów*, ed. Renata Dutkowa (Kraków: Krajowa Agencja Wydawnicza, 1991), which contains an entire section (part 4, consisting of fifteen articles) entitled "Ateny polskie w stylu zakopiańskim" (The Polish Athens in Zakopane style).

4. A fine introduction is Justyna Bajda, *Młoda Polska* (Wrocław: Wydawnictwo Dolnośląskie, 2003).

5. For more, see Justyna Bajda and Małgorzata Łoboz, *Młoda Polska* (Wrocław: Wydawnictwo Dolnośląskie, 2004), 85.

6. The reference to the mud has also been published in Jan Reychman, *Peleryna, ciupaga i znak tajemny*, 2nd ed. (Kraków: Wydawnictwo Literackie, 1976), 180.

7. This development is covered in Mieczysław Świerz, "Zarys dziejów taternictwa polskiego," *Pamiętnik Towarzystwa Tatrzańskiego* 34 (1913): 49–69.

8. Ewa Roszkowska, *Taternictwo polskie: Geneza i rozwój do 1914 roku* (Kraków: Akademia Wychowania Fizycznego im. Bronisława Czecha w Krakowie, 2013), 105–14. Much was published in the Hungarian Carpathian Society's yearbook.

9. Roszkowska, *Taternictwo polskie*, 106. Worth noting: Englisch's mother Antonina also summited (as did two guides).

10. An excellent introduction to Polish taternictwo is Roszkowska, *Taternictwo polskie*.

11. For basic information, see Tomasz Kowalik, "Zapomniany Uniwersytet Zakopiański," *Rocznik Podhalański* (Zakopane: Wyd. Muzeum Tatrzańskie, 1992), 5:181–99.

12. Mieczysław Orłowicz, *Moje wspomnienia turystyczne* (Wrocław: Ossolineum, 1970), 267–74.

13. On the rails—a spray of hot water from the train got them to move. Irena Homola, "Od wsi do uzdrowiska: Zakopane w okresie autonomii galicyjskiej 1867–1914," *Zakopane: Czterysta lat dziejów*, ed. Renata Dutkowa (Kraków: Krajowa Agencja Wydawnicza, 1991), 1:191.

14. Orłowicz, *Moje wspomnienia turystyczne*, 131–32.

15. Stanisław Witkiewicz, *Bagno*, in *Pisma tatrzańskie* (Kraków: Wydawnictwo Literackie, 1963), 1:222.

16. Witkiewicz, *Bagno*, 222–23.

17. There is a huge literature on the subject. See Jill Steward, "The Spa Towns of the Austro-Hungarian Empire and the Growth of Tourist Culture: 1860–1914," in *New Directions in Urban History: Aspects of European Art, Health, Tourism and Leisure since the Enlightenment*, ed. Peter Borsay, Gunther Hirschfelder, and Ruth-E. Mohrmann (Münster: Waxmann, 2000), 87–125 and elsewhere.

18. Andrzej Chramiec, *Wspomnienia dr Andrzeja Chramca*, ed. Barbara Wysocka (Kórnik and Zakopane: Biblioteka Kórnicka Polskiej Akademii Nauk and Urząd Miasta, 2004), 45.

19. Chramiec, *Wspomnienia*, 1. In the early 1890s it housed approximately one-sixth of the summer guests. E-n, "Zakład Dra Jędrzeja Chramca," *Almanach Tatrzański* (1894–95), 14–27, esp. 25.

20. E-n, "Zakład Dra Jędrzeja Chramca," 18.

21. I borrow this designation for Dłuski's sanatorium from Urszula Makowska, "Zakopiański Berghof," *Konteksty*, no. 1 (2013): 147–66, who compares it to Thomas Mann's creation.

22. Paderewski's investment of 110,000 crowns amounted to more than one-fifth of the sanatorium's initial capital, per the list of shareholders in the Central State Historical Archive of L'viv [TsDIAL], 146/58/2501: 22–23.

23. Chramiec, *Wspomnienia*, 102.

24. Chramiec, *Wspomnienia*, 2.

25. Witkiewicz, *Bagno*, 116. Sznapik, *Tatrzańska Arkadia*, 232–80, is an authoritative source on the role played by the Zakopane periodicals in the *Quagmire* debacle and elsewhere.

26. The influential *Przegląd Zakopiański* had long supported Witkiewicz and his Zakopane Style. *Tygodnik Zakopiański*—certainly at least one anonymous author of an article in the weekly addition to the Kraków newspaper *Głos Narodu*—eventually came out on the side of Chramiec. See [delta], "Letnia stolica Polski," *Tygodnik Zakopiański*, nos. 8–10 (1903): 60–61, 69–70, 73–75.

27. Per Witkiewicz, *Bagno*, 287.

28. Witkiewicz, *Bagno*, 226.

29. *Na Bagno Stanisława Witkiewicza odpowiedź radnych gminy Zakopane* (Zakopane: nakładem radnych gminy, 1903).

30. This was hardly a novelty in the world of spas, where local conservatism in places like Meran sometimes clashed with developers' wishes. On this see Steward, "Spa Towns," 103.

31. "Proces o 'Bagno,'" *Przegląd Zakopiański*, no. 26 (1903): 191–92, cited in Jan Majda, *Góralszczyzna i Tatry w twórczości Stanisława Witkiewicza* (Kraków: Universitas, 1998), 99.

32. Timothy J. Cooley, *Making Music in the Polish Tatras: Tourists, Ethnographers, and Mountain Musicians* (Bloomington: Indiana University Press, 2005), 3, 6–8 and passim, argues for the creation of the Górale as an ethnic group.

33. Włodzimierz Wnuk and Andrzej Kudasik, *Podhalański ruch regionalny* (Kraków: Oficyna Podhalańska, 1993), 11.

34. Details on the Union of Highlanders in Wnuk and Kudasik, *Podhalański ruch*, and Włodzimierz Wnuk, "Ruch regionalny," in *Zakopane: Czterysta lat dziejów* (Kraków: Krajowa Agencja Wydawnicza, 1991), 1:712–36.

35. The work of Celia Applegate and others on the connection between regionalism and nationalism is important here. Celia Applegate, *A Nation of Provincials: The German Idea of Heimat* (Berkeley: University of California Press, 1990).

36. Witkiewicz, *Bagno*, 225.

37. Ferdynand Hoesick, *Tatry i Zakopane: Przeszłość i teraźniejszość* (Poznań: Księgarnia Św. Wojciecha), 4:133.

38. Society for the Promotion of Foreign Travel in Galicia, *Short Guide trough* [sic] *Zakopane and surroundings with illustrations and 1 map*, [b.d.—1913?], 6–8, 15–16.

39. Nikodem Bończa-Tomaszewski, *Źródła narodowości: Powstanie i rozwój polskiej świadomości w II połowie XIX i na początku XX wieku* (Wrocław: Wydawnictwo Uniwersytetu Wrocławskiego, 2006), 357.

40. Walery Eljasz, "Kilka wrażeń z Tatr," *Pamiętnik Towarzystwa Tatrzańskiego* 4–6 (1879–81): 76. "Kulturtreger" comes from the original Polish text—apparently a Polish phonetic spelling of the German "Kulturträger" (bearer of culture).

41. Cited in Jan Majda, "Środowisko literackie Zakopanego," in *Zakopane: Czterysta lat dziejów*, ed. Renata Dutkowa (Kraków: Krajowa Agencja Wydawnicza, 1991), 2:335.

Chapter 5. The Hutsul Region and the Hand of Civilization

1. The fundamental ethnographic work on the Hutsuls is Volodymyr Shukhevych, *Hutsul'shchyna* (L'viv: Nakl. Naukovoho tovarystva im. Shevchenka, 1899–1908), 5 vols.; in Polish translation, Włodzimierz Szuchiewicz, *Huculszczyzna* (Lwów: Muzeum im. Dzieduszyckich, 1902–1908), 4 vols.

2. While Habsburg Galicia has been claimed as the Piedmont of both the modern Polish and the modern Ukrainian nations, there were various interpretations of both identities vying with each other at this time. Only the identities associated with the Greek Catholic East Slavs had a choice of terms. In this part of the chapter I will use "Ruthenian," as it best reflects the usage on the part of all parties at this time.

3. Per Article 19 of the Fundamental Laws of 1867.

4. For more information about the Hutsuls and their economy, see Anthony Amato, "In the Wild Mountains: Idiom, Economy, and Ideology among the Hutsuls, 1849–1939" (PhD diss., Indiana University, 1998), esp. part I.

5. See, for example, Volodymyr Shukhevych, *Hutsul'shchyna* (L'viv: nakladom Naukovoho Tov. imeny Shevchenka, 1899); 1997 reprint ed., 21–24. See the opening note for more on the original publication in Ukrainian and in Polish.

6. Balthasar Hacquet, *Neueste physikalisch-politische Reisen in den Jahren 1788–1795 durch die Dacischen und Sarmatischen oder Nördlichen Karpathen*, 1-IV (Nuremberg, 1790–1796). A Polish translation of a section pertaining to the Hutsul region of this raritas (chap. 9 of vol. 3), with a note about the author, has been published in *Dawne Pokucie i Huculszczyzna w opisach cudzoziemskich podróżników: Wybór tekstów z lat 1795–1939*, ed. Janusz Gudowski et al. (Warsaw: Wydawnictwo Akademickie DIALOG, 2001), 10–22; the original German can also be found in Oskar Kolberg, *Dzieła wszystkie*, vol. 54: Ruś Karpacka, part 1 (Wrocław-Poznań: Polskie Towarzystwo Ludoznawcze, 1970), 67–8, 108–10, 113–14, 136–37, 176–78, 186–87, 201–5. Hacquet, interestingly, referred to the Hutsuls only as "Ruthenian highlanders" (*Gebirgrussen*).

7. Aleksander Zawadzki; see Alex. Zawadzki, "Rzut oka na osobliwości, we względzie historyi naturalney, widzianej w podróży przedsięwziętey przez Karpaty stryyskiego i stanisławowskiego obwodu," *Rozmaitości*, no. 21 (27 May 1825): 161–63.

8. Whole books have been devoted to the origins of the Hutsuls, with—as far as I can tell—no consensus in the academic community. Those interested in the problem might consult Magocsi's no longer current, but still useful bibliography: Paul Robert Magocsi, *Galicia: A Historical Survey and Bibliographic Guide* (Toronto: University of Toronto Press, 1983).

9. This Hungarian word made its way into the vernacular through the intermediacy of Romanian. See, for example, S. Hrabec, *Nazwy geograficzne Huculszczyzny* (Kraków: Polska Akademia Umiejętności, 1950), cited in Janusz Gudowski, *Ukraińskie Beskidy Wschodnie* (Warsaw: DIALOG, 1997), 1:19n*.

10. Henryk Gąsiorowski, "O przeszłości i teraźniejszości Burkutu," *Wierchy* 10 (1932): 89–90.

11. Denys [Il'nyts'kyi, V.], "Z Karpat kolomyiskykh," *Zoria: lyteraturno-naukove dlia rus'kykh rodyn* (L'viv) 1, nos. 2–4 (15 January–February 1880).

12. Pol, cited in Gąsiorowski, "O przeszłości," 91–94.

13. Gąsiorowski, "O przeszłości," 94.

14. Gudowski, *Ukraińskie Beskidy Wschodnie*, 1:12, mistakenly gives this date as 1884.

15. Jan A. Choroszy, *Huculszczyzna w literaturze polskiej* (Wrocław: Jan A. Choroszy, 1991), 9–13.

16. Choroszy, *Huculszczyzna*, 19; Larry Wolff, *The Idea of Galicia: History and Fantasy in Habsburg Political Culture* (Stanford: Stanford University Press, 2010), 117–19, 390.

17. For more on the fascinating Vahylevych, see Peter Brock, *Folk Cultures and Little Peoples: Aspects of National Awakening in East Central Europe* (Boulder: East European Quarterly, 1992), chap. 2, esp. 57n23. Holovats'kyi was a colleague of Vahylevych and a coauthor of *Rusalka Dnistrovaia* (Nymph of the Dniester). See Mariia Andriïvna Val'o, ed., *Podorozhi v Ukraïns'ki Karpaty: Zbirnyk* (L'viv: Kameniar, 1993), 22–113, for a Ukrainian translation of the texts.

18. K[azimierz] W[ładysław] Wójcicki, "Nad-Prucie: Wyjątek z opisu Pokucia," *Kwartalnik Naukowy* (1835), 2: 94, cited in Choroszy, *Huculszczyzna*, 23.

19. For discussion of this transformation, as well as the overall plight of the Hutsul, see Amato, "In the Wild Mountains." Regarding the deforestation by Germans/ Prussians, see Marceli Antoni Turkawski, *Wspomnienia Czarnohory* (Warsaw: nakład Filipa Sulimierskiego, 1880), 50.

20. A recent issue of *Płaj* has focused on this fascinating individual: Andrzej Wielocha and Leszek Rymarowicz, "Sofron Witwicki (1819–1879): Zapomniany proboszcz Huculów," *Płaj* 57 (spring 2019): 5–40; Andrzej Wielocha, "Delegat Towarzystwa Tatrzańskiego pod Czarnohorą," *Płaj* 57 (spring 2019): 41–62; Leszek Rymarowicz, "W poszukiwaniu Sofrona Witwickiego," *Płaj* 57 (spring 2019): 63–71.

21. Żabie occupied 596.12 square kilometers while having a population (in 1890) of only 6,216. Lu.Dz., "Żabie," *Słownik geograficzny Królestwa Polskiego i innych krajów słowiańskich* (Warsaw: nakł. Filipa Sulimierskiego i Władysława Walewskiego, 1895) 14:711–12.

22. Sofron Witwicki, *Rys historyczny o Hucułach zdołączeniem mapy geograficznej obecnej siedziby Huculów* (Lwów: nakładem i drukiem M.F. Poremby, 1863). The date, from Mykola Vasyl'chuk's introduction to his (unfortunately bowdlerized) Ukrainian translation of Witwicki's book: "Hutsul's'kyi entsyklopedyst," in Sofron Vytvyts'kyi, *Istorychnyi zarys pro hutsuliv*, trans. Mykola Vasyl'chuk (Kolomyia: Vydavnytstvo "Svit," 1993), 5. In his introduction to the Ukrainian translation, Mykola Vasyl'chuk wrote that this work "discovered for Europe" [!] the Hutsuls (Vasyl'chuk, "Hutsul's'kyi entsyklopedyst," 10). Unfortunately, I do not have any indication that this term was used by any contemporary of Witwicki, which would make the parallel between him and Tytus Chałubiński greater.

23. Witwicki's letters to the Tatra Society are found in the folder entitled AR ON 184, 1875/1: Komisja Wykonawcza T.T. w Żabiu, Muzeum Tatrzańskie, Zakopane. The Tatra Society excerpted some of the letter in question in "Sprawozdanie z czynności wydziału Towarzystwa Tatrzańskiego za czas od 27 maja 1877 do 5 maja 1878 r. . . . ," *Pamiętnik Towarzystwa Tatrzańskiego* 3 (1878): 32n*.

24. Letter of Witwicki to the Tatra Society of 14 October 1875, AR ON 184, 1875/1: Komisja Wykonawcza T.T. w Żabiu, Muzeum Tatrzańskie, Zakopane. Other options for the province's Ruthenes included Old Ruthenianism, Russophilism, and Ukrainophilism.

25. Sofron Witwicki, "Hucuły," *Pamiętnik Towarzystwa Tatrzańskiego* 1 (1876): 73–86; Witwicki, "Zwyczaje, przesądy, i zabobony Huculów," *Pamiętnik Towarzystwa Tatrzańskiego* 2 (1877): 73–82.

26. Letters of Witwicki to the Tatra Society of 14 October, 6 and 14 November 1875, AR ON 184, 1875/1: Komisja Wykonawcza T.T. w Żabiu, Muzeum Tatrzańskie, Zakopane.

27. Minutes of the first meeting of the Executive Commission, AR ON 184, 1875/1: Komisja Wykonawcza T.T. w Żabiu, Muzeum Tatrzańskie, Zakopane.

28. AR NO 185, 1876/1:33–4, Komisja Wykonawcza T.T. w Żabiu, Muzeum Tatrzańskie, Zakopane.

29. Per Sprawozdanie z III. walnego zgromadzenia, 28 December 1879 and 11 January 1880, AR NO 187, 1880/5: Oddzial Czarnohorski T.T., 74.

30. Barring words to that effect in the introduction to a Ukrainian translation—if a bowdlerized one—of Witwicki's book on the Hutsuls: see Vasyl'chuk, "Hutsul's'kyi entsyklopedyst."

31. AR NO 185, 1876/1:33–4, Komisja Wykonawcza T.T. w Żabiu, Muzeum Tatrzańskie, Zakopane.

32. Minutes of the second session, 7 January 1876, in AR ON 184, 1875/1: Komisja Wykonawcza T.T. w Żabiu, Muzeum Tatrzańskie, Zakopane.

33. From the list of regular members (no date), cited in Andrzej Ruszczak, "Oddział Czarnohorski Towarzystwa Tatrzańskiego: Zarys działalności," Płaj 25 (2002): 156.

34. Ruszczak, "Oddział Czarnohorski," 157.

35. AR NO 187, 1878/4: 39, 41, Oddział Czarnohorski T.T., Muzeum Tatrzańskie.

36. Marceli Eminowicz, "Sprawozdanie Zarządu oddziałowego Towarzystwa Tatrzańskiego w Stanisławowie z wycieczki w Karpaty obwodu Stanisławowskiego i Kołomyjskiego odbytej r. 1876," Pamiętnik Towarzystwa Tatrzańskiego 2 (1877): 33–39; and Turkawski, Wspomnienia Czarnohory.

37. See Turkawski, Wspomnienia Czarnohory, 36.

38. See, for example, Turkawski, Wspomnienia Czarnohory; Jan Gregorowicz, "O koniu huculskim," Pam. Tow. Tatrz. 4 (1879), and "Słownik wyrazów huculskich," Pam. Tow. Tatrz. 5 (1880); and Leopold Wajgiel, "O Burkucie i jeziorach czarnohorskich," Pam. Tow. Tatrz. 5 (1880).

39. The first mention of this idea in the Tatra Society archives comes from March 1879 (AR NO 188, 1879/3: 45, Oddział Czarnohorski T.T., Muzeum Tatrzańskie).

40. Per Marceli Turkawski, "Wystawa etnograficzna Pokucia w Kołomyi," Czas 244 (23 October 1880). See also Jan Bujak, "Towarzystwo Tatrzańskie prekursorem zbieractwa etnograficznego w Polsce," Rocznik Podhalański 2 (Zakopane 1979): 91–99 and Ryszard Brykowski, "W setną rocznicę pierwszej polskiej wystawy etnograficznej w Kołomyi," Polska Sztuka Ludowa 36, no. 2 (1981): 117–22.

41. Daniel Unowsky has written extensively on the subject of the imperial tour of 1880, although he devotes little time to the Kołomyja events. Daniel L. Unowsky, The Pomp and Politics of Patriotism: Imperial Celebrations in Habsburg Austria, 1848–1916 (West Lafayette, IN: Purdue University Press, 2005), chap. 3.

42. News of the rash of donations made its way to the readership of the Warsaw journal Tygodnik Illustrowany (Władysław Zawadzki): "Korespondencya Tygodnika ilustrowanego. Z Galicyi. W marcu. [Dokończenie]," Tygodnik Illustrowany, no. 225 (17 April 1880): 243.

43. Aleksander Nowolecki, Pamiątka podróży Cesarza Franciszka Józefa I. po Galicyi i dwudziesto-dniowego pobytu Jego w tym kraju (Kraków: nakładem Wydawnictwa Czytelni ludowej H. Nowoleckiej, 1881), 11.

44. To be sure, as Unowsky argues, in some places they had come not only to see their beloved emperor but also to voice their grievances, even preparing written documents for him.

45. This doubtless was the group for whom the district captain of Kosów had asked the provincial authorities for additional funding to transport them to Kołomyja (Unowsky, "Pomp and Politics," 120n2).

46. From an article by Teofil Merunowicz in Gazeta Narodowa, cited in Nowolecki, Pamiątka, 200.

47. The phrase was given in English (yes, in the Polish text): Stanisław Tarnowski, "Z Kołomyi," Niwa 9, no. 144 (1880): 768.

48. Józef Korzeniowski, "O Hucułach," in Korzeniowski, Karpaccy górale: Dramat w trzech aktach (Kraków: Nakładem Krakowskiej Spółki Wydawniczej, 1923), 29. The emperor was given a beautifully carved and inlaid Hutsul hatchet by the exhibition committee. "Podróż Najjaśniejszego Pana [Kołomyja, 15 września]," Czas, no. 214 (18 September 1880).

49. For more on Bohosiewicz's collection, see Katalog przedmiotów Wystawy Etnograficznej Oddziału Czarnohorskiego, Tow. Tatrzańskiego obejmującej powiaty: kołomyjski, kossowski, śniatyński, horodeński, zaleszczycki i borszczowski połączonej z wystawą płodów górskich która zaszczycona obecnością Najjaśniejszego Cesarza i Króla Franciszka Józefa I. otwarta została w dniu 15 września 1880 roku w Kołomyi (Lwów 1880), 8–9.

50. Reported in numerous articles; see, for example, Teofil Merunowicz, "Wystawa etnograficzna Czarnohorskiego Oddziału Towarzystwa Tatrzańskiego w Kołomyi. II Dział etnograficzny. Słówko o pp. inspektorach podatkowych, tkaniny, hafty, wyroby ozdobne," Gazeta Narodowa, no. 22 (1880), with the correction by Kolberg published in Kolberg, Dzieła, 54: 226, 228.

51. See Hermann Bausinger, Folk Culture in a World of Technology (Bloomington: Indiana University Press, 1990), chap. 5, for an important discussion of the commodification of folklore, also known as "folklorism."

52. According to Marceli Turkawski, "Wspomnienie Wystawy etnograficznej Pokucia w Kołomyi," Kłosy, no. 832 (1881): 364–65; no. 833: 379; no. 834: 388–89, cited fragment from Kolberg, Dzieła, 54:229.

53. Of course, tourism leads to the "inevitability of the inauthentic," according to Bausinger, Folk Culture, 137.

54. Evidence of the problems that could arise comes from a young woman from Scotland visiting the region a decade later. She observed that, while the Hutsul artisans were masters of their traditional craft, when they came into contact with new things—for example, new colors of wool provided to employees of a local textile factory—they by no means automatically came up with happy combinations. Ménie Muriel Dowie Norman, A Girl in the Karpathians, 5th ed. (London: George Philip & Son, 1892), 273ff.

55. Tarnowski, "Z Kołomyi," 843.

56. As expressed, for example, in Marceli Turkawski, "Wspomnienie," cited in Kolberg, Dzieła, 54:231–32.

57. The reference to a "forest of hundreds of oil rigs" comes from J. Badeni, "W huculskich górach," Przegląd Powszechny 10, no. 4 (1894): 11, cited in Choroszy, Huculszczyzna, 101. The story of the Galician oil industry has been engagingly told by Alison Fleig Frank, Oil Empire: Visions of Prosperity in Austrian Galicia (Cambridge, MA: Harvard University Press, 2005).

58. Which the emperor examined, by the way; he also spent almost twice as much time in the capital of Galician oil industry, Borysław (Boryslav), than he had in Kołomyja.

59. Paul Robert Magocsi, "The Kachkovs'kyi Society and the National Revival in Nineteenth-Century East Galicia," originally published in *Harvard Ukrainian Studies* 15, nos. 1–2 (1991): 48–87, cited here from his collection of essays, *The Roots of Ukrainian Nationalism: Galicia as Ukraine's Piedmont* (Toronto: University of Toronto Press, 2002), 119–58.

60. From the report on the second general assembly, cited in Magocsi, *Roots of Ukrainian Nationalism*, 132.

61. Descriptions can be found, for instance, in Tarnowski, "Z Kołomyi," 846–47; and Nowolecki, *Pamiątka*, 203–4.

62. Tarnowski, "Z Kołomyi," 846.

63. The Poles were very conscious of the approaching two hundredth anniversary of the battle.

64. This term was used in Tarnowski, "Z Kołomyi," 768, as well as in a number of other articles.

65. The committee reportedly had well over ten thousand guldens at its disposal, according to Turkawski, "Wystawa etnograficzna," *Czas*, no. 272 (26 November 1880); see AR NO 189 1880/5: 69, 70, 76, 79, Oddział Czarnohorski T.T., Muzeum Tatrzańskie.

66. Nowolecki, *Pamiątka*, 203.

67. This chivalrous tradition is discussed in Witwicki, "Huculy," 83–84.

68. Eugen Weber, *Peasants into Frenchmen: The Modernization of Rural France, 1870–1914* (Stanford: Stanford University Press, 1976), chap. 1, 9.

69. Choroszy, *Huculszczyzna*, 108; Grzegorz Niewiadomy, "Huculszczyzna oczami artystów," in *Odkrywanie Huculszczyzny: Katalog wystawy, październik 2002-luty 2003* (Pelplin-Gdańsk: "Bernardinum" and Muzeum Narodowe, 2002), 41.

70. Elizabeth Clegg, *Art, Design and Architecture in Central Europe 1890–1920* (New Haven: Yale University Press, 2006), 122–23.

71. Clegg, *Art, Design and Architecture*; Niewiadomy, "Huculszczyzna"; Zofia Weiss-Albrzykowska, "The Myth of Hucul Culture in Polish Art up to the Twenties," *Seminaria Niedzickie/Niedzica Seminars: Polish-Czech-Slovak-Hungarian Artistic Connections* (Kraków: Secesja, 1991), 79–83. A recent book dealing with Jarocki, Sichulski, and Pautsch is Agnieszka Jankowska-Marzec, *Między etnografią a sztuką: Mitologia Huculów i Huculszczyzny w kulturze polskiej* [sic] *XIX i XX wieku* (Kraków: Universitas, 2013).

72. Ruszczak, "Oddział Czarnohorski," 161.

73. "Jubileusz Towarzystwa Tatrzańskiego (1873–1913)," *Pamiętnik Towarzystwa Tatrzańskiego* 35 (1914): LIX.

74. See his letter of 14 November 1875, AR NO 184, 1875/1: Komisja Wykonawcza T.T. w Żabiu, Muzeum Tatrzańskie, 10–17.

75. Tomasz Kowalik has written extensively about this organization. See, for example, his "Rodowód Akademickiego Klubu Turystycznego," *Gościniec* 2 (2006): 114–18.

76. Mieczysław Orłowicz, *Moje wspomnienia turystyczne* (Wrocław: Ossolineum, 1970), 333–46, 398–400.

77. Orłowicz, *Moje wspomnienia turystyczne*, 354–72.

78. Orłowicz, *Moje wspomnienia turystyczne*, 470.

Chapter 6. The Advent of the Railway

1. Laurence Cole, "The Emergence and Impact of Modern Tourism in an Alpine Region: Tirol c. 1880–1914," *Annali di San Michele* 15 (2012): 31–40, 31.

2. Stanisław Tarnowski, "Z Kołomyi," *Niwa* 9, no. 144 (1880): 893.

3. Antony Amato, "In the Wild Mountains: Idiom, Economy and Ideology among the Hutsuls, 1849–1939" (PhD diss, Indiana University, 1998), 41. See also the story of the origins of Worochta/Vorokhta, in Mykola Sankovych, *Vorokhta: Istoriia, liudy, tradytsiï* (Vorokhta: ZAT "Nadvirnians'ka drukarnia," 2001), 7–9.

4. See, for example, "Kolej ze Stanisławowa do Woronianki [sic]," *Gazeta Kołomyjska* 4, nos. 9 and 10 (6 January 1892).

5. "Stanisławów-Woronienka," *Kurjer Lwowski* (16 November 1894).

6. Comments of Heinrich von Wittek in K.C., "Urocza kolej," *Tygodnik Illustrowany*, no. 50 (3–15 December 1894), 381–82; and "Uroczyste otwarcie nowej kolei Stanisławów-Woronienka," *Kurjer Lwowski* 12, no. 321 (21 November 1894), 5.

7. "Die größte Eisenbahnbrücke der Welt," *Neue Freie Presse*, 29 May 1894.

8. On the engineer, see Stanisław Sławomir Nicieja, *Kresowa Atlantyda: Historia i mitologia miast kresowych* (Opole: Wydawnictwo MS, 2013), 2:96–100. For more on the bridges, see Janusz Jankowski, *Mosty w Polsce i mostowcy polscy (od czasów najdawniejszych do końca I wojny światowej)* (Gdańsk: Zakład Narodowy im. Ossolińskich, Oddz. w Gdańsku, 1973), 218. On the cholera outbreak: "Uroczyste otwarcie nowej kolei Stanisławów-Woronienka."

9. Wolfgang Schivelbusch, *The Railway Journey: The Industrialization of Time and Space in the 19th Century* (Berkeley: University of California Press, 1986), 10.

10. For the impact of the railroad on the American West, see the insightful Hal K. Rothman, *Devil's Bargains: Tourism in the Twentieth-Century American West* (Lawrence: University Press of Kansas, 1998), 44–45.

11. "Po sezonie II," *Gazeta Kołomyjska*, 17 September 1899. On how important Delatyn was for the Hutsuls, see Kazet, "Jarmark w Delatynie (obrazek z życia dzisiejszych huculów)," *Kurjer Stanisławowski*, 17 April 1904.

12. Zakopane comparison from "Z naszych uzdrowisk," *Gazeta Kołomyjska*, 28 May 1898; Swiss comparison from "Kronika: Nowa miejscowość klimatyczna," *Kuryer Lwowski* 13, no. 126 (7 May 1895); "Kronika," *Gazeta Kołomyjska*, 7 April 1897. On Jaremcze's desirable Alpine location, see also Hoffbauer, *Przewodnik*, 2:70. Switzerland was the gold standard: a similar comparison—"the Switzerland of America"—had been made to the White Mountains of New Hampshire earlier that century. See Dona Brown, *Inventing New England: Regional Tourism in the Nineteenth Century* (Washington, DC: Smithsonian Institution Press, 1995), 66.

13. "Po sezonie III," *Gazeta Kołomyjska*, 24 September 1899. David Stradling, *Making Mountains: New York City and the Catskills* (Seattle: University of Washington Press, 2007); on New Hampshire, see Brown, *Inventing New England*.

14. "Kronika: Nowa miejscowość klimatyczna," *Kuryer Lwowski* 13, no. 126 (7 May 1895).

15. Yet accommodations in the hamlet were also advertised in the Viennese press: see, for example, "Kleine Anzeigen," *Neues Wiener Journal*, 29 June 1897.

16. "Po sezonie III," *Gazeta Kołomyjska*, 24 September 1899. On the billboard: Kazet, "Jaremcze w zimie," *Kurjer Stanisławowski*, 3 January 1904.

17. Tadeusz Smarzewski, "Wycieczka do kraju Hucułów," *Gazeta Kołomyjska*, 8 October 1899. The article was originally published in St. Petersburg's Polish-language newspaper *Kraj* 17, no. 42 (15–27 October 1898): 10–12, and no. 43 (22 October–3 November 1898): 15–18; then it was republished in the organ of the Tatra Society, *Pamiętnik Towarzystwa Tatrzańskiego* 20 (1899): 73–86, only after which it appeared in *Gazeta Kołomyjska*, 17 September, 24 September and 8 October 1899.

18. "Wycieczka w góry," *Gazeta Kołomyjska*, 5 August 1899.

19. "Przeciw wyzyskiwaczom," *Gazeta Kołomyjska*, 25 May 1902.

20. Klewe, "Moje plotki," *Kurjer Stanisławowski*, 22 July 1900.

21. "Kronika: Do Jaremcza," *Kurjer Stanisławowski* 15, no. 777 (12 August 1900).

22. The two cities functioned for the Prut River Valley as New York City had for the Catskills: Stradling, *Making Mountains*.

23. "Z Nadprucia," *Gazeta Kołomyjska*, 2 June 1901.

24. Listy z kraju: Jaremcze, 9 sierpnia," *Kuryer Lwowski* 17, no. 221 (11 August 1899), 1–2; "Katastrofy żywiołowe. Powodzie w Galicji wschodniej," *Kuryer Lwowski* 29, no. 309 (10 July 1911), afternoon edition, 1; "Kleine Nachrichten," *Agramer Zeitung*, 2 April 1896, 6; "Usunięcie się góry w Jaremczu," *Kurjer Stanisławowski* 22, no. 1136 (16 June 1907): 2; "Usunięcie się góry w Jaremczu," *Kurjer Stanisławowski* 23, no. 1195 (2 August 1908): 2.

25. See for example: "Listy z kraju: Jaremcze. (Zakusy spekulantów)," *Kurjer Lwowski* 23, no. 100 (10 April 1905): 1–2.

26. "Jaremcze," *Nasze Zdroje* 1, no. 13 (24 July 1910). At least one observer complained that one heard too much German—the language of upper-class Jews. See gw., "Z letnisk i zdrojowisk," *Kurjer Lwowski* 27, no. 350 (29 July 1909), afternoon edition.

27. "Kronika," *Gazeta Kołomyjska*, 26 May 1901.

28. Mieczysław Orłowicz, "Turystyka w dawnym Lwowie (Urywek z przemówienia wygłoszonego na uroczystem Zebraniu jubileuszowem, odbytem w dniu 27.6. b.r. w sali Politechniki lwowskiej dla uczczenia 25 lecia założenia Akademickiego Klubu Turystycznego)," *Kurjer Lwowski*, 3 July 1931.

29. s.b., "List z Worochty (od naszego korespondenta)," *Kurjer Lwowski* 25, no. 379 (16 August 1907), afternoon edition.

30. Another Galician example would be Gabriela Zapolska's play *The Assistant*—about which later this chapter.

31. Kw., "Z Jaremcza (list oryginalny)," *Kurjer Stanisławowski* 15, no. 776 (5 August 1900).

32. Not until 1910, after eight years of negotiations and bureaucratic foot-dragging, was Jaremcze allowed to secede from Dora. Only then could some of the plans for the resort be realized.

33. From a petition sent to the provincial executive, published in "W sprawie rozwoju Jaremcza," *Gazeta Kołomyjska*, 6 October 1906.

34. *Miejscowość klimatyczna "Jaremcze" (525 metrów nad poziomem morza): Przewodnik dla zwiedzających, ułożony staraniem Komitetu Redakcyjnego Klubu "Jaremczańskiego"* (Lwów: n.p., 1913). And I know of only one villa, the Makarewiczes', built with Hutsul motifs: K.Z., "Z Jaremcza," *Kurjer Stanisławowski* 23, no. 1189 (21 June 1908). That said, there was no dearth of literary works dealing with the Hutsuls, including Juljusz Turczyński's *Dzieci puszczy* and *Taras z Worochty*; see "Teatr, literatura

i sztuka," *Kurjer Lwowski* 18, no. 294 (23 October 1900). See also Jan A. Choroszy, *Huculszczyzna w literaturze polskiej* (Wrocław: Jan A. Choroszy, 1991).

35. "W sprawie rozwoju Jaremcza," *Gazeta Kołomyjska*, 6 October 1906. Others voiced concerns that the Hutsuls, like the Tatra highlanders, were becoming greedy: E. M. Ł., "Listy z kraju: Jaremcze, 4. sierpnia," *Kuryer Lwowski*, 6 August 1899. This, although they apparently had not learned how to build houses for guests: b., "Listy z kraju," *Kurjer Lwowski* 30, no. 394 (29 August 1912).

36. "Z naszych gór. Jaremcze, w maju 1910," *Kurjer Stanisławowski*, no. 1291 (5 June 1910).

37. "Visty z Hutsul'shchyny (Dopys' z Dory)," *Stanïslavivs'ki Visty*, no. 1 (4 January 1912).

38. Stanisław Lewicki, Mieczysław Orłowicz and Tadeusz Praschil, *Przewodnik po zdrojowiskach i miejscowościach klimatycznych Galicyi* . . . (Lwów: Związek Zdrojowisk i Uzdrowisk we Lwowie, 1912), 61–65, 18.

39. Nicieja, *Kresowa Atlantyda*, 2:121. There is a great anecdote of a Hutsul hitching a ride with the archducal pair in their car from Jaremcze to Mikuliczyn, not realizing with whom he was traveling: "Tagespost: Der Fahrgast des Erzherzogs," *Bukowinaer Post* 19, no. 2855 (13 June 1912).

40. *Przewodnik po Galicyi zawierający opis zdrojowisk, uzdrowisk* [sic] *zakładów leczniczych polskich oraz miast Krakowa i Lwowa*, ed. Zenon Pelczar, 8th ed. (Kraków: nakład "Polskiego Towarzystwa Balneologicznego," June 1911), 15.

41. "Pol's'ke misto" from "U hory do 'Dory'," *Stanïslavivs'ki Visty*, no. 24 (13 June 1912). There were 15 Poles resident in Jaremcze in 1880, 296 in 1912; 1912 statistics: "Jaremcze jakiem ono jest dzisiaj," *Kurjer Stanisławowski*, no. 1402 (21 July 1912).

42. "U hory do 'Dory'," *Stanïslavivs'ki Visty*, no. 24 (13 June 1912).

43. From "Z-nad Pruta," *Stanyslavivs'ki visti*, 1 August 1937. "Dopysy: Z Dory," *Stanïslavivs'ki Visty* 1, no. 36 (5 September 1912), speaks of a festival there bedecked with the Ukrainian colors (blue and yellow), with the participation of the Ukrainian Sokil group.

44. That they wanted to "Ukrainianize" Dora: "Dopysy: Z Dory," *Stanïslavivs'ki Visty* 1, no. 36 (5 September 1912). Some twenty-five outsiders did invest in a cooperative in Dora, per "Visty z Hutsul'shchyny (Dopys' z Dory)," *Stanïslavivs'ki Visty*, no. 1 (4 January 1912).

45. Interlaken, per *Przewodnik po Galicyi*, 15. Of the 24 members of the communal council of Jaremcze in 1912, reportedly there were (by religion) 19 Christians and 5 Jews, (by nationality) 16 Poles and 8 Ruthenes (6 of whom were peasant farmers). This suggests that 3 Jews had declared themselves as Poles, 2 as Ruthenes. "Korespondencja. Jaremcze, 20. września 1912," *Kurjer Stanisławowski*, no. 1411 (22 September 1912).

46. Perhaps the Jews in Jaremcze were more politically inclined: there was a "flower day" organized by the Zionist Youth from Stanisławów to help fund a Hebrew high school in Jerusalem. "Rundschau," *Wiener Jüdische Volksstimme* (5 September 1912).

47. The sole monograph on the sanatorium is Natalia Tarkowska, *Lecznica narodu: Kulturotwórcza rola zakładu przyrodoleczniczego doktora Apolinarego Tarnawskiego w Kosowie na Pokuciu (1893–1939)* (Kraków: Scientia Plus, 2016). On Kosów, including the famous sanatorium, see also Stanisław Sławomir Nicieja, *Kresowa Atlantyda: Historia i mitologia miast kresowych* (Opole: Wydawnictwo MS, 2013), 3:87–132; also Maciej

Górny, "Exotische Sommerfrische: Das Huzulenland im unabhängigen Polen und die Karpatoukraine im tschechoslowakischen Staat," in *Wiedergewonnene Geschichte. Zur Aneignung von Vergangenheit in den Zwischenräumen Mitteleuropas*, ed. Peter Oliver Loew, Christian Pletzing, and Thomas Serries (Wiesbaden: Harrassowitz 2006), 187–204.

48. *Program lecznicy Dra Tarnawskiego w Kosowie* (Lwów: n.p., 1933), 5.

49. s.b., "Nasze uzdrowiska," *Gazeta Kołomyjska*, 20 August 1899. For more on Meran as a tourist destination, see Cole, "The Emergence and Impact of Modern Tourism in an Alpine Region," 33.

50. Although Tarkowska mentions the utopian aspect of the sanatorium, she does not develop this observation further (Tarkowska, *Lecznica narodu*, 279).

51. Tarkowska, *Lecznica narodu*, 67–69.

52. Dr. Tarnawski, "Łaźnia słoneczna pomysłu Dra Tarnawskiego," *Nasze Zdroje* 3, no. 11 (1 June 1912): 178.

53. See, for example, "Kronika," *Gazeta Kołomyjska* (9 September 1896). In this he was different from Dr. Andrzej Chramiec of Zakopane, who by 1910 had also acquired some of these modern methods, offering a full smorgasbord of treatments. See *Zakład wodoleczniczy dra. A Chramca w Zakopanem* (Kraków: druk W.L. Anczyca i Spółki, 1910).

54. "Polish method," from Tarkowska, *Lecznica narodu*, 64.

55. This loosely woven clothing was reminiscent likewise of Sebastian Kneipp's institute. On this, see Jill Steward, "Travel to the Spas: The Growth of Health Tourism in Central Europe, 1850–1914," in *Journeys into Madness: Mapping Mental Illness in the Austro-Hungarian Empire*, ed. Gemma Blackshaw and Sabine Wieber (New York: Berghahn, 2012), 82.

56. Ignacy Wieniewski, *Kalejdoskop wspomnień* (London: nakładem Polskiej Fundacji Kulturalnej, 1970), 81; Wit Tarnawski, *Mój ojciec* (London: Polska Fundacja Kulturalna, 1966), 118.

57. Romualda Tarnawska and Apolinary Tarnawski, *Kosowska kuchnia jarska* (Warsaw: Wydawnictwo M. Arcta w Warszawie, 1929). A still earlier cookbook (without the doctor's commentary) was published in 1901: Romualda Tarnawska, *Kuchnia jarska stosowana w lecznicy dr Apolinarego Tarnawskiego w Kosowie* (Lwów: n.p.).

58. *Program lecznicy Dra Tarnawskiego w Kosowie.*

59. Tarkowska, *Lecznica narodu*, 88–91.

60. "Po powrocie z Kossowa," *Gazeta Kołomyjska* (17 November 1901). That the same author remarked on it being a Christian institute—and indeed Jews were not welcome—suggests that Tarnawski's antipathy to Jews may well have predated the debacle of him being wrongly accused of treason by Jews during World War I. More about this complicated, dark episode in Tarkowska, *Lecznica narodu*, 44–47 and 265ff. That said, he had treated them as a district doctor in Kosów before he opened his sanatorium.

61. Wieniewski, *Kalejdoskop wspomnień*, 79. Tarnawski had little positive to say about the center of Kosów, which he labeled a "dingy (niechlujne) Jewish town": Dr. A. Tarnawski, "Z Kosowa," *Nasze Zdroje* 3, no. 25 (15 November 1912): 372.

62. As reported in Helena Duninówna, *Ci, których znałam* (Warsaw: Czytelnik, 1957), 125.

63. "Asystent," in *Niedrukowane dramaty Gabrieli Zapolskiej*, ed. Jan Jakóbczyk (Katowice: Wydawnictwo Uniwersytetu Śląskiego, 2012), 2:121–326.

64. Wieniewski, *Kalejdoskop wspomnień*, 77.

65. H.L., "Z naszych letnisk," *Gazeta Kołomyjska*, 19 July 1913. See also Janina Surynowa Wyczółkowska, *W cieniu koronkowej parasolki* (London: Nakładem Katolickiego Ośrodka Wydawniczego "Veritas," n.d.), esp. 134–45.

66. The Kosów institution was an important early hub of Polish scouting. Wieniewski, *Kalejdoskop wspomnień*, 82; Mariusz Martyniak, "Harcerstwo polskie w Karpatach Wschodnich: Zarys działalności," *Płaj* 15 (1992): 5–34.

67. Tarkowska (*Lecznica narodu*, 229–68) devotes a whole chapter to famous patients.

68. *Prospekt lecznicy hygienicznej Dra A. Tarnawskiego w Kosowie (Za Kołomyją, st. kolei Zabłotów lub Wyżnica na Bukowinie) W Galicyi Wschodniej* (Kraków: n.d.) (before 1918), 37, cited in Tarkowska, *Lecznica narodu*, 257.

69. Wieniewski, *Kalejdoskop wspomnień*, 85.

70. "Wiadomości bieżące," Nasze Zdroje 3, no. 5 (1 March 1912): 75. For the actual statute, approved in 1914, see Tarkowska, *Lecznica narodu*, 303–22.

71. "Wiadomości bieżące," Nasze Zdroje 2, no. 9 (2 July 1911); Dr. A[polinary] T[arnawski], "Z Kosowa," Nasze Zdroje 3, no. 27 (15 December 1912): 393.

72. An automobile connection had already been established: "Wiadomości bieżące," Nasze Zdroje 2, no. 4 (23 May 1911).

73. "Kolej lokalna Kołomyja-Kossów," *Gazeta Kołomyjska* (3 February 1894); "Kronika," *Gazeta Kołomyjska* (9 September 1896); "Potrzeba nowej kolei lokalnej," *Gazeta Kołomyjska* (29 April 1900).

74. Wsaz, "Z Kosowa," Nasze Zdroje 3, no. 24 (1 November 1912): 358.

75. Apolinary Tarnawski, "Powiat Kosowski, jako teren letniskowy i uzdrowiskowy," in Mieczysław Orłowicz and Stanisław Lenartowicz, *Ankieta w sprawie Karpat Wschodnich 1931 r.* (Warsaw: nakładem Ministerstwa Robót Publicznych, 1932), 220; James C. Scott, *Weapons of the Weak: Everyday Forms of Peasant Resistance* (New Haven: Yale University Press, 1985).

76. Thomas M. Prymak, *Hrushevsky: The Politics of National Culture* (Toronto: University of Toronto Press, 1987), 60–62.

77. Volodymyr Shukhevych, *Hutsul'shchyna* (L'viv: Nakl. Naukovoho tovarystva im. Shevchenka, 1899–1908), 5 vols.; in Polish translation, Włodzimierz Szuchewicz, *Huculszczyzna* (Lwów: Muzeum im. Dzieduszyckich, 1902–8), 4 vols.

78. On Ivan Franko, see Ivan Denysiuk, "Hutsul's'ki opovidannia Ivana Franka," in *Istoriia Hutsul'shchyny*, ed. Mykola Domashevs'kyi (Chicago: Hutsuls'kyi doslidnyi instytut, 2001) 6:158–68; Petro Arsenych, "Fol'klorno-etnohrafichna diial'nist' I. Franka na Hutsul'shchyni," in *Istoriia Hutsul'shchyny*, ed. Mykola Domashevs'kyi (L'viv: Lohos, 2001), 6:65–66, 70.

79. Biographies of Khotkevych include Fedir Pohrebennyk, "Hnat Khotkevych: Krytyko-biohrafichnyi narys," in Hnat Khotkevych, *Tvory v dvokh tomakh*, 1 (Kyïv: Dnipro, 1966) and Anatolii Bolabol'chenko, *Hnat Khotkevych: Biohrafichni narysy* (Kyïv: Litopys, 1996).

80. In this they were similar to the Tatra Mountain highlanders, who—in the words of one Polish observer—were "perfect artists, although they had never stood on the stage." Władysław Ludwik Anczyc, "Zakopane i lud podhalski," *Tygodnik Illustrowany*, no. 341 (11 July 1874): 28. Secondary works dealing with the Hutsul Theater include Petro Arsenych, *Hutsul's'kyi teatr Hnata Khotkevycha* (Kolomyia: "Svit," 1993); Vasyl' Stef'iuk, *Kermanych Hutsul's'koho teatru: Narys zhytiia i tvorchosti*

H. Khotkevycha; Spohady pro n'oho (Kosiv: Pysanyi Kamin', 2000); Ol'ha Shlemko, "Mystets'ki zasady 'Hutsul's'koho teatru' Hnata Khotkevycha," in *Dyvosvit Hnata Khotkevycha: Aspekty tvorchoï spadshchyny* (Kharkiv: "Fort," 1997); Ol'ha Shlemko, "Hastrol'na diial'nist' hutsul's'koho teatru H. Khotkevycha," *Zapysky naukovoho tovarystva imeny Shevchenka. Pratsi Teatroznavchoï komisiï* 245 (2003): 174–217; Volodymyr and Roman Sinitovych, *Teatral'na perlyna Hnata Khotkevycha* (Verkhovyna: Redaktsiia zhurnalu [vydavnytstvo] "Hutsul'shchyna," 2010).

81. Even today, Poles—and Ukrainians—not familiar with Józef Korzeniowski's play itself know at least one of the songs it popularized, depicting the carefree life of the Hutsul, with his red cape, firearms, and shiny hatchet, free and happy in the mountains. Mykola Ustyianovych wrote Ukrainian lyrics to the Polish song; the Hutsuls would ultimately embrace the resultant "Verkhovyno, svitku ty nash" as their own official hymn. Leszek Rymarowicz, "Wokół historii Teatru Huculskiego z Żabiego (1933–1939)," *Płaj* 54 (fall 2017):1–23, 3.

82. Teodoziia Jasel's'ka-Mel'nychuk, in Stef'iuk, *Kermanych Hutsul's'koho teatru*, 64.

83. Khotkevych, "Hutsulskyi teatr," in Khotkevych, *Tvory* 2:497.

84. Quotation from Rolicz, "Kronika," *Głos Narodu* 74 (31 March 1911). See also "'Karpaccy gorale' i oryginalni bohaterzy [sic]," *Głos Narodu* 74 (31 March 1911): 3; *Nowa Reforma*, no. 138 (24 March 1911), p.m. issue, and no. 142 (28 March 1911), p.m. issue, 2; and *Nowości Illustrowane* 8 (1911), no. 13, 13, with a photograph of the troupe.

85. Shlemko, "Hastrol'na diial'nist' hutsul's'koho teatru," 187.

86. Petro Shekeryk-Donykiv, "Pershyi hutsulskyi teater opered' svitovov voinov (uryvok yz spomyniv)," *Hutsulskyi kaliendar na rik* (1937).

87. Clearly no one in the region saw the acting of peasants as a potential tourist draw, as was the case in the Austrian spa of Meran, where the local authorities and even the regional railway lent financial support to such things. See Jill Steward, "The Spa Towns of the Austro-Hungarian Empire," *New Directions in Urban History: Aspects of European Art, Health, Tourism, and Leisure since the Enlightenment*, ed. Peter Borsay (Münster: Waxmann, 2000), 117.

88. Dmytro Mynailiuk, "Teatral'ni spomyny," in Vasyl' Stef'iuk, *Kermanych Hutsul's'koho teatru, Narys zhyttia i tvorchosti H. Khotkevycha; Spohady pro n'oho* (Kosiv: Pysanyi Kamin', 2000), 161–63, 167–68.

89. Locations from Sinitovych, *Teatral'na perlyna*, 17.

90. Words of Khotkevych, according to Mynailiuk, in Stef'iuk, *Kermanych Hutsul's'koho teatru*, 165.

91. Khotkevych, "Spohady," in Khotkevych, *Tvory* 2:576.

92. Shekeryk-Donykiv, "Pershyi hutsulskyi teater," 110–11.

93. The words of Donia Jasel'ska, cited in Stef'iuk, *Kermanych Hutsul's'koho teatru*, 115. One wonders what kinds of "uncivilized" Europeans the Hutsuls had already encountered, or whether they were referring to their treatment at times during the tours.

94. Khotkevych, in Khotkevych, *Tvory*, 2:496.

95. Stef'iuk, *Kermanych Hutsul's'koho teatru*, 68–9.

96. Lewicki, Orłowicz, and Praschil, *Przewodnik*, 9.

97. I thank Martin Rohde for fruitful discussions on this subject of the missing terminology of "discovery" in the Ukrainian case.

Chapter 7. A New Alpine Club

1. Jerzy K[onrad] Maciejewski, "Odkrywamy Huculszczyznę," in *Huculskim szlakiem II Brygady Legionów Polskich* (Warsaw: Wydawnictwo Towarzystwa Przyjaciół Huculszczyzny, 1934), 28. Maciejewski—who declared that "We are discovering the Hutsul region"—was affiliated with the Military Scientific Publishing Institute (W.I.N.W.) as well as the Propaganda Section of the Society of Friends of the Hutsul Region, also writing novels and articles under the pseudonym Konrad Jotemski. State Archive of the Ivano-Frankivs'k Region in Ukraine (henceforth DAIFO), 370/1/2: 14–18.

2. Henryk Gąsiorowski took Maciejewski to task for claiming discovery, when the Czarnohora Branch of the Polish Tatra Society had been working in the region for sixty years. Henryk Gąsiorowski, "Karpaty Wschodnie jako teren walk legjonowych w świeżych publikacjach," *Wierchy* 12 (1934): 133–40, 139. In another publication the Society of Friends of the Hutsul Region was more circumspect, writing that the region was "as if discovered anew" ("jakby na nowo odkryta"): Towarzystwo Przyjaciół Huculszczyzny, *Projekt organizacji stacji naukowej i muzeum huculskiego w Żabiem* (Warsaw: n.p., 1934), 1.

3. For a Ukrainian story of development, see Patrice M. Dabrowski, "Hutsul Art or 'Hutsul Art'? Ukrainians, Poles, and the 'Discovery' of the Hutsul Kilim in the Interwar Period," *Canadian-American Slavic Studies* 50 (2016): 313–31.

4. Dr. Eduard Kaufmann, "Dem Siege nach (Eine Fahrt ins wiedereroberte Gebiet)," *Pester Lloyd* 62, no. 59 (28 February 1915): 8–9; Volodymyr Klapchuk and Ol'ha Klapchuk, "Z istoriï iaremchans'koï kurortnoï zony (pervisnoobshchynnyi lad-1930-ti roky)," in *Khrestomatiia z hutsul'shchynoznavstva. Dlia zahal'noosvitnikh shkil, himnaziï, litseïv ta vyshchykh navchal'nykh zakladiv* (Kosiv: Pysanyi Kamin' and Prut Prynt, 2001), 248.

5. See the results of the 1921 and 1931 censuses in Joseph Rothschild, *East Central Europe between the Two World Wars* (Seattle: University of Washington Press, 1977), 36.

6. Timothy Snyder, *Sketches from a Secret War: A Polish Artist's Mission to Liberate Soviet Ukraine* (New Haven: Yale University Press, 2005). For a different view of Polish attitudes, see Kathryn Ciancia, "Borderland Modernity: Poles, Jews, and Urban Spaces in Interwar Eastern Poland," *Journal of Modern History* 89 (September 2017): 531–61.

7. Jotsaw [Jadwiga Sawicka], *Z Łodzi do Wschodnich Karpat* (Łódź: [czcionkami Drukarni Państwowej w Łodzi], 1927), 12.

8. Jotsaw, *Z Łodzi*, 57.

9. Jotsaw, *Z Łodzi*, 60.

10. Mieczysław Orłowicz and Stanisław Lenartowicz, *Ankieta w sprawie Karpat Wschodnich 1931 r.* (Warsaw: nakładem Ministerstwa Robót Publicznych, 1932), 10–12.

11. All the same, a handful of Hutsul region cooperatives (including "Hutsul Art") and organizations were ransacked, although nothing incriminating was found. *Polish Atrocities in Ukraine*, ed. Emil Revyuk (New York: printed by the Svoboda Press, 1931), 330. That the Hutsul region was less troubled than other regions inhabited by Ukrainians is likewise suggested by the fact that the English consul and an editor of the London *Times* were taken on a trip to Jaremcze and Tatarów during the pacification, where the beauty of the region was admired and yet its poverty noted. This, per *Dilo*, October 28, 1930, according to *Polish Atrocities*, 83.

12. Walery Goetel, "Zagadnienie ochrony przyrody w Karpatach Wschodnich i ich stosunek do turystyki," in *Ankieta w sprawie Karpat Wschodnich 1931 r.* (Warsaw: nakładem Ministerstwa Robót Publicznych, 1932), 25. The Czarnohora National Park would be established in 1933.

13. See the discussion in Orłowicz and Lenartowicz, *Ankieta*, 46–47.

14. Szymon Wierdak, "Ochrona przyrody w Karpatach Wschodnich ze szczególnem uwzględnieniem Parku Narodowego na Czarnohorze," in Orłowicz and Lenartowicz, *Ankieta*, 34. Some of the terrain was in foreign hands: for example, Kizie Ułohy, prized for the peat bog in its ravine, belonged to lawyer Dr. Landau of Vienna.

15. From the discussion following the presentations on nature preservation, in Orłowicz and Lenartowicz, *Ankieta*, 44.

16. Wacław Majewski, "Zagadnienia turystyki letniej i zimowej," in Orłowicz and Lenartowicz, *Ankieta*, 51–52; Emiljan Bürgel, "Zagadnienia z dziedziny komunikacji kolejowej, drogowej, automobilowej, autobusowej, lotniczej, pocztowej i telefonicznej," in *Ankieta*, 86; Zygmunt Klemensiewicz, "Turystyka zimowa i sporty zimowe w Karpatach Wschodnich," in *Ankieta*, 56–57.

17. For mention of Żabie's potential, see the comment of Wit Tarnawski, in Orłowicz and Lenartowicz, *Ankieta*, 167. On the roads, see Bürgel, "Zagadnienia," 98–99.

18. Apolinary Tarnawski, "Powiat Kosowski jako teren letniskowy i uzdrowiskowy," in Orłowicz and Lenartowicz, *Ankieta*, 218. Emphasis his.

19. Opinions of Dr. Waclaw Majewski and Apolinary Tarnawski's son (also a physician) Wit Tarnawski, in Orłowicz and Lenartowicz, *Ankieta*, 226 and 86, respectively.

20. According to Jotsaw, *Z Łodzi*, 28.

21. Regarding bottled mineral water, Poles shipped around 1 million bottles annually, while the numbers grew astronomically for France (150 million) and Germany (300 million). Włodzimierz Kryński, "Program inwestycji i potrzeba kredytu dla uzdrowisk," in Orłowicz and Lenartowicz, *Ankieta*, 79–80.

22. Henryk Gąsiorowski, "Ochrona swojszczyzny, przemysł i styl ludowy Huculszczyzny; sprawy szkolnictwa zawodowego," in Orłowicz and Lenartowicz, *Ankieta*, 137.

23. Adam Fischer, "Ochrona sztuki ludowej i przemysłu ludowego w Województwie Stanisławowskiem," in Orłowicz and Lenartowicz, *Ankieta*, 125.

24. Gąsiorowski, "Ochrona swojszczyzny," 137–60.

25. Fischer, "Ochrona sztuki ludowej," 133; Gustaf Bolinder, *Underliga Volk i Europas mitt* (Uncommon Peoples of Central Europe) (Stockholm: n.p., 1928).

26. Fischer, "Ochrona sztuki ludowej," 126.

27. Fischer, "Ochrona sztuki ludowej," 127.

28. Fischer, "Ochrona sztuki ludowej," 130.

29. Fischer, "Ochrona sztuki ludowej," 124–26, quotations from 125 and 126, respectively.

30. Fischer, "Ochrona sztuki ludowej," 125. On the Boikos, see the work of Mykhailo Zubryts'kyi, per Frank Sysyn, "Mykhailo Zubryts'kyi: The Nestor of the Ukrainian Village," in Mykhailo Zubryts'kyi, *Zibrani tvory i materialy u triokh tomakh*, vol. 1, *Naukovi pratsi* (L'viv: Litopys, 2013).

31. Orłowicz and Lenartowicz, *Ankieta*, 131–2.

32. Gąsiorowski, "Ochrona swojszczyzny," 140.

33. Gąsiorowski, "Ochrona swojszczyzny," 140, 161.

34. Gąsiorowski, "Ochrona swojszczyzny," 141. Gąsiorowski did not specify what this "element" was, but surely it was clear to those present at the survey.

35. Gąsiorowski, "Ochrona swojszczyzny," 138.

36. From Gąsiorowski, "Ochrona swojszczyzny," 152–53.

37. That said, since the end of the war, several hospitals had been founded, in Żabie and other localities, to fight this epidemic (Gąsiorowski, "Ochrona swojszczyzny," 138).

38. Gąsiorowski, "Ochrona swojszczyzny," 139.

39. 12 August 1931 letter of MSW to Woj. Stan. PILNE, DAIFO 2/5/330: 14; letter of 22 August 1931, DAIFO 2/5/330: 15.

40. Zygmunt Nowakowski, "Kolorowy kraj," Ilustrowany Kurier Codzienny (henceforth IKC), 24 July 1931.

41. See the discussion following the presentation of Henryk Gąsiorowski, in Orłowicz and Lenartowicz, Ankieta, 163.

42. The minutes are found in Protokół z obrad Zjazdu odbytego w 6 listopada 1932 w sali Urzędu wojewódzkiego w Stanisławowie, pod przewodnictwem Wojewody Zygmunta Jagodzińskiego, w sprawie rozwoju turystyki i letnisk w Karpatach Wschodnich, Stanisławów 1932, DAIFO 368/1/32, ark. 1–31.

43. For reference to the Provincial Social Committee (Wojewódzki Komitet Społeczny), see the Orbis brochure, "Święto Huculszczyzny," Centralne Archiwum Wojskowe (henceforth CAW) I.300.1.644, 523–24.

44. DAIFO 368/1/40: 32. (Letter of 9 June 1933 of Teodor Cais, Chair of the Communications-Excursion Section of the District Committee of the Hutsul Holiday in Nadwórna, to the administration of the Stanisławów Branch of the PTT.) The so-called Hutsul region was not coterminous with any one administrative district.

45. The tiny and remote Jabłonica was prepared to house more than four hundred guests, while they had comfortable bedding for one hundred. For more on this, see Patrice M. Dabrowski, "Reinforcing the Border, Reconfiguring Identities: Polish Initiatives in the Carpathians in the Interwar Period," European Review of History: Revue européenne d'histoire 27, no. 6 (Special issue: The Dissolution of the Austro-Hungarian Monarchy: Border Making and Its Consequences) (December 2020): 847–65.

46. From the secret report on the Hutsul Holiday prepared for General Tadeusz Kasprzycki by Captain Adam Kowalski, CAW I.300.1.644, ark. 518.

47. Per the printed Program Święta Huculszczyzny w powiecie kosowskim, CAW I.300.1.644 (between ark. 516 and 517); CAW I.300.1.644, 520.

48. CAW I.300.1.644, 520. For more on 1880, see chapter 5.

49. Reported by the Kosów district captain in the June 1933 secret reports for the Stanisławów province, in DAIFO 2/1/958, ark. 11.

50. CAW I.300.1.644, 519; DAIFO 2/1/958, ark. 30–1; on OUN, DAIFO 2/1/959, ark. 156–57, 270.

51. Secret report on the Hutsul Holiday prepared for General Tadeusz Kasprzycki by Captain Adam Kowalski, CAW I.300.1.644, 520.

52. "Z życia ukraińskiego w R.P. i w Świecie: Święto Huculszczyzny," Biuletyn Polsko-Ukraiński 2, no. 11 (16 July 1933): 11–12, citations from 11.

53. More about that later in this chapter.

54. P[etro] Arsenych, "Uchast' hutsuliv u national'no-vyzvol'nykh zmahanniakh XX stolittia," in *Hutsul'shchyna: perspektyvy ï sotsial'no-ekonomichnoho i dukhovnoho rozvytku v nezalezhnïï Ukraïni* (Ivano-Frankivs'k: n.p., 1994), 3–4.

55. [Piotr Kontny], "Stosunki gospodarcze na połoninach wschodnio-karpackich (Beskidy Huculskie)," DAIFO 869/1/68: 42, ark. 44.

56. This paragraph is based on an account by Petro Shekeryk-Donykiv, who himself had escaped to Czechoslovakia, and thus did not witness the terror inflicted on his family and neighbors. The level of detail and sheer length of the account, penned in April 1921 (perhaps on his return to his homeland, which took place that year), lends credibility. In the possession of Shekeryk's son, this account was first published in 1996–97 in Toronto. See Petro Shekeryk-Donykiv, "Hutsul'shchyna v pol's'komu iarmi," in Shekeryk-Donykiv, *Rik u viruvanniakh Hutsuliv: vybrani tvori* (Verkhovyna: "Hutsul'shchyna," 2009), 217–56.

57. Some labeled this a "Hutsul uprising." See secret letter no. PN 1662/1/ tjn/33 of the Ministry of Internal Affairs to the Governor in Stanisławów, 15 February 1933, signed by M[ikołaj]. Dolanowski, Podsekretarz Stanu/Undersecretary of State, DAIFO 2/1/977. Shekeryk-Donykiv asserted that no uprising took place, and that the original killing of the two policemen was provoked (Shekeryk-Donykiv, "Hutsul'shchyna," 241).

58. [Piotr Kontny], "Stosunki gospodarcze na połoninach wschodnio-karpackich (Beskidy Huculskie)," DAIFO 869/1/68: 42, ark. 44.

59. Secret letter no. PN 1662/1/tjn/33 of the Ministry of Internal Affairs to the Governor in Stanisławów, 15 February 1933, DAIFO F. 2, op. 1, spr. 977. Shekeryk-Donykiv makes no mention of this murder.

60. Secret letter no. PN 1662/1/tjn/33.

61. The attitude of the Hutsuls is clearly stated by Shekeryk-Donykiv, "Hutsul'shchyna," 239.

62. These and other rather outlandish theories are presented, for example, in F. Antoni Ossendowski, *Huculszczyzna: Gorgany i Czarnohora* (Poznań: Wydawnictwo Polskie [R. Wegner)], 1936), 80ff. Of course, in the nineteenth century various other theories had been advanced, including Asiatic, Scandinavian, and Cossack roots— just to mention some presented by Ruthenes/Ukrainians during that period.

63. Nataliya Nechayeva-Yuriychuk, "National Identity and its Role in State Building: The Example of the Hutsul Republic," in *Blick ins Ungewisse: Visionen und Utopien im Donau-Karpaten-Raum 1917 und danach*, ed. Angela Illić, Florian Kührer-Wielach, Irena Samide, and Tanja Žigon (Regensburg: Friedrich Pustet, 2018), 33–50.

64. Karol Stojanowski, "Głód na Huculszczyźnie," *Myśl Narodowa: Tygodnik poświęcony kulturze twórczości polskiej* 12, no. 27 (19 June 1932), 389–40; later republished in full in *Kurjer Lwowski*, 1 July 1932.

65. Jagodziński, in DAIFO 368/1/32, 3.

66. See the secret report on the Hutsul Holiday prepared for General Tadeusz Kasprzycki by Captain Adam Kowalski, CAW I.300.1.644, ark. 518.

67. Andrzej Chojnowski notes the existence of the organization but does not think it was very active—something that this and the next chapter seek to disprove. Andrzej Chojnowski, *Koncepcje polityki narodowościowej rządów polskich w latach 1921– 1939* (Wrocław: Zakład Narodowy imienia Ossolińskich, Wydawnictwo Polskiej Akademii Nauk, 1979), 198. More recently Daniel Fedorowycz has also made note of

what he called "Society of Friends of Hutsulshchyna"—using the Ukrainian form of the name for the Hutsul region—using Ministry of the Interior documents: Daniel Fedorowycz, "Quelling Ukrainian Opposition in Interwar Poland: The Ministry of Interior's Divide and Rule Strategy," *East European Politics and Societies and Cultures* 34, no. 2 (May 2020): 351–74, 363–65.

68. See the first two notes to this chapter.

69. See, for example, "Kasprycki, Tadeusz Zbigniew," in Piotr Stawecki, *Słownik biograficzny generałów Wojska Polskiego 1918–1939* (Warsaw: Bellona 1994), 161–63; Wacław Jędrzejewicz, "Ś.p. Generał Tadeusz Kasprzycki," *Niepodległość* 8 (1980): 225–27; CAW, Akta personalne, K-6749. Kasprzycki himself penned *Kartki z dziennika oficera I Brygady* (Warsaw: Wojskowy Instytut Naukowo-Wydawniczy, 1934).

70. After Piłsudski's death Kasprzycki would become minister for military affairs. Piłsudski had also been inspector general of the Armed Forces.

71. From § 2 of the statute, DAIFO, 370/1/42: 1.

72. DAIFO 370/1/12:2–14. There were approximately forty military men of the two hundred or so on the membership list.

73. DAIFO, 370/1/42: 1, § 4.

74. DAIFO, 370/1/42:2. Serving as intermediary between Warsaw and the Hutsul region was the main branch of the society, in Stanisławów. DAIFO, 370/1/42:18 verte. Much of the extant archival documentation shedding light on the society's activities stems from the archive of the main branch in Stanisławów, presently housed in the State Archive of the Ivano-Frankivs'k Region in Ukraine (DAIFO).

75. DAIFO, 370/1/42:1.

76. DAIFO, 370/1/42:18. The first six were thematic: economic, social hygiene, tourist-health resort, propaganda, the preservation of nativeness, and cultural-educational.

77. The society wished to avoid the haphazard development found in the Tatra Mountain region to the west. DAIFO, 370/1/42: 19. In these competitions, prizes included cows, pigs, and sheep. DAIFO, 370/1/17:24; 370/1/7:1.

78. DAIFO, 370/1/42: 20ff.

79. DAIFO, 370/1/42:22 verte.

80. Bertold Merwin wrote that the temperature fell to minus 25 degrees already in the middle of November, with thick snow cover. Bertold Merwin, *Mit den polnischen Legionen in den Karpathen 1914* (Munich: G. Müller, 1915], 64. For the history of the Second Brigade (if very brief on the Hutsul region), see Stanisław Czerep, *II Brygada Legionów Polskich*, 2nd ed. (Warsaw: Bellona, 2007), 86. The Hutsul campaign is described in detail in *Szlakiem II Brygady Legionów Polskich w Karpatach Wschodnich* (Warsaw: Wojskowy Instytut Naukowo-Oświatowy, 1937), 201–15; Henryk Lewartowski, Bol. Pochmarski and J. A. Teslar, *Szlakiem bojowym Legionów: Krótki zarys organizacyi i dziejów 2. Brygady Legionów Polskich w Karpatach, Galicyi i na Bukowinie* (Lwów: Nak ł. Funduszu Wdów i Sierot po Legionistach, 1915), 74–76.

81. Built on wooden trestles, this four-mile-long road required the construction of nearly thirty bridges by a workforce of about one thousand, composed of Legionnaires as well as workers. Per Captain Stanisław Librewski, "Legjony na Huculszczyźnie," in *Huculskim szlakiem II Brygady Legjonów Polskich* (Warsaw: Wydawnictwo Towarzystwa Przyjaciół Huculszczyzny, 1934), 9–19. The proper name of the Pantyr Pass was Rogodze Pass, but it has gone down in World War I history as Pantyr Pass and is thus referred to here as such.

82. "Młodzieży polska, patrz na ten krzyż! / Legiony Polskie dźwignęły go wzwyż, / Przechodząc góry, lasy i wały, / Do Ciebie Polsko i dla Twej chwały." Published in various secondary sources, including Marek Olszański and Leszek Rymarowicz, *Powroty w Czarnohorę: Nie tylko przewodnik* (Pruszków: Rewasz, 1993), 116.

83. The following section (except where otherwise noted) is based on the report of the man behind the recruitment, Captain Edward Szerauc (Relacja kpt. Szerauca Edwarda: Oddziały huculskie przy Legjonach Polskich, CAW 1.300.28, t. 8, 145–47). For a recent account, see Andrzej Wielocha, "Dzieje kompanii huculskiej 2 pułku piechoty Legionów Polskich," *Płaj* 38 (spring 2009): 63–78.

84. In publications other than Szerauc's (perhaps unpublished) reminiscences, the total is given as 136 (for example, in Wielocha, "Dzieje kompanii huculskiej," 67).

85. Wielocha, "Dzieje kompanii huculskiej," 65.

86. See P[etro] Arsenych, "Uchast' hutsuliv u national'no-vyzvol'nykh zmahanniakh XX stolittia," in *Hutsul'shchyna: perspektyvy ïï sotsial'no-ekonomichnoho i dukhovnoho rozvytku v nezalezhniï Ukraïni* (Ivano-Frankivs'k: n.p., 1994), 3–6.

87. On the first platoon, Wielocha, "Dzieje kompanii huculskiej," 75, where a pay list with their names has been reproduced.

88. For further details, see Patrice M. Dabrowski, "Poles, Hutsuls, and Identity Politics in the Eastern Carpathians after World War I," in special issue "War and Identity," edited by Stephan Lehnstaedt and Marta Ansilewska-Lehnstaedt, *Zeitschrift für Genozidforschung* 16, no. 1 (2018): 19–34.

89. Basic information about the event was laid out in a pamphlet, *Huculskim szlakiem II Brygady Legionów Polskich* (Warsaw: Wydawnictwo Towarzystwa Przyjaciół Huculszczyzny, 1934). More recently, see Dariusz Dyląg, "Marsz zimowy Huculskim szlakiem II Brygady Legionów Polskich," *Płaj* 38 (spring 2009): 139–53. Archival information comes from DAIFO as well as the fond of the command post of the Eastern Małopolska District/Precinct of the Border Guard in Lwów, in the Central State Historical Archive in L'viv (TsDIAL), F. 204, op. 2.

90. TsDIAL, 204/2/279: 1.

91. TsDIAL, 204/2/279: 42.

92. DAIFO, 368/1/42: 26.

93. DAIFO 2/1/10234: 8 verte; Konrad Jotemski, "Śladami legjonistów Żelaznej Brygady," *Żołnierz Polski* 16, no. 7 (1 March 1934), 132. Also addressing the crowds was the mayor of Żabie, Petro Shekeryk-Donykiv.

94. That first year two Hutsul patrols took part.

95. Jotemski, "Śladami legjonistów," 131–33.

96. See, for example, DAIFO 370/1/17:110, 114. DAIFO 370/1/3, ark. 22–23 notes that elements of pro-state propaganda were introduced into the courses, over meals, etc.

97. DAIFO, 370/1/2:19–22, 27, 113–15; 370/1/3:45ff.; 370/1/22: 4–11. More on the Ukrainian reaction in the next chapter. On the deluxe ski trip, see Jarosław Skowroński, *Tatry międzywojenne* (Łódź: Galaktyka, 2003), 59–60; "Zapowiedzi zimowe," *Turystyka* (October 1936): 11–12. The route was Kraków-Worochta-Sławsko-Krynica-Zakopane-Wisła-Kraków.

98. DAIFO 2/1/1023: 40 verte. Orłowicz provided the higher estimate: DAIFO 370/1/4: 61–2.

99. DAIFO 370/1/22: 31–3.

100. DAIFO 370/1/22: 15; DAIFO 3701/22: 16.

101. *Program Święta Huculszczyzny*, 4–8; Henryk Gąsiorowski, *Przewodnik po Beskidach Wschodnich*, vol. 2, *Pasmo Czarnohorskie* (Lwów: Książnica-Atlas, 1933).

102. *Program Święta Huculszczyzny*, 8.

103. DAIFO, 370/1/42:19 verte.

Chapter 8. A Poland of Regions

1. For more on this subject, see Patrice M. Dabrowski, "Borderland Encounters in the Carpathian Mountains and Their Impact on Identity Formation," in *Shatterzone of Empires: Coexistence and Violence in the German, Habsburg, Russian, and Ottoman Borderlands*, ed. Omer Bartov and Eric D. Weitz (Bloomington: Indiana University Press, 2013), 193–208.

2. Among the numerous accounts of the event is Walery Goetel, "Święto Gór," *Turysta w Polsce* 1, no. 7 (1935): 6–7.

3. Goetel, "Święto Gór."

4. Archival material on this event is found in the archive of the Muzeum Historyczne w Sanoku: collection 21a. Zjazd Górski w Sanoku. See also the article by Edward Zając, "Zjazd Ziem Górskich w Sanoku, 14–17 sierpnia 1936 r," *Płaj* 8 (spring 1994): 102–9. Elsewhere I have rendered this as the Union of Highlands (Dabrowski, "Borderland Encounters," 204ff). Jagoda Wierzejska has termed it the Union of Highland Terrains: Jagoda Wierzejska, "A Domestic Space: The Central and Eastern Carpathians in the Polish Tourist and Local Lore Discourse, 1918–1939," *Philological Studies. Literary Research (PFLIT)*, 9, no. 12, part 1: 33–62, 46.

5. Minutes from the ZZG Congress, April 1937, 23–24 in the Centralne Archiwum Turystyki Górskiej, COTG PTTK Kraków: Związek Ziem Górskich (ZZG), 1937, quotation on 24.

6. ZZG Congress, April 1937, 2, 6.

7. The words of Professor Jerzy Smoleński, in ZZG Congress, April 1937, 8.

8. Historian Pieter Judson sees the successor states such as the Second Polish Republic as little empires in their own right: Pieter M. Judson, *The Habsburg Empire: A New History* (Cambridge, MA: Belknap Press of Harvard University Press, 2016). For the slogan, see Walery Goetel, "Zagadnienia regionalizmu górskiego w Polsce," *Wierchy* 14 (1936): 164.

9. On this see Wierzejska, "A Domestic Space," 48, who in this regard speaks of the "Janus face of regionalism" (43). Indeed, soon enough it would give way at the top to a push for national assimilation, while advocating a kind of Hutsul separatism. Andrzej Chojnowski, *Koncepcje polityki narodowościowej rządów polskich w latach 1921–1939* (Wrocław: Zakład Narodowy imienia Ossolińskich, Wydawnictwo Polskiej Akademii Nauk, 1979), esp. 197–98; Waldemar Kozyra, *Polityka administracyjna ministrów spraw wewnętrznych Rzeczypospolitej Polskiej w latach 1918–1939* (Lublin: Wydawnictwo Uniwersytetu Marii Curie-Skłodowskiej, 2009), 549–51; Kozyra, "Regionalizm administracyjny w Polsce w latach 1926–1939," *Res Historica*, no. 37 (2014): 125–38.

10. Daniel Fedorowycz has seen moves of the Polish state vis-à-vis "Ukrainian ethnic subgroups" (the Old Ruthenians, Lemkos, and Hutsuls) as ploys to "divide and rule the Ukrainian minority." Daniel Fedorowycz, "Quelling Ukrainian Opposition in Interwar Poland: The Ministry of Interior's Divide and Rule Strategy," *East European Politics and Societies and Cultures* 34, no. 2 (May 2020): 370, 365.

NOTES TO PAGES 123–127

11. Terry Martin, *The Affirmative Action Empire: Nations and Nationalism in the Soviet Union, 1923–1939* (Ithaca: Cornell University Press, 2001).

12. Health centers were opened in Kosów, Hryniawa, Kosmacz, Zielona, and Sołotwina. The Society of Friends of the Hutsul Region helped finance the construction of wells in Kosmacz, Berezów, Sokołówka, Pistyń, Pasieczna, Worochta, and Nadwórna; bathhouses in Szeszory, Hryniawa, Mikuliczyn, and Żabie; and the provision of running water in Kosów and Żabie. State Archive of the Ivano-Frankivs'k Region in Ukraine (henceforth DAIFO) 370/1/5, ark. 82.

13. DAIFO 370/1/22: 7. For more on the Hutsul Museum, see Łukasz Quirini-Popławski, "Muzeum Huculskie w Żabiem: Historia powstania, funkcjonowanie, współczesne próby reaktywacji," *Płaj* 36 (spring 2008): 111–31; as well as Stanisław Sławomir Nicieja, *Kresowa Atlantyda: Historia i mitologia miast kresowych* (Opole: Wydawnictwo MS, 2014) 4:166–69.

14. Towarzystwo Przyjaciół Huculszczyzny, Projekt organizacji stacji naukowej i Muzeum Huculskiego w Żabiem, Warsaw 1934, Centralne Archiwum Wojskowe (henceforth CAW) I.300.28, t. 8, 2, 8.

15. Quirini-Popławski, "Muzeum Huculskie," 114, 117.

16. DAIFO 370/1/18, ark. 12.

17. "Plan pracy na Huculszczyźnie," CAW, Departament Dowodzenia Ogólnego MSWojsk., I.300.22.109, no date, no archival pagination. The next section is based on this document.

18. Underscoring in the original typescript.

19. This statement helps to date the document to 1933 or earlier.

20. Protokół z zebrania organitacyjnego [sic] Zarządu Gł. Leg. Koła T.P.H. dnia 2 marca 1934, CAW I.300.28, t. 8: 128; Protokół z zebrania organizacyjnego Zarządu Gł. Koła T.P.H. z dnia 16 marca 1934 r., CAW I.300.28, t. 8: 118.

21. "Otwarcie wysokogórskiej szkoły rolniczej w Żabie," *Polska Zbrojna*, 14 February 1937.

22. Briefly on the observatory: Nicieja, *Kresowa Atlantyda*, 2:106–9; Jerzy M. Kreiner, "Dzieje obserwatorium meteorologiczno-astronomicznego na Popie Iwanie," *Urania*, no. 4 (1989).

23. "Obserwatorjum na szczycie Popa Iwana," *Kurjer turystyczno-zdrojowy i komunikacyjny*, dodatek do *IKC*, 19 April 1935. One route went from Kołomyja to Żabie to Zełene by road, after which the traveler was faced with an hour-and-a-half climb up the mountain from the forester's house by the Pohorylec brook, some twelve miles away; the forty-five-mile-long route from Foreszczenka, via Worochta, required a full day of hiking, much across the Czarnohora ridge, to reach the summit.

24. "Nowe obserwatorjum w Czarnohorze: Na granicy dwóch klimatów," *IKC*, 13 April 1935.

25. Kreiner, "Dzieje obserwatorium," 100.

26. Kreiner, "Dzieje obserwatorium," 101. Given the fact that the building had two floors in its basement, cut into the mountain, perhaps the Hutsuls—doubtless some of whom worked on the building or had witnessed the construction—were justified in being suspicious.

27. Władysław Midowicz, "O białym słoniu na Czarnohorze," *Płaj* 2 (1988): 103–12, esp. 109. One needed a pass from the State Meteorological Institute, the actual owner of the building, to gain admittance.

28. That story in Midowicz, "O białym słoniu na Czarnohorze," 103–12, and elsewhere. For more on the fourteen-month career of the observatory, see Władysław Midowicz, *Narracja karpacka (Wspomnienia)* (maszynopis), R-4, Centralna Biblioteka PTTK im. K. Kulwiecia, Warsaw.

29. That this materialistic approach might not suffice, and warranted an ideological approach as well, was discussed at a meeting by Colonel Ryziński, if only noted in the handwritten minutes, not the typewritten ones: DAIFO 370/1/3: 64–70.

30. Report on the Ukrainian press in DALO 121/1/348:21.

31. So according to a secret monthly report to the Stanisławów governor: DAIFO 2/1/1030: 140.

32. "Do aktyvnoi pratsi na Hutsul'shchyni," *Hutsul's'ke Slovo*, 3 June 1934; DAIFO 2/1/1030: 140.

33. Al'fred Budzynovs'kyi, "Nebezpeka zahybeli," *Dilo*, 17 June 1934, commented on in DALO 121/1/348:32, and its Kołomyja version, "Nebezpeka zahybeli," *Hutsul's'ke Slovo*, 24 June 1934.

34. M.L., "Z-nad Pruta," *Stanislavivs'ki Visti*, 1, 8, and 15 August 1937.

35. DAIFO 2/1/1319: 115. For more on the priest, Myroslav Haiduchek, see also DAIFO 2/1/1051:92 and DAIFO 2/1/1317: 139.

36. DALO 121/1/117: 27.

37. B. Li-ch, "Karpaty hovoriat," *Stanislavivs'ki Visti*, chap. 2 (18 July 1937).

38. Brendan Karch, "Instrumental Nationalism in Upper Silesia," in *National Indifference and the History of Nationalism in Modern Europe*, ed. Maarten Van Ginderachter and Jon Fox (London: Routledge, 2019), 180–203; Karch, *Nation and Loyalty in a German-Polish Borderland: Upper Silesia, 1848–1960* (Cambridge: Cambridge University Press, 2018). On national indifference, see works such as those by Tara Zahra, "Imagined Noncommunities: National Indifference as a Category of Analysis," *Slavic Review* 69, no. 1 (spring 2010): 93–119; and Zahra, *Kidnapped Souls: National Indifference and the Battle for Children in the Bohemian Lands, 1900–1948* (Ithaca: Cornell University Press, 2008). On another such case in the Polish lands, see Morgane Labbé, "National Indifference, Statistics, and the Constructivist Paradigm: The Case of the Tutejsi ('The People from Here') in Interwar Polish Censuses," in *National Indifference and the History of Nationalism in Modern Europe*, ed. Maarten Van Ginderachter and Jon Fox (London: Routledge, 2019), 161–79.

39. Examples in DAIFO 2/1/964: 45; DAIFO 2/1/1327: 12; DAIFO 2/1/1047: 60; DAIFO 2/1/1434: 93.

40. On ski clubs: DAIFO 2/1/1464: 99.

41. Sygnały alarmowe z Huculszczyzny," *IKC*, 27 February 1936.

42. James C. Scott, *Weapons of the Weak: Everyday Forms of Peasant Resistance* (New Haven: Yale University Press, 1985).

43. This was pointed out in "Sygnały alarmowe z Huculszczyzny," *IKC*, 27 February 1936.

44. Such as Ivan-vel-Jan Kitleruk, who also wrote of his legionary experience: Jan Kitleruk z Żabiego, "Jak wstąpiłem do Legjonów Polskich," *Żołnierz Polski* 7 (1934): 136–38.

45. Protokół z II Walnego Zjazdu Delegatów towarzystwa Przyjaciół Huculszczyzny, odbytego w Worochcie 16 lutego 1935, DAIFO 370/1/4: 43–47; Protokół Pierwszego Zjazdu Walnego Delegatów T.P.H., odbytego w Jaremczu, dnia 9 lipca 1934 o godz. 9,30, Odpis, DAIFO 370/1/2: 156.

46. Jalu Kurek, "Góralu, czy ci nie żal? O zachłystywaniu się ciupagą," *Wiadomości Literackie* 42 (1937): 7. Kurek was writing in general about highlanders, or even more about the Górale, not about the Hutsuls in particular.

47. Biographical information on Shekeryk can be found in Ivan S[en'kiv?], "Hutsul-pys'mennyk," *Chornohora* (Vienna 1921) 1, no. 2: 54–62; Petro Arsenych, "Samouk z Hutsul'shchyny," *Halychyna*, 18 May 1999; and Arsenych, "Narodoznavets' i hromads'kyi diiach Hutsul'shchyny," in Petro Shekeryk-Donykiv, *Dido Yvanchik: Roman* (Verkhovyna: Hutsul'shchyna, 2007), 476–95; Andrzej Wielocha, "Petro Szekeryk-Donykiv: Biografia nie całkiem kompletna," *Płaj* 35 (fall 2007): 96–122; Maria Sonevytsky, "Three Perspectives on Ethnography from Ukraine: The Mysterious Tale of a Lost Hutsul Manuscript, its Recovery, and the Dialogue that Ensued," *Harriman Review* 17, no. 2 (March 2010): 15–21; Nicieja, *Kresowa Atlantyda* 4: 178–82. Wielocha's is the most complete extant biography.

48. His appearance in Hutsul garb was sensational enough to make the newspapers: "Poseł, który swym strojem wzbudził sensację w Sejmie," *IKC*, no. 90 (30 March 1928), 2 (photograph included).

49. DAIFO 2/1/1031, ark. 141.

50. Taken from a *Hromads'kyi Holos* article under that title of 10 March 1934, no. 9, reported on in secret monthly report of the Kosów district captain: DAIFO 2/1/1044: 96; DAIFO 2/1/1049: 81.

51. Brendan Karch, *Nation and Loyalty*, 19 and passim.

52. Both quotations from Vasyl' Virlynyi, "Ukraintsi-hutsuly i ukraïns'ka inteligentsiiia: Reflieksiï z prohulanky," *Stanyslavivs'ki visti*, cont., 8 August 1937.

53. "Ludność huculska składa pieniądze na zakup samolot 'Hucul,'" *IKC*, 31 July 1937.

54. Jehoschua and Danek Gertner, *Home Is No More: The Destruction of the Jews of Kosow and Zabie* (Jerusalem: Yad Vashem, 2000), 59.

55. Kalèvale, from "Zapiski," *Wiek przyrodniczy i techniczny*, supplement to *Wiek Nowy*, 20 February 1936. More broadly on Vincenz in Mirosława Ołdakowska-Kuflowa, *Stanisław Vincenz pisarz, humanista, orędownik zbliżenia narodów: Biografia* (Lublin: Towarzystwo Naukowe Katolickiego Uniwersytetu Lubelskiego Jana Pawła II, 2006), 20–24.

56. Ołdakowska-Kuflowa, *Stanisław Vincenz pisarz*, 117, 169.

57. See, for example, Ołdakowska-Kuflowa, *Stanisław Vincenz pisarz*, 174 (Cipriani), 126 (Holzapel), 131 (Zbinden). On Ehrenpreis, see Leon Weinstock, "Śladami dróg Baal Szema: O badanianch rab. Dra M. Ehrenpreisa w gniazdach górskich Huculszczyzny," *Chwila*, 10 August 1933.

58. This is visible from Jerzy Konrad Maciejewski's text of "discovery," mentioned in the first note to chapter 7, which in the next paragraph lists Cipriani, Ehrenpreis, and Zbinden.

59. From an interview with Vincenz: Simsund, "Europa i Polska wobec Huculszczyzny," *Gazeta Poranna*, 18 February 1934. For more on Gertner, see his son Danek's chapters in Gertner, *Home Is No More*, 147–85.

60. Stanisław Vincenz, "Uwagi o kulturze ludowej," *Złoty Szlak*, no. 2 (1938): 5–21, esp. 7–8, 17.

61. Simsund, "Europa i Polska."

62. The military authorities behind the society did not share Vincenz's inclusive attitude toward the Ukrainian intelligentsia, which it saw only in its separatistic

incarnation. For Vincenz's positive view of the old Jagiellonian state, the Polish-Lithuanian Commonwealth, see the telling quotation in Ołdakowska-Kuflowa, *Stanisław Vincenz*, 122. It has been translated into English in Patrice M. Dabrowski, "On Forgetting, Displacement, and Historical Error in Polish History," *The Polish Review* (forthcoming 2021).

63. St[anisław] Kostka, "Odkrywamy Huculszczyznę," *Podchorąży* nr 13, 1.04.1937(?): 22–23, copy in Ossolineum rkp 17276/III: 20b–21.

64. He was on an early list of members. DAIFO 370/1/12: 12 and reportedly served as the head as the Section for the Protection of Nativeness of the Kołomyja branch of the society, according to Ołdakowska-Kuflowa, *Stanisław Vincenz*, 177. Yet Vincenz did not lead the overall organization, as Maciej Górny claimed: Maciej Górny, "Exotische Sommerfrische: Das Huzulenland im unabhängigen Polen und die Karpatoukraine im tschechoslowakischen Staat," in *Wiedergewonnene Geschichte. Zur Aneignung von Vergangenheit in den Zwischenräumen Mitteleuropas*, ed. Peter Oliver Loew, Christian Pletzing, and Thomas Serries (Wiesbaden: Harrassowitz 2006), 187–204, esp. 202.

65. For a look at the extant correspondence between Kasprzycki and Vincenz after World War II, see "Obraz Huculszczyzny w liście Stanisława Vincenza do gen. Tadeusza Kasprzyckiego," ed. Andrzej Ruszczak, *Płaj* 40 (spring 2010): 65–71. On Witkiewicz, see chaps. 1–4.

66. Plan piśmiennictwa huculskiego na najbliższe czasy, CAW I.300.1.644, ark. 546–48. Although Vincenz's name does not appear in this document, the details betray the author's identity. Regular calendars were published in the even years.

67. Plan piśmiennictwa huculskiego, ark. 547.

68. Plan piśmiennictwa huculskiego, ark. 547. Vincenz had nothing against Ukrainians, a number of whom he counted among his friends; rather, he preferred that Poland be a multiethnic country, with room for Ukrainians and Hutsuls alike.

69. Piotr Kontny, "Polska na międzynarodowej giełdzie turystyki: Licytacja piękna naszego kraju," *Gazeta Poranna*, 8 August 1933.

70. Petro Shekeryk-Donykiv, "Pershyi hutsulskyi teater opered' svitovov voinov (uryvok yz spomyniv)," *Hutsulskyi kaliendar na rik 1937*, 117–18.

71. A conversation noted in Józef Kuropieska, *Wspomnienia oficera sztabu 1934–1939* (Kraków: Krajowa Agencja Wydawnicza, 1984), 251.

72. Ivan Sen'kiv, *Hutsul's'ka spadshchyna* (Kyïv: Ukraïnoznavstvo, 1995), 465.

73. On the digging up and publishing, see Sonevytsky, "Three Perspectives." Petro Shekeryk-Donykiv, *Dido Yvanchik: Roman* (Verkhovyna: vydavnytstvo "Hutsul'shchyna," 2007).

74. Here I render as "native landscape" (krajobraz rodzimy) that which Jagoda Wierzejska in her perceptive article translated as "domestic landscape": Wierzejska, "A Domestic Space," 33–62.

75. For information on the Carpathian huts, see Władysław Krygowski, "Gospodarka turystyczna w Karpatach," *Wiadomości Ziem Górskich* 6 (June 1939): 2–6. A more recent assessment of the region is Łukasz Quirini-Popławski, "Najważniejsze ośrodki ruchu turystycznego w Czarnohorze w dwudziestoleciu międzywojennym," *Prace geograficzne*, 117 (Kraków: Instytut Geografii i Gospodarki Przestrzennej UJ, 2007): 113–24.

76. See, for example, "Połonina Maryszewska" and "Nowe schroniska w górach Czywczyńskich," both in *IKC*, 10 January 1936. A review of these accomplishments is found in Andrzej Ruszczak, "Oddział Czarnohorski Towarzystwa Tatrzańskiego: Zarys działalności," *Płaj* 25 (2002): 155–65.

77. Łukasz Quirini-Popławski, "Początki zorganizowanego ratownictwa górskiego w Czarnohorze i Tatrach," *Stan i perspektywy rozwoju turystyki w Tatrzańskim Parku Narodowym*, ed. J. Pociask-Karteczka, A. Matuszyk, P. Skawiński (Kraków-Zakopane: AWF-TPN, 2007): 111–20, 115–16.

78. See the account in Józef Stasko, *Huculskim szlakiem* (Chorzów: n.p., 1938), 31ff.

79. Maria Dulęba, *Na turystycznych ścieżkach* (Warsaw: Nasza Księgarnia, 1975), 171; description of trips 164ff.

80. Although travel restrictions were lifted for certain health resort-spa destinations in May 1939, per *Wiadomości Ziem Górskich* 5 (May 1939): 9–10. For the restrictions on real estate, see the Polish translation of Dr. Stefan Baran, "Kraina, która zamiera," *Dilo*, no. 157 (21 July 1938), found in DALO 121/1/350.

81. Quotations from "K. Pawlewski, " 'Tydzień Gór' wielką manifestacją patriotyczną ludu górskiego," *Wiadomos'ci Ziem Górskich*, no. 8 (August 1939), 2. It was also advertised as the "International 'Highland Week' in Zakopane," as highlanders from other countries—Hungary, Romania, even Scotland—were scheduled to participate. "III. Mie˛dzynarodowy 'Tydzien' Gór' w Zakopanem," *Wiadomos'ci Ziem Górskich*, no. 4 (April 1939), 11, as well as in later issues of the same journal.

Chapter 9. A Novel Wilderness

1. There was also an occasional German settlement, dating from the time of Joseph II of Austria. Stanisław Kryciński, "Kolonizacja 'jozefińska' w Galicji," *Połoniny* 14 (1984): 20–32.

2. For more on the distribution of the Jewish population, see Maria Soja, "Jewish Population in the Polish Carpathian Mountains in the 19th and 20th Centuries," *Region and Regionalism* 2, no. 6 (2003): 51–57. One should not forget Polish noble estates or landholdings either: for the wartime fate of one of them, see Józefa Renata Dąmbska-Gedroyć, *Tajemnice Bieszczad: Placówka AK Żubracze* (Warsaw: Muzeum Niepodległości, 2001).

3. In correspondence with Piotr Kontny before the war, a young ethnographer named Roman Reinfuss said that it was "nonsense" (*bujda*) to make of these peoples separate "tribes": the differences between them had emerged only in the last 100 to 150 years. Letter of Roman Reinfuss to Piotr Kontny of 21 October 1936, in Arkhiv Petra Kontnoho, Tsentralnyi Derzhavnyi Istorychnyi Arkhiv u L'vovi [henceforth TsDIAL], 869/1/14, 130.

4. Stanisław Kłos, *Bieszczady* (Wrocław: Wydawnictwo Dolnośląskie, 2000), 126. The multiethnic and contested nature of the borderlands was of course typical of Eastern Europe. For their relation to the development of tourism see the chapters by Alexander Vari and Aldis Purs ("From Friends of Nature to Tourist-Soldiers: Nation Building and Tourism in Hungary, 1873–1914" and " 'One Breath for Every Two Strides': The State's Attempt to Construct Tourism and Identity in Interwar Latvia," respectively), in *Turizm: The Russian and East European Tourist under Capitalism and*

Socialism, ed. Anne E. Gorsuch and Diane P. Koenker (Ithaca: Cornell University Press, 2006).

5. See, for example, relations in Terka, discussed in Artur Brożyniak and Małgorzata Gliwa, "Terka—Wołkowyja 1939-1947: Mikrohistoria krwawego konfliktu ukraińsko-polskiego," in *Bieszczady w Polsce Ludowej 1944-1989*, ed. Jakub Izdebski, Krzysztof Kaczmarski, and Mariusz Krzysztofiński (Rzeszów: IPN Oddział w Rzeszowie, 2009), 62.

6. Grzegorz Motyka, *W kręgu "Łun w Bieszczadach": Szkice z najnowszej historii polskich Bieszczad* (Warsaw: Oficyna Wydawnicza Rytm, 2009), 52.

7. For more detail, see Timothy Snyder, *The Reconstruction of Nations: Poland, Ukraine, Lithuania, Belarus, 1569-1999* (New Haven: Yale University Press, 2003), esp. chap. 8; Orest Subtelny, "Expulsion, Resettlement, Civil Strife: The Fate of Poland's Ukrainians, 1944-1947," in *Redrawing Nations: Ethnic Cleansing in East-Central Europe, 1944-1948*, ed. Philipp Ther and Ana Siljak (Lanham, MD: Rowman & Littlefield, 2001), 155-72; and Marek Jasiak, "Overcoming Ukrainian Resistance: The Deportation of Ukrainians within Poland in 1947," in *Redrawing Nations: Ethnic Cleansing in East-Central Europe, 1944-1948*, ed. Philipp Ther and Ana Siljak (Lanham, MD: Rowman & Littlefield, 2001), 173-94.

8. Motyka, *W kręgu*, 56-59.

9. Małgorzata Gliwa, "Przesiedlenia ludności ukraińskiej z Bieszczad Zachodnich w latach 1944-1947," in *Bieszczady w Polsce Ludowej 1944-1989*, ed. Jakub Izdebski, Krzysztof Kaczmarski, and Mariusz Krzysztofiński (Rzeszów: Instytut Pamięci Narodowej, Komisja Ścigania Zbrodni przeciwko Narodowi Polskiemu, Oddział w Rzeszowie, 2009), 46.

10. Gliwa, "Przesiedlenia ludności ukraińskiej," 45-60.

11. The timing of this move is noteworthy: the communists set about dealing with the UPA only once they had sounded the death knell for the noncommunist opposition of the Polish peasant-populist leader Stanisław Mikołajczyk.

12. Grzegorz Ostasz, "Śmierć generała 'Waltera' i jego legenda," in *Bieszczady w Polsce Ludowej 1944-1989*, ed. Jakub Izdebski, Krzysztof Kaczmarski, and Mariusz Krzysztofiński (Rzeszów: Instytut Pamięci Narodowej, Komisja Ścigania Zbrodni przeciwko Narodowi Polskiemu, Oddział w Rzeszowie, 2009), 115-22; Motyka, *W kręgu*, esp. 122-40; Jasiak, "Overcoming Ukrainian resistance," 189.

13. Snyder, *Reconstruction of Nations*, 189.

14. "Przechodniu! / Spójrz na ten krzyż / Żołnierze polscy wznieśli go w zwyż / Ścigając faszystów / przez lasy gory i skały / Dla ciebie Polsko / i dla twojej chwały." Photograph of the tablet in Motyka, *W kręgu*, 85. "Fascists" was a synonym for "Ukrainians" at that time.

15. Bart Nabrdalik, "South-eastern Poland between 1939 and the Final Soviet Frontier Demarcation in 1951—the Destruction of an Ethnic Mosaic," *Journal of Slavic Military Studies* 21 (2008): 32.

16. Kazimierz Pudło, "Dzieje Łemków po drugiej wojnie światowej (Zarys problematyki)," *Łemkowie w historii i kulturze Karpat*, ed. Jerzy Czajkowski (Rzeszów: Editions Spotkania, 1992), 355-56, 360. Tadeusz Andrzej Olszański claims that most of the inhabitants of the highland regions in the Bieszczady escaped deportation to the USSR but, after the UPA had been routed, did not escape Operation Vistula. Olszański, in *Bieszczady: Przewodnik*, 8th rev. ed. (Pruszków: Rewasz, 2001), 65.

17. Mieczysław Orłowicz, *Bieszczady* (Warsaw: Sport i Turystyka, 1954), 28.

18. *Bieszczady: Przewodnik*, 70–71, 76–77; Zbigniew K. Wójcik, "Zmiana granicy wschodniej Polski Ludowej w 1951 r. (zarys problematyki)," in *Bieszczady w Polsce Ludowej 1944–1989*, ed. Jakub Izdebski, Krzysztof Kaczmarski, Mariusz Krzysztofiński (Rzeszów: IPN Oddział w Rzeszowie, 2009), 125–30. As with previous population transfers, the inhabitants had been given no prior notice of the exchange; that cold December day they had not been allowed to take with themselves more than they could carry.

19. The Bieszczady (more specifically, Ustrzyki Dolne) gained only a thousand individuals to replace the four thousand Ukrainians who had been displaced. See Nabrdalik, "South-eastern Poland," 33–35.

20. Peter Coates, "Borderland, No Man's Land, Nature's Wonderland: Troubled Humanity and Untroubled Earth," *Environment and History* 20, no. 4 (November 2014): 499–526.

21. The words of Władysław Krygowski, "Przymierze z Bieszczadami," in Archiwum Państwowe w Rzeszowie, Polskie Towarzystwo Turystyczno-Krajoznawcze, Zarząd Okręgowy w Rzeszowie 1950–1976 (henceforth APRz PTTK) 218: 13. Some of the prose is reminiscent of that of Stanisław Witkiewicz.

22. The Tatra National Park was established in 1954. For more on its rather convoluted history, see Bianca Hoenig, *Geteilte Berge: Eine Konfliktgeschichte der Naturnutzung in der Tatra* (Göttingen: Vandenhoeck & Ruprecht, 2018).

23. Shades of the region in centuries past: the seventeenth and eighteenth centuries in the mountains were characterized by brigandage, with bands of so-called *beskidnicy* and lawless nobles from both sides of the Polish-Hungarian border on the rampage. On this see Władysław Łoziński, *Prawem i lewem: Obyczaje na Czerwonej Rusi w pierwszej połowie XVII wieku*, 4th ed. (Lwów: Nakładem Księgarni Gubrynowicza i syna, 1931).

24. A gendered reading of this is apt: for many more men came to inhabit the region than did women. Even today, there are only 96 women per 100 men in the region at large, with the communes of Cisna and Lutowiska at only 76 and 69 women, respectively, per 100 men (*Bieszczady: Przewodnik*, 34).

25. *Bieszczady: Przewodnik dla prawdziwego turysty*, 11th rev. ed. (Pruszków: Oficyna wydawnicza "Rewasz," 2006), 142.

26. Daniel H. Cole, *Instituting Environmental Protection: From Red to Green in Poland* (Houndmills, UK: Macmillan Press, 1998), 94–95.

27. This successor to the Polish Tatra Society and the Polish Local Studies Society has sometimes been translated as the Polish Association for Tourism and Knowledge of the Country; see Barbara Hicks, *Environmental Politics in Poland: A Social Movement Between Regime and Opposition* (New York: Columbia University Press, 1996), 84. More commonly it is given as the Polish Tourist Country-Lovers' Association, which appears to be the translation of choice in the PTTK's organ, *Wierchy*.

28. W[ładysław] Krygowski, "Główny szlak wschodnio-beskidzki Krynica-Halicz," *Wierchy* 22 (1953): 238–43.

29. In Polish, this type of tourism was called "tourism with a hatchet" (*turystyka z siekierą*). *Bieszczady: Przewodnik*, 145.

30. Władysław Krygowski, "Spotkanie z inną ziemią," *Wierchy* 21 (1952): 126.

31. Krygowski, "Spotkanie z inną ziemią," 125.

32. Krygowski, "Spotkanie z inną ziemią," 127.

33. Jacek Kolbuszewski, *Kresy* (Wrocław: Wydawnictwo Dolnośląskie, 1995), 208.

34. For their routes and reminiscences, see Andrzej Potocki, *Bieszczadzkimi i beskidzkimi śladami Karola Wojtyły* (Brzozów: n.p., 1992), 17–28. Basic information is also in Tadeusz Szewczyk, "'Te góry są mi dobrze znane': Jan Paweł II w Bieszczadach," *Bieszczad* 12 (2005): 202–31.

35. Witness Stanisław Staszic, already in the early nineteenth century, or parish priests Wojciech Roszek, Jędrzej Pleszowski, and Józef Stolarczyk, all in the Tatra Mountain region of the Polish Carpathians.

36. In later years, already as pope, he would famously travel to hike—albeit without the same verve of these earlier years—in various segments of the Polish Carpathians. And late in his life he repeatedly said he wanted to visit the Bieszczady again. Szewczyk, "'Te góry są mi dobrze znane,'" 221 and passim.

37. Maria Dulęba, *Na turystycznych ścieżkach* (Warsaw: Nasza Księgarnia, 1975), 288–90.

38. A number of Greek Catholic churches were treated this way—and worse. See Olga Kurzynoga, "Utracone dobra kultury w Bieszczadach w latach 1944–1989," *Bieszczady w Polsce Ludowej 1944–1989*, ed Jakub Izdebski, Krzysztof Kaczmarski, and Mariusz Krzysztofiński (Rzeszów: IPN Oddział w Rzeszowie, 2009), 399–401.

39. Dulęba, *Na turystycznych ścieżkach*, 291–93.

40. To be sure, responsibility for the Bieszczady and Low Beskids would in 1956 be assigned to Warsaw student hikers. (Students in other cities would take responsibility for other parts of the Polish Carpathians.) On this, see Tomasz Kowalik, "W pięćdziesiąt lat później—złoty jubileusz," *Pół wieku w górach 1957–2007, czyli dzieje Studenckiego Koła Przewodników Beskidzkich w Warszawie*, ed. Andrzej Wielocha (Warsaw: Studenckie Koło Przewodników Beskidzkich, 2007), 40.

41. "Górale spod Warszawy"—for example, in Jerzy Korejwo, "Przewodnicy z błękitnym krzyżem," in *Pół wieku w górach 1957–2007, czyli dzieje Studenckiego Koła Przewodników Beskidzkich w Warszawie*, ed. Andrzej Wielocha (Warsaw: Studenckie Koło Przewodników Beskidzkich, 2007), 94.

42. Grzegorz Woroszyłło, "Góry wspólnie odnalezione," *Połoniny* 3 (1973): 7–11.

43. Witold Michałowski and Janusz Rygielski, *Spór o Bieszczady* (Warsaw: Sport i Turystyka, 1979), 18. For more about the organization, see *Pół wieku w górach 1957–2007, czyli dzieje Studenckiego Koła Przewodników Beskidzkich w Warszawie*, ed. Andrzej Wielocha (Warsaw: Studenckie Koło Przewodników Beskidzkich, 2007). The name dates from 1963. A chronological list of all members can be found at SKPB Warszawa, Wszechlista Koła: http://www.skpb.waw.pl/przewodnicy/wszechlista. html, last accessed 2 September 2020.

44. Dariusz Piątkowski, "Bieszczadzkie perspektywy," *Światowid*, no. 24 (8 October 1961): 10–13, 10.

45. Until 1959, students spending the night in Ustrzyki Górne slept in a chicken coop near the border guard station. Witold Michałowski and Janusz Rygielski, *Spór o Bieszczady*, 2nd ed. (Warsaw: Sport i Turystyka, 1986), 146–47.

46. Kowalik, "W pięćdziesiąt lat później," 42.

47. For more on the beginnings, see Witold Cygan, "Początek," *Pół wieku w górach 1957–2007, czyli dzieje Studenckiego Koła Przewodników Beskidzkich w Warszawie*, ed. Andrzej Wielocha (Warsaw: Studenckie Koło Przewodników Beskidzkich, 2007),

95–98. In addition to students, it attracted a lot of characteristic Bieszczady types—about whom more later.

48. Uchwała nr17/65 Wojewódzkiej Rady Narodowej w Rzeszowie z dnia 21 września 1965 r. w sprawie zatwierdzenia sprawozdania z realizacji uchwał rządowych dotyczących zagospodarowania Bieszczadów oraz głównych kierunków rozwoju terenów południowo-wschodnich województwa rzeszowskiego w latach 1966–1970, in Archiwum Akt Nowych (henceforth AAN), GKKFiT 2/168: 88.

49. GKKFiT, Uchwała podkomitetu turystyki w sprawie podniesienia społeczno-wychowawczej roli turystyki (Warsaw, 9 November 1962), 22–30, in AAN, GKKFiT 1/399: 24.

50. Some such excursions (likely smaller ones) were called *wczasy wędrowne*, literally "wandering vacations." Some examples of these are found in APRz PTTK 371/217: 36–39.

51. *Bieszczady: Przewodnik*, 148. The second ever rajd in the Bieszczady already had 786 participants. E.M., "II Ogólnopolski Raid Bieszczadzki," *Wierchy* 24 (1955): 182–83.

52. The rules governing participation in the All-Poland Highland Rajd in the Bieszczady of 1954 filled nine typed pages. APRz PTTK 371/205: 87–91.

53. See, for example, AAN, GKKFiT, 1/397: 63.

54. For information on the first rajd in the Bieszczady, also in 1954, see E. Moskała, "Pierwszy Górski Raid w Bieszczadach," *Wierchy* 23 (1954): 240–42. This appears to be the Year of the Rajd—so many were organized in various parts of the Polish Carpathians. And that same year a four-person group traversed the route Komańcza-Cisna-Ustrzyki Górne on skis. Paweł Czartoryski, "Grzbietami Bieszczadów na nartach," *Wierchy* 23 (1954): 247–48.

55. APRz PTTK 218: 46 verte.

56. Capitalization in the original. Per the Regulamin I-go Okręgowego Raidu Górskiego w Bieszczadach, APRz PTTK 218: 1.

57. Sprawozdanie z odbytego Rajdu Górskiego w Bieszczadach Zachodnich w dniach od 13–19 września 1954 zorganizowanego przez Zarząd Okręgu PTTK i Zarząd Woj. TPPR w miesiącu Pogłębienia Przyjaźni Polsko-Radzieckiej, APRz PTTK 218: 89ff.

58. Sprawozdanie z odbytego Rajdu Górskiego . . . APRz PTTK 218.

59. APRz PTTK 218: 1. An inheritance from the brief period when Ustrzyki Dolne (then Shevchenkovo) had been part of the USSR (before the border revision of 1951), the Stalin monument was one of only three monuments to Stalin in the East Bloc. Krzysztof Potaczała, *Bieszczady w PRL-u* (Olszanica: BOSZ, 2012), 17.

60. APRz PTTK 218: 15.

61. Dariusz Jarosz, *"Masy pracujące przede wszystkim": Organizacja wypoczynku w Polsce 1945–1956* (Warsaw-Kielce: Instytut Historii PAN-Akademia Świętokrzyska, 2003), 286.

62. APRz PTTK 218: 14.

63. See, for example, the Patrol March of Youth via the Last Trail of the General-Revolutionary Karol Świerczewski that took place from 24–28 March 1954. It was fully militarized, with participants asked—among other things—to throw a grenade at a target. Per Regulamin, APRz 43/21641: 4–9.

64. Not only subsequently: an atypical part of his biography was the Pole Świerczewski's participation in the Polish-Soviet War of 1920 on the side of the Soviets.

65. On him supplanting Piłsudski, see Świerczewski's biographer and apologist Franciszek Kusiak, *Generał Karol Świerczewski Walter—życie i po życiu 1897–1947–2017* (Wrocław: Wydawnictwo Eurosystem, 2017), 10. On the cult of Piłsudski, see Heidi Hein-Kircher, *Kult Piłsudskiego i jego znaczenie dla państwa polskiego 1926–1939* (Warsaw: Neriton, 2008).

66. On the former point, see Tadeusz Andrzej Olszański in *Bieszczady: Przewodnik*, 68. On the latter point, see Tadeusz Graba, "Śmierć generała [Karola Świerczewskiego]," *Kamena* 34, no. 6 (1967): 1, 3.

67. The first quotation comes from the title of Janina Broniewska's popular children's book about Świerczewski, *O człowieku, który się kulom nie kłaniał* (Warsaw: "Prasa Wojskowa," 1948) (multiple editions); the second, from Jan Gerhard, "O generale Walterze, pomniku i pamięci," *Życie literackie* 8, no. 14 (1964): 1–2.

68. Cited in Ostasz, "Śmierć generała," 123.

69. x.y., "Odsłonięcie pomnika ku czci gen. Karola Świerczewskiego," *Wierchy* 31 (1962): 215–16. It would stand there for fifty-five years, to be torn down by a post-communist government in early 2018.

70. Words of Aleksander Zawadzki, the chair of the General Polish Committee of Defenders of Peace, cited in Henryk Pasławski, "W Bieszczadach stanął pomnik generała Waltera," *Kamena* 29, no. 15 (1962): 2.

71. Protokół Nr 5 / 66 z posiedzenia Prezydium Wojewódzkiego Komitetu Kultury Fizycznej i Turystyki odbytego w dniu 20 maja 1966 r., in AAN, GKKFiT 2 / 170: 184. In 2018 the monument was torn down.

72. See *Bieszczady: Przewodnik*, 148, for the timing; Artur Bata, *Jabłonki: Miejsce śmierci Generała Karola Świerczewskiego* (Rzeszów: Krajowa Agencja Wydawnicza, 1987), 66–70, and Zbigniew Kresek, *Szlak im. Gen. Karola Świerczewskiego w Bieszczadach: Przewodnik turystyczny* (Warsaw: Wydawnictwo PTTK "Kraj," 1985), provide details on the trail.

Chapter 10. Tourism for the Masses

1. This was clearly the Party line already as of the early 1950s. See Walery Goetel, "Turystyka polska na nowych drogach," *Wierchy* 20 (1950–51): 5–41, esp. 32.

2. W. Krygowski, "Góry nasze—góry dla wszystkich," *Wierchy* 19 (1949): 1–12.

3. Often the term used was *universal tourism*, even though it early on became a reward for shock workers and other especially deserving workers or communist functionaries. Paweł Sowiński, *Wakacje w Polsce Ludowej: Polityka władz i ruch turystyczny (1945–1989)* (Warsaw: TRIO, 2005), 59.

4. Words of Zbigniew Kulczycki, Stenogram z posiedzenia Podkomitetu Turystyki GKKFiT 15 XI 1961 r., Archiwum Akt Nowych (henceforth AAN) 1 / 398: 24.

5. Kulczycki, Stenogram . . . AAN 1 / 398: 24–25.

6. Founded in the 1920s, Orbis was the main Polish tourist bureau; it was allowed to resume activity in the 1940s. Aleksy Chmiel, *Turystyka w Polsce w latach 1945–1989* (Warsaw: ALMAMER, 2007), 389.

7. The law of the Economic Committee of the Council of Ministers (no. 271 / 59 of 27 June 1959) addressed the "matter of developing the Bieszczady" (*sprawę zagospodarowania Bieszczad*), not only tourism, during the period 1959–65. Wilhelm Dębicki,

"Jeszcze wokół problemu zagospodarowania Bieszczadów," *Wierchy* 37 (1968): 169, among other sources.

8. State-owned farms and enterprises outweighed privately owned farms and businesses, a phenomenon which in Poland reflected the fact that the social and economic structure of the prewar period had been destroyed here.

9. Prezydium Wojewódzkiej Rady Narodowej w Rzeszowie, "Realizacja uchwał rządowych w sprawie aktywizacji gospodarczo-społecznej rejonu Bieszczadów oraz wnioski zmierzające do dalszego rozwoju tych terenów," 24 April 1965, in AAN, GKKFiT 2/168: 22. See also APRz 43/21703: 71; APRz 43/21703: 101–2.

10. Worth noting: of the 1959 law's four main thrusts, investment in tourism came in a distant last.

11. For more on the construction of the dam at Solina, see Janusz Dziewański, "Morze Bieszczadzkie: Budowa zapory wodnej i elektrowni w Solinie," *Bieszczad: Rocznik Towarzystwa Opieki nad Zabytkami, Oddział Bieszczadzki* 10 (2003): 317–58. For more on the roads, see Bronisław Bremer, "Od traktu winnego do 'obwodnicy' i 'cięciwy,'" *Połonina* (1973): 41–46.

12. Loren Graham, *The Ghost of the Executed Engineer* (Cambridge, MA: Harvard University Press, 1993), discussed in Paul R. Josephson, *Industrialized Nature: Brute Force Technology and the Transformation of the Natural World* (Washington, DC: Island Press/Shearwater Books, 2002), 22–23.

13. Krzysztof Potaczała, *Bieszczady w PRL-u* (Olszanica: BOSZ, 2012), 118; Paul Josephson, "Industrial Deserts: Industry, Science, and the Destruction of Nature in the Soviet Union," *Slavonic and East European Review* 85, no. 2 (April 2007): 294–321. On "brute force technology," see Josephson, *Industrialized Nature*.

14. Potaczała, *Bieszczady*, 111–24.

15. Phrase borrowed from David Blackbourn, *The Conquest of Nature: Water, Landscape, and the Making of Modern Germany* (New York: W. W. Norton, 2006), 66.

16. Jan Malczewski, "Inwestycje w Bieszczadach i ich geneza," in *Bieszczady w Polsce Ludowej 1944–1989*, ed. Jakub Izdebski, Krzysztof Kaczmarski, and Mariusz Krzysztofiński (Rzeszów: IPN w Rzeszowie, 2009), 433.

17. Quoted from Blackbourn, *The Conquest of Nature*, 239.

18. Blackbourn, *The Conquest of Nature*, 7.

19. Potaczała, *Bieszczady*, 103–10.

20. The authorities admitted as much. See Prezydium Wojewódzkiej Rady Narodowej w Rzeszowie, "Realizacja uchwał rządowych w sprawie aktywizacji gospodarczo-społecznej rejonu Bieszczadów oraz wnioski zmierzające do dalszego rozwoju tych terenów," 24 April 1965, in AAN, GKKFiT 2/168: 15. In the 1970s, it actually cost more to produce the lumber than it was worth (*Bieszczady: Przewodnik dla prawdziwego turysty*, 11th revised ed. [Pruszków: Oficyna wydawnicza "Rewasz," 2006], 35 and passim).

21. Adolf Jakubowicz, "Reklamowa pocztówka . . . z cieniem," *Kamena*, no. 19 (15 October 1962): 12, decries the situation he encountered. See also the report in APRz 43/21703: 118–19.

22. Paweł Sowiński, *Wakacje w Polsce Ludowej: Polityka władz i ruch turystyczny (1945–1989)* (Warsaw: TRIO, 2005), 65. Whereas previously the Workers' Vacation Fund (Fundusz Wczasów Pracowniczych) had a monopoly over the organization

of leaves from work, as of 1958, individual enterprises could develop their own rest facilities for their workers (Sowiński, *Wakacje w Polsce Ludowej*, 92). For more on the various permutations of *wczasy*, see, for example, Główny Urząd Statystyczny Polskiej Rzeczypospolitej Ludowej, *Statystyka turystyki 1950–1966* (Warsaw: Główny Urząd Statystyczny, 1967).

23. Protokół z XI posiedzenia Prezydium Polskiego Komitetu Ochrony Środowiska Człowieka, 23 October 1971, AAN, GKKFiT 19/7: 35.

24. "Wild" tourism is discussed usefully by Christian Noack, "Coping with the Tourist: Planned and 'Wild' Mass Tourism in the Soviet Black Sea Coast," in *Turizm: The Russian and East European Tourist under Capitalism and Socialism*, ed. Anne E. Gorsuch and Diane P. Koenker (Ithaca: Cornell University Press, 2006). For a complaint that camping was endangering the environment, see Archiwum Państwowe w Rzeszowie—Sanok (henceforth APRz-Sanok), 68/3433:12.

25. Interview with Adolf Maciołek, in W. Juzwik and B. N. Lopieńska, "W Bieszczadach mowią," *Kultura* 12, no. 38 (22 September 1974): 7.

26. Władysław Juzwik, "Stawka Bieszczady," *Kultura* 12, no. 33 (18 August 1974): 10.

27. Potaczała, *Bieszczady*, 173–92.

28. After ten years of activity in the region, the PTTK in Sanok finally felt that the national councils were becoming more understanding of the value of tourism. Sprawozdanie z działalności Powiatowego Komitetu Kultury Fizycznej i Turystyki w Sanoku na rok 1962, AAN, GKKFiT, 2/163: 216.

29. See the Uchwała KERM nr 181/59 w sprawie programu zagospodarowania turystycznego kraju dla turystyki zagranicznej w latach 1959–1962.

30. On the basin: Dębicki, "Jeszcze wokół problemu," 181; on the Swiss-style resort: Wilhelm Dębicki, "Problem zagospodarowania Bieszczadów," *Wierchy* 35 (1966): 203.

31. Sprawozdanie z realizacji zadań w zakresie upowszechniania i rozwoju kultury fizycznej i turystyki w województwie rzeszowskim, 11 March 1965, in AAN, GKKFiT 2/169: 11.

32. *Bieszczady: Przewodnik*, 149. New opportunities for travel abroad starting in the 1970s made domestic tourism less attractive. Recent historiography on tourism in People's Poland underscores the fact that the 1970s represented "the golden decade" of vacationing in the country (quotation from Sowiński, *Wakacje*, 282; see also Chmiel, *Turystyka*, 395).

33. For an example of this, see Patrice M. Dabrowski, "Encountering Poland's 'Wild West': Tourism in the Bieszczady Mountains under Socialism," in *Socialist Escapes: Breaks from the Everyday in Cold War Eastern Europe*, ed. Cathleen Giustino, Catherine Plum, and Alexander Vari (New York: Berghahn Press, 2013), 75–97, esp. 88.

34. See, for example, Jerzy Fałkowski, "W imieniu stonki," *Walka Młodych*, no. 41 (13 October 1963).

35. *Bieszczady: Przewodnik*, 11th ed., 64.

36. Rosa Lehmann, "Social(ist) Engineering: Taming the Devils of the Polish Bieszczady," *Communist and Post-Communist Studies* 42 (2009): 423–44, 431.

37. Ewa Beynar-Czeczott, "49 lat z Bieszczadami w tle," in *Pół wieku w górach 1957–2007, czyli dzieje Studenckiego Koła Przewodników Beskidzkich w Warszawie*, ed. Andrzej Wielocha (Warsaw: Studenckie Koło Przewodników Beskidzkich, 2007), 71–76.

38. Elżbieta Misiak-Bremer, "Wspomnienie o Bronku," in *Pół wieku w górach 1957– 2007*, 277–80.

39. SKPB Warszawa, Wszechlista Koła: http://www.skpb.waw.pl/przewodnicy/ wszechlista.html, last accessed 31 January 2019.

40. Witold Michałowski and Janusz Rygielski, *Spór o Bieszczady*, 1st ed. (Warsaw: Sport i Turystyka, 1979), 20; *Bieszczady: Przewodnik dla prawdziwego turysty*, 11th rev. ed. (Pruszków: Oficyna wydawnicza "Rewasz," 2006), 145; Jerzy Korejwo, "Przewodnicy z błękitnym krzyżem," in *Pół wieku w górach 1957–2007*, 91.

41. Recounted by Ewa Beynar-Czeczott, "49 lat z Bieszczadami w tle," 76.

42. Adam Teneta, "Cowboye w Bieszczadach," *Przekrój*, no. 659 (1957): 8–10. Reactions in "Cowboyska sprawa," *Przekrój*, no. 667 (19 January 1958): 4–5 (quotation from "Dzikuska," 4); "avalanche," from "Cowboyskiej sprawy ciąg dalszy," *Przekrój*, no. 672 (23 February 1958): 15.

43. Andrzej Burghardt, "Bieszczady w filmie fabularnym," *Wierchy* 64 (1998): 29–56, 31–32. Other films include *Baza ludzi umarłych* (1959), *Ogniomistrz Kaleń* (1961), *Zerwany most* (1963), *Chudy i inni* (1966), and *Wszyscy i nikt* (1977).

44. See the previous note for a list of major Polish films of the late 1950s through the 1970s. I thank Patryk Wasiak for turning my attention to some of the smaller forms. Some are also listed in Patrycja Trzeszczyńska-Demel, "Pisanie Bieszczadu: O mityzacji i narracji na peryferiach," in *W krainie metarefleksji: Księga poświęcona Profesorowi Czesławowi Robotyckiemu*, ed. J. Barański, M. Golonka-Czajkowska, and A. Niedźwiedź (Krakow: Wydawnictwo Uniwersytetu Jagiellońskiego, 2015), 514n6.

45. See Cygan, "Początki," 97; Szymon Wdowiak, "Akademicy zapraszają na Łopiennik," *Pół wieku w górach 1957–2007*, 101–2, first published in *Światowid* 15, no. 49 (4 December 1966). The film (PKF 2B/66) is available at http://www.repozytorium.fn.org.pl/?q=pl/node/6577, last accessed 2 September 2020.

46. *Pionierzy: Pamiętniki osadników bieszczadzkich* (Rzeszów: Rzeszowskie Towarzystwo Przyjaciół Nauk, 1975).

47. Andrzej Potocki, *Majster Bieda czyli zakapiorskie Bieszczady*, 5th expanded ed. (Rzeszów: Wydawnictwo "Carpathia," 2014), 5. That there were hippie communes in the Bieszczady is attested by Wojciech Tarzan-Michalewski, *Mistycy i narkomani* (Olsztyn: Ethos, 1992).

48. Lehmann, "Social(ist) Engineering," 440.

49. The "great transhumance" into the Bieszczady and the usage conflict in the Tatras are given thorough treatment in Bianca Hoenig, *Geteilte Berge: Eine Konfliktgeschichte der Naturnutzung in der Tatra* (Göttingen: Vandenhoeck & Ruprecht, 2018), 128–35, 169–93.

50. Potaczała, *Bieszczady*, 94.

51. Potaczała, *Bieszczady*, 98, 34.

52. Waldemar Ufnalski "Kaczor," "Kilka wspomnień," *Pół wieku w górach 1957– 2007*, 52–53, 52.

53. Potocki, *Majster Bieda*.

54. Potocki, *Majster Bieda*, 9–19, esp. 10.

55. If not in the Bieszczady: he was too undisciplined at that point.

56. Mountain Eden: Jan Bazyl Lipszyc, "Tam, gdzie nie było szosy," *Politechnik* 27–28, nos. 887–88 (July 1980): 1, 13.

57. Diane P. Koenker, "The Proletarian Tourist in the 1930s: Between Mass Excursion and Mass Escape," in *Turizm: The Russian and East European Tourist under Capitalism and Socialism*, ed. Anne E. Gorsuch and Diane P. Koenker (Ithaca: Cornell University Press, 2006), 119–40.

Chapter 11. Battling for the Soul of the Bieszczady

1. Hal K. Rothman, *Devil's Bargains: Tourism in the Twentieth-Century American West* (Lawrence: University of Kansas Press, 1998), 11.

2. See, for example, Artur Pawlowski, "The Historical Aspect to the Shaping of the Sustainable Development Concept," in *Environmental Engineering*, ed. Lucjan Pawlowski, Marzenna R. Dudzinska, and Artur Pawlowski (London: Taylor & Francis, 2007), 25–26.

3. Witold Michałowski and Janusz Rygielski, *Spór o Bieszczady*, 1st ed. (Warsaw: Sport i Turystyka, 1979), 54. For students' actions vis-à-vis nature preservation in 1972, see Janusz Rygielski, "Idea—przeciw folwarkom," *Politechnik*, no. 18 (6 May 1973): 5.

4. Both the international concern with nature preservation and the opening of Poland's borders are discussed in Michałowski and Rygielski, *Spór o Bieszczady*, 54.

5. This is akin to the definition of the tourist being "only that traveler who embarked on a purposeful journey, a circuit (tour) using one's own physical locomotion." Anne E. Gorsuch and Diane P. Koenker, "Introduction," *Turizm: The Russian and East European Tourist under Capitalism and Socialism* (Ithaca: Cornell University Press, 2006), 2–3.

6. See, for example, Attachment #1 to Law no. 35/69 of the Council of Ministers of 28 January 1968, in Archiwum Akt Nowych (henceforth AAN), GKKFiT 26/137: 8.

7. Article 1 of draft Ustawa z dnia . . . 1961 o zagospodarowaniu turystycznym, in AAN, GKKFiT 1/397: 72.

8. So claim Kazimierz Zabierowski and Henryk Jadam, "Bieszczady nie są pustynią," *Kultura*, no. 37 (15 September 1974). For more on the region, see Tomasz Kowalik, "Wschodnio-Beskidzki Obszar Chronionego Krajobrazu," *Połoniny* (1973): 38–40.

9. See *Dziennik Ustaw* 43 (6 October 1972); "Utworzenie powiatu bieszczadzkiego," *Nowiny Rzeszowskie*, no. 279 (8 October 1972).

10. Andrzej Ziemski, "Nasze boje o Bieszczady," *Politechnik*, no. 7 (18 February 1980): 4, 5, 6.

11. Redakcja, "Odkrywamy powtórnie Bieszczady," *Politechnik*, nos. 38–39 (17–31 December 1972). The consulting, according to Janusz Rygielski, "Spór o Bieszczady," in *Turystyka akademicka 1906–2016: 60 lat BPiT Almatur* (Warsaw: Wydawnictwo "Kto jest Kim," 2016), 154–268, 264.

12. Redakcja, "Odkrywamy powtórnie Bieszczady."

13. Facts on the weekly from Janusz Rygielski, "Pismo 'czerwonej Politechniki'," *Literatura* 11, no. 213 (11 March 1976).

14. Citations from Redakcja, "Odkrywamy powtórnie Bieszczady."

15. See, for example, Władysław Krygowski, "Park czy parking?" *Politechnik*, no. 6 (11 February 1973): 10; Artur Bata, "Z plecakiem i . . . rysownicą," *Politechnik*, no. 9

(4 March 1973): 12; Stanisław Smolski, "Chrońmy Bieszczady," *Politechnik*, no. 11 (18 March 1973): 9; Witold St. Michałowski, "Nie dajmy odejść legendzie," *Politechnik*, no. 12 (25 March 1973): 10; and Jacek Mazur, "Pora na mądre decyzje," *Politechnik*, no. 14 (8 April 1973): 11.

16. Jacek Mazur and Janusz Rygielski, "Chwila uzasadnionej fantazji," *Politechnik*, no. 18 (6 May 1973): 3. The ideas in the next paragraphs all come from this piece. For more on Rygielski, see Patrice M. Dabrowski, "Dla kogo Bieszczady? Janusza Rygielskiego wkład w dyskusję (lata 70. do wczesnych lat 80. XX w.)," *Góry—Literatura—Kultura* 13 (forthcoming, 2020).

17. Michałowski and Rygielski, *Spór o Bieszczady*, 1st ed., 5.

18. On the interwar connection, see Janusz Rygielski, "Dla kogo Bieszczady?" *Gościniec* nos. 2–3–4 (1978): 22–25; 14–16, 23–25, 14.

19. Mazur and Rygielski, "Chwila uzasadnionej fantazji," 3.

20. Mazur and Rygielski, "Chwila uzasadnionej fantazji."

21. Mazur and Rygielski, "Chwila uzasadnionej fantazji."

22. Oscar J. Martinez, "The Dynamics of Border Interaction: New Approaches to Border Analysis," in *Global Boundaries*, ed. Clive H. Schofield (London: Routledge, 1994), 1–15.

23. On the big Swiss-style resort, see Wilhelm Dębicki, "Problem zagospodarowania Bieszczadów," *Wierchy* 35 (1966): 203. For "basin of health," see J.A., " 'Zagłębie zdrowia' w Bieszczadach?" *Wierchy* 35 (1966): 216.

24. As early as 1961, one encountered assertations such as "This corner 'was discovered' in about 1957," as in Dariusz Piątkowski, "Bieszczadzkie perspektywy," *Światowid*, no. 24 (8 October 1961): 10.

25. Studenckie Koło Przewodników Beskidzkich w Lublinie, "Nasz lubelski program," *Politechnik*, no. 24 (17 June 1973): 11.

26. Tadeusz Kowalik, "Studencka rzeczpospolita bieszczadzka," *Politechnik*, no. 36 (2 December 1973): 11.

27. Krygowski, "Park czy parking?" As early as 1955 Krygowski had proposed that a national park be established in the Bieszczady; and various projects were prepared in 1957 and 1961. J.I.D., "Nowy projekt parku narodowego w Bieszczadach," *Wierchy* 30 (1961): 254–5; x.y., "Utworzenie Bieszczadzkiego Parku Narodowego," *Wierchy* 43 (1974): 221.

28. Rygielski, "Idea—przeciw folwarkom," 5.

29. Studenckie Koło Przewodników Beskidzkich, "Nasz program działania," *Połonina* (1973): 16–17. For more on the periodical, see Andrzej Wielocha, "O Komisji Wydawniczej," *Pół wieku w górach 1957–2007, czyli dzieje Studenckiego Koła Przewodników Beskidzkich w Warszawie*, ed. Andrzej Wielocha (Warsaw: Studenckie Koło Przewodników Beskidzkich, 2007), 229–32.

30. On the village fair as well as the overall arrangement, see Edmund Kuna "Mundek," "Jarmarki bieszczadzkie w Komańczy," *Pół wieku*, 125–29.

31. Witold St. Michałowski, "Nie dajmy odejść legendzie," 10, republished in *Połonina* (1973): 19–20. More on the Witkiewicz connection in Zbigniew Święch, "Styl bieszczadzki," *Dziennik Polski* 29, no. 262 (4–5 November 1973): 4.

32. Rygielski, "Idea—przeciw folwarkom."

33. Rygielski, "Idea—przeciw folwarkom."

34. Andrzej Okólski, "Musimy iść za ciosem," *Politechnik*, no. 20 (20 May 1973): 11.

35. From the title of the article, J. Mazur and J. Rygielski, "Chwila uzasadnionej fantazji."

36. Lech Stefański, Marta Wesołowska, and Andrzej Krzysztof Wróblewski, "Bieszczady i cała Polska," *Polityka* (26 May 1973).

37. "pięknym poletkiem doświadczalnym nowej, dynamicznej i sprawnej polityki społecznej," from Stefański et al., "Bieszczady i cała Polska." Shades of Stanisław Witkiewicz in the Tatras, who spoke of an "experimental workshop" there.

38. For a list of vacation houses from 1971, see APRz-Sanok 68/3428: 4–5.

39. Witold Michałowski, *Hajże na Bieszczady* (Michalin-Lutowiska: nakład Fundacji "Odysseum," 1993), 116–17.

40. Jan Bazyl Lipszyc, "Spór o Bieszczady," *Historia studenckiej turystyki górskiej* (Warsaw: n.p., 1977), 42–48, chronicles much of this debate. See also Lipszyc, "Spór o Bieszczady," *Pół wieku w górach 1957–2007, czyli dzieje Studenckiego Koła Przewodników Beskidzkich w Warszawie*, ed. Andrzej Wielocha (Warsaw: Studenckie Koło Przewodników Beskidzkich, 2007), 119–20, where Lipszyc lists names of student mountain guides who took part. Janusz Rygielski also was involved with a nature program on television during this period, per correspondence with the author.

41. Michałowski, *Hajże na Bieszczady*, 117 and earlier (for discussion of the meeting).

42. Henryk Jadam, "Idei przeciwko folwarkom ciąg dalszy," *Politechnik*, no. 24 (17 June 1973): 11. This was clearly wishful thinking: the organization was not founded until late February 1974, according to (b), "Powołanie do życia Towarzystwa Rozwoju Bieszczadów," *Nowiny Rzeszowskie* 26, no. 59 (1 March 1974): 2.

43. (b), "Powołanie do życia"; (tur), "W trosce o dalszy rozwój Bieszczadow [sic]," *Podkarpacie*, no. 46 (18 November 1976): 1, 2.

44. Taking credit for the competition: "II Zjazd Towarzystwa Rozwoju Bieszczadów," *Podkarpacie*, no. 22 (2 June 1977): 2. The volume, to be the first volume in a series titled Bieszczady Library, was *Pionierzy: Pamiętniki osadników bieszczadzkich* (Rzeszów: Rzeszowskie Towarzystwo Przyjaciół Nauk, 1975). Although the competition reportedly took place in 1972, the author of the preface to the published work took direct aim at those on the other side of the dispute over the Bieszczady.

45. Interview with Maria Tetera, in W. Juzwik and B. N. Lopieńska, "W Bieszczadach mówią," *Kultura*, no. 38 (22 September 1974): 7. These interviews are among the few published voices from within the Bieszczady region.

46. Interview with Henryk Suszek, in W. Juzwik and B. N. Lopieńska, "W Bieszczadach mówią," 7.

47. Views of Tadeusz Domorzyk, Ewa Blasiak, and Władysław Pepera, in W. Juzwik and B. N. Lopieńska, "W Bieszczadach mówią," 7. The director of one of the vacation houses admitted they were too urban in style: he had a Zakopane-Style fence built around his to soften the look. See the interview with Witold Wierciak, director of the "Solinka" vacation house in Polańczyk, in Juzwik and Lopieńska, "W Bieszczadach mówią," 7.

48. Interview with Adolf Maciołek, in W. Juzwik and B. N. Lopieńska, "W Bieszczadach mówią," 7.

49. Interview with Andrzej Nowaczyk, in W. Juzwik and B. N. Lopieńska, "W Bieszczadach mówią," 7.

50. Interview with Maria Czerwińska, school director, in W. Juzwik and B.N. Lopieńska, "W Bieszczadach mówią," 7.

51. Janusz Rygielski, "Czego chcą młodzi?," *IMT Światowid*, no. 8 (1973).

52. Reaching out to youth: Janusz Rygielski, "Czego pragniemy w Bieszczadach?," *Magazyn młodzieżowy Prometej* 24 (July 1973). On the Plenum: Janusz Rygielski, "Jedna jest ziemia," *Politechnik*, nos. 25–26 (24 June 1973).

53. On this, see Waldemar Siwiński, "W Komańczy nie lubią obcych," *Politechnik*, no. 37 (9 December 1973): 1, 4; Redakcja, "Bieszczady i 'Politechnik'," *Politechnik*, no. 38 (16 December 1973): 1, 4.

54. Jan Romaszkan, "O bieszczadzkim stylu budownictwa," *Politechnik*, nos. 25–26 (24 June 1973): 11; Mieczysław Mysiak, "Szkoda, że nie pomyślano wcześniej," *Politechnik*, nos. 25–26 (24 June 1973): 11; and Jerzy Olek, "Koszmar Bieszczadów," *Politechnik*, no. 30 (21 October 1973): 6–7.

55. For early use of the term *republic*, see Michałowski, "Nie dajmy odejść legendzie."

56. Michałowski and Rygielski, *Spór o Bieszczady*, 22.

57. Tomasz Kowalik, "Chata ciasna, ale własna," *Politechnik*, no. 32 (4 November 1973): 10; Kowalik, "Studencka rzeczpospolita bieszczadzka."

58. Andrzej Wielocha, "Olgierd Łotoczko: W trzydziestą rocznicę śmierci," *Płaj* 33 (fall 2006); accessed at karpaccy.pl/olgierd-lotoczko/, 12 February 2013. Only after 1989 would the situation change. In 1990 the Społeczna Komisja Opieki nad Zabytkami Sztuki Cerkiewnej (Social Commission of Care for Monuments of Church Art), with the initiative of Zbigniew Kaszuba, gained permission to fix the church up, which it did with financing from the Ministry of Culture and Art until that dried up in 1995. As of 1997 the Towarzystwo Karpackie assumed responsibility for the church in Łopienka and has continued work on the church. Further updates can be found at http://karpaccy.pl/lopienka/, last accessed 2 September 2020.

59. Michałowski, *Hajże na Bieszczady*, 244; discussed in Wywiad 1: transcript of interview of Ernestyna Kuriat Kozek of *Puls Polonii* (Australia) with Janusz Rygielski, circa 2005–6 (scan in possession of author).

60. Redakcja, "Bieszczady i 'Politechnik,'" *Politechnik*, no. 38 (16 December 1973).

61. This was the Law no. 35/73, referred to as the "Second Bieszczady Law" for its similarity to the first such law of 1959 (*Pionierzy*, 38).

62. And it was, throughout the 1970s. It even produced furniture. Jan Malczewski, "Inwestycje w Bieszczadach i ich geneza," in *Bieszczady w Polsce Ludowej 1944–1989*, ed. Jakub Izdebski, Krzysztof Kaczmarski, and Mariusz Krzysztofiński (Rzeszów: IPN w Rzeszowie, 2009), 442.

63. Malczewski, "Inwestycje w Bieszczadach," 443.

64. x.y., "Utworzenie Bieszczadzkiego Parku Narodowego," *Wierchy* 43 (1974): 221.

65. x.y., "Utworzenie Bieszczadzkiego Parku Narodowego."

66. Michałowski, *Hajże na Bieszczady*, 85.

Chapter 12. Power, Ecology, and the Public Sphere

1. The Archive of the Main Command of the Union of Polish Scouting (Archiwum Komendy Głównej Związku Harcerstwa Polskiego—henceforth AKG ZHP), "Bieszczady-40," B-40 2/16, 5. See also articles such as Artur Bata, "Harcerze Bieszczadom," *Podkarpacie*, no. 10 (9 May 1974).

2. AKG ZHP, "Bieszczady-40," B-40 2/7, 1–2.

3. Sprawozdanie z przebiegu harcerskiej "Operacji Bieszczady-40" za rok 1974, AKG ZHP, "Bieszczady-40," B-40/2, 8, 11.

4. For more detail, see Patrice M. Dabrowski, "Transforming Poland's 'Wild West,'" *Herito: Dziedzictwo, Kultura, Współczesność* 36 (fall 2019): 52–65. With side-by-side Polish translation: "Jak zmieniano polski 'Dziki Zachód,'" translated by Aga Zano.

5. According to the deputy director of the Forest Executive in Krosno, cited in Jan Bazyl Lipszyc, "Spotkanie ludzi o czystym sumieniu," *Politechnik*, no. 2 (11 January 1981), 10.

6. Sprawozdanie z Harcerskiej operacji "Bieszczady-40" w r. 1975, AKG ZHP, "Bieszczady-40," OB-40–11, 2–3, 14–15.

7. Operacja 'Bieszczady 40" Program na lata 1975–1984. AKG ZHP, "Bieszczady-40," B-40–2/21, 10.

8. Związek Harcerstwa Polskiego, "Operacja Bieszczady 40" Ustrzyki Dolne 29 czerwca 1974, AKG ZHP, "Bieszczady-40," B-40/1. By 1981, some 54,000 scouts had taken part in the operation, in the process completing over 2.5 million work-hours worth approximately 25 million zloty. Związek harcerstwa Polskiego, Komenda Operacji. Informacja o przebiegu i wynikach Operacji "Bieszczady—40" (lata 1974–1984), Ustrzyki Dolne 15.08.1984 r., in AKG ZHP. "Bieszczady-40," 1984 Informacja o wynikach i przebiegu operacji 1974–1984 (77), 2, 7.

9. See, for example, the recollections of one of the group leaders, present during the highly choreographed visit of Edward Gierek in 1979, http://obserwato riumedukacji.pl/esej-wspomnieniowy-moj-rok-1979-czyli-tez-oboz-ale-naukowy-w-bieszczadach/, last accessed 2 September 2020.

10. Timothy Garton Ash, *The Polish Revolution: Solidarity* (New York: Vintage, 1985), 125.

11. Krzysztof Potaczała, *Bieszczady w PRL-u* (Olszanica: BOSZ, 2012), 31.

12. For more on this complex individual, see Potaczała, *Bieszczady*, 243–62; Witold Michałowski and Janusz Rygielski, *Spór o Bieszczady*, 2nd ed. (Warsaw: Sport i Turystyka, 1986), 42–43.

13. Potaczała, *Bieszczady w PRL-u*, 50.

14. Potaczała, *Bieszczady w PRL-u*, 48. Yugoslavia's Josip Broz Tito was another famous guest. For more on his visit, see Potaczała, *Bieszczady w PRL-u*, 203–5 as well as Mirosław Surdej, "Między polityką a wypoczynkiem—wizyta Josipa Broz-Tito w Polsce w 1975 r. w aktach aparatu bezpieczeństwa PRL," in *Bieszczady w Polsce Ludowej 1944–1989*, ed. Jakub Izdebski, Krzysztof Kaczmarski, and Mariusz Krzysztofiński (Rzeszów: IPN w Rzeszowie, 2009), 197–209.

15. Potaczała, *Bieszczady w PRL-u*, 51–66.

16. Potaczała, *Bieszczady w PRL-u*, 250.

17. Under the 1952 legislation, poaching was a felony, while the killing of endangered species was only a misdemeanor. Daniel H. Cole, *Instituting Environmental Protection: From Red to Green in Poland* (Houndmills, UK: Macmillan, 1998), 32–33.

18. In Hungary, more of the nomenklatura was able to participate. See György Péteri, "*Nomenklatura* with Smoking Guns: Hunting in Communist Hungary's Party-State Elite," in *Pleasures in Socialism: Leisure and Luxury in the Eastern Bloc*, ed. David Crowley and Susan E. Reid (Evanston, IL: Northwestern University Press, 2010), 311–44.

19. Although seen as exotic by visitors, the bison population had grown quite large, thus already in 1968 a West German couple was allowed to shoot an old one. Surdej, "Między polityką," 198–99.

20. Already in the late 1960s a tendency to gently Polonize some of the Bieszczady toponyms—for example, Brzegi Górne instead of Berehy Górne—seemed to have been allowed by the Commission for the Establishment of Names, under the Council of Ministers. W.K., "Jeszcze raz o urzędowym nazewnictwie," *Wierchy* 36 (1967): 215–16.

21. Michałowski and Rygielski, *Spór o Bieszczady*, 2nd ed., 82.

22. Details of what he envisaged are found in Jan Gerhard, "O generale Walterze, pomniku i pamięci," *Życie literackie* 8, no. 14 (1964): 1–2.

23. For a list of the names and their replacements, see Potaczała, *Bieszczady w PRL-u*, 228–29.

24. See, for example, "Miejscowości wydarte historii," *Słowo Powszechne* (20–22 February 1981): 1–3.

25. Although the second edition of *Spór o Bieszczady* does discuss the changes in the names of the Bieszczady toponyms.

26. Witold Michałowski and Janusz Rygielski, *Spór o Bieszczady*, 1st ed., 5–6, quotation from 5.

27. Michałowski and Rygielski, *Spór o Bieszczady*, 1st ed., 94. Capitalization from the original.

28. Krzysztof Czabański, "Spór jeszcze aktualny," *Kultura* (16 September 1979); Jan Bazyl Lipszyc, "Sporu ciąg dalszy," *Politechnik*, no. 25 (24 June 1979); Bogdan Kujawa, "Spór o Bieszczady," *Fundamenty*, no. 33 (19 August 1979); Marek Rymuszko, "Rodowód pewnego sporu: Recenzje," *Prawo i Życie*, no. 38 (23 September 1979).

29. Jan Bazyl Lipszyc, "Sporu ciąg dalszy," *Politechnik*, no. 25 (24 June 1979).

30. Janusz Rygielski, "Prosto z buszu: Spór o Bieszczady (Part One)," *Puls Polonii* (9 January 2014). http://www.zrobtosam.om/PulsPol/Puls3/index.php?sekcja=1&arty_id=13220, last accessed 29 August 2020.

31. "Środowisko," *Przekrój* 1801 (14 October 1979).

32. "Rzeszów," *Politechnik*, no. 3 (20 January 1980).

33. Jan Bazyl Lipszyc, "Nie ma sporu o Bieszczady," *Politechnik*, no. 7 (18 February 1980): 8–9.

34. Wywiad 1: transcript of interview of Ernestyna Kuriat Kozek of *Puls Polonii* (Australia) with Janusz Rygielski, circa 2005–6 (scan in possession of author), 31.

35. Most important here are Redakcja, "Odkrywamy Bieszczady po raz trzeci," *Politechnik*, no. 7 (18 February 1980): 1; Andrzej Ziemski, "Nasze boje o Bieszczady," *Politechnik*, no. 7 (18 February 1980): 4–6; Jerzy Burtan, "W zasadzie wszyscy są za," *Politechnik*, no. 7 (18 February 1980): 6–7; and Jan Bazyl Lipszyc, "Nie ma sporu o Bieszczady," *Politechnik*, no. 7 (18 February 1980): 8–9.

36. On his approval, see Stanisław Szczepański, "Z tego może być chleb. Rozmowa z tow. Wojciechem Grochalą, sekretarzem KW PZPR w Rzeszowie, I sekretarzem Bieszczadzkiego Komitetu Powiatowego PZPR," *Politechnik*, no. 1 (619), 6 January 1974: 1, 4; Ziemski brought him up in his article (see previous footnote.)

37. Ziemski, "Nasze boje o Bieszczady," 4–6. Ziemski had been editor-in-chief until 1978.

38. For more on Rygielski, see Patrice M. Dabrowski, "Dla kogo Bieszczady? Janusza Rygielskiego wkład w dyskusję (lata 70. do wczesnych lat 80. XX w.)," *Góry—Literatura—Kultura* 13 (forthcoming, 2020).

39. Per the Dyploma "Nagroda za calokszalt.pdf," scan in the author's possession; *Gościniec* 5 (1981); scan of the diploma (Turystyka.pdf) in the author's possession.

40. Michałowski and Rygielski, *Spór o Bieszczady*, 1st ed., 27.

41. Janusz Rygielski, "Hunowie w Tatrach" ["Technika i ty"], *Politechnik*, no. 35 (1969).

42. "Warszawa," *Politechnik*, no. 15 (13 April 1980).

43. Cited in Jerzy Burtan, "W zasadzie wszyscy są za," *Politechnik*, no. 7 (18 February 1980), 7.

44. Assessment of Krzysztof Ołtarzewski, former student, writing as a resident of Komańcza, in letters to the editor, *Politechnik*, no. 19 (11 May 1980): 10. Jan Bazyl Lipszyc also mentions Muczne in his elegy to what the Bieszczady had been like in 1968, contrasted with a snapshot of the present situation: "Tam, gdzie nie było szosy," *Politechnik*, nos. 27–28 (July 1980): 1, 13.

45. Janusz Rygielski, "Być turystą," *Polityka* (5 July 1980).

46. Bronisław Bremer had been on rescue duty deep in the Bieszczady during those heady days and was surprised to find how much Poland had changed upon his return to "civilization" in September. Elżbieta Misiak-Bremer, "Wspomnienie o Bronku," in *Pół wieku w górach 1957–2007, czyli dzieje Studenckiego Koła Przewodników Beskidzkich w Warszawie*, ed. Andrzej Wielocha (Warsaw: Studenckie Koło Przewodników Beskidzkich, 2007), 279.

47. Jacek Kolbuszewski, "Krajobraz pełen znaczeń," *Politechnik*, no. 29 (5 October 1980): 10.

48. Roman Lewandowski, "O Kazku z Bieszczadów opowieść," *Politechnik*, no. 29 (5 October 1980): 5. For a fascinating retort, followed by yet another, see Roman Lewandowski, "Patriotyczna koncepcja rozwoju Bieszczadów," *Politechnik*, no. 37 (30 November 1980): 12.

49. Jan Bazyl Lipszyc, "Spotkanie ludzi o czystym sumieniu," *Politechnik*, no. 2 (11 January 1981): 10.

50. Zob. list Andrzeja Trojnara, Zastępcy Przewodniczącego Głównego Komitetu Turystyki w Warszawie do wicewojewody krośnieńskiego Wiesława Skałkowskiego z 30 marca 1981 r., Archiwum Państwowe w Rzeszowie Oddział w Skołyszynie, 2993: 27.

51. KFT.-5620/6/81 copy of letter to Edgar Kaczmarek, Deputy Chair of the Main Tourism Committee in Warsaw, July 81, Archiwum Państwowe w Rzeszowie Oddział w Skołyszynie, 2993: 39.

52. Tomasz Bereza, "Strajk ustrzycki (grudzień 1980-luty 1981)," in *Bieszczady w Polsce Ludowej 1944–1989*, ed. Jakub Izdebski, Krzysztof Kaczmarski, and Mariusz Krzysztofiński (Rzeszów: IPN w Rzeszowie, 2009), 380.

53. For more on the strike, see Mariusz Głuszko, *Bieszczadzkie karty historii* (Sandomierz: Wydawn. Armoryka, 2008), 149–54.

54. Bereza, "Strajk," 381. The strike lasted from 29 December to 12 January.

55. The danger of this last point is discussed in Michałowski and Rygielski, *Spór o Bieszczady*, 2nd ed., 102ff. Various farmers' groups were ready to demand this even before the Solidarity movement. *Politechnik* published in full the protocol of the agreement signed by the government commission and the strike committee: "Protokół Porozumienia zawartego dnia 20 lutego 1981 roku pomiędzy Komisją rządową a Komitetem Strajkowym w Ustrzykach Dolnych działającym w imieniu Komitetu

Założycielskiego Związku Zawodowego Rolników Indywidualnych oraz członków NSZZ 'Solidarność' z terenu Bieszczadów przy udziale Krajowej Komisji Porozumiewawczej NSZZ 'Solidarność,'" *Politechnik,* nos. 12–13 (22–29 March 1981): 14–15.

56. I thank Janusz Rygielski for bringing this point to my attention.

57. Bereza, "Strajk," 384–85, 386.

58. Michałowski and Rygielski, *Spór o Bieszczady,* 1st ed., 12.

59. The Solidarity movement did make some demands relative to the environment, but they were not as high-priority as many others. See Barbara Hicks, *Environmental Politics in Poland: A Social Movement Between Regime and Opposition* (New York: Columbia University Press, 1996), 86.

60. Jan Bazyl Lipszyc, "Widziane z Warszawy," *Politechnik,* no. 15 (12 April 1981): 1, 11.

61. Władysław Krygowski, "Przymierze z Bieszczadami," in APRz PTTK 218: 13.

62. From List otwarty X Zjazdu Krajowego PTTK do Sejmu z 14 listopada 1981, published in Janusz Rygielski, *Niekochane Góry* (Warsaw: Wydaw. PTTK Polskiego Towarzystwa Turystyczno-Krajoznawczego "Kraj," 1984). Prior to that Rygielski had been a member of the Commission of Mountain Tourism of the Main Executive of the PTTK.

63. Bereza, "Strajk," 383.

64. Janusz Rygielski, *Fiatem na Rysy* (Warszawa: Krajowa Agencja Wydawnicza, 1981), 95.

65. Janusz Rygielski, "Prosto z buszu: Spór o Bieszczady (dokończenie)," *Puls Polonii* (9 January 2014). http://www.zrobtosam.com/PulsPol/Puls3/index.php?sekcja=16&arty_id=13221, last accessed 22 August 2020.

66. "krainy wolnej od zalewu kulturowych tandet," from Jacek Kolbuszewski, "Krajobraz pełen znaczeń," *Politechnik,* no. 29 (5 October 1980): 10.

67. Władysław Krygowski, "Wokół sporu o Bieszczady," *Wierchy* 49 (1981): 373–75, quotation from 375.

68. Witold St. Michałowski, *Hajże na Bieszczady* (Michalin-Lutowiska: nakład Fundacji "Odysseum," 1993). Foreword by Stefan Bratkowski.

Conclusion

1. Redakcja, "Odkrywamy Bieszczady po raz trzeci," *Politechnik,* no. 7 (18 February 1980): 1.

2. Tytus Chałubiński, *Sześć dni w Tatrach: Wycieczka bez programu* (Kraków: Wydawnictwo Literackie, 1988), 41.

3. Stanisław Witkiewicz, *Bagno,* in *Pisma tatrzańskie* (Kraków: Wydawnictwo Literackie, 1963), 1:222.

4. Hnat Khotkevych, "Spohady," in *Tvory v dvokh tomakh* (Kyïv: Dnipro, 1966), 2:576.

5. Jacek Mazur and Janusz Rygielski, "Chwila uzasadnionej fantazji," *Politechnik,* no. 18 (6 May 1973): 3.

6. Stanisław Witkiewicz, cited in Zbigniew Moździerz, ed., *Stanisław Witkiewicz: Człowiek—artysta—myśliciel* (Zakopane: TMT, 1997), 310, which in turn has been cited in Edward Manouelian, "Invented Traditions: Primitivist Narrative and Design in the Polish Fin de Siècle," *Slavic Review* (summer 2000): 391–405, 393.

NOTES TO PAGES 200–203

7. According to Dmytro Mynailiuk, "Teatral'ni spomyny," in Vasyl' Stef'iuk, *Kermanych Hutsul's'koho teatru: Narys zhyttia i tvorchosti H. Khotkevycha; Spohady pro n'oho* (Kosiv: Pysanyi Kamin', 2000), 165.

8. Andrzej Wielocha, "O Komisji Wydawniczej," in *Pół wieku w górach 1957–2007, czyli dzieje Studenckiego Koła Przewodników Beskidzkich w Warszawie*, ed. Andrzej Wielocha (Warsaw: Studenckie Koło Przewodników Beskidzkich, 2007), 229–32.

9. Jost Krippendorf, "The Capital of Tourism in Danger: Reciprocal Effects between Landscape and Tourism," in *The Transformation of Swiss Mountain Regions: Problems of Development between Self-reliance and Dependency in an Economic and Ecological Perspective*, ed. Ernst A. Burgger et al. (Bern: Verlag Paul Hupt, 1984), 437.

10. More on him and other Polish climbing elites in Bernadette McDonald, *Freedom Climbers* (Victoria, BC: Rocky Mountain Books, 2011).

✿ INDEX

Academic Tourist Club, 80–81
Akcja Wisa. *See* Operation Vistula
alpine clubs, 3, 27–28, 69, 175; *See also*
Czarnohora Branch of the Tatra Society;
Hungarian Carpathian Society; Tatra
Society/Polish Tatra Society
alpinism, Polish. *See* mountain climbing
Archduke Charles, 89, 230n39
architecture, Zakopane Style (Polish
Style): beyond Zakopane, 45, 79, 87,
200, 256n47; in Zakopane, 45–46,
59–62, 222n26
Arłamów. *See under* tourism, secret
Communist Party
Armenians, 68, 70, 78, 103, 200

Bałucki, Michał, 19, 209n22
Balzer, Oswald, 49
Bellon, Wojtek, 164, 253n55
Beshchady. *See* Bieszczady
Beynar, Ewa, 160–61
Bieszczady, 9; demographics, postwar, 146,
160, 163–64, 247n24; demographics,
prewar, 139, 141, 245n2; farmers, 160,
162, 191–94; growth, of tourism under
socialism, 145, 147, 155–57, 159, 166,
251n8; Jews and Roma, World War II,
141; location name changes, 185–86,
191, 259n20, 259n25; location/physical
description, 139, 145; numbers of
tourists, 9, 159, 166; Polish/East Slav
relations, 141; popularization of, 145–46,
161–62; repopulation/resettlement of,
145–46, 162–63, 202; socialist vision/
building in, 146, 152, 167, 173–74,
182–83; trail development, 147, 152–53;
transportation, 157, 171; Ukrainian
national cause and, 141 (*see also*
Organization of Ukrainian Nationalists;
Ukrainian Insurgent Army); wilderness,
9, 145–47, 161, 164, 167; wildness as
attraction, 164–65

Bieszczady, competing visions for tourism
under socialism: "Bieszczady-40", 182–83,
188, 258n8; central authorities, 168–69,
175, 178, 182–83, 187, 189–91, 194–95; *The
Dispute over the Bieszczady*, 186–88, 190,
194–95; farmers/Rural Solidarity, 191–92,
260n55; locals, 177–79; Warsaw Polytechnic
students/ *Politechnika*, 169–75, 178–79,
188–90, 192–94, 199; Warsaw press,
175–76, 190. *See also* Rygielski, Janusz
Bieszczady, population transfers from,
142–44, 163–64, 247nn18–19; Operation
Vistula, 143–44, 164, 246n16
Bieszczady, socialist development/industry,
146, 155–56, 160–61, 165, 177–78,
180, 251n8; dams/reservoirs (Solina
and Myczkowce), 156–57, 160–61,
178, 180; highway loops, 156–57, 161;
road development, 161, 180; State
Agricultural Farms, 146, 155, 180, 162,
189, 251n8; Ustianowa lumber mill,
180–81, 194; workers on projects/
working conditions, 156, 160–61;
zagospodarowanie/reclaiming, 168–69,
176, 187. *See also* "Bieszczady-40"
"Bieszczady-40", 182–83, 188, 258n8
Bieszczady National Park, 171, 181, 191–92
Bieszczady Society, 170–71, 174, 176,
190–91, 193
Bohosiewicz, Bohdan, 75–76
Boikos, 6, 9, 122, 139, 198, 200, 245n3; as Poles,
141; resettlement from Bieszczady, 142–44,
163, 202; in Ukrainian Insurgent Army, 143;
as Ukrainians, 106, 123, 141, 143
borderlands/border, 7; Bieszczady, 144, 146,
150, 155, 245n4; Carpathian region, 6–7,
10, 35, 122–23, 197, 200; contestation/
challenges in, 6–7, 48; Hutsul region,
100, 108, 113, 120, 134, 139, 201; Polish
elite visions of, 37–38; security of, 8, 120,
136, 147, 160, 198; Tatras, 7, 13, 15, 19,
22, 34–35, 37–38, 42